This second volume of *Sources of Dramatic Theory* includes major theoretical writings on drama and theatre from the eighteenth and early nineteenth centuries, focusing on issues that are still relevant to our understanding of the genres. Among the writers represented by their own essays or substantial extracts from longer works are Voltaire, Diderot, Goldoni, Dr. Johnson, Lessing, Goethe, Schiller, Hegel, and Coleridge. Mlle Dumesnil, Carlo Gozzi, and Joanna Baillie are among the less frequently cited theorists, and there is also a selection of decrees from the French Revolution. Many of the texts have been newly translated for this volume and all have been newly annotated and introduced. Recurrent topics and allusions are traced by a system of cross-references.

Michael Sidnell's introduction explores some of the perennial issues surfacing in these writings, such as: the nature of imitation, the relationship between writing and acting, the role of theatre in making and sustaining cultural and national cohesion, and the effects of performance on audience behavior.

SOURCES OF DRAMATIC THEORY

Volume 2

Previously published

Volume 1: Plato to Congreve

Forthcoming

Volume 3: Hebbel to Bond
Volume 4: Performance Theory

SOURCES OF DRAMATIC THEORY

2: Voltaire to Hugo

Edited and annotated by

MICHAEL J. SIDNELL

University of Toronto

with

Barbara Kerslake, Lawrence Kerslake, Domenico Pietropaolo,
Natalie Rewa, and Jean Wilson

CAMBRIDGE
UNIVERSITY PRESS

Published by the Press Syndicate of the University of Cambridge
The Pitt Building, Trumpington Street, Cambridge CB2 IRP
40 West 20th Street, New York, NY 10011–4211, USA
10 Stamford Road, Oakleigh, Melbourne 3166, Australia

First published 1994

Printed in Great Britain at the University Press, Cambridge

A catalogue record for this book is available from the British Library

Library of Congress cataloguing in publication data

Sources of dramatic theory.
Collaborators: v. 2: With Barbara Kerslake ... [et al.].
Includes bibliographical references and indexes.
Contents: 1. Plato to Congreve – 2. Voltaire to Hugo.
1. Drama.   2.Theater.   I. Sidnell, Michael J.
PN1631.86   1991   801'.952   90–1564
ISBN 0 521 32694 X (v. 1)
ISBN 0 521 32695 8 (v. 2)

ISBN 0 521 32695 8 hardback

CONTENTS

ACKNOWLEDGMENTS

The following permissions are gratefully acknowledged:

University of Nebraska Press for the use of John W. Miller's translation of Goldoni's *The Comic Theatre, a Comedy in Three Acts*; reprinted from *The Comic Theatre: A Comedy in Three Acts*, by Carlo Goldoni, translated from the Italian by John W. Miller, by permission of the University of Nebraska Press. Copyright © 1969 by the University of Nebraska Press. Suhrkamp Verlag (1986) for the use of Ellen and Ernest H. von Nardroff's translation of Goethe's *Essays on Art and Literature*; Oxford University Press for the use of T. M. Knox's translation of Hegel's *Aesthetics: Lectures on Fine Art*; Penguin Books Ltd. for the use of the Prologue from *The Robbers and Wallenstein* by Friedrich Schiller, translated by F. J. Lamport (Penguin Classics, 1979) copyright © F. J. Lamport, 1979.

The encouragement and support of Professor C. J. McDonough has been most welcome, as has the material assistance given by Trinity College, Toronto. Michael Sidnell once more expresses his appreciation of continuous and stimulating discussion with the members of his seminar in the Graduate Centre for the Study of Drama at the University of Toronto. He also thanks the staff of Cambridge University Press for their resourceful expertise and their constant courtesy, particularly Sarah Stanton for her initial and continuous encouragement, and Victoria Cooper and Lindeth Vasey for their valuable contributions to this volume.

NOTE ON THE TEXTS

Many of the translations included in this volume have been specially made for it by the editors, as indicated below. The other translations used are: John W. Miller's of Goldoni; Ellen and Ernest H. von Nardroff's of the selections from Goethe's "Shakespeare: A Tribute," "On Epic and Dramatic Poetry," "Shakespeare Once Again," and "On Interpreting Aristotle's *Poetics*"; Thomas Carlyle's of Goethe's *Wilhelm Meister's Apprenticeship*; F. J. Lamport's of Schiller's Prologue to *Wallenstein*; John Black's of Schlegel (with revisions by A. J. W. Morrison and Jean Wilson); and T. M. Knox's of Hegel.

The primary responsibilities for the notes, commentary, and the new translations are as follows:

Barbara Kerslake: the translations of, the introductory notes to, and the annotation of, the selections from: Voltaire and Diderot.

Lawrence Kerslake: the translations of, the introductory notes to, and the annotation of, the selections from: Beaumarchais, Stendhal, and Hugo.

Domenico Pietropaolo: the translations of, the introductory notes to, and the annotation of, the selections from: Metastasio and Gozzi, and the introductory notes to, and the annotation of, the selection from Goldoni.

Natalie Rewa: the translations of, the introductory notes to, and the annotation of, the selections from: Decrees and Documents of the French Revolution, Dumesnil, and de Staël.

Michael J. Sidnell: the general introduction, including the translations from Diderot and Beaumarchais; the introductory notes to, and the annotation of, the selections from: Steele, Johnson, Hume, Baillie, Hegel, Coleridge, and Hazlitt; and the cross-references and Bibliography.

Jean Wilson: the translations of, the introductory notes to, and the annotation of, the selections from: Lessing, Schiller (except for the translation from *Wallenstein*), and Kleist; the introductory notes to, and the annotation of, the selections from Goethe and Schlegel.

ABBREVIATIONS

Throughout the volume a system of cross-references has been used to signal and locate for comparison passages that appear either in this volume or in volume 1. These cross-references are in the form < 1:Cv/129>, which refers to p. 129 of the Castelvetro entry in volume 1, or <Gt/136>, which refers to p. 136 of the Goethe entry in this volume. In the case of Horace's *The Art of Poetry* the line number follows the page number: < 1:Hr/69:180>. The abbreviations used are:

Ar	Aristotle	Hz	Hazlitt
Bl	Baillie	Ig	Ingegneri
Bm	Beaumarchais	In	Introduction to volume 1
Cd	On *Le Cid*		or 2, as indicated
Cg	Congreve	Jh	Johnson
Cn	Corneille	Jn	Jonson
Co	Coleridge	Kl	Kleist
Cv	Castelvetro	Lg	Lessing
Db	D'Aubignac	Lp	Lope de Vega
Dd	Dryden	Mt	Metastasio
Dl	Dumesnil	Nh	Torres Naharro
Dn	Donatus	Od	Oddi
Dt	Diderot	Pl	Plato
Ed	Edwards	Rb	Robortello
Fr	Decrees of the French Revolution	Rc	Racine
Gd	Giraldi	Rm	Rymer
Gl	Goldoni	Sa	de Staël
Gm	Giacomini	Sd	Stendhal
Go	Gozzi	Se	Saint-Evremond
Gt	Goethe	Sg	Scaliger
Gu	Guarini	Sl	Schlegel
Gz	Grazzini	Sr	Schiller
Hg	Hegel	St	Steele
Hm	Hume	Sy	Sidney
Hr	Horace	Tm	Tirso de Molina
Hu	Hugo	Vt	Voltaire
Hw	Heywood	Wh	Whetstone

1

INTRODUCTION

In this final decade of the twentieth century, having survived a phase in which its very existence was in question, Western theatre flourishes; and it does so despite the dominance of dramatizations in other artistic media. One reason for this renewed vitality is that, having all but lost certain historic communicational and social functions to television, video, and film, theatre has reaffirmed its distinctiveness as a Hegelian mode of knowing through involvement <Hg/206; Hz/241>, a medium for live actors performing for present spectators in real time. On this understanding, it has drawn on the performance traditions of many cultures as sources for renewal,[1] and has partly thrown off the old submission to playwrights – or rather to writing – that has shaped its history for nearly five hundred years. But Western theatre has by no means surrendered its claims to the performance of literature: on the contrary, it has tended to widen its scope to include the staging of novels and other kinds of non-dramatic writing, in addition to the playscripts which remain its staple material.

The fourth volume in this series will attempt to match the intercultural emphasis on performance that animates contemporary theatre, but this second volume (and the third) will be concerned, like the first, with ideas about drama as a social practice that assumes – sometimes questionably – the stage performance of works written for that purpose; and assumes also that the dramatic literary genre and theatrical performance are congruent. In Schlegel and Hegel <Sl/193; Hg/209> especially, this supposed congruence is founded on (performed) drama's unique capacity for combining the sensuous with the ideal.

Before the end of the eighteenth century, "dramatic" usually referred to theatrical performance but during the nineteenth the term acquired more literary connotations and, in the course of the present century, began to provide English with the handy though insufficient distinction, now commonly used, between written texts ("drama") and performance

---

[1] See Barba and Savarese 1991 and Fischer-Lichte, Riley, and Gissenwehrer 1990.

I

("theatre").[2] In France, Mlle Dumesnil had tried much earlier to establish an equivalent verbal and conceptual distinction <Dl/95> by way of asserting the performer's claims to a creativity equivalent to that of the playwright.[3] In their wider uses, the two terms frequently imply different evaluations: "dramatic" words and deeds being generally more estimable than "theatrical" ones.[4] This distinction, and the greater flexibility of the term "drama" – sometimes embracing film, television, and theatre, as well as literature – are consistent with the emphasis on the linguistic and literary components in most European dramatic theory <1:In/6–7>; and also with an actual practice in which the written text has aspired to dominate theatre. The valuation that Castelvetro, in the sixteenth century, gives to non-verbal theatrical expression <1:Cv/129> is exceptional in the context of theoretical writings of his time and earlier, and it remains so long afterwards.

If the traditional assumptions – or prejudices – about the fundamental literariness of drama are clearly limiting, they have also proved highly productive in the context of Western drama and theatre, sustaining theatrical, as well as literary efforts; and supplying the concepts and analytical methods for a theoretical discourse that has been in progress, now, for over two thousand years. In this discourse, the tripartite division of three genres of literature remains remarkably stable until, with Hugo, the neo-classical distinctions between lyric, epic, and dramatic begin to break down and the genres to fuse <Hu/260>. But, if the genre of dramatic literature is stable, the assumed literary-theatrical compound of drama in performance is less so, especially in the period covered by this volume, from the early eighteenth to the early nineteenth century, when the separation of its literary and theatrical constituents is sometimes quite unsettling for theorists of drama and playwrights. "Theatre is literature in action," says de Staël <Sa/184> but Baillie <Bl/178> is only one of many playwrights who find in the theatre action that is anything but literary.

The importance commonly attached to dramatic literature is associated with that of language itself in instantiating cultural coherence and expressing national sentiments; and, when one adds to the literary and linguistic aspects of drama, the theatrical ones of culturally specific non-verbal conventions and manners, and immediate, collective reception, there is good reason for theatre to be more bound up with ideas (and prejudices) about ethnicity and nationhood than other fine arts; and for national theatres to be seen as vital political institutions: "if we had a national theatre," says Schiller, "we would also be a nation" <Sr/161>.

---

[2] See also the brief account of "dramatic" in Williams 1983, 109–10.

[3] François Riccoboni, similarly motivated, attempted to distinguish "l'art du théâtre" and "le poëtique du théâtre", the latter signifying the art of *writing* tragedies and comedies, and the former signifying the art of performance, Riccoboni 1750/1971, 4–5.

[4] See Barish 1981, 323ff.

Such ideas are by no means new – in Lope de Vega <1:Lp/184> and Dryden <1:Dd/285> they are fundamental – but they are especially common in the dramatic theory of the period covered by this volume; and they are subject to critical scrutiny in the writings of Schlegel and de Staël, especially.

The usual privileging of the literary genre is founded on three main assumptions: first, that the writing precedes the playing; second, that what is essential in drama is, as Aristotle insisted – but with respect to tragedy only – accessible through reading <1:Ar/7>; and third, that written drama can actually inscribe theatricality and is thus distinct from other literary genres – lyric, for instance – that theatre uses. The first of these assumptions is founded on a general practice in Western theatre. In Diderot's theory, however, allowance is made for a non-verbal content supplied by actors: "We talk too much in our plays, and consequently the actors have little chance to act," says Diderot's Dorval <Dt/42>. He also allows his actors to "rearrange the text" somewhat, with the idea that such freedom enables that strong emotional involvement of the spectators which is stirred by representations of moments of silence and incapacity for speech. More oppositionally, we see writing set off against playing in Gozzi's defense of the *commedia dell'arte* <Go/103> from Goldoni's attempt <Gl/72> to reform the genre by bringing theatre more firmly under the control of literature, and thus making it socially critical. We also have the extraordinary dramatic spectacle – as it was conceived in its own time and has been since (Butwin 1975) – of the French Revolution, in which theatrical performance is regarded as, first and foremost, a political activity. Rather paradoxically, though, the officially preferred basis for such celebrations of republican citizenship was old tragedies <Fr/173>. In England, we hear the reiterated complaint <Bl/180> that "legitimate drama" is being driven from the theatre by all manner of "illegitimate" shows, about how ill-accommodated dramatic literature is by actual theatre practice.

The second assumption privileging the literary genre is tersely articulated by Dr. Johnson: "A play read, affects the mind like a play acted" <Jh/86>. The epigrammatic certitude of this statement is enabled by the ambiguity of "play," as it has developed in English usage from a word signifying such physical activity as dancing and leaping for joy to a term for a literary text: reading a "play" is rather like eating a bill of fare, from a certain etymological point of view. The French language does something similar in entitling a playwright's collected writings *le théâtre de* ... somebody or other. In such usages there may be lurking the understanding that, if the staged play represents the world, the read play represents not the world but the stage <Sl/193>. Shakespeare's plays are particularly prone to be praised as dramas for which staging is superfluous.

As to the third assumption privileging writing, the idea that it can inscribe theatre, Steele asserts that "the greatest effect of a play in reading is to excite the reader to go see it," but what the spectators saw of his *The Conscious Lovers* was not what he had devised for them, and he made publication an occasion for pointing out, and doing his best to make good, the stage production's substitution of instrumental music for a song <St/18>. Goethe remarks that "a good play can be in fact only half transmitted in writing, a great part of its effect depending on the scene, the personal qualities of the actor, the powers of his voice, the peculiarities of his gestures, and even the spirit and favorable humour of the spectators" (Goethe/Eastlake 1967, xxviii). Hazlitt agrees with him <Hz/241> but, on the other hand, mostly prefers his Shakespeare read, rather than performed. And, on this point, Goethe agrees with *him*, claiming that Shakespeare's "living world" is better conveyed by reading aloud than by stage performance <Gt/146>. Either way, to define what may be and cannot be transmitted in the theatre, or what may be and cannot be "committed to paper" – that is to say, what the relationship might be between the inscripted and unscripted parts of a "play" proves a compelling, intractable, and often contentious problem.

One thing is certain, though: in an age deeply preoccupied with the theory and practice of acting, ideas about acting are critical to the understanding of what belongs to writing and what to the stage. The different views and practices of the Riccobonis, father and son, bear on this issue, as do those of the rival French players Clairon and Dumesnil <Dl/94>, or of two later players commonly paired, Bernhardt and Duse.[5] François Riccoboni and Hippolyte Clairon both advocate systematic study and conscious application of acting technique, and tend thus towards the idea of the actor as an interpretive medium bodying forth the character drawn by the writer. On the other hand, Luigi Riccoboni's insistence on real feelings on stage, like Dumesnil's reliance on passion, intuition, and nature, comes from the conviction that the actor is a creator – not just an interpreter – of roles; one who introduces into the work an *authentic subject*, another author.

This key issue of the collaboration, intervention, or suppression of the performer as a distinct creative source and subject-presence arises in many forms. Diderot's fictional-theoretical actors of *Le Fils naturel* play themselves: in the most intimate possible relation between acting and living they *are* the characters they play <Dt/35>. Lessing discovers that mediocre plays leave more room for the actor-subject than great ones <Lg/115>, a view shared by Hazlitt <Hz/241>. In Goethe's *Wilhelm*

---

[5] In his *Réflexions historiques et critiques sur les différents théâtres de l'Europe, avec les pensées sur la declamation* (1738) the *commedia dell'arte* actor Luigi Riccoboni (1676–1753) advocated the achievement of illusion through the actor's emotional immersion in the role: his son, Antonio Francesco Riccoboni (1707–72), in his *L'Art du théâtre: à Madame xxx* (1750), favored detachment, technique, and control. On Sarah Bernhardt (1844–1923) and Eleonora Duse (1858–1924), see States 1987, 166–70.

Meister, the Manager, Serlo, insists that the actor give himself utterly to the character but also considers how Shakespeare's *Hamlet* might best be adapted to the demands of the public <Gt/143>! Elsewhere Goethe contrasts the epic narrator, who should be invisible, with the actor who should be intensely present to the audience, but only as the embodiment of the character represented <Gt/145>. Hegel insists that actors should be regarded as genuine artists but, at the same time, that the actor should be a "sponge," bound by the conditions of theatrical art to immolate all selfhood in the realization of the character drawn by the playwright <Hg/213>. Most insidious, because it appears to be a truism, is the view that the actor's person should conform with the playwright's imagination; that typecasting (as it has come to be called) is a given of theatrical performance. On this understanding, the playwright (or director) may rightly require that the actor not only "match as far as possible the prevalent conceptions of his fictitious original in sex, age, and figure, but assume his entire personality" <Sl/193>. In such matching of gender, age, and physique the theatre performs silently its office of imitating life and, at the same time, confirms prejudices, stereotypes, and ideals; as when Goethe's Wilhelm Meister persuades himself that Hamlet must be blue-eyed, blonde, and plump <Gt/140>. But Diderot – the later Diderot, at least – would not have found it impossible to accept today's conventions (which are not operative in the non-theatrical media and not ubiquitously on the stage, of course) whereby a black actor may be cast as an eighteenth-century European, a woman play a male role, or an adult actor represent a child. In the period covered by this volume, the discussion is about how actor and character might merge – whether by empathy or technique – rather than whether they should; though there is also a recognition that the spectators go to see a David Garrick or an Edmund Kean more than the characters they play <Hz/246>.

Garrick, indeed, was for many spectators the outstanding example of what, in theory, acting should be. Diderot, who became acquainted with him during Garrick's Continental tour of 1763–65, found in the English actor's performances the model for an art whereby the character's emotions might be conveyed through technique and control, rather than through the personal emotion or empathy of the actor. So, in the posthumously published *Paradoxe sur le comédien*, he writes:

> As far as I am concerned, [a great actor] must have excellent judgment; he must have within him a cool and detached observer; it follows that what I require of him is perspicuity and not sensitivity, the art of imitating everything or, what is the same thing, an equal aptitude for all sorts of characters and roles. ... What confirms me in this opinion is the unevenness of actors who play from the heart. Expect no unity from them; their acting is alternately strong and weak, hot and cold, flat and sublime.

Tomorrow they will miss the moment that they have excelled in today; they will make up for this by excelling where they failed on the previous occasion. On the other hand, the actor who plays from premeditation, from the study of human nature, from a consistent imitation of some concrete conception, from imagination, from memory, will be coherent, the same at every performance, always equally proficient: everything has been weighed, combined, learnt, and mentally ordered. In his delivery there is neither monotony nor dissonance. Passion is progressive with its peaks and abatements, its beginning, its middle, and its end. The intonations are the same, the positions are the same, the movements are the same; if there is any difference from performance to performance, it is usually in the superiority of the most recent. He will not change day by day; he is a mirror, always poised to reflect actualities and to show them with the same precision, the same power, and the same truth. Every bit as much as the poet he will draw from nature's inexhaustible depths rather than confronting the exhaustion of his own resources.[6]

For Lessing, another admirer of Garrick, the sustained analysis of acting and theatrical production was the motive for initiating the series of papers later collected as *Hamburg Dramaturgy* <Lg/107>. His abandonment of this original intention in favor of a series of more abstractly theoretical discussions of drama, though it opened the way to achievements of other kinds, was a significant failure, anticipating some of the difficulties that have confronted later attempts to make objective analyses of the intersubjective arts of the theatre. But, in the early numbers of the periodical, Lessing does make really penetrating observations on the relation between writing and acting. For him, this relation is fundamentally a dialectical one, whereby the speech, gesture, and expression of the actor far from offering simply to reiterate, illustrate, or interpret anterior verbal meanings, should register, even resist, the impact of the given (abstract) words on a natural being – the actor <Lg/109>. In Kleist's subtle and prophetic meditation on marionettes, however, naturalness, knowledge, and self-awareness are antithetical to a non-human performative perfection <Kl/235>.

For Lessing, it would appear, the transformation of the playwright's words into the utterances and other physical expressions of the actor (in dialogue with the spectators) is the second stage of a transformation of the arbitrary signs of language into the natural signs of speech <Lg/126>. The first stage of this transformation (which is the antithesis of the *de*familiarization associated with Brechtian theory) is writing in dialogue form, from which the supremacy of drama among the arts (for Lessing as for Hegel) derives; dramatic dialogue being the medium that, to a greater extent than

---

[6] Newly translated from Diderot 1967, 128–29. See Burwick 1991, 44ff. for a succinct discussion of the levels of paradox in the *Paradoxe*.

any other, effects a sensuous, natural representation of abstract ideas (or spirit) <Hg/211>.

In Lessing, the processes of dramatic and theatrical naturalization serve to disclose the operations of a providential nature, which all proper art necessarily reveals <Lg/121>. Diderot (to whose thought Lessing is so heavily indebted) illustrates theatrical mediation between providence and human society in an extraordinarily subtle and complex work, of which it might be said that its mixture of genres is its message. The play it contains (*Le Fils naturel*) is deliberately – and perhaps rather deceptively – non-theatrical in that it is incorporated in a narrative context and is the occasion for a theoretical dialogue <Dt/45>. Overall, the work is generically less theatrical than narrative, more theoretical than theatrical. In it, Diderot envisages a role for the playwright as the (reluctant) dramaturge of his family's crisis, which he scripts for performance by its members, who play themselves for themselves alone. This performance is intended by its supposed originator to be a kind of secular, domestic ritual (celebrating the avoidance of unconscious incest) and it should be a more inspiring legacy than painted family portraits can ever be. Given in the privacy of the family drawing-room, such a performance is altogether different from others of its day but not radically different, in terms of its social function, from ancient theatre, perhaps. The kind of theatre envisaged by Diderot would be immune, incidentally, to the strictures against public theatres and professional players that Jean-Jacques Rousseau re-invokes in his *Lettre à d'Alembert sur les spectacles* (1758).[7] But a better match for Rousseau is the unpuritanical Hazlitt, who sees actors as exemplars of style and grace and who experiences the theatre as matter for conversation, as a medium of history and morality, and as an engine of civility <Hz/243>.

As playwright, Diderot's Dorval has the office of giving performable shape to actual events, which in practice requires that the thoughts and feelings of the players, who have incomparably the most intimate understanding – but also a too involved and self-reflexive one – of the roles they play, be not only articulated but restrained by formal requirements. This playwright mediates between the personal involvement of the participants in the actual events and their mimetic reiteration of it, in order to make representation possible; but the playwright in Diderot's narrative is not "really writing for the stage" <Dt/38> and, what is more important, the players in it are unable, finally, to sustain the detachment necessary for the re-enactment of what they have lived through and are still, therefore, living. And this, perhaps, is the salient point: that the representation is *not*

---

[7] Jean-Jacques Rousseau (1712–78) wrote it in response to d'Alembert's article on Geneva in Diderot's *Encyclopedia*. Rousseau uses some standard and some ingenious arguments <Lg/116> in favor of the prohibition of theatre in Geneva. His argument that drama ineluctably presents vice in an attractive form is echoed by Schiller in "Preface to *The Robbers*" <Sr/155>.

quite possible. Actual stagings of *Le Fils naturel*, or attempts to evaluate its "stage-worthiness," negate this theme of the work, of course.

Conflicts between the needs of representation and the circumstances of performance necessarily arise in a medium founded on intersubjective relations amongst performers, and between performers and spectators. Lessing was surprised to discover what Hazlitt so acutely realized, that even writing about performances interferes with performances, and that acting does not consist of objective phenomena. Goethe's Wilhelm Meister <Gt/137> comes to understand, through his intimate involvement in it, the modifications that theatrical performance undergoes in response to the pulsating emotional life of the occasions in which it is immersed. A very direct channel between the work and life is the dialogue with the audience that Hegel supposes to be a necessary characteristic of all works of art <Hg/209>. In the theatre, playwrights and actors may compete for control over that dialogue <Sl/194>, especially if they do not share with the audience, and with each other, an understanding about a creative polyphony <Dl/100>.

For playwrights, one radical solution to the problems of theatrical intersubjectivity is to avoid the theatrical medium. Dramatic form is employed without theatrical restraints or contamination for an audience of readers. This closeting of drama becomes a practice commoner in the nineteenth century than at any earlier time. Fears about the social effects of the theatre, contempt for its degenerate condition, a pre-cinematic drive toward visual images more fluid, extensive, and objective than scenography can match, and even, ultimately, the conviction that the compelling action in drama is an imaginative one that can only be hampered by physical action on the stage, and will be brought to a halt by dancing – all these conspire, in various combinations, to make "drama" separated from the theatre a viable and estimable literary genre.

Insofar as Joanna Baillie was a closet dramatist, she was so by default and her critique <Bl/178> of architectural determinants of performance, of the obstacles imposed by enormous theatres to certain kinds of plays and acting, discloses significant incongruities between ideas about dramaturgy on the one hand and about performance (and economy) on the other. This was a matter of concern for many writers but few inquired into it as closely as Baillie did. More commonly, contemporary theatrical practice was proposed as a major cause of the perceptible "decline of the drama."

Many poets write plays, they say, without ambitions for the theatre; or not, at least, for the theatre of the day. Schiller's *The Robbers* is a renowned example of a play intended for the closet, using the literary methods of drama in order to "catch the most secret operations of the soul," as Schiller says in his Preface <Sr/154>. Schiller's implication that dramatic form is an analogue of these "most secret operations" harks back to Plato and anticipates many modern attempts (such as the Nighttown episode in Joyce's *Ulysses*) to dramatize subjective life. But the main reason Schiller gives for not staging the play is that its portrayal of vice is too realistic and (necessarily) too attractive for a proper decorum of the stage, given theatre's peculiarly immediate appeal to the spectators. (In the event, though, *The Robbers* proved immensely successful in the performance it was soon given.) Verse drama, especially, tends to retire to the closet, where the "supersensuous" ambitions of poetry <Sr/153> may be least inhibited. Byron, despite his personal and official (though brief) attachment to the theatre, and despite the fact that many of his plays were staged, often disavows any theatrical intentions in writing them. In the Preface to *Marino Faliero, Doge of Venice* (produced at Drury Lane in 1821) he insists that he "never made the attempt, and never will" to write "a play which could be deemed stage-worthy" (Byron 1844, 196). But Byron encouraged Drury Lane to produce Joanna Baillie's plays <Bl/177> and urged Coleridge to write for the stage <Co/219>, in the belief that playwrights with the requisite poetic ability were in a position to reform the theatre.

But the theatre's shortcomings are not always the reason for insulating "drama" from it. Sometimes the best artistry of the stage, especially acting, is what makes it an uncongenial medium. Charles Lamb takes both views in his commentary on the "painful and disgusting" spectacles offered by productions of Shakespeare's *Macbeth* and *King Lear*. On the one hand, theatrical presentation may be all too effective; on the other hand, it may demonstrate the hopeless representational inadequacy of the theatre. Lamb's undisguised susceptibilities to theatrical (as opposed to literary) effects are apparently founded on fundamental differences between reading and spectating:

> The state of sublime emotion into which we are elevated by those images of night and horror which Macbeth is made to utter, that solemn prelude with which he entertains the time till the bell shall strike which is to call him to murder Duncan, – when we no longer read it in a book, when we have given up that vantage-ground of abstraction which reading possesses over seeing, and come to see a man in bodily shape before our eyes actually preparing to commit a murder, if the acting be true and impressive, as I have witnessed it in Mr. K[ean]'s performance of that part, the painful anxiety about the act, the natural longing to prevent it while it yet seems unperpetrated, the too close pressing semblance of reality, give a pain and an uneasiness which totally destroy all the delight which the words in the book convey, where the deed doing never presses upon us with the painful sense of presence . . . .

But, as with attempts to stage *King Lear*, the inherent feebleness of theatrical representation may also be an insuperable obstacle:

> The contemptible machinery by which they mimic the storm which
> he goes out in, is not more inadequate to represent the horrors of
> the real elements, than any actor can be to represent Lear . . . .[8]

Lamb's rather ingenuously emotive responses to book and stage, like
Schiller's rationalist concern with stage decorum, are not inconsistent with
Lessing's developed theory in his *Laocoön*, published in 1766. This work
may be said to ground such intuitions in a theory of the non-transferability
of the content of representations, all such content being radically affected
by the particular artistic medium.

Lessing argues for the distinct potentialities of the visual arts and of
poetry: the first are founded on spatial arrangements of bodies (which also
exist in time, however), and the second, poetry, on temporal sequences of
actions (which are, however, embodied). He was frustrated by the opposing current of Romanticism in his attempt to arrest a tendency towards the
confusion of the arts and did not himself follow up the question with
respect to drama's apparent *fusion*, if not confusion, of the arts. In Coleridge, we find the common understanding of the stage as "a combination
of several, or of all the fine arts to an harmonious whole having a distinct
end of its own" <Co/224>; in Hegel the stage is comprised by a totalizing
conception of an art of drama, which is now "liberated" from dance and
music. The idea of a single art of drama appears to gather strength through
the nineteenth and early twentieth centuries. In the mid-twentieth century
it was still current, as in the following instance:

> People are so used to defining each art by its characteristic medium
> that when paint is used in the theatre they class the result as "the
> painter's art," and because the set requires building, they regard
> the designer of it as architect. Drama, consequently, has so often
> been described as a synthesis of several or even all the arts that its
> autonomy, its status as a special mode of a great single art, is
> always in jeopardy.   (Langer 1953, 320–1)

The habit of "defining each art by its characteristic medium" is precisely
what Lessing hopes to encourage in *Laocoön*. He makes discriminations
between the semiotics of the various artistic media in order to further the
appreciation and interpretation of particular works employing them (Wellbery 1984). So, in the art of acting, the particular sensuous expression in
itself, apart from (and in addition to) the fictive or other content of the
representation is a major concern:

> The reporting of someone's scream produces one impression and
> the scream itself another. The drama, designed for living presen-
> tation by the actor, might perhaps for that very reason have to
> conform more strictly to material representation [as?] in painting.

---

[8] "On the tragedies of Shakespeare, considered with reference to their fitness for stage
representation," in Lamb/Lucas 1912, 123–24.

> ... The closer the actor approaches nature, or reality, the more our
> eyes and ears must be offended; for it is an incontrovertible fact
> that they are offended in nature itself when we perceive loud and
> violent expressions of pain.   (Lessing/McCormick 1962, 24)

Lessing's analysis in the *Laocoön* is a considerable theoretical clarification
– or transformation – of earlier ideas about decorum and reception; an
analysis that also presents them in a more aesthetic, less socio-political,
context. But, regrettably, *Laocoön* offers only a few glimpses of the impli-
cations for theatre of Lessing's analysis.

One such is that the proclivities of different artistic media for respectively
temporal and spatial arrangement bears on the long and mostly barren
discussion of the "unities" <1:In/10>. But though, in *Hamburg Dramaturgy*, Lessing observes that the actor's art "stands midway between the
plastic arts and poetry" <Lg/110; Hg/214>, his ideas about spatial and
temporal dynamics in various arts are never given the theatrical application that they invite. Their potential for a revitalized conception of the
unities went unnoticed, even by Lessing himself, for though his theory
strongly implies a distinctive coordination of poetic-temporal and scenic-
spatial media in the theatre, he pays little attention to scenography and his
attack on the neo-classical unities was conventionally rationalistic.

In the sixteenth and seventeenth centuries the achievement of verisimilitude is frequently a main reason given for adherence to the unities of
time, place, and action <1:In/8–9>, as is respect for what was supposed to
be the practice of the ancients and the doctrine of Aristotle <1:In/9–10>.
But Antoine Houdar de la Motte (1672–1731), who ranged himself on the
side of the Moderns against the Ancients in the so-called "Quarrel"
between them, proposed a general "unity of interest" <Vt/25; Dt/52;
Sl/202; Co/232> and, in theory, made the spectators' pleasure decisive in
the judging of plays, rather than formal criteria. Voltaire and, more
pragmatically, Diderot <Dt/37> defend the unities. For Diderot the unity
of place is the necessary recourse of a theatre incapable of the rapid
changes of scene that he would welcome. De Staël sensibly remarks that
the discussion of the unities is "overworked" but finds it necessary to
engage in it <Sa/185>, as do most theorists of the period. Even Hegel finds
it necessary to work them into his paradigm of dramatic art <Hg/207>,
though Schlegel had effectively dealt with the matter <Sl/201> on terms
that are more consistent, probably, with Hegel's own conception of
drama. Voltaire defends the unities against de la Motte partly out of
reverence for the great practitioners of the previous generation – Corneille
<1:Cn/234>, Racine <1:Rc/257>, and Molière – and also as the means of
achieving credibility founded on an implacable rationality: "a single
action cannot occur in several places at once," he says. "If the characters I
see are in Athens in the first act, how can they be in Persia in the second?"
<Vt/24>

Dr. Johnson answers Voltaire with an opposite and equal rationalism of his own:

> an action must be in some place; but the different actions that complete a story may be in places very remote from each other; and where is the absurdity of allowing that space to represent first Athens, and then Sicily, which was always known to be neither Sicily nor Athens, but a modern theatre. <Jh/84–5>

Coleridge views this encounter of rationalists as a meeting of extremes <Co/230> and seeks to shift the discussion away from disputes about the structures of plays to consideration of audiences' states of mind. Following in Lessing's and, more particularly, in Schlegel's footsteps <Sl/198>, he regards theatrical illusion as a matter of conventional and volitional responses to the medium rather than as the consequence of a relation between the stage representation and the world, or as the product of certain formal characteristics of drama.

If questions about illusion and delusion are fundamental to the experience and understanding of theatre, the answers are such as to lead one to suppose that different individuals, or the same individuals on different occasions – or even at different moments – are infinitely various in their responses; and that problems concerning theatrical illusion pertain to all representation and hence to life itself.[9] For Lessing, like Robortello before him <1:Rb/86>, the language of poetry is distinguished from ordinary language by virtue of making its audience forget the linguistic means by which a mental image is sustained – so strongly sustained that it arouses feelings like those produced by its equivalent in reality. This being his view of theatrical images also, interruptions of the illusion, such as references to the theatre itself, are to be avoided <Lg/118; Bm/132>. In Schlegel and Coleridge, on the other hand, the voluntariness of the theatrical illusion, which depends on a degree of sophistication in the spectator, is cardinal.

Theatrical illusion is a theme for fiction, as well as theory. Diderot makes it such in his *Les bijoux indiscrets* (1748), in which compelling illusion is conceived as the chief source of theatrical pleasure. Henry Fielding, also, satirizes perfect theatrical illusion in *The History of Tom Jones: A Foundling* (1749), in which Mr. Partridge, the very model of a naive, deluded spectator, gives more entertainment than the stage performance does to all those within earshot of him. Partridge's opinions on the acting are, in their own way, a great tribute to the star:

> ... Jones asked him, "Which of the players he had liked best?" To this he answered, with some appearance of indignation at the question, "The King, without doubt." – "Indeed, Mr. Partridge," says Mrs. Miller. "You are not of the same opinion with the town; for they are all agreed that Hamlet is acted by the best player who

---

[9] For an excellent study of this issue throughout the period see Burwick 1991.

ever was on the stage." – "He the best player!" cries Partridge, with a contemptuous sneer; "why, I could act as well as he myself. I am sure, if I had seen a ghost, I should have looked in the very same manner, and done just as he did. And then, to be sure, in that scene, as you called it, between him and his mother, where you told me he acted so fine, why, Lord help me, any man, that is any good man, that had such a mother, would have done exactly the same. I know you are only joking with me; but indeed, madam, though I was never at a play in London, yet I have seen acting before in the country: and the king for my money; he speaks all his words distinctly, half as loud again as the other. – Anybody may see he is an actor."[10]

As has been remarked, the converse equivalent of Partridge's response to David Garrick's acting was felt throughout Europe, Garrick being the supreme example of an art of acting that, by concealing art, achieved moving effects of "naturalness."

Whether Partridge's reception of *Hamlet* is proper or not is easier to judge, perhaps, than whether he gets more or less pleasure than his fellow-spectators. Dr. Johnson has no time for Partridgery: "The delight of tragedy proceeds from our consciousness of fiction; if we thought murders and treasons real, they would please no more" <Jh/85>. But Partridge accepts both the reality of the Ghost and the theatricality of the presentation; and his enjoyment of his emotional involvement with the action includes fear. His responses are, in fact, quite complex, and, like those of more experienced spectators, strongly emotional.

David Hume's view of the pleasure in tragedy has something in common with Johnson's but adds a specifically aesthetic dimension. For Hume, the pleasure in tragedy comes from the "consciousness of the fiction" together with its emotional truth. It arouses passions which correspond with those excited by real occasions but these passions are transmuted by art and felt with a certain detachment. So we may weep and find pleasure at the same time. Hume anticipates Kant's theory of the disinterestedness of art and of aesthetic response. In doing so, he mediates between doctrines positing real emotions aroused by close imitations, as expounded by Diderot, for whom "the real world [is] the only source of pleasure for the mind" <Dt/45> and, on the other hand, Schiller's, Hugo's, and the Romantic conception of an autonomous art reaching for a realm of moral freedom <Sr/165>. Access to such a realm can be inhibited by theatrical illusion, naturalism, and prose and may be enabled by deliberate artificiality, such as Schiller's use of the chorus as a wall to preserve the poetic freedom of the theatre from the real world <Sr/167> by symbolism and, for Hugo <Hu/258>, by the mixture of the grotesque and sublime. Drama that partakes of the poetic, says Schlegel, should express "thoughts and feelings which . . . are

[10] Fielding 1950, 761.

eternally true, and soar above this earthly life" and yet it must also "exhibit them embodied before us" <Sl/193>. These demands may seem the more mystical in their origins when we recall Schiller's assertion that "Nature itself is only an idea of the spirit" <Sr/166>.

Much of the theoretical discussion, in this period, is conducted, as usual, in terms of genre: the new genres of serious and bourgeois drama proposed by Diderot <Dt/57; Bm/127>, traditional tragedy and comedy, and romantic drama. Beaumarchais works both sides of a generic street, experimenting with the new genre of *drame* and, more successfully, with traditional comedy. In the dedication to the reader of his *The Barber of Seville* (1772) he repudiates (in a rather double-edged way) his earlier conception of serious drama and his practice of it:

> What writer ever had more need of the indulgence of the reader than I? In vain I would like to conceal it. I once had the weakness, Sir, to offer you, at different times, two sad *drames*, monstrous productions, as is well known, for it is no longer possible to deny that there is no genre between tragedy and comedy. That's a settled issue: the Master [Aristotle?] has said so, the school re-echoes it and, as for me, I am so thoroughly convinced of it that if today I wanted to put on the stage a mother bathed in tears, a betrayed wife, a distraught sister, a disinherited son, in order to present them decently to the public, I should begin by inventing for them a fine kingdom where they would have reigned to the best of their ability. It would be somewhere near one of the archipelagos or in some other such corner of the world. After that I would make sure that the implausibility of the tale, the extravagance of the deeds, the turgidity of the characters, the immensity of the ideas and the overblown language, far from being imputed to me as a reproach, would underwrite my success.
>
> Present middling men despondent and miserable – not on your life! One should never put such types on display except for ridicule. Ridiculous citizens and unhappy kings – there you have all the theatre that there is and can be, and I take it as a given; that is how it is and I do not want to quarrel with anyone.
>
> So, I once had the frailty, Sir, to compose *drames* which were not well-conceived as to genre, and I now deeply regret it.[11]

Redefinitions of tragedy, which posit, as in Hume, a special aesthetic pleasure in it <Hm/89> or, as in Schlegel and Hegel, its revelation of a spiritual realm in which human suffering and conflict are transcended <Sl/193–4; Hg/215>, recuperate the traditional genre by differentiating sharply between the classical and modern practice of it, between Aristotelian and Romantic poetic theory; that is to say, the discussion of the classical genres is historicized and neo-classical formalism is thus overtaken.

---

[11] Newly translated from Beaumarchais/Allem & Courant 1973, 160.

Associated with questions about genre are those about appropriate linguistic forms: whether prose is appropriate for tragedy, as de la Motte argues in the preface to *Inès de Castro* (1723); whether rhyme and metre <Vt/26; Sr/166> are essential to poetry (as opposed to verse); whether French alexandrine is more or less viable than English blank verse <Sa/185>; whether verse is mimetically restrictive <Bm/131; Sd/254> or imaginatively liberating <Sr/166–7; Hu/264>. In Schlegel such questions are transformed by the infusion of historical awareness into critical discussion <Sl/189>, and in Hegel by a fusion of historical with aesthetic theory <Hg/206>. An open dialectics of "Romantic" and "Classical" displaces the implacable oppositions of "Ancient" and "Modern." But there remain irresolvable tensions between the possibilities of representation and those of performance, in both writing and playing.

Throughout this period (and later) one playwright comes more and more to dominate, and is often employed to subvert, the theoretical discussion. Standing as a mighty opposite to antiquity and the corrective of neo-classical rigidity, his works supreme examples of "organic form" <Sl/204> or even utterances of nature <Co/220>, Shakespeare supposedly confirms the expendability of all theoretical reflection on drama and even drama's transcendence of the stage, which cannot be "a vehicle worthy of his genius" <Gt/150>. In this way, Shakespeare transcends even Schlegel's multicultural historicism <Sl/202>. For Victor Hugo "Shakespeare is drama," and, in the name of such creative genius, Hugo asserts "the freedom of art against the despotism of systems, codes and rules" <Hu/265>. Lessing, though no less an admirer of Shakespeare's work than Hugo, had warned against taking genius as a model <Lg/106>, but the warning went largely unheeded, alas, by playwrights and theorists alike.

In the writings included in this volume major conceptual transformations are evident, mostly associated with the transition from neo-classical to Romantic modes of thought. But, as in the first volume, certain issues are recurrent, such as: the relations between representation, illusion, and performance; or those between writing and staging; the sources and paradoxes of emotional response, as in their moral effects, or the pleasure taken in painful spectacles; how dramatic literature and theatrical production are or should be coordinated; whether actors are creators or interpreters, what effects they may properly aim for, and how these might best be achieved; and what the possibilities might be in dramatic genres old and new. In representing such issues, whole documents or substantial extracts have been preferred over a wider-ranging selection of writers and works and, though the arrangement is, for convenience, chronological, each selection has been made for its intrinsic theoretical interest.

Michael J. Sidnell, Toronto, 1993.

2

SIR RICHARD STEELE
(1672–1729)

The two things Steele had uppermost in mind in his writing of *The Conscious Lovers* were money and a new example for comedy. He hoped that the play would supply both, relieving him of his considerable debts and demonstrating the efficacious wholesomeness of a comedy which would move the audience to tears rather than laughter and emphasize virtue rather than vice. Steele succeeded amply on both counts.

The comedy, which was Steele's fourth, was some six years in the writing and was further delayed in its arrival on stage by his difficulties – extraneous to the play – with the Lord Chamberlain, or so it appears (Loftis 1952, 121ff.). But the interval between the writing of the play and its performance was not wholly disadvantageous since great expectations were built up in advance of the production not only through Steele's own references to the play in his journalism but also through other published news and views about it, not the least of which was John Dennis' <Jh/76> savage pre-performance critical attack.[1]

The Conscious Lovers was based on Terence's *Andria*,[2] though with very extensive transformations, modernization, and elaboration of the classical model. Colley Cibber, who played the servant Tom, apparently had more of a hand in reshaping the play for performance than the Preface below indicates, though Steele would later claim that Cibber's alterations were for the worse (Steele/Kenny 1971, 278). The production, when it came, was lavish, with new costumes and sets, and vastly successful, running for eighteen nights and bringing in the biggest gross in the history of Drury Lane. The critical reception was by no means of the same order, the play being vigorously attacked and ridiculed, and more moderately defended. Frequently printed and much translated, the play was not only widely read but remained popular for another fifty years and more in the English theatre, enjoying many revivals in London and the provinces. As Steele had intended, *The Conscious Lovers* established itself as a model of the kind of didactic, sentimental comedy that he commends in the Preface.

For further reading
Loftis 1952; Steele/Kenny 1971.

---

[1] "A Defense of Sir Fopling Flutter," Dennis 1943, II:241–50. John Dennis (1657–1734) was the chief, often controversial, critic of the day, as well as a playwright and poet.

[2] Terence's first comedy, *Andria* (*Woman of Andros*), was produced in 166 B.C. Though the *mores* in the two plays are very different, both have to do with the conflict between the older and younger generations about whom the latter shall marry.

Preface to *The Conscious Lovers*[3]

This comedy has been received with universal acceptance, for it was in every part excellently performed; and there needs no other applause of the actors, but that they excelled according to the dignity and difficulty of the character they represented. But this great favor done to the work in acting, renders the expectation still the greater from the author to keep up the spirit in the representation of the closet, or any other circumstance of the reader, whether alone or in company: to which I can only say, that it must be remembered a play is to be seen, and is made to be represented with the advantage of action, nor can appear but with half the spirit, without it; for the greatest effect of a play in reading is to excite the reader to go see it; and when he does so, it is then a play has the effect of example and precept.

The chief design of this was to be an innocent performance, and the audience have abundantly showed how ready they are to support what is visibly intended that way; nor do I make any difficulty to acknowledge that the whole was writ for the sake of the scene of the fourth act, wherein Mr. Bevil evades the quarrel with his friend,[4] and hope it may have some effect upon the Goths and Vandals that frequent the theatres, or a more polite audience may supply their absence.

But this incident, and the case of the father and the daughter,[5] are esteemed by some people no subjects of comedy; but I cannot be of their mind; for anything that has its foundation in happiness and success, must be allowed to be the object of comedy, and sure it must be an improvement of it, to introduce a joy too exquisite for laughter <Dt/59; Go/103; Lg/115; Bm/130>, that can have no spring but in delight, which is the case of this young lady. I must therefore contend, that the tears which were shed on that occasion flowed from reason and good sense, and that men ought not to be laughed at for weeping, till we are come to a more clear notion of what is to be imputed to the hardness of the head, and the softness of the heart; and I think it was very politely said of Mr. Wilks[6] to one who told me there was a general weeping for Indiana, I'll warrant he'll fight ne'er the worse for that. To be apt to give way to the impressions of humanity is the excellence of a right disposition, and the natural working of a well-turned spirit. But as I have suffered by critics who are got no further than to inquire whether they ought to be pleased or not, I would

---

[3] 1723. Spelling and punctuation have been modernized.

[4] In Act 4, scene 1, Bevil Junior courageously and kindly avoids the acceptance of a challenge to a duel made by his jealous and rash friend Charles Myrtle. Steele's dialogue moralizes the situation.

[5] In Act 5, scene 3, Mr. Sealand and his long lost daughter rediscover each other, with much emotion.

[6] Robert Wilks (1665–1732) was well known as an actor in spirited and refined roles. In Steele's play he acted Myrtle and also spoke the Prologue. Wilks was also one of the joint managers of Drury Lane.

willingly find them properer matter for their employment, and revive here a song that was omitted for want of a performer, and designed for the entertainment of Indiana; Sig. Carbonelli instead of it played on the fiddle, and it is for want of a singer that such advantageous things are said of an instrument which were designed for a voice. The song is the distress of a love-sick maid, and may be a fit entertainment for some small critics to examine whether the passion is just, or the distress male or female.

I

From place to place forlorn I go,
    With downcast eyes a silent shade,
Forbidden to declare my woe;
    To speak, till spoken to, afraid.

II

My inward pangs, my secret grief,
    My soft consenting looks betray.
He loves, but gives me no relief;
    Why speaks not he who may?

It remains to say a word concerning Terence, and I am extremely surprised to find what Mr. Cibber told me, prove a truth, that what I valued myself so much upon, the translation of him, should be imputed to me as a reproach. Mr. Cibber's zeal for the work, his care and application in instructing the actors, and altering the disposition of the scenes, when I was, through sickness, unable to cultivate such things myself, has been a very obliging favor and friendship to me.[7] For this reason, I was very hardly persuaded to throw away Terence's celebrated funeral,[8] and take only the bare authority of the young man's character; and how I have worked it into an Englishman, and made use of the same circumstances of discovering a daughter, when we least hoped for one, is humbly submitted to the learned reader.

---

[7] Usually, the author himself would have overseen the staging of the work.
[8] On Cibber's advice Steele substituted a masquerade for the funeral in Terence's *Andria*, as the occasion on which the lovers' attachment to each other is revealed.

3

VOLTAIRE
(FRANÇOIS-MARIE
AROUET)
(1694–1778)

Voltaire's interest in the theatre was lifelong. He began writing tragedies at an early age, enjoyed acting, and built several private theatres, including one at Ferney, his home. His version of *Oedipus* was begun when he was eighteen and completed during his eleven-month sojourn in the Bastille. It was first performed in 1718, achieving considerable success, and remained popular for some years (Voltaire/ Moland 1877, II:47). When it was published, in 1719, it was accompanied by several letters, giving Voltaire's ideas on tragedy, and the difficulties he sees in trying to imitate ancient authors, as well as answering or anticipating criticism of his own play. He evaluates and compares three different versions of *Oedipus*, by Sophocles, Corneille <1:Cn/234>, and himself.

The Preface to the 1730 edition of *Oedipus* was in part a reply to Houdar de la Motte <In/11>, who wanted to free tragedy from the tyranny of the unities and of rhymed verse. With his admiration for Corneille and Racine and his insistence on the use of poetry in tragedy, Voltaire reasserts traditional values.

The "Discourse on Tragedy," which accompanied his tragedy *Brutus* and which was dedicated to Lord Bolingbroke,[1] brings English influence into the equation. Having spent over two years in England, and having had a taste of greater intellectual freedom, Voltaire seeks to broaden the experience of French audiences and show them new possibilities of action and spectacle on the stage. He walks a delicate line between the loosening of the rules of *bienséance* – decency and what is suitable to be shown on the stage – and insistence on the classical rules of the unities. As in the previous century, verisimilitude <1:In/9> is still highly prized.

For further reading

Cardy 1982; Williams 1966.

---

[1] Henry St. John Bolingbroke (1678–1751), the Tory Secretary of State, philosopher, and essayist. At the accession of George I, he was convicted of treason and fled to France. It is from this time that most of his essays date. Having been pardoned, he returned to England in 1725 (where Voltaire himself was in exile from 1726 to 1729). Bolingbroke's collected works, posthumously published in 1754, revealed his religious skepticism.

From letters on *Oedipus*[2]

Letter III: Containing the Critique of the Work of Sophocles

Sir,

My lack of erudition prevents me from determining "whether Sophocles' tragedy imitates by language, number, and harmony, which Aristotle explicitly calls pleasingly heightened language" < 1:Ar/42 >. Nor will I discuss "whether it is a play of the first kind, simple and complex, simple because it has only a single catastrophe and complex because it has both recognition and peripety" < 1:Ar/46–47 >.

I will simply point out to you in all candor the passages which I did not like, and for which I require assistance from those with greater knowledge of the ancients, who can better excuse all of their defects. . . .[3]

M. Dacier,[4] who translated Sophocles' *Oedipus*, maintains that the spectators are very impatient to find out what stand Jocasta will take, and how Oedipus will carry out against himself the maledictions he has uttered against the murderer of Laius. I had allowed myself to be swayed by this argument because of my respect for this learned man, and I was of his opinion when I read his translation. The performance of my play has clearly disabused me, and I realize that there is no harm in praising the Greek poets to our heart's content, but that it is dangerous to imitate them <Sd/251>. . . .

You see that in my criticism of Sophocles' *Oedipus*, I have concentrated on pointing out only those weaknesses which are commonly recognized at all times and in all places. Contradictions, examples of absurdity, or speeches that merely strive for effect without advancing the plot or revealing character, are considered weaknesses in every country. I am not surprised that, in spite of so many imperfections, Sophocles should have won the admiration of his contemporaries. The harmony of his verse and the pathos of his style were able to captivate the Athenians, who, for all of their intellect and high degree of civilization, could not possibly have an accurate idea of the perfection of an art which was still in its infancy.

. . . Thus Sophocles and Euripides, with all of their imperfections, were as successful with Athenian audiences as Corneille < 1:Cn/234> and Racine < 1:Rc/257> were with us. While we may find fault with Greek tragedies, we must still respect the genius of their authors. Their weaknesses can be ascribed to the time when they lived; their beauty is theirs alone. And it is probable that, had they been born in our time, they would have perfected the art that they practically invented in their own.

---

[2] Newly translated from Voltaire/Moland 1877, II:18–46.

[3] Here follows a detailed reckoning of the formal inadequacies of the play and absurdities of the plot.

[4] André Dacier (1651–1722) was an editor and translator of classical texts. His edition of Aristotle's *Poetics* (1692) was regarded as authoritative in England as well as France.

Letter IV: Containing the Criticism of Corneille's *Oedipus*[5]

... Certainly I have much more respect for this French author than for the Greek playwright, but I have even more respect for the truth, to which I owe the highest consideration. Indeed, I believe that those who are unable to recognize the weaknesses of great men, are also incapable of appreciating their perfections. I therefore dare to criticize Corneille's *Oedipus* <1:Cn/250>....

Corneille was well aware that the simplicity, or rather the sterility of Sophocles' tragedy was unable to provide the entire scope of action that our plays require. It is a great mistake to think that all of these subjects which were used successfully in the past by Sophocles and Euripides – *Oedipus*, *Philoctetes*, *Electra*, and *Iphigenia in Tauris* – are suited for dramatic treatment and easy to handle. They are, on the contrary, the most unrewarding and impracticable subjects, yielding material for one or two scenes at the very most, but not for an entire tragedy. I realize that more terrible or more touching events than these are scarcely to be seen on the stage, and for that very reason it is more difficult to achieve success with them. They must be combined with passions that prepare for them and make them credible. If these passions are too strong, they overpower the subject, and if they are too weak, they fall flat. Corneille had to make his way between these two extremes and from his own fertile imagination make up for the aridity of the subject....[6]

Letter V: Containing the Critique of the new *Oedipus*

Sir,

I have arrived at the easiest part of my treatise – the criticism of my own work. In order not to waste time, I shall begin with the first problem, which is that of the subject. According to the rules, the play ought to end in the first act. It is unnatural for Oedipus not to know how his predecessor died. Sophocles made no effort at all to solve this problem. In trying to avoid it, Corneille does even worse than Sophocles, and I was no more successful at correcting it than either of them....

Here is a more glaring fault, having nothing to do with the subject, and for which I alone am responsible; it is the character of Philoctetes. He seems to have come to Thebes solely in order to be accused, and even so, there may be little ground for suspicion against him. He arrives in the first act, and leaves again in the third. He is mentioned only in the first three acts, and not a word is said about him in the last two. He contributes to some extent to the central complication of the play, and the dénouement

---

[5] The play was first produced in 1659 at the Hotêl de Bourgogne.
[6] Voltaire's critique begins with Corneille's choice of subject (the episode of Thésée and Dircé, ending with their marriage, to which Oedipus' misfortunes are subordinated) and continues with detailed remarks on the shortcomings of the treatment.

occurs without him. Thus there appear to be two separate tragedies, one
revolving around Philoctetes and the other around Oedipus.

I wanted to give Philoctetes the character of a hero, but I greatly fear
that I exaggerated his nobility of soul to the point of turning him into a
braggart....

His ignorance about events in Thebes, when he arrives there, is no less
reprehensible, in my view, than that shown by Oedipus. Mount Oeta,
where he witnessed the death of Hercules, was not so far away from
Thebes that he could not easily have found out what was happening in
that city. Fortunately this deplorable ignorance gave me the opportunity
for an exposition of the subject which was very well received. I am thus
persuaded that the excellent qualities of a work sometimes stem from a
weakness.

The usual pitfall in tragedies is exactly the opposite. The exposition of the
play's subject is addressed to a character who knows just as much about it
as the speaker. In order to let the audience know what is happening, the
author must have the main characters say things to each other that they
have probably said a hundred times before. The perfect technique would be
to combine events in such a way that the actor who is speaking would
never have had to say the lines he is given until the very moment when he
is uttering them. One example among others of this kind of perfection, is
found in the first scene of [Racine's] tragedy *Bajazet* < 1:Rc/263–64 >.
Acomat cannot possibly be aware of what is going on in the army; Osmin
has no way of knowing about events in the harem. Each one tells the other
his secrets, which are both informative and interesting to the audience.
And this clever exposition is handled with a subtlety of which I believe
Racine alone was capable.

It is true that there are some tragic plots in which one is so hampered by
the strangeness of the events, that it is almost impossible to achieve this
degree of naturalness and probability in the exposition. I believe ... that
the subject of Oedipus is one of this kind, and when one has so little control
of the material, one must always try to be interesting rather than accurate.
For audiences can forgive everything except tedium, and once their
emotions have been touched, they rarely question the reasons behind these
feelings.

As for the memory of an earlier love between Jocasta and Philoctetes, I
venture to say that it is a necessary defect. The subject by itself did not
provide me with anything to fill the first three acts; in fact I scarcely had
enough for the last two....

The first scene of the fourth act was the most successful, but I still blame
myself, nevertheless, for having Oedipus and Jocasta reveal everything
that they should have told each other much sooner. The plot is based
entirely on a lack of knowledge that seems scarcely credible....

It remains for me to speak about a few rhymes that I experimented with in this tragedy. . . . I find it intolerable that all other qualities of poetry are subordinate to the richness of rhyme, and that poets try to appeal to the ear, rather than to the heart or the mind. This tyranny extends even to requiring that words must rhyme to the eye even more than to the ear . . . .

It seems to me that French poetry would gain a great deal if we wished to shake off the yoke of this unreasonable and tyrannical custom. Giving new forms of rhyme to writers would be tantamount to giving them new thoughts. For being forced to use limited rhymes, means that often one finds only one word in the language that can finish a line. Rarely does one say what one wants to say; the right word cannot be used <Sa/185>. One is obliged to find a thought to fit the rhyme, because one cannot find a rhyme to express one's thought. . . .

Letter VI: Containing a Dissertation on Choruses
Sir,

It only remains for me to speak about the chorus <Sr/164> which I have introduced into my play. I made it into a character, appearing in its place like the other characters. Sometimes it appears on the stage without speaking, merely to add interest to the scene and to contribute to the general magnificence of the spectacle . . . .

In ancient drama, the chorus filled the interval between the acts and never left the stage. This practice had several disadvantages, for between the acts it either spoke about what had already happened, thereby tiring the audience with tedious repetition, or it told what was to happen in the following acts, thus depriving the audience of the pleasure of surprise, or finally it might go on at length with no relation to the main subject, which would therefore be very boring.

The continual presence of the chorus on the stage in a tragedy seems to me even more impracticable. In order for a play to be interesting, the plot usually requires that the main characters have secrets to divulge to one another. How can they possibly tell their secrets in front of a whole crowd? . . . One may well ask why people in ancient times could take such care to maintain a custom so open to ridicule. They did so because they were convinced that the chorus was the root and foundation of tragedy. How typical this is of human beings, who almost always mistake the origin of a thing with the essence of the thing itself. . . .

I shall always believe, therefore, until I am convinced otherwise, that one cannot risk using a chorus in a tragedy without taking the precaution of introducing it in the appropriate place, and only when its presence adds to the beauty of the staging. Furthermore, there are only a very few subjects where this innovation can be used. . . . it is only suitable for plays which concern the destiny of an entire nation. . . .

Preface to *Oedipus*[7]

... The principles of all the arts that depend on the imagination are all easy and simple, all taken from nature and arrived at through reason. Pradon and Boyer[8] knew them just as well as did Corneille and Racine. The only difference was, and will always be, in their application.... It therefore seems just as needless to speak of rules in the preface to a tragedy as it would be for a painter to influence his public by writing dissertations on his paintings, or for a musician to try to demonstrate why his music must be pleasing.

But, since M. de la Motte wishes to establish rules that are in complete opposition to those that guided our great masters, it is right to defend these ancient laws, not because they are ancient, but because they are good and necessary, and could have a formidable adversary in a man of his merit.

The Three Unities
To begin with, M. de la Motte wants to abolish the unities of action, place, and time.

The French were the first among the modern nations to revive these sensible rules. For a long time other countries were reluctant to take on a yoke that seemed restrictive, but since these rules were correct, and since reason triumphs over all, they gradually gave in over the years. In fact, today in England dramatists take pleasure in mentioning in the prefaces to their plays, that the length of the action is the same as the length of the performance....

If I had nothing else to say to M. de la Motte except that Messieurs Corneille, Racine, Molière, Addison, Congreve ... have all observed the laws of the stage, that would be enough to stop anyone who would like to break these laws. But M. de la Motte deserves to be refuted with reasons, rather than with authority.

What is a play? The representation of an action. Why of only one action, and not two or three? It is because the human mind cannot encompass several objects simultaneously, and when the interest is divided it cannot be maintained. ... And finally, Nature alone has shown us this precept, which must be as invariable as Nature itself.

For the same reason unity of place is essential, for a single action cannot occur in several places at once <Jh/85>. If the characters I see are in Athens in the first act, how can they be in Persia in the second? ...

The unity of time is naturally linked to the first two, as I believe I can prove very simply. I go to see a tragedy that is the representation of an

---

[7] From the edition of 1730. Newly translated from Voltaire/Moland 1877, II:47–52.

[8] Nicolas (Jacques) Pradon (1644–98) was persuaded to write *Phèdre et Hippolyte* (1677) to compete with Racine's *Phèdre*. L'Abbé Claude Boyer (1618–98) wrote many mediocre tragedies and tragicomedies on classical and biblical subjects.

action. The subject is the accomplishment of this single action. There is a plot against Augustus in Rome. I want to know what will happen to Augustus and the conspirators. If the playwright makes the action last for two weeks, he must tell me everything that happens during those two weeks, since I am there to find out what happens, and nothing must occur that does not advance the plot. Now if he shows me two weeks of events, then there are at least fourteen different actions, no matter how insignificant they might be. It is no longer only the carrying out of a conspiracy, towards which the action needed to proceed rapidly. Instead it is a long story, which will lose its interest ... because everything has moved away from the moment of decision, which is my only reason for being there. I did not come to the theatre to hear the life story of a hero, but to see one single event in his life. In addition, the playgoer is only in the theatre for three hours; therefore the action should not last more than three hours. ...

We often extend the unity of time to twenty-four hours <1:Dd/277>, and the unity of place to include the precincts of an entire palace. Stricter limits than this would sometimes mean that good subjects could not be shown on the stage, and allowing more freedom would open the way for too many abuses. ...

M. de la Motte thinks that one can transcend all of these rules, by confining oneself to the unity of interest <In/11; Dt/52; Sl/202; Co/232>, which he calls a paradox and claims to have invented. But to me this unity of interest seems to be nothing more than unity of action. ...

All one has to do is to read the best French tragedies, and one will always find that the main characters have different interests, but these various interests are all related to the interest of the central character, and then there is unity of action. If, on the contrary, all of these different interests have nothing to do with the main character, if they do not create lines converging on a common center, the interest is double, and what we call action in the theatre is also double. With the great Corneille, let us confine ourselves to the three unities, within which the other rules, that is to say, the other refinements are contained. ...

"Discourse on Tragedy"[9]

To my lord Bolingbroke.

If I dedicate a work performed in Paris to an Englishman, my lord, it is not for lack of enlightened critics or cultivated minds in my own country, to whom I could have paid this homage; but as you know, the tragedy of *Brutus* <Fr/173> was begun in England. You will remember that when I had retired to Wandsworth, at the home of my friend Mr. Falkener, that

[9] Newly translated from Voltaire/Moland 1877, II:311–24.

worthy and virtuous citizen, I occupied my time there by writing in English prose the first act of this play, more or less as it now exists in French verse. Occasionally I discussed it with you, and we were both astonished that no Englishman had ever written a play on this subject, which of all others is perhaps the most suited to your stage. You encouraged me to continue this work, which was fertile ground for such noble feelings. Allow me to present to you *Brutus*, although it is written in another language . . . to you who would teach me at least to give to my own language that strength and energy inspired by the noble freedom of thought. For the powerful feelings of the soul always find expression in the language, and those who think mighty thoughts speak in the same way. . . .

On Rhyme and the Difficulties of French Versification

What frightened me the most in taking up this career again, was the strictness of our poetry and the restrictions imposed by the rhyme. I missed that freedom you enjoy, of being able to write your tragedies in blank verse, to lengthen, and especially, to shorten almost all your words, to allow lines to flow over into one another, and when required, to create new terms. These are always accepted by your countrymen, as long as they are sonorous, intelligible, and necessary. . . . The French poet is a slave to rhyme, who is sometimes obliged to write four lines to express a thought that an English writer could render in a single line. English writers say what they want; French writers say what they can . . . .

Despite all of these reflections and complaints, we shall never be able to rid ourselves of the enslavement to rhyme; it is essential to French poetry. . . .

Prose Tragedies

Some people[10] have tried to give us prose tragedies; but I do not believe that this undertaking will ever succeed . . . . In fact, it is this very restriction of rhyme and the strictness of our versification which has given us the excellent works we have in our language. . . .

The Nature of English Plays

Since I was unable, my lord, to risk blank verse, such as is used in Italy and in England, on the French stage, I would have liked, at least, to introduce into our theatres some of the excellent qualities of your plays. It is true, and I admit it, that the English theatre certainly has its faults. I have heard you say yourself, that you did not have a single good tragedy; but to make up for this, within these unwieldy monstrosities you have some admirable scenes. Up to the present time, almost all of the tragic authors of your nation have lacked that purity, that orderly conduct of the plot, those proprieties of action and style, that elegance and all of those artistic refinements which have established the reputation of the French theatre

---

[10] De la Motte <In/11> being the most prominent.

since the time of the great Corneille. But your most irregular plays have one great quality, which is their action.

The Weakness of French Plays

In France we have highly acclaimed tragedies which are more like conversations than the representation of an event.... Our excessive delicacy sometimes forces us to narrate what we would like to let the audience see. We are afraid to risk showing new sights on the stage before a nation that is in the habit of ridiculing anything that is contrary to custom.

The conditions under which our comedies are performed, and the abuses that have crept into these performances are another reason for that sterility for which some of our plays may be criticized. The seats for spectators that are on the stage reduce the playing space, and make it almost impossible to show any kind of action.[11] This state of affairs means that stage décor, so highly recommended by ancient authors, is seldom appropriate to the play. Above all, it prevents the actors from moving from one room into another in full view of the audience, as was the practice in Greek and Roman theatre, so that the unity of place and the rule of verisimilitude should both be respected....

Critique of Shakespeare's *Julius Caesar*

What great pleasure it gave me to see in London your tragedy of *Julius Caesar*, which has been delighting your countrymen for a hundred and fifty years! Assuredly I have no intention of approving of the many examples of barbaric vulgarity it contains. It is only surprising that there are not more of them in a work which was written in an age of ignorance, by a man who did not know Latin and whose only teacher was his own genius. But in the midst of so many clumsy breaches of the rules, with what delight I saw Brutus,[12] still holding a dagger stained with Caesar's blood, call together the Roman people and say to them...: "Friends, Romans, countrymen..." [*Julius Caesar* 3.2.12,78].

... Perhaps the French would not allow a chorus made up of Roman artisans and plebeians to be shown on their stages, or the bloody corpse of Caesar to be put on display before the eyes of the people, or the crowd to be incited to vengeance.... Custom alone, which is the sovereign of this world, must change the taste of nations and make us find pleasure in objects for which we now feel aversion.

Horrible Spectacles in Greek Drama

I am well aware that the Greek writers of tragedy, who were moreover superior to the English, made the mistake of often confusing horror with terror and what was disgusting and unbelievable with the tragic and the marvellous. ... But if the Greeks and your nation have gone beyond the

---

[11] Voltaire campaigned successfully against this practice.

[12] Compare the openings of Brutus' and Mark Anthony's addresses.

limits of decency, and if the English in particular have shown appalling spectacles while trying to achieve what was terrifying, we French, as full of scruples as you are daring, hold back, for fear of being carried away. Sometimes, in our fear of going too far, we fall short of tragedy.

I have no intention of suggesting that the stage should become a place of carnage <Hm/93>, as it is in Shakespeare and his successors, who, lacking his genius, imitated only his defects. I dare say, however, that there are some situations the French may still consider merely disgusting and horrible, which, if handled tastefully and artistically, and above all tempered by beautiful poetry, would give us a kind of pleasure we have not previously experienced....

Decorum and the Unities

Can anyone tell me why, in our plays, heroes and heroines are allowed to kill themselves, and yet are prohibited from killing anyone else? Is there any less bloodshed on the stage when Atalide[13] stabs herself for her lover's sake, than there is when Caesar is murdered? ...

All of these rules, about not showing bloodshed on the stage, about not allowing more than three people to speak etc., are rules to which, it seems to me, some exceptions could be made in our plays, as they were in Greek drama. The rules of decorum, which are always somewhat arbitrary, are quite different from the fundamental rules of the drama, the three unities. The result of extending an action beyond the fitting limit of time and space would be a weak and tedious play. ... Ask an author who has crammed too many events into his play, the reason for this error. He will tell you, if he is honest, that he did not have enough talent to find one single occurrence that could fill his play. And if he spread his action over two days and two different cities, you will know that is because he lacked the skill to compress it into a length of three hours and within the confines of a palace, as the rules of verisimilitude require. It would be quite different for an author who dared to present a terrifying spectacle on stage. This would not be a breach of verisimilitude, and far from indicating a dearth of talent, such courage would require instead great gifts as a poet, to imbue with true greatness an action that, without a sublime style, would be merely heinous and disgusting.

The great Corneille dared try such a thing once, in his play *Rodogune*. He depicts a mother who, in the presence of the entire court and an ambassador, tries to poison her son and her daughter-in-law, after having killed her other son with her own hands. She presents the poisoned cup to them, and when they refuse to drink and express their suspicions, she drinks it herself and dies from the poison intended for them. Such terrible events should be shown only sparingly, and it is not for everyone to venture to carry them out....

---

[13] A slave loved by the hero in Racine's *Bajazet*.

Pomp and Dignity of the Spectacle in Tragedy

The more awesome or terrifying a dramatic spectacle is, the more insipid it would become if it were often repeated ....

The more one wishes to dazzle the spectators with a brilliant spectacle, the more one is obliged to say great and unforgettable things ....

The English are much more inclined to action than we are; they appeal to the visual sense. The French are more given to elegance, to harmony, and to the charm of poetry. It is certainly more difficult to write well than to fill the stage with assassinations, tortures, gallows, sorcerers, and ghosts <Lg/113>....

On Love

Discerning critics might ask me why I spoke of love in a tragedy entitled *Junius Brutus*, and why I allowed that passion to mingle with the austere virtue of the Roman senate and ambassadorial politics <Fr/173>.

Our nation has been criticized for having diluted drama with too much tenderness, and the English have earned more or less the same reproach for nearly a century. For to some extent you have always copied our fashions and been contaminated by our vices. But will you allow me to give my opinion on this matter?

It seems to me, that the desire to introduce love into all tragedies betrays an effeminate taste <Jh/78>, while the determination to exclude it completely is unreasonable and curmudgeonly <1:Dd/275-6>.

The drama, whether tragic or comic, is the living portrait of human passions. ... Love is no more a major defect in a tragedy than it is in the *Aeneid*. It is reprehensible only when it is inappropriate to the main action or unskillfully handled.

The Greeks rarely ventured to show this passion in the theatre of Athens. This was firstly because, in the beginning their tragedies were based only on such horrifying stories that the minds of the audience had become accustomed to such spectacles. Secondly, Greek women led a much more secluded life than our women, and thus the language of love was not the subject of every conversation as it is today. There was less demand for poets to write about this passion, which, of all others, is the most difficult to represent, requiring the utmost care and delicacy. A third reason, which seems quite convincing to me, is that there were no actresses in ancient Greece; the roles of women were played by men wearing masks. Words of love would have seemed ridiculous coming from them.

It is just the opposite in London and in Paris, and admittedly authors would have been in conflict with their own interests and the taste of the audience if they had made actresses such as Oldfield, Duclos, and Lecouvreur[14] speak only of politics or of ambition.

---

[14] Anne Oldfield (1683–1730) was the leading London actress of her time, playing in both comedy and tragedy. She was also a considerable social figure. Marie-Anne Duclos

The difficulty is that for our dramatic heroes, love is no more than dalliance, and in your plays it sometimes degenerates into debauchery. . . .

In order for love to be worthy of the tragic theatre, it must be the essential pivot of the play, and not an external element that is arbitrarily dragged in to fill up the empty spaces of your tragedies and ours, which are all too long. It must be a truly tragic passion, considered as a weakness and resisted with remorse. Love must either lead to crimes and misfortunes, to show how dangerous it is, or else be vanquished by virtue, to show that it is not invincible. Failing that, it is no more than love in a pastoral eclogue of a comedy.

It is up to you, my lord, to decide whether I have fulfilled some of these conditions. . . .

(1668–1748) was known for her tempestuous personality and for a declamatory style, which Adrienne Lecouvreur's style <Dl/98> challenged. Lecouvreur's last part was the role of Jocasta in the March 1730 production of Voltaire's *Oedipus*.

4

PIETRO METASTASIO
(1698–1782)

Few writers have enjoyed during their lifetime the success of Pietro Metastasio. Born in Rome as Pietro Trapassi to a family of modest means, he had the good fortune of being adopted by the celebrated scholar Gianvincenzo Gravina, professor of law, literary theorist, student of the classics, and unyielding critic of opera and modern drama, who had seen him as a young boy entertain a group of people by improvising verses. Gravina immediately changed his surname to Metastasio, a word consisting of two Greek roots meaning Trapassi, and began to tutor him in the austere philosophy of art and life of which he was a master, keeping him away as much as he could from the corruptive influence of contemporary dramatic fashion, especially opera. But no sooner was Gravina dead that Metastasio began his career as a prolific librettist, achieving such success as others could only dream of. In 1730 he moved to Vienna to assume the post of imperial poet, and there he remained basking in undiminished glory until his death.

Gravina's lessons, however, had not been entirely lost on him, for Metastasio was also a learned scholar and a careful reader of Aristotle as well as a cogent theorist himself. Of course he could not share his teacher's sense of allegiance to the ancients, championing as he did the new art form that had made him famous and the refined sensitivity of contemporary high society which had made that fame possible. The chief concern of his theory is the opera libretto as a dramatic form, and this motivates his revisitation of Aristotle, whose *Poetics* <1:Ar/3–61> had been generalized by the Aristotelian tradition to cover not only tragedy but all the dramatic genres <1:In/7>. The following passage on catharsis illustrates at once the scope of his theory of the libretto, which must be concerned with all the passions, and his acute awareness that modern times call for a more complex understanding of the psychology of artistic composition and reception.

For further reading

Arcari 1902; Binni 1963; Burney 1796; Russo 1921; Smith 1970.

From *Extract from the Poetics of Aristotle and Considerations on the Same*[1]

... As for me, I would rather that Aristotle had explained himself more clearly with regard to the cure <1:In/7–8> that he proposes. In the first

---

[1] Newly translated from Pietro Metastasio, *Estratto dell'arte poetica di Aristotile e considerazioni su la medesima*, in Metastasio/Brunelli 1951.

place I do not know whether with the term catharsis or purgation he wanted us to understand the total destruction of the passions or simply their rectification. I cannot imagine that he meant the total destruction of the passions, since in the process one would also destroy man, given that it is without fail the passions, good or evil though they may be, that excite men to action. Nor do I believe, as some critics do, that Aristotle wanted to say that, through exposure to terrifying and moving representations, the spectators become accustomed to such acts as move men to fear and pity, with the result that they would have little power over men confronted by real disaster <1:Cv/135>, for these same passions are indeed useful in bringing men to reciprocal assistance in times of need. If however by this purgation of the passions, which is the product and chief purpose of tragedy, we must understand, not their destruction, but their rectification, then I need to be instructed regarding both the way in which terror and pity can actually achieve this end and the reason why only these two medicaments are employed in the treatment. But if the fear of such horrible punishments as in the end ought always to befall wretched men were constantly to restrain us from imitating them, and if the compassion that in the end should always be accorded to good men were constantly to stimulate us to be deserving of it ourselves, then my first doubt would have been cleared away. But this could not possibly have been Aristotle's intention, because the heroes of the tragedies that he commends and proposes as exemplary are for the most part wretched persons who end up happy, as are the likes of Orestes, Electra, Clytemnestra, and Aegisthus;[2] or else they are good men in extreme unhappiness, as is the unfortunate son of Laius, in whom (Plutarch and his learned disciples notwithstanding[3]) there is no real crime other than his having so unjustly and cruelly punished an innocent man in himself. But what I find most difficult to understand is the reason why fear and pity are considered the only two remedies <Lg/121-2> in this cure, to the exclusion of all other human passions, from which our actions also derive. Human passions are the necessary winds with which we sail the sea of life; and if our journeys are to be prosperous, we should not set ourselves on learning the impossible art of stopping them. Rather we should study the art of advantageously using them, gathering or opening our sails to this one or to that one, in accordance with the useful or harmful efficacy that they exhibit as they lead us along a straight route or as they force us away from it. Our passions do not include only fear and pity: admiration, glory, aversion, friendship, love, jealousy, envy, emulation, avidity in the ambition to acquire, and anxiety in the fear of losing what we have acquired, and thousands of others, which are formed by the concurrence and mixture of

---

[2] Metastasio would seem to be considering the fortunes of the characters in *Agamemnon* separately, as well as in the *Oresteia* of Aeschylus overall.

[3] Plutarch, *De Curiositate* 552c, attributes Oedipus' tragedy to his curiosity.

these, are also among those winds which move us to action and which we must learn how to govern if we wish to attain public and private tranquillity. Experience shows that even the most wicked spectator admires great examples of heroic virtue, which result from useful passions and triumph over harmful ones, and he takes pleasure in seeing them represented on stage. Whenever we see an innocent son generously sacrifice his own glory and his own life in order to save his father, or a friend forget all about himself in order not to displease his friend, or a citizen subordinate his personal happiness to that of his country, or a beneficiary decline a kingdom or a dear, worthy, and much yearned for object in order not to be ungrateful to his benefactor, or someone who has unjustly suffered bloody offense neglect an opportunity of easy vengeance and not only forgive his enemy but also offer him his hand in help if he should find him in grave danger: whenever we see (I say) the representation of actions so laudable and luminous as these, our soul is magnified in the glory of which we believe our species to be capable. We take the liberty of believing that we too are suitable subjects for the pursuit of such actions, and, nourished by these noble ideas, we hope that at some time we can actually enable ourselves to imitate them. However, I do not know of what passion we are cleansed or towards what virtue we are drawn by the representation of an inhuman daughter who, instead of being moved by the suffering voice of her dying mother imploring her to take pity on her and to help her, horrifies nature by encouraging her assassin to strike her, and is then happy and contented.[4] Nor do I know what teaching is imparted to us by the much commended spectacle of lacerated corpses, by the ostentation of Oedipus' torment, and the howlings and putrid sores of Philoctetes.[5] Neither can I understand why the passion of love – which is less avoidable, more common, and more in need of a tight rein than any other – cannot give rise on stage to tender and admirable examples, capable of teaching us which are the sacred duties that make every sacrifice at once necessary and glorious. And why should such heroines full of love, victorious over themselves, be deemed unworthy of the cothurnus when incestuous Phaedras[6] and adulterous Clytemnestras are instead deemed most worthy? What advantage or delight is there in preferring tragedies that represent wretchedness that goes unpunished rather than virtues that are rewarded < 1:Gd/126 >? Yet Aristotle maintains that the essence of tragedy itself demands that the horrid and deathly be found in it, since, in his view, tragedy must produce a pleasure peculiar to it alone by means of these very qualities < 1:Ar/50 >. This is a pleasure that must derive from sight of the physical torments to which others are subjected, that is to say the pleasure of seeing blows, wounds, and the laceration of corpses, new and old, on

---

4 Sophocles, *Electra* 1410–15.
5 In *Oedipus the King* 1268–79, and *Philoctetes* 732ff., both by Sophocles.
6 In the *Hippolytos* of Aeschylus, Phaedra falls in love with her stepson.

exhibit. If he means to say that these ingredients are useful in achieving purgation, I do not understand in what way they are so. In fact I believe that for many people such a treatment is worse than any infirmity. And if he advises us to make use of them because he believes them to be efficacious in creating a sense of pleasure, then the wisdom of his advice needs to be very carefully examined.

5

DENIS DIDEROT
(1713–84)

Diderot was a man of astonishing breadth of knowledge and an insatiable curiosity. He wrote novels, plays, art criticism, and essays, and was the moving spirit behind the *Encyclopédie* (the volumes published between 1751 and 1772).

The Natural Son (*Le Fils naturel*), the first of his two plays, was written in 1757. It purports to depict an actual event, reenacted by the people to whom it has happened. The drama itself is framed by a Prologue and an Epilogue followed by three conversations (*entretiens*) about the play and drama in general. Giving "the true history of the play," the Prologue sets it up as the reenactment in the drawing-room of the house where the supposed events actually occurred. Dorval, the protagonist, has written the play at the behest of his late father, who believed that the dramatization of the family's experience would be a source of moral edification. Diderot is secretly present at the performance, and afterwards has a series of discussions with Dorval on the merits and shortcomings of the play, expressing – through Dorval – his ideas about modern drama and the new course it should take. Thus the three conversations embed dramatic theory in a lively narrative that refers it to a particular play and particular occasion.

A brief summary of the plot of *Le Fils naturel* will help fill out the context of the conversations. Dorval is visiting his best friend Clairville and the latter's sister Constance. Rosalie, Clairville's fiancée, is also staying with them until her father returns from abroad. Realizing that he is in love with Rosalie, Dorval decides to leave, rather than betray his friend. But Clairville begs him to dissuade Rosalie from breaking off their engagement. Dorval discovers that Rosalie returns his love, and is even more tormented by guilt. Constance also reveals that she is in love with Dorval. Clairville is nearly killed in a fight with two ruffians, who have been spreading rumors about Dorval and Rosalie. Dorval saves Clairville's life. Constance believes that Dorval is in love with her, and Clairville offers Dorval his sister's hand in marriage. Rosalie is devastated. News arrives that Rosalie's father has lost his fortune. Dorval determines to transfer his fortune secretly to Rosalie and to become a recluse. But Constance, accepting the fact that Dorval is illegitimate and now without a fortune, overcomes all of his objections to marriage with her, and further persuades him to help reunite Rosalie and Clairville. Rosalie publicly accuses Dorval of perfidy towards Clairville, but Dorval persuades her to give up her love for him and marry Clairville. At that moment, Rosalie's father arrives. He turns out to be Dorval's father also. Incestuous love has been avoided, friendship and good faith preserved. The father blesses the respective unions of his offspring and the play ends.

In the interweaving of play and commentary, Dorval is the riveting figure of a melancholy, idealistic hero, who champions virtue, family values, and also passion and truth in literature. Through him, Diderot introduces his innovative ideas about

35

staging, the use of what he calls "pantomime"[1] and scenic tableaux and the new serious genre halfway between comedy and tragedy. He is ahead of his time in foreseeing the development of the new, more specialized, genres of "grand" opera and ballet. He also considers the relation of drama to the novel, the burlesque, and the marvellous.

Given his strong visual sense and his preoccupation with painting, art criticism, and aesthetic theory, it is not surprising that Diderot uses terms borrowed from art criticism in these writings on the theatre – tableau, nuance, tone, color – as well as frequent analogies between the playwright and the painter. In *The Natural Son* itself, the stage directions give precise descriptions of movement, placement, and even the expressions on the characters' faces. This was all part of the "panto-mime," and it includes much of what today would be worked out in a stage production. Here, the playwright is shown to be fully in control, although Diderot also was inclined to give the actors considerable leeway.

A second play, *Le Père de famille* (*The Father*), written in 1758 and performed in 1760, illustrated the theories presented in the "Discourse on Dramatic Poetry" ("Discours sur la poésie dramatique"). In the "Discourse", Diderot takes a more systematic approach to dramatic theory than in the *Conversations*. There are twenty-two sections or chapters, each dealing with a specific aspect of the play-wright's art, providing a useful reference tool for aspiring practitioners. The definitions of the new genres are elaborated here, and there is a further discussion of illusion in drama. To a certain extent, the discourse retains the character of a dialogue, since Diderot is addressing his friend Grimm, whose arguments and objections are anticipated.

The posthumously published *Paradoxe sur le comédien* <In/5–6> is, once more, a dialogue; it began as a review[2] of a pamphlet about Garrick's acting and became something of an argument by Diderot against himself (or his earlier self), modifying and even reversing, his earlier views on the uses of emotion and sensibility in performance.

For further reading

Burwick 1991; Chouillet 1973; Davis 1967; Jones & Nicol 1976; Niklaus 1963.

From "Conversations on *The Natural Son*"[3]

Dorval and Myself

First Conversation

MYSELF

... I have read [your play] but either I am much mistaken, or you did not

---

[1] The Greek word "pantomime," originally denoted an actor who performed in dumb show. In Diderot's text it sometimes means the art of miming or representing actions or gestures without words, in which case it has been translated as "pantomime" or "mime." Diderot also uses it to mean the notation in the dramatic text of actions, gestures, movements, and facial expressions to be performed by the actors, and this has been translated as "stage directions."

[2] *Observations sur une brochure intitulée Garrick ou les acteurs anglais* (1770).

[3] Newly translated from Diderot/Caput 1973. The conversations are introduced by narrative sections giving the locations of the discussions and some context for them. Within the dialogues there are also narrative links, which this translation does not include.

try to comply scrupulously with your father's intentions. It seems to me, that his recommendation to you was to record the events exactly as they had happened. Several things struck me as having the characteristics of fiction, which would be impressive only on the stage, where illusion and applause may be said to belong by convention.

To begin with, you have bound yourself by the rule of the unities, and yet it is difficult to believe that so many events happened in the same place, within the space of only twenty-four hours, and that in actual fact one event followed as quickly on the heels of another as you have linked them together in your play.

DORVAL

You are right. But do you really believe that if the situation lasted for two weeks, the performance had to go on for the same length of time? And if the events of the story were interspersed with other events, would it be correct to show this confusion? And if they happened in different parts of the house, would I be obliged to spread them over the same area?

The rules of the three unities are difficult to observe, but they are reasonable.

In society, situations are sustained only by small incidents, which would provide authenticity in a novel, but would sap a dramatic work of all its interest. In a novel our attention can be divided among an infinite number of different objects, but in the theatre, where only specific moments of real life are represented, we must focus all of our attention on one thing only.

I prefer a play to be simple, rather than filled with incidents. However, I am more concerned with the way the incidents hang together than with their number. I am less inclined to believe in two events that occur successively or simultaneously by chance, than in a large number of events that are similar to our everyday experience, which is the invariable standard for dramatic probability. These events would seem to me to be linked together by the requirements of necessity.

The art of creating successful dramatic plots consists in joining the events in a way that will always provide intelligent spectators with a reason they find satisfying. The more unusual the events of the play are, the more convincing this reason must be. . . .

. . . I believe that unity of place is absolutely essential. Without it, the conduct of the action is almost always confused or muddled. If only we had stages where the scenery could be changed every time the action has to shift to a different place <Jh/84–5>! . . .

MYSELF

And why do you think that would be such a great advantage?

DORVAL

It would be easy for the audience to follow the complete movement of the play. The performance would be clearer, more varied, and more interesting. The only time the scenery can be changed is when the stage is empty; this can happen only at the end of an act < 1:Lp/187>. Thus, whenever a change of scene was required between two incidents, they would be in two different acts. . . .

Here are my further thoughts on these theatrical conventions. Anyone who is ignorant of the poetical requirement behind the convention, since he is unaware of the basis for the rule, will be unable either to abandon it or to follow it properly. He will have either too much disdain or too much respect for it, two opposite, but equally dangerous pitfalls. One attitude negates the observations and experience of past centuries and reduces the art to its infancy. The other brings it to a standstill and prevents its further development < 1:Jn/193>. . . .

. . . If I confined all of the action within a single place, it was because I was able to do so without hindering the conduct of the plot and without depriving the events of their probability < 1:In/8>.

MYSELF

That is all well and good, but in arranging the place, time, and order of events, you should have avoided anything that was not in keeping with our customs or your own character.

DORVAL

I believe I did so.

MYSELF

Do you mean to tell me that you actually had the conversation with your valet in the second scene of the first act? . . . You listened calmly to his reprimands? The austere Dorval, unwilling to unburden himself even to his friend Clairville, conversed so easily and familiarly with his valet, Charles? That is neither probable nor true.

DORVAL

I must admit you are right. The words I had Charles say are more or less what I said to myself. But Charles is a good servant, who is loyal to me. . . . He was there when it all happened. I could see very little objection to giving him a small part in the play, and it gave him so much pleasure!— Just because they are our servants, does that mean they are no longer human?— If they serve us, there is another we all serve.

MYSELF

But what if you were really writing for the stage?

DORVAL

I would set aside my moral principles and would take care not to give too much importance on the stage to people who have no status in society. The Davus characters[4] played a pivotal role in ancient comedy, because

---

[4] Davus, the cunning slave in Terence's *Woman of Andros*, became the epitome of all such character types in drama.

they were in fact the driving force behind all domestic discord. Are we supposed to imitate the social customs of two thousand years ago, or those of our own time? The valets in our comedies are always amusing, indisputable proof that they are indifferent. If the author leaves them in the antechambers, where they belong, the action between the main characters will be all the more interesting and intense. .... Subplots involving valets and maidservants that interrupt the main plot, are a sure way to make the play less interesting. There can be no pause in dramatic action. Mixing two plots together means that one must be stopped, while the other proceeds.

MYSELF

I would beg your indulgence for maidservants. It seems to me, that for young ladies, who have so many constraints on their speech and their conduct, these women are the only ones to whom they can open their hearts and confide the overwhelming feelings that custom, propriety, fear, and prejudice force them to conceal.

DORVAL

Well then, let them remain on the stage until our education improves, and fathers and mothers become the confidants of their children— What else have you observed?

MYSELF

Why is the entrance of Clairville announced while you are talking to Rosalie? People are never announced in their own homes, and this seems exactly like a deliberate *coup de théâtre*.[5]

DORVAL

No, that was exactly the way it happened, and the way it had to happen....
I would much prefer to see tableaux on the stage, where they are so rarely seen, and would produce such a pleasing and unmistakable effect, rather than these *coups de théâtre*, which are introduced in such an artificial way, based on so many singular suppositions, that for every appropriate and natural combination of events, there are a thousand others that must offend any man of taste.

MYSELF

But what difference do you see between a tableau and a *coup de théâtre*?

DORVAL

It would be much easier for me to give you examples, rather than definitions. The second act of the play opens with a tableau, and closes with a *coup de théâtre*.

---

[5] There is no satisfactory English equivalent for the term *coup de théâtre*, which is a sudden, unexpected turn of events, or reversal, occurring at a moment of tension in a play.

MYSELF

I understand. An unforeseen incident that takes the form of an action, and that suddenly changes the situation of the characters, is a *coup de théâtre*. The placement of these characters on the stage, so natural and so true to life that it would please me as a painting, is a tableau.

DORVAL

More or less.

MYSELF

I would almost be willing to wager that in the fourth scene of the second act, every single word is true. . . . What a beautiful tableau, for that is what I believe it is, to see the unhappy Clairville, leaning on the bosom of his friend, as if it were his last refuge. . . .

DORVAL

You must admit that such a scene would not have taken place on the stage, and that the two friends would not have dared look each other in the face, turn their backs to the audience, move close together, move apart, and come together again. All of their movements would have been very controlled, very stiff, very affected, and very cold.

MYSELF

I believe so.

DORVAL

How can anyone fail to realize that unhappiness has the effect of bringing people closer together? Especially in moments of turmoil, when passions are running high and the action is at its most frenetic, it is ridiculous for actors to stand in a circle, symmetrically placed at some considerable distance apart from one another.

Stage action must still be far from perfect, since hardly any situations are shown on the stage which would make a tolerable composition for a painting. Does this mean that truth is less essential on the stage than on canvas? . . .

I myself think that if a dramatic work were well written and well performed, the spectator would see as many real tableaux on stage as there would be moments in the action that would make good paintings. . . .

MYSELF

You do not like *coups de théâtre?* . . .

DORVAL

No.

MYSELF

And yet here is one[6] that is very well thought out. .... Your whole plot is based on it.

DORVAL

I agree.

MYSELF

And is that a bad thing?

DORVAL

No doubt it is.

MYSELF

Then why did you use it?

DORVAL

Because it is not fiction, but actual fact. ...

MYSELF

There is nothing that rings false.

DORVAL

And nothing plausible enough. Do you not see that it would take centuries to bring together so many different circumstances? ... The simpler a play is in its unfolding, the more beautiful it is. A poet who might have imagined both this *coup de théâtre* and the situation in the fifth act, where I approach Rosalie and point out to her the figure of Clairville, at the other end of the drawing-room, collapsed on a sofa in the attitude of a man in despair, would show very little sense if he preferred the *coup de théâtre* to the tableau. One is an almost infantile piece of work, while the other is a stroke of genius. I speak with impartiality, having invented neither. The *coup de théâtre* is a fact. The tableau is a fortunate circumstance that occurred by chance and I was able to use to advantage. ...

MYSELF

While we are on the subject of that scene of despair, it is extraordinary. It had a strong effect on me as I watched it in the drawing-room. Imagine my surprise, on reading it, to find gestures described, and no speeches.

DORVAL

Here is an anecdote I would be sure not to tell you if I attached any value to this play or took much pride in having written it. When I came to that moment in our story and in the play, I had in my mind only a strong

---

[6] Myself is referring to Act II, scenes vii, viii, and ix, where Dorval begins a letter intended for Rosalie, and is suddenly called away to rescue Clairville. Constance comes in, sees the letter, thinks it is for her, reads it, and is convinced that Dorval is in love with her. This misconception, based on a series of "coincidences", is a prime example of the *coup de théâtre*.

impression of what had happened, and not the least idea of how to express
it in dialogue. Remembering certain scenes in comedies I had seen inspired
me to make Clairville very articulate in his despair. But as he was glancing
over his part, he said to me, "Brother, this is no good. There isn't a single
word of truth in all this rhetoric." "I know," said I. "But why don't you go
over it and see if you can improve it." "That will not be difficult," he said.
"All I have to do is to put myself back into the situation, and listen to my
feelings." ... The next morning he brought me the scene exactly as you
read it, word for word. I read and reread it several times, and recognized
that it had the ring of truth. Tomorrow, if you like, I will tell you some of
the thoughts on the passions, the tone in which they are expressed,
declamation and pantomime, that this scene suggested to me. ...

Second Conversation

DORVAL

The ... author must not make his characters clever, but know how to
create circumstances that will bring out their cleverness. ... A peasant
woman from the village you see between those two mountains ... sent her
husband to visit her relatives who lived in a neighboring hamlet. While he
was there, the poor man was killed by one of his brothers-in-law. The next
day, I went to the house where the accident had occurred. There I saw a
tableau and heard words that I have not forgotten. The dead man was laid
out on a bed, with his bare legs protruding over the edge. His distraught
wife was kneeling on the ground. She was holding her husband's feet, with
tears streaming down her face, and with a gesture that brought tears to the
eyes of everyone in the room, she cried, "Alas! When I sent you here, little
did I know that these feet were carrying you to your death." Do you think
that a woman of a different class would have been more touching? No. The
same situation would have inspired the same speech. Her heart would
have been at one with the moment. The artist must find exactly what
everyone would say in the same situation, so that all who hear it will
immediately recognize it within themselves.

Matters of great importance, and strong passions. These are the source
of great speeches that express truth. Almost everyone is eloquent at the
moment of death.

What I like in the Clairville scene is that it contains nothing except
precisely what one would say in a moment of extreme passion. Passion
becomes associated with an essential idea. The passion is silent and returns
to this idea, which is almost always expressed in an exclamation.

Pantomime, which has been so neglected on our stages, is used in this
scene. You yourself experienced how effective it was.

We talk too much in our plays, and consequently the actors have little
chance to act <In/3>. We have lost an art whose resources were well
known to the ancients. In former times mimes played characters of all sorts

and conditions – kings, heroes, tyrants, rich people, poor people, city dwellers, and country folk, choosing what was appropriate to each social position, and what was most striking in each action. . . .

What an effect this art <Lg/109–10> would have if it were used in conjunction with speech! Why did we separate what nature joined together? At any given moment do our gestures not correspond to our words? I was never more aware of this than when writing this play. I tried to remember what I had said and what others had said to me, and since all that came to mind were the movements, I put down the name of the character and beneath it the action. In Act two, Scene two, I say to Rosalie, "If it happened – that your heart, taken unawares – was suddenly seized by a desire that your reason regarded as a crime – I have experienced this same cruel state!— How I would pity you!"

She answers, "Pity me then—." I express my pity for her, not in words, but with a gesture of commiseration; and I do not believe that a man who is capable of feeling would have acted any differently. But how many other situations there are in life where silence is forced upon us! What if someone asked you for advice, which, if followed, might cause him to lose his life, or if disregarded, to lose his honor? . . . You would indicate your perplexity with a gesture, and you would allow the man to make up his own mind.

In this scene I also saw that there are places where everything must be left almost entirely in the hands of the actor. It is up to him to rearrange the text of the scene, repeating certain words, emphasizing certain ideas, leaving out some, and adding still others. . . . When we see someone in the grip of a strong passion, what is it that touches our emotions? Is it the words that are spoken? Sometimes. But what invariably moves us are the cries, the inarticulate phrases, spoken in a faltering voice, the few monosyllabic words that come out between moments of silence, and indescribable mutterings that barely escape from the throat or between the teeth. Overpowered by the violence of the emotion, the speaker forgets to breathe regularly, thus experiencing agitation in the mind, words are broken into dislocated syllables, the speaker darts from one idea to another, beginning many different speeches, without finishing any. And with the exception of a few feelings expressed in the first onslaught of emotion, to which he constantly returns, the rest is nothing but a series of inarticulate and confused sounds, dying away or choked back, that the actor understands better than the dramatist. Voice, tone, gesture, and action are all part of the actor's repertoire. He is the one who brings all of the energy to the dialogue. . . . Nothing could be farther removed from the true voice of passion than those arias we call *tirades* <Gl/70; Hu/264>.[7] Nothing receives more applause or is in worse taste. Having no part in the perform-

---

7 This word has no exact equivalent in English. It is a long speech, usually in high-flown language, an exhibition of the playwright's virtuosity, and usually a test of the actor's breath control. It could be directed either to the audience or to other characters.

ance, the spectator might as well not exist. When speeches are directly addressed to the audience, then the playwright has departed from his subject, and the actor has stepped out of the role. To me it is as if they had both left the stage and come down into the audience. As long as the monologue continues, the action is suspended for me and the stage is empty.

In the composition of a play there is a unity of discourse which corresponds to a unity of tone in the delivery. These two systems vary, not from comedy to tragedy, but from one comedy or tragedy to another. Without this unity, either the play or its performance would be deficient. There would be no affinity between the characters, no standards of appropriate behavior to which they must all conform, even in their nonconformity < I:Ar/52 > . . . .

It is the actor's task to be aware of the unity of tone, and he will devote his entire life to perfecting this ability. Without it, he will sometimes underplay his part, sometimes overact, but rarely will he achieve exactly the right tone. His acting will be occasionally good, but on the whole mediocre.

If an actor is seized by the desire for applause, he exaggerates. This affects the way another actor plays his part. There is no longer unity in his delivery of his lines, nor in the delivery of the entire play. Before long, I see no more than a noisy tumult on the stage, with each actor using whatever tone he or she feels like; I am overcome by boredom, I put my hands over my ears and make my escape.

I should very much like to talk to you about the tone that is appropriate for each passion. But this tone changes in so many different ways. It is such a subtle and elusive subject, that I know of no other which can make us more aware of the shortcomings of all languages, living or dead. . . .

MYSELF

That is another reason for writing in "pantomime" [stage directions].

DORVAL

Gesture and intonation doubtless have an influence on one another.

MYSELF

But gesture can easily be written down, and intonation cannot. . . .

DORVAL

. . . Poets, actors, musicians, great dancers, and singers, all of these enthusiastic and impassioned people feel keenly and think but little. They are not guided and enlightened by precepts, but by something more immediate, more private, more mysterious, and more certain. I cannot tell you how much I admire a great actor, or a great actress. How proud I would be if I possessed this talent! . . .

MYSELF

You believe that your play would not succeed on the stage?

DORVAL

Only with difficulty. Either the dialogue would have to be cut in certain places, or the dramatic action and the stage would have to be changed.

MYSELF

What would you do to change the stage?

DORVAL

I would get rid of everything restricting a space that is already too small. I would have set decoration, and allow us to use other tableaux besides the ones we have seen for the last hundred years. In other words, it would be possible to recreate on the stage Clairville's drawing-room exactly as it is.

MYSELF

It is very important then to have a stage set?

DORVAL

Undoubtedly. Imagine a French theatre where set decoration was as lavish as in the lyric theatre,[8] but more pleasing, because instead of the world of make-believe, suitable for entertaining children, it would show the real world, the only source of pleasure for the mind— Without stage effects and scenery our imaginations will not function. Writers of genius will lose interest. Mediocre writers will succeed by servile imitation. We will become ever more rigid in observing petty rules of decorum and the national taste will degenerate— Have you seen the theatre in Lyons?[9] If we had a theatre like that in Paris, it would inspire our dramatists to produce a host of new works, and perhaps some new genres. . . .

All I would ask for, to completely transform the dramatic genre, would be a very extensive stage area, so that when the subject of a play required it, we could show a large square with its adjacent buildings, such as the front of a palace, the entrance to a temple, or other places spread out in such a way that the audience can follow all of the action. Part of the stage should also be enclosed so that the actors' movements are not seen by the audience.

This may have been the kind of stage setting that was used in Aeschylus' *Eumenides*. On one side was a space where the relentless Furies were looking for Orestes, who had managed to escape from them while they were dozing. On the other side of the stage Orestes, with a bandage around his head, could be seen clinging to the feet of the statue of Minerva, begging

---

[8] "French theatre" here could refer either to the Théâtre Français, now known as the Comédie-Française, or to French dramatic theatre in general, as opposed to musical theatre or opera of the Théâtre Lyrique, where very elaborate sets and costumes were used.

[9] A new theatre, designed by Germain Soufflot (1713–80), the architect of the Pantheon in Paris, was opened in Lyons in the summer of 1756.

for her assistance. ... Finally, one of [the Furies] cries out, "Here are the bloody tracks made by the murderer— I can smell him, I am on his trail— " She advances, followed by her merciless sisters. They move across the stage, from the place where they were, until they reach Orestes' place of refuge. They surround him, screaming, trembling with rage, and brandishing their torches. What a moment of terror and pity, when we hear the victim's moans and supplications intermingled with the hideous shrieks and terrifying movements of the implacable creatures who are after him. Will we ever achieve such an effect on our stages? We can never show more than one action at a time, whereas in nature things almost always happen simultaneously. If they were shown close together, each making the other more striking, the effect on us would be terrifying. Then we would tremble at the thought of going to the theatre, but nothing could keep us away. Instead of being satisfied with the insipid, fleeting emotions, the indifferent applause, and the occasional tears they now elicit, dramatists would overwhelm the minds of the audience and would fill their hearts with terror and distress. Once again we would see the incredible, but not impossible effects of ancient tragedy coming to life on our stages. It requires only a man of genius, with the ability to combine pantomime with dialogue, to intermingle a spoken scene with a scene in mime, to make the most of the fusion of these scenes, and above all, to emphasize the comic or terrifying moments leading up to this inevitable fusion. ...

MYSELF

Alternating spoken and mimed scenes, that I understand. But would it not lead to confusion?

DORVAL

A scene without dialogue is a tableau, a living scene painting. Does the visual effect detract from listening to the music in the lyric theatre?

MYSELF

No— But is this what we are to understand when we are told that in ancient drama music, spoken text, and pantomime were sometimes combined and at other times separate?

DORVAL

Sometimes. ... Let us see what would be possible today, taking an example from everyday domestic life.

A father has lost his son in a duel. It is night. A servant who has witnessed the duel arrives with the bad news. He enters the bed chamber, where the father is fast asleep. ... The sound of his footsteps wakes the father. ... "What is it?" "Nothing." ... "That is not true. You are shaking, you turn your head away, and you won't look me in the eye. Once again, what is the matter? I *will* know. Tell me! I order you." "I tell you, sir, it is nothing," the servant replies again, with tears streaming down his face.

"Wretched man!" cries the father, leaping out of bed. "You are lying, something terrible has happened— Is my wife dead?" "No, sir." "My daughter?" "No, sir." "Is it my son, then?" The servant says nothing.— The father throws himself to the ground and the room is filled with his cries of pain and despair. He does and says everything one would expect of a father who has lost his son, the only hope of his family.

The same man rushes to the mother's room. . . . Here is the tableau of the pious woman; soon we shall see the tableau of the loving wife and the bereaved mother. . . .

In the meantime, the son's body has been brought into the father's chamber, and a scene of despair has been going on there, while the mother's piety was expressed in pantomime.

You see how pantomime and spoken text alternate from one place to another. This is what we must substitute for the practice of asides spoken to the audience. But now comes the moment when the two scenes are about to be brought together. The mother, supported by the servant, moves toward her husband's chamber— What does the audience feel as she approaches?— The sight of a husband and father, prostrate over the body of his son is about to be seen through the eyes of a mother. She has crossed the space separating the two playing areas. The terrible cries have reached her ears. She looks and recoils from what she sees. Her strength fails her, and she faints in the arms of the servant. . . .

There is little dialogue in this plot summary, but a talented writer who had to fill in the empty spaces, would put in only a few scattered monosyllabic words, an exclamation here, an unfinished sentence there. Rarely would he put in a continuous speech, however brief it might be.

These are my thoughts on tragedy. But in order to achieve true tragedies, we need dramatists, actors, a theatre, and perhaps a nation of playgoers.

MYSELF

What? Do you mean to say that in a tragedy you would have a bed, a sleeping mother and father, a crucifix, a dead body, two scenes alternately mimed and spoken? And what about the rules of decorum [*bienséances*]?

DORVAL

O, cruel decorum, that makes plays respectable and mediocre!

. . . we must hope that someday a talented playwright will realize the impossibility of competing with the great dramatists of the past on the well-trodden paths of the ancient genres, and in a fit of pique will blaze a new trail for himself. Only when that happens will we be freed from a number of prejudices that philosophy has tried in vain to challenge. Reasons are no longer needed: we now require a production. . . .

MYSELF

And what name would you give to this new genre?

DORVAL

Domestic, bourgeois tragedy. The English have *The London Merchant*
<Hz/243> and *The Gamester*,[10] which are both prose tragedies. Shake-
speare's tragedies are half in verse and half in prose. The first dramatist to
use prose to make us laugh, introduced prose into comedy. The first author
who uses prose to make us cry, will introduce prose into tragedy.

But, in art, as in nature, everything is linked together; if we approach the
truth from one direction, we will approach it from many other directions.
Then we will begin to see on the stage realistic situations, which have
hitherto been prohibited by an overzealous conventionality, hostile to
artistic genius and to great dramatic effects. . . .

We have spared no effort to corrupt the drama. We have retained the
extravagant versification of the ancients, which was so well-suited to . . .
strongly accented languages, to large theatres, and to a marked delivery
that was accompanied by musical instruments, and we have abandoned
the simplicity of plot and dialogue and the authenticity of tableaux.

I would not want to bring back to our stages the great socks and high
buskins,[11] the monumental costumes, the masks, and the megaphones,
although all of these things were merely necessary elements in a theatrical
system. But were there not in this system some valuable resources? . . .

MYSELF

What kind of resource do you mean?

DORVAL

The presence of a large number of spectators. Strictly speaking, there are
no more public entertainments. There is no comparison between the
audiences who attend our theatres for the most popular performances and
those in Athens or Rome. Those ancient theatres could hold up to eighty
thousand people. . . .

But if the presence of a huge audience must have magnified the emotions
felt by each spectator, imagine what an influence it had on the dramatists
and on the actors! What a difference there is between providing entertainment for a few hundred people, on a given day, within certain hours, in
some crowded, dimly-lit nondescript space, and holding an entire nation
transfixed, on solemn national occasions, in the most magnificent buildings, and seeing these buildings surrounded and filled with vast numbers of
people whose pleasure or boredom will depend on our talents alone! . . . But
where were we in your critique of my play? . . .

---

[10] *The London Merchant; or, the History of George Barnwell* by George Lillo (1693–1739) was
first played at Drury Lane in 1731 and frequently revived. *The Gamester* is a domestic
tragedy by Edward Moore (1712–57), written in collaboration with Garrick, who produced it at Drury Lane in 1753; Diderot translated it in 1760.

[11] The light shoes (socks) and thick-soled boots (buskins) worn by comic and tragic actors
respectively.

MYSELF

There is little more to say about your play, except to praise it . . . . But can you tell me why in a play which you did not make up, every single thing that happens is prepared for?

DORVAL

The art of play writing does not prepare for events, except by making them follow inevitably one from another. And they are only linked together in plays because that is how they are in real life. Art imitates nature even to the point of capturing the subtle ways in which nature conceals the connections between events.

MYSELF

It seems to me that pantomime would sometimes foreshadow events in a very natural and clever way.

DORVAL

No doubt. And there is an example of it in the play. While André was telling us about the misfortunes that had befallen his master, it occurred to me many times that he was talking about my father. My foreboding was expressed in my movements, so that any attentive member of the audience could easily have guessed my suspicion. . . .

MYSELF

That is all I have to say on the specific details of your play. As far as the structure is concerned, I see one weakness, which may be inherent in the subject matter. The nature of the interest changes. From the first act until the end of the third, we see virtue in distress, and in the rest of the play we see virtue triumphant. It would have been better (and this would not have been difficult) to maintain the turmoil, and to prolong virtue's discomfort and ordeal. . . . Exacerbating the passions of Clairville and of Rosalie would have exposed you to even greater risks, perhaps, than the ones you faced before. From time to time you would have been tempted to reveal everything. You might indeed have done so at the end.

DORVAL

I see your point, but it completely changes our story. And what would my father have said? Besides, are you really convinced that the play would have been improved? By placing me in such desperate straits, you would have turned a fairly simple adventure into an extremely complicated play. I would have become more theatrical—

MYSELF

And more commonplace, it is true; but the play would definitely have been successful.

DORVAL

No doubt, and lacking in taste. It would certainly have been less difficult to maintain a heightened state of agitation, but also less truthful and less pleasing than to continue to support one another in calmness. That is when the sacrifices of virtue begin and are inevitably linked together. Observe how the exaltation of the speeches and the emotional impact of the scenes emerge from the pathos of the situation. Nevertheless, in the midst of this calm, the destinies of Constance, Clairville, Rosalie, and myself remain uncertain. What I propose to do is clear, but my chances of success are small. Indeed, I do not succeed with Constance, and it is even less likely that I will fare any better with Rosalie. What significant event would have replaced these two scenes in the plan that you just outlined? None that I can think of.

MYSELF

I have only one last question to ask you. What genre does your play fit into? It is neither a tragedy, nor a comedy. What is it then, and what name would you give it?

DORVAL

Whatever name you please. But if you like, we will put our heads together tomorrow and find one that is suitable. . . .

Third Conversation

DORVAL

. . . In all moral objects we can distinguish a middle and two extremes. Since all dramatic plots are moral objects, it seems that there should therefore be a middle genre and two extremes. These two are comedy and tragedy, but people are not always plunged in sorrow or exalted with joy. There is therefore a point separating the distance between the comic and the tragic genres <Bm/130>.

Terence wrote a play[12] with the following subject. A young man marries. Shortly afterwards, he must travel far away on business. He is absent, and then he comes back. Thinking that he detects certain undeniable signs of infidelity in his wife, he is in despair, and wishes to send her back to her parents. We may imagine the state of mind of the father, the mother, and their daughter. There is, however, one character, a cunning slave, who is essentially a comic character. What does Terence do with him? He keeps him off the stage for the first four acts and only brings him on to liven up the dénouement.

What genre does this play belong to? Is it comedy? No, there is nothing funny in it. Is it tragedy? We do not feel terror, pity, or other strong emotions. But there is human interest, and the same will be true, if there is nothing ridiculous to make us laugh or any danger to frighten us, in any dramatic composition where the subject matter is important, where the author assumes the tone used in dealing with serious matters, and where

---

[12] The allusion is to *The Mother-in-Law* (*Hecyra*). In its concern with married life it is a more serious work than Terence's other five plays.

the dramatic action is driven by perplexity and obstacles. It seems to me, that since these are the most common actions in real life, the genre that depicts them must be the most useful and the most wide-ranging. I will call this the *genre sérieux* [serious drama].

Once this genre is established, there will be no social condition, no important event in real life which cannot be assigned to some part of the dramatic spectrum.

If you want to make this system as broad as possible, to include truth, reality, and the realms of fantasy, you may add the burlesque genre below the comic genre, and the marvellous above the tragic genre.

MYSELF

I see what you mean. The burlesque— the comic genre— the serious genre— the tragic genre— the marvellous.

DORVAL

A play is never strictly confined to only one genre. All works in the comic and tragic genres contain some elements that are appropriate to the serious genre, and conversely, there will be elements in this genre that will be identified with either comedy or tragedy.

The advantage of this serious genre is that being in between the two other genres, it has resources to draw on by either raising or lowering its tone. This is not true of tragedy and comedy. All of the nuances of what is comic are included between comedy itself and the serious genre, and all tragic possibilities fall between serious drama and tragedy. The burlesque and the marvellous are equally beyond the realm of nature; nothing can be borrowed from them without distorting the work. Painters and poets have the right to try anything, but this does not include the license to combine different species within a single individual < 1:Tm/210>. . . .

Comedy and tragedy are the actual limits of dramatic composition. But if it is impossible for comedy to draw on the burlesque without degrading itself, or for tragedy to encroach on the territory of the marvellous without becoming unrealistic, it follows that being placed at the two ends of the spectrum, these genres are the most striking and the most difficult.

Every man of letters who feels he has some talent for the theatre, should begin by working in the serious genre. . . . The author who has spent many years studying human nature in the serious genre may choose, according to his talent, to work in either tragedy or comedy, clothing his characters in royal robes or legal gowns, but the human being must always be recognizable beneath the outer trappings.

If the serious drama is the easiest of all, it is, on the other hand, less subject to the vicissitudes of time and place. . . . If you excel in the serious genre, you will be successful in all ages and with all nations. . . .

You see that tragicomedy cannot be a proper genre, because it is a confused mixture < 1:Gu/150> of two quite distant genres that are separated by a natural barrier. There are no subtle nuances here, but only jarring contrasts, so that all sense of unity disappears. . . .

The poetics of tragedy and comedy have been discussed many times. The serious genre also has its own poetics, which are undoubtedly quite extensive. But I will mention to you only those ideas that occurred to me as I was working on my play.

Since this genre lacks the strong emotional colors of the two extreme genres on either side of it, no detail must be neglected which will give it power.

The subject should be important. The plot should be simple, deal with domestic matters, and be modelled on real life.

I do not want to see any valets in this genre. Respectable people do not make them privy to their affairs, and if all of the scenes take place with no servants present, they will be all the more interesting. If a servant speaks on stage as he does in society, he will be sullen; if he speaks any other way, it will not sound authentic.

If the nuances borrowed from the comic genre are too strong, the play will make its audience laugh and cry at the same time, and there will cease to be unity of interest <In/11; Vt/25; Sl/202; Co/232> or of emotional tone.

Since the serious genre includes monologues, this leads me to conclude that it leans more toward tragedy than to comedy, in which monologues are rarely used or very short.

It would be risky to use elements borrowed from both tragedy and comedy in the same play. Thoroughly understand the nature of your subject and your characters and follow it consistently.

Let the moral import of your play be universal and clear.

Avoid episodic characters, or if the plot requires such a character, he or she should be remarkable enough to add interest to the action.

Take time to work out all the details of the pantomime. Forget about those *coups de théâtre*, which have only a momentary effect, and look for tableaux. The longer we look at an excellent tableau, the greater the effect it has on us.

Movement almost always detracts from dignity; therefore, the main character should generally not be the moving force of the action.

And above all, remember that there is no fixed rule. There is not a single one of the guidelines I have just indicated, that cannot be infringed successfully by a writer with genius. . . .

Comedy deals with human types, and tragedy depicts individuals. Let me explain what I mean. The hero of a tragedy is one particular man – Regulus, Brutus, or Cato[13] – and no other. On the other hand, the main

---

[13] As in Voltaire's *Brutus* (1730) and Addison's *Cato* (1713).

character of a comedy must represent a large number of men. If, by chance, he was given such a unique personality that only one individual in society matched that description, comedy would regress to its infancy, and would degenerate into satire <Lg/124>....

In serious drama the character types are often as universal as in comedy, but they are invariably less individual than in tragedy.

Sometimes people say that a very amusing event happened at court, or an extremely tragic event occurred in the city, from which it may be concluded that comedy and tragedy exist at all levels of society. There is this difference, that sorrow and distress are even more frequent in the homes of humble folk, than are mirth and jollity in royal palaces. It is not so much the subject that makes a play comic, serious, or tragic, as the tone, the emotions, the temperament of the characters, and the interest. The effects of love, jealousy, gambling, profligacy, ambition, hatred, and envy can make us laugh, give us something to think about, or fill us with dread....

... Write comedies in the serious genre and write domestic tragedies, and your work will assuredly be appreciated now and in future generations. Above all, avoid *coups de théâtre*, use tableaux, get as close to real life as you can, and make sure you have a large enough playing space to use pantomime to the fullest advantage— People say that there are no more great tragic passions to be awakened, and that it is impossible to present noble feelings in a new and striking way. That may be true for tragedy as it was written by the Greeks, Romans, French, Italians, English, and all other nations in the past. But domestic tragedy will have a different plot, another emotional tone, and a sublime effect that will belong to it alone. I can feel this sense of the sublime in the words of an old man who said to the son who took care of him in his old age, "My son, now we are even. I gave you life, and you have paid me back." ...

MYSELF

But will we find this tragedy interesting?

DORVAL

What do you think? It is much closer to us. It depicts the misfortunes that surround us. Can you not imagine the effect that would be created by realistic scenery and costumes, words that are in keeping with actions, simple plots, and dangers as real as those that must at some time have threatened your relatives, your friends, or yourself? An abrupt change of fortune, the fear of public humiliation, the effects of poverty, a passion which leads to moral or financial ruin, from ruin to despair, from despair to violent death— these are not uncommon occurrences. Do you not think they would affect you as much as the death of a tyrant or the sacrifice of a child to Greek or Roman gods?— But ... you are not listening to me.

MYSELF

I am obsessed by your outline for a tragic version of the play.[14] ... I do
not believe an audience could stand to watch it; and this entire action may
be one of those that should be narrated. ...

DORVAL

No improbable event should either be shown on stage or narrated in the
dialogue. Among those actions that are probable, it is easy to determine
which the audience should actually see, and which should occur offstage. I
must apply my ideas to familiar tragedies, since it is impossible to cite
examples from a genre which does not yet exist.

When an action is simple, I think it preferable to show it on stage,
instead of presenting it indirectly through narration. The sight of Mahomet
with his dagger poised above the heart of Irene[15] is a striking tableau. He is
torn between his ambition, which prompts him to stab her, and his
passion, which stops him from doing so. My soul will be profoundly moved
by compassion, which always puts us in the place of the victim, and never
of the aggressor. I will see the dagger suspended and vacillating over my
own heart, rather than that of Irene— This action is too simple to be badly
imitated— But if the action becomes more complicated, with many incidents, some of them may easily remind me that I am sitting in a theatre,
that all of these characters are really actors, and that what is happening is
not a real event. Narration, on the other hand, will carry me into a realm
beyond the stage. I will follow all of the details of the story; my imagination
will bring them to life, as I have seen them in nature. ...

But there is another factor. Our overriding desire for order, which we
discussed earlier, impels us to see beings in proportion to one another. If
some detail is presented to us that is larger than life, the rest will then
become correspondingly larger in our minds. ...

Those are the guidelines. Apply them yourself to the action of my tragic
outline. Is the action not simple?

MYSELF

It is.

DORVAL

Is there any circumstance that cannot be shown on the stage?

MYSELF

None.

---

[14] Dorval had given Diderot the outline of a possible tragic ending for the play, in which
Dorval committed suicide by falling on his sword.
[15] In *Mahomet II* (1739) by Jean-Baptiste Sauvé (1701–c. 1761), an actor and dramatist,
known as La Noue. Voltaire admired this play and promoted its production at the
Comédie-Française.

DORVAL

Will its effect on the audience be devastating?

MYSELF

Too much so, perhaps. Would we really seek out such experiences in the theatre? We want to be moved, touched, and frightened, but only up to a certain point.

DORVAL

... What is the purpose of a dramatic work?

MYSELF

I believe it is to inspire in us the love of virtue and the horror of vice—

DORVAL

Therefore, saying that people should not be moved beyond a certain point is tantamount to saying that they should not leave the theatre too enamored of virtue or too repelled by vice. There would be no art of poetry for such a pusillanimous nation. What would become of taste and of art if we rejected its energy and imposed arbitrary limits on its effects? ...

MYSELF

But what are the subjects of this serious comedy that you see as a new kind of drama? Human nature does not seem to offer at the most more than a dozen truly distinct types of comic character.

DORVAL

I agree.

MYSELF

The slight differences that are to be seen in human character are more difficult to handle than more clear-cut personality types.

DORVAL

I agree. But do you realize what that means? It is no longer, strictly speaking, character types that are to be shown on stage, but social roles. Hitherto, character was the main subject of comedy, and the place in society was merely secondary. Today social rank must become the main concern and character must be incidental. The entire plot was based on character. Writers generally tried to find events which emphasized character and then strung these events together. The play must now be based on occupation, with all of its responsibilities, advantages, and drawbacks. This seems to me a richer, broader, and more useful source than that of character. If the character was the least bit exaggerated, the spectator could say to himself, "That is not me."

But he cannot deny that the profession he sees depicted on the stage is his own. He cannot fail to recognize his responsibilities. He is absolutely obliged to apply what is said to himself. ...

MYSELF

Are there not tax-collectors in our plays?

DORVAL

No doubt there are, but tax-collectors have not really been done.

MYSELF

It would be difficult to mention a play that does not have a father in it.

DORVAL

That is true, but fathers have not really been done. In short, I would ask you if the responsibilities, advantages, disadvantages, and dangers inherent in these social roles have been shown on the stage. And if they are the basis for the plots and the moral conclusions of our plays. ...

MYSELF

Therefore you would like playwrights to show us men of letters, philosophers, shopkeepers, judges, lawyers, politicians, citizens, magistrates, tax-collectors, aristocrats, and stewards in our plays.

DORVAL

Add to that, all of the family relationships— fathers, husbands, sisters, brothers <Lg/114>. Fathers! What a subject <Dt/57>, in a society such as ours, when we do not seem to have the slightest idea of what a father really is!

Just think that new professions are being invented every day. Perhaps nothing is as unfamiliar to us as these various roles in society, and nothing should be of greater interest to us. Each of us has our own role in society, but we also have to deal with people from all walks of life.

What a wealth of important details, public and private actions, undiscovered truths, and new situations are to be drawn from these social roles! And they offer the same contrasts and differences as are to be found among character types, so that the poet can juxtapose them <Gl/72>.

But these subjects do not belong to the serious genre alone. They will become tragic or comic, depending on the talent of the writer who uses them. ...

Well then, do you still believe that the last century has left us nothing further to do in this one?

Domestic, middle-class tragedy has to be created.

The serious genre needs to be developed.

Social roles and occupations should be substituted for temperament or character types, perhaps in all genres.

Pantomime has to be closely interwoven with the dramatic action.

The stage must be modified, and *coups de théâtre* replaced by the use of tableaux. This will provide a new source of inspiration for playwrights and a new field of study for actors. Obviously, it is of little use for authors to invent tableaux, if the actors remain attached to their symmetrical placement and limited scope of action.

From "Discourse on Dramatic Poetry"[16]
To Monsieur Grimm[17]

On Dramatic Genres

Imagine a nation where the only kind of dramatic entertainment was amusing and happy, and where someone tried to introduce another type that was moving and serious. Do you know, my dear friend, what the citizens of that nation would think of it? Unless I am much mistaken, once they had become aware of the possibility, reasonable people would undoubtedly say, "Why do we need this new genre? Are there not enough real difficulties in life without bringing in other imaginary ones? Why do even our amusements have to be suffused with sorrow?" They would speak in the manner of people unacquainted with the pleasure to be derived from feeling compassion and shedding tears. . . .

When one genre already exists, it is difficult to introduce a new one. Once this second genre is accepted, another misconception arises; soon people imagine that both genres are similar and are very close together. . . .

In *The Natural Son* I tried to give the idea of a drama that was midway between comedy and tragedy.

The Father, which I had promised to write next, but whose composition was delayed by constant distractions, is halfway between the serious drama of *The Natural Son* and comedy.

And if ever I have the time and the courage, I hope to write a play that falls between serious drama and tragedy.

Whether or not these two plays are well received, they still clearly demonstrate that there is a real and perceptible distance between these two established genres of tragedy and comedy.

On Serious Comedy

Here then is the complete range of the types of drama. Lighthearted comedy, which has as its aim ridicule and human folly; serious comedy, dealing with virtue and our duties as human beings; tragedy which would involve our domestic misfortunes; and the tragedy which treats of public disasters and the misfortune of important people.

But who will be capable of giving us a clear and accurate picture of our

---

[16] 1758. Newly translated from Diderot/Chouillet 1980.

[17] Friedrich-Melchior, Baron von Grimm (1723–1807) was a literary critic and friend of Diderot. His periodical *Correspondance littéraire, philosophique et critique*, to which Diderot was a contributor, was intended to keep its readers informed about literary and artistic trends in Paris.

duties? What qualities must be possessed by the poet who sets out to do this?

He must be a philosopher, who has gone deeply within himself to discover his true human nature. He must also be thoroughly conversant with the various professions in society, so that he is familiar with the tasks and responsibilities, the drawbacks and advantages of each one. . . .

The fact that what people do for a living has given us such plays as Molière's *The Bores*[18] is already a considerable achievement, but I believe we can make even better use of this material. The obligations and disadvantages of a profession are not all equally important. It seems to me that one could concentrate on the main ones, making them the basis for the play, and the others could be filled in as details. This is what I set out to do in *The Father*, where the plot hinges on arranging suitable marriages for the son and daughter. Financial situation, family background, upbringing, the duties of fathers toward their children, and children's obligations to their parents, marriage, the single life, everything that has to do with being a father comes in through the dialogue. . . .

Our duties as human beings are as rich a source of inspiration for the playwright as are our foibles and vices, and plays that are honest and serious will be successful anywhere, but especially in a society that is corrupt. These people will escape from the company of the evil companions who surround them by going to the theatre. There they will find the kind of people with whom they would like to live. There they will see humankind as it is, and will become reconciled with it. . . .

We should always have virtue and virtuous people in mind when we write. . . .

When I heard the scenes about peasant life in *The Feigned Benefactor*,[19] I said, "Here is something that will please people at all times and in all places, and everyone will shed tears to hear it." . . . This episode was undoubtedly an example of the honest and serious genre.

"The example of a single successful episode proves nothing," some people will say, "and if you do not break up the monotony of speeches about virtue with some boisterous, ridiculous, and even somewhat exaggerated characters, as all the other writers have done, whatever you may say about the honest and serious genre, I am still afraid you will merely produce scenes that are flat and colorless, moralizing that will bore and depress the audience, and little more than dramatized sermons."

Let us examine the parts of a play and see. Should it be judged by the subject matter? In the honest and serious genre, the subject is no less important than in lighthearted comedy, and it is handled in a more

---

[18] *Les Fâcheux*, a *comédie-ballet*, produced in 1661, in which the hero's courtship is interrupted by a series of insistent bores.

[19] *Le Faux Généreux* by Antoine Bret was performed in January 1758. The play was condemned by Grimm.

realistic way. Should we judge by the characters? They can be just as varied and original, and the poet is obliged to make them even more forceful. Is it to be judged by the emotions? They will be all the more dynamic since the interest will be greater. Is it to be judged by style? It will be more spirited, more serious, more elevated, more tempestuous, and more conducive to what we call feeling; without this quality no style can touch the heart. Is it by the absence of ridicule? When foolish actions and words are prompted by misplaced self-interest or by emotional turmoil, is this not the real absurdity of life? . . .

Let us take two comedies, one serious and one humorous. Let us construct from them, scene by scene, two picture galleries, and see in which one we will continue to walk the longest and with the greatest pleasure, where we will feel the strongest and most delightful emotions, and to which we will be most eager to return.

I repeat, the honest [and serious] genre. It touches us more nearly and more tenderly than work that elicits derision and laughter <St/17; Lg/115>. Poets, if you are sensitive and of subtle understanding, strike this chord and you will hear it resonate in every heart.

"Does this mean that human nature is good?"

Yes, my friend, very good indeed. . . .

It is the miserable conventions that pervert humankind, and not human nature that is to blame. . . .

The theatre is the only place where the tears of the virtuous and of the wicked are mingled. There the wicked take umbrage at the kind of injustice they themselves may have committed, feel compassion for the kind of suffering they may have caused others, and are filled with indignation by a person whose character resembles their own. But the impression is received and remains indelibly within us, whether we like it or not. And the wicked leave their seats in the theatre less inclined to wrongdoing than if they had been chastized by a harsh and unyielding moralist. . . .

On a Kind of Moral Drama

Sometimes it has occurred to me that the most important tenets of morality might be discussed on stage without hindering the flow of the dramatic action.

How could this be done? The conduct of the plot would be organized in such a way that moral questions would arise naturally, as for example, the abdication of the empire is central to the action of *Cinna*.[20] Thus a playwright would discuss the questions of suicide, of honor, of duels, of fortune, of the dignities of office as well as countless others. Our plays would take on a seriousness that they now lack. . . .

When I leave the theatre, it is not words I want to take away with me, but impressions. . . .

---

[20] Tragedy by Corneille, written in 1640.

Playwrights, the true applause that you must aim to elicit, is not the clapping of hands that suddenly erupts after a dazzling line, but the deep sigh that comes from the depths of our hearts releasing the tension after a long silence. . . .

On Simple and Complex Plays

As for me, I prefer a passion or a character that develops gradually until it finally can be seen in all its power, rather than those combinations of incidents that are woven together into a play that is equally unsettling for the characters and the audience. . . . However, that is what we call movement. The Ancients had quite a different idea. A simple plot line, an action selected as close as possible to its ending, so that everything was at its height, a catastrophe that was always imminent and always avoided by an event that was simple and believable. Speeches full of power, strong passions, tableaux, one or two clearly delineated characters, that was all they needed. . . .

If a play is to be performed only once and never published, I would say to the poet: "Make it as complicated as you like. You will certainly stir the audience up and keep them entertained. But keep your work simple if you want your play to be read and to remain for posterity." . . .

Any author who undertakes to carry on two plot lines at the same time will be obliged to untangle them both at the same moment. If the main action is resolved first, the remaining subplot cannot stand on its own. If, on the contrary, the subplot finishes first, there is another disadvantage; characters either disappear suddenly, or else reappear for no reason, and the play is truncated or becomes boring. . . .

There is no middle ground; what you gain on one side, you lose on the other. If you achieve interest and momentum by combining many incidents, you will have no more dialogue; your characters will barely have time to speak. They will be in constant movement instead of developing. I speak from experience.

On Burlesque Drama (Farce)

There cannot be too much action and movement in farce; . . . in humorous comedy there will be less, even less in serious comedy, and almost none in tragedy.

The more improbable a genre is, the easier it is to make it fast-paced and lively. Liveliness and excitement mean that there is less truth and decorum. . . . In the serious genre the choice of incidents makes it difficult to sustain liveliness. . . .

While the movement varies from one genre to another, the action always continues. It does not even stop in the intervals. It is a piece of rock falling from the top of an escarpment; it gains momentum as it falls, bouncing from one place to another with every obstacle in its path.

If this is an accurate comparison, if it is true that there is proportionately less dialogue when there is more action, there should be more talk than action in the first acts, and more action and less talk in the later acts. . . .

On the Plan and the Dialogue

Is it more difficult to establish the plan than to write the dialogue? . . .

A person who is at home in the company of other people, who speaks with ease, who knows other people, has studied and listened to them, finds it difficult to write the plan.

Another person, who has breadth of mind, has reflected on the art of poetry, who knows the theatre, who has learned from experience and the development of taste what situations are inherently interesting, and who knows how to arrange events, will easily be able to compose the plan, but will have trouble writing the scenes. . . .

Moreover, both require talent, but it is not the same kind of talent. The plan is essential to a complex play; it is the art of discourse and dialogue that make a simple play compelling to see or to read.

Plans are worked out using the imagination, while dialogue is based on nature. . . .

Listen to [other] people and carry on conversations with yourself; these are the ways to train yourself in writing dialogue.

Have a fertile imagination, observe the order and sequence of things in reality, do not be afraid of difficult scenes or of hard work, enter into the heart of the subject, see clearly the moment when the action must begin, know what can properly be left aside, know what situations have the most impact. With these abilities you will be able to work out the plan.

Above all, make it a rule not to write down on paper a single idea about the details before you have completed your plan < 1:Lp/188>. . . .

On the Outline

. . . But how to formulate your plan? In Aristotle's *Poetics* there is an excellent idea on this subject < 1:/Ar/55>. . . . Whether you are working on a familiar subject, or are trying to make up a new one, begin by making an outline of the plot; later you will think of the episodes or details that will fill it out. . . .

On the Incidents

If the poet has imagination and adheres to his outline, he will find it a source of inspiration for a host of incidents, so that his only problem will be to choose among them. . . .

He should be scrupulous in his choice of incidents, and abstemious in his use of them. They should fit the importance of his subject, and the links between them should seem almost necessary. . . .

If you use a small number of incidents, you will have a small number of characters. Use no superfluous characters, and make sure that all your incidents are imperceptibly held together. Above all do not lay false trails. If

you raise my anticipation with a problem that does not materialize, you
will distract my attention. . . .

On the Plan of Tragedy and Comedy

. . . "A plan is a fanciful story, distributed according to the rules of drama.
This story is partially made up by the tragic playwright, and completely
made up by the comic playwright."

Very good. What then is the basis of dramatic art?

"The art of history."

Nothing is more reasonable. Poetry (literature) has rightly been compared to painting <Lg/110>, but a more useful and more revealing
comparison would have been to compare history to poetry <1:Cv/130>.
We would thus have arrived at more exact notions about what is true,
what is probable, and what is possible, and we would have clarified
precisely what is meant by the idea of the marvellous, a term common to
all poetic genres, but which most poets are unable to define properly.

Not all historic events are suitable for use in tragedy, nor are all domestic
events suitable subjects for comedy. . . .

It sometimes happens that the natural order of things brings together
extraordinary events. This same natural order marks the difference
between the marvellous and the miraculous. Rare occurrences are marvellous; occurrences that are naturally impossible are miraculous. Dramatic art rejects miracles <Lg/108>.

If nature never linked events together in an extraordinary way, all that
the poet might imagine beyond the plain, cold uniformity of mundane
affairs, would be unbelievable. But this is not the case. What then does the
poet do? He either seizes upon these extraordinary sequences of events, or
he imagines ones that are similar. But, whereas we often fail to see the
causal link between events in nature <Lg/121>, and without knowing all
of the factors, we merely see an inevitable simultaneity in the facts, the
poet, for his part, is determined that the entire texture of his work will be
linked together in a clear and understandable way. Thus he is less accurate, but more credible than the historian. . . .

The role that is played by the gods in tragedy, must be played by human
beings in comedy. Fatality and malice are the bases for dramatic interest in
tragedy and comedy respectively.

"What is the novelistic veneer that has been criticized in some of our
plays?"

A work will be novelistic if the marvellous element stems from the
simultaneity of the events, if there are gods, or if the people involved are
either too wicked or too good, if the situations or characters deviate too
greatly from what we know from history or experience, and particularly if
the connection between events is too improbable or complicated.

Hence we may conclude that any novel which would not make a good play, may still be a good novel; but there is no good play which would not make an excellent novel. These two types of literature differ by their rules.

Illusion is their common goal, but on what does illusion depend? On the circumstances, which make illusion more or less difficult to achieve.

May I be permitted for a moment to speak the language of geometry? We know what is meant by an equation. Illusion is on one side of the equation, by itself. It is a constant quality that is equal to a sum of terms, some positive and some negative, whose number and arrangement may be infinitely varied, while their total value is always the same. The positive terms represent ordinary circumstances, and the negative terms are extra-ordinary circumstances. They must balance each other out. . . .

When I say that illusion is a constant quality, I mean that it remains constant within one individual judging different works of art, and not from one person to another. On the entire surface of the earth, there may not be two people who have the same degree of certainty, and yet the poet is obliged to make them all believe in illusion. He overcomes the intelligent, experienced, and educated person as easily as a governess outwits a dull child. A good piece of literature is a tale fit to be told to sensible people. The novelist has the time and space that are denied to the playwright. Given two works of equal merit, I would appreciate the play more than the novel. . . .

The Ancients had tragedies in which everything was made up by the playwright. Not even the names of the characters were taken from history. And what does it matter, as long as the poet does not go beyond the true measure of the marvellous. . . .

Domestic tragedy would involve the problems inherent in two genres: to produce the emotional effect of heroic tragedy and to make up the entire story as in comedy. . . .

Without imagination, one is neither a poet, nor a philosopher, nor an intelligent person, nor one capable of reason, nor a human being. . . . Imagination is the ability to remember images. Anyone who was completely lacking in this faculty would be an imbecile, whose intellectual functions would be limited to producing the sounds learned in childhood, and to applying them mechanically to the circumstances of life. . . . [The playwright] has received from nature, to a high degree, the quality that distinguishes a genius from an ordinary person and an ordinary person from an imbecile: imagination. . . .

But the poet cannot surrender completely to the power of his imagination. There are certain limits imposed on him. The model for his conduct is found in the rare occurrences within the general order of nature. This is his guiding principle.

The more strange and singular these occurrences are, the more he will require art, time, space, and ordinary circumstances to compensate for the marvellous element and give the illusion a basis in reality.

If the historic fact is not sufficiently marvellous he will reinforce it with extraordinary incidents. If it is too remarkable, he will tone it down with ordinary incidents. ...

The art of poetry would certainly be greatly advanced, if we had completely dealt with the question of historic certainty. The same principles would apply to the story (*conte*), to the novel, to the opera, to farce, and to all types of poetry, including fables. ...

Once the poet has drawn up his plan, by expanding his outline to a suitable length, and his drama has been divided into acts and scenes, he may now set to work. He should begin with the first scene and finish with the last. He will be mistaken if he believes he can follow his whims, jumping back and forth from one section to another, wherever his talent may inspire him to go. He has no idea of the trouble he will have later, if he wants his work to be unified. ... Scenes have an influence on one another, that he will not have understood. ... Before going from one scene to the next, one should be thoroughly rooted in the previous scenes. ...

On [Dramatic] Interest

In plays with complicated plots, the interest comes more from the plan than the dialogue. In simple plays, on the other hand, it resides more in the dialogue than in the plan. But should the interest be viewed in relation to the characters or to the spectators?

The spectators are merely unacknowledged witnesses of the events.

"It is the characters who must be considered then?"

So I believe. They must create the complications without realizing it. Everything should remain unfathomable to them. They should move toward the outcome unawares. If they are in a state of agitation I will have to follow them and experience the same emotions.

I disagree so completely with most dramatic theorists, who believe that the audience must not suspect the outcome < 1:Lp/188>, that I would not consider it a task too far beyond my abilities to try to write a drama where the outcome was announced in the first scene, and I would elicit the most intense interest based on this very circumstance.

Everything must be clear to the spectator. ... People may find as many paradoxes as they like in my ideas, but I shall persist in believing that for every instance where it is advisable to keep the audience from knowing about an important incident before it happens, there are several others where dramatic interest requires the opposite.

By keeping it secret, the playwright has given me a moment of surprise. By letting me know, he would have kept me in a state of anxiety for a long time.

I will have only a moment of pity for someone who is struck down in a moment. But what do I experience if the fatal blow is long awaited, or if I see the storm clouds gathering above my head or above someone else's head, and hanging suspended there for a long time? ...

All of the characters may be unaware of their true relationships with each other, if you like, but the audience must know who they all are. . . .

Why do certain monologues have such striking effects? It is because they reveal to me the secret plans of a character, and this revelation immediately fills me with fear or hope.

If the identities of the characters are unknown, the spectator can take no more interest in the action than the characters do. But the interest will double for the spectator if he knows enough to understand that the words and actions would be very different if the characters knew each other's true identity. Thus you will create in me an intense expectation of how they will feel when they are able to compare what they are with what they have done or have tried to do. . . .

Moreover, the more I reflect on dramatic art, the more angry I become with those who have written about it. It is a muddle of particular rules, from which general precepts have been drawn. People have seen that certain incidents produced great effects, and have immediately concluded that the dramatist must use the same means to achieve the same effects. Whereas, if they had looked more closely, they would have noticed even greater effects to be produced by completely opposite means. . . .

Whether you are a playwright or an actor, take no more thought for the spectator than if he did not exist. Imagine, at the edge of the stage, a great wall separating you from the audience. Act as if the curtain did not go up. . . .

On Exposition

The first part of the dramatic structure is the exposition, according to our critics. In tragedy, where the story is familiar, the exposition can be a single word. If my daughter sets foot in Aulis, she will die.[21] . . . I would be just as happy if they asked the dramatist to arrange his first scenes so that they contain the actual outline of his play. . . .

To achieve clarity, everything must be explained. The nature of drama requires rapidity. How can we explain everything and keep the action moving rapidly?

The incident chosen to begin the action will be the subject of the first scene. It will naturally lead to the second, the second scene will lead to the third, and the act will be filled out. The important point is for the action to gather momentum and to be very clear. Here is where the audience must be considered. Thus we see that the exposition must be given gradually, as the drama unfolds, and the audience does not know or see everything until the final curtain. . . . The more rapid the pace and the more complete the exposition, the more careful the dramatist must be. Beyond a certain point he cannot put himself in the spectator's place. His plot is so familiar to him,

---

[21] Iphigenia, the daughter of Agamemnon and Clytemnestra, was to be sacrificed to the gods by her father. This was the subject of Euripides' *Iphigenia in Aulis* (c. 405 B.C.) and of Racine's *Iphigénie en Aulide*, produced in 1674.

he can easily think things are clear when they are not. It is up to his reader-critic [*censeur*] to point this out to him, for however talented a writer may be, he needs an impartial reader or critic. . . .

Explain everything that requires an explanation, and nothing more. . . .

Nothing is beautiful if it lacks unity, and the first incident will set the tone for the whole work.

If the play begins with a strong situation, everything else must have the same energy, or it will begin to drag. How many plays have been ruined by their beginnings! The dramatist was afraid of a weak beginning, and his situations were so strong he could not sustain the impressions made on the audience.

On Character Types[22]

If the structure of the drama has been well worked out, if the dramatist has correctly chosen the first moment, has started in the center of the action, if he has accurately portrayed the temperament of his characters, why should he not succeed? But it is the situations that must determine the nature of the characters. . . .

The characters will be well drawn if the situations become more difficult and more upsetting by virtue of the temperaments of the people involved. Imagine that the next twenty-four hours for your characters are the most critical and painful moments of their lives. You must therefore keep them in the greatest possible agitation. Make your situations extreme, creating conflict for the characters. Go even farther and create opposition between one person's interest and that of another, so that one cannot reach his goal without obstructing someone else's plans, and when all are concerned in one event, each one wishes it to go according to his own desires.

True contrast is between personalities and situations, between one person's interest and that of another.

"But why not add to these the contrast between opposing character types? This is such a useful resource for the playwright!"

And so commonplace . . . I want characters to be different, but I must admit I dislike the deliberate use of contrast. . . . Is it not true that one of the most important and most difficult parts of the dramatist's task is to conceal the art? What more glaring revelation of the author's technique than to set one type of character off against another? . . . It seems to me that the more serious a genre is, the less contrast should be used. It is seldom seen in tragedy, except perhaps between minor characters. The hero stands alone. . . . Contrast is unnecessary in comedies of character. In other kinds of comedy it is superfluous. . . .

---

[22] "Character type" is used to translate "caractère," meaning nature, character, or disposition, as in the (Horatian) theoretical tradition that Diderot appears to be invoking.

On Customs and Mores

... In general, the more polite and civilized a nation is, the less poetic its manners and customs will be. ... What does the dramatist require? Is it nature in its wild or cultivated state, tranquil or in torment? ... Poetry needs something vast, uncivilized, and wild. ...

We may marvel at the peculiarities of civilized nations, where fastidiousness may be exaggerated to the point of prohibiting dramatists from using situations, even though they are part of their experience, and have beauty, simplicity, and truth. Who in our society would dare to spread straw on the stage and show a newborn baby lying there? If the playwright put a cradle on the stage, some lout in the pit would undoubtedly imitate the crying baby, the people in the boxes would burst out laughing, and the play would be a failure. ...

A nation's taste must be very dubious, if it acknowledges the existence in nature of things which artists are not permitted to imitate, or when it admires in art, things which it disdains in nature. ...

On Stage Décor

... You expect your dramatist to abide by the unity of place, and yet you abandon the stage to the ignorance of an incompetent scene painter.

If you want to bring your dramatists closer to truth in their plot structure and dialogue, if you want your actors to bring more naturalness and true emotion to their parts, raise your voices and simply demand that the place represented on stage be shown as it ought to be. ...

Once you have decided that the dramatist's play is worthy of being performed for you, let him send for the stage designer and read his play to him. Once the latter is familiar with the place where the action occurs, he should reproduce it exactly as it is, being particularly aware that scene painting must be much more rigorous and authentic than any other kind of painting. ... There must be no distractions, no suppositions that awake in my mind any impressions other than those the dramatist wants me to have. ... Scene painting is limited to those details that serve the illusion. ...

On Costume

... Comedy should be performed in ordinary clothes. On stage one should not be more elaborately nor more casually dressed than one would be at home. Actors, if you spend a fortune on clothes <Dl/98> to impress the audience,[23] you have no taste, and you forget that the audience should not exist for you. The more serious the genre, the more sober and restrained the style of dress should be. How realistic is it, in a moment of tumultuous action, for people to take the time to dress up as if they were going to a parade or a celebration. ...

---

[23] At this time, actors still provided their own costumes.

On Stage Directions (Pantomime)

... The description of movements and gestures must be written down every time it constitutes a tableau, whenever it intensifies or clarifies the dialogue, whenever it reveals character, when it is some subtle form of byplay that cannot be guessed at, whenever it represents an answer, and almost always at the beginning of scenes. ...

I admit, nevertheless, that if the art of mime were highly developed on our stages, we could often dispense with writing it down <In/3; Gl/72>, and that may be the reason why the Ancients did not do so. ... For a reader, does it not bring added pleasure to see the actions described as the playwright visualized them? ...

Stage directions reveal the picture that existed in the dramatist's mind as he was writing, and that he would like to see reproduced on stage throughout the performance. It is the simplest way to teach the audience what they have a right to expect from their actors <Hg/213>. ...

Moreover, when I write down the stage directions, it is as if I were saying to the actors, "This is the way I say the lines; these are the things I saw in my imagination as I was writing. ...

"Actors, take advantage of your rights. Do what the moment and your talent inspire you to do. If you are made of flesh and blood and have feelings, all will go well, without my interference. It will be useless for me to interfere, and all will go badly, if you are made of wood or marble. ..."

6

CARLO GOLDONI
(1707–93)

At the end of the 1750 season, Carlo Goldoni promised his Venetian audience sixteen new plays for the following year. *The Comic Theatre* was the first of these, and aptly enough, it is a play on the art of playwriting and on the status of Italian comic theatre in that period of history. But as he himself suggests in the address to the reader of the 1753 edition, it could figure as a foreword, not only to the other fifteen plays of 1751, but to all of Goldoni's earlier comedies, too.[1] *The Comic Theatre* is a dramatized poetics of drama and an outline of the reform of Italian theatre which Goldoni had initiated some years before and which was currently in progress. The chief ideas expounded in the play, quickly stated, are: Italian comic theatre has long been dominated by the *commedia dell'arte* tradition of improvised comedies with masked characters but, since this tradition has now exhausted its artistic creativity, the theatre is in need of a complete reform, especially in such areas as composition, performance, and public taste. Whereas the principles of a new art of composition may be taught in a short period of time by means of a sufficiently detailed poetics of comedy, the changes that this would entail in performance methods and in public taste would be such as to arouse resistance to reform in both actors and audience. The reform must therefore be slow enough to be acceptable to acting companies, without whose collaboration no reform can take place, and to the audience, without whom there can be no theatre at all.

The plays that Goldoni wrote prior to, and immediately after, the 1751 season reveal that it is indeed with calculated slowness that he moves away from the compositional principles of the *commedia dell'arte* and towards those of what he calls "character comedies," that is to say, comedies in which the well-known stock characters of tradition are replaced by social types, all with a number of well-defined personal psychological traits, arising entirely from the dialogue, that distinguish them as individuals: as types they espouse the principles of their social class <Dt/55>, and hence become for Goldoni instruments of social criticism, carried out from a perspective sensitive to Enlightenment views; as individuals they are the agents of an action characterized by verisimilitude <1:In/8–9>. Yet despite the gradualism of his reform, Goldoni met with stiff opposition, first from Pietro Chiari (1711–85), who was always ready to assess the market conditions of the theatre and to adapt borrowed plots to the current taste of theatre-goers for the sake of easy success, and later from Carlo Gozzi <Go/69>, who championed the cause of the *commedia dell'arte* as well as a counter-Enlightenment ideology.

Goldoni was a man of the theatre, who wrote over two hundred plays and who, throughout his life, was associated with the actors, impresarios, and directors who

---

[1] Goldoni/Miller 1969, 3.

determined the course of Italian theatre for many years. In 1762 he moved to Paris, where he became playwright for the Comédie italienne, and never returned to Italy.

For further reading

Chatfield-Taylor 1913; Fido 1977; Fido 1984; Goldoni/Miller 1969; Herry 1976; Nicastro 1974.

From *The Comic Theatre*[2]

Act 2, Scene 1

LELIO: Signor Anselmo, I'm desperate.

ANSELMO: But my dear man, you come here and you propose such a rag of a subject that even a company of puppets would refuse to act it.

LELIO: Well, I won't insist about the subject, but they never should have cut the dialogue to shreds that way.

ANSELMO: But don't you understand that stock dialogues, witticisms, soliloquies, insults, conceits, lamentations, tirades <Dt/43; Hu/264>, and such[3] are no longer used?

LELIO: Then what do they use these days?

ANSELMO: Character comedies.

LELIO: Well, in that case I have as many character comedies as you wish.

ANSELMO: Then why didn't you propose one to our director?

LELIO: I had no idea that Italians liked character comedies.

ANSELMO: Why, this is the only kind of play Italians want nowadays; and what is more, in no time at all these character comedies have so improved everyone's taste that now even common people have definite opinions about whether a play is well or badly written.

LELIO: This is remarkable indeed!

ANSELMO: And let me tell you why. Comedy was created to correct vice and ridicule bad customs; when the ancient poets wrote comedies in this manner, the common people could participate, because, seeing the copy of a character on stage, each found the original either in himself or in someone else. But when comedies became merely ridiculous, no one paid attention any more, because with the excuse of making people laugh <Lg/115>, they admitted the worst and most blatant errors. But now that we have returned to fish comedies from nature's *Mare Magnum* [Great Sea], men feel their hearts touched again. They can identify with the characters or passions and discern whether a character is well observed and developed, and whether a passion is well motivated.

LELIO: You sound more like a poet that an actor.

ANSELMO: I'll tell you, sir. With the mask I'm Brighella,[4] without the mask I'm a man who may not have enough invention to be a poet, but at least

---

[2] The text is from Goldoni/Miller 1969, with revisions.
[3] All features of *commedia dell'arte* plays.
[4] A stock character (a servant) in the *commedia dell'arte*.

has enough discernment to understand his own craft. An ignorant actor never plays any character well.

Act 2, Scene 3

LELIO: Here we are. This is a play translated from the French and called . . .

ANSELMO: Wait. Don't say any more. If it's a translation I've no use for it.

LELIO: Why not? Don't you like French works?

ANSELMO: On the contrary; I praise them, esteem them, venerate them; but they don't suit my needs. The French have triumphed in the art of drama for an entire century; I think the time has come for Italy to show the world that it can still give birth to good authors, such as those who, after the Greeks and Romans, were the first to enrich and ennoble the theatre. One cannot deny that in their plays the French have created fine and well depicted characters, that the passions are well handled and the ideas are keen and witty and brilliant; but their public is satisfied with very little. An entire French play can rest on the shoulders of a single character. Around one single passion – of course, well developed throughout the play – they spin out so many words, conveying an air of novelty by mere strength of expression. Our Italians demand much more. They expect that the principal character be strong, original, and recognizable; that virtually all the figures in the episodes be characters in their own right; that the plot be reasonably rich in surprises and innovations. They want the moral mixed with the spice of jokes and banter. They want an unexpected ending < 1:Lp/188>, yet one deriving from the play in its entirety. Their demands are too numerous to list; and only with experience, practice, and time can we ever come to know them and satisfy them.

LELIO: But once a play contains all these good qualities, will everyone in Italy like it?

ORAZIO: No, by no means. Every individual has his own peculiar manner of thinking, and this will naturally affect his reaction to a given play. If he's melancholy, he won't like jokes; if jolly, he won't like moralizing. For this reason plays have never had, and never will have, universal appeal < 1:Hr/74>. Nevertheless, when a play is good, most people like it, and when it's bad nearly everyone dislikes it.

LELIO: In that case I have a character comedy of my own invention that I'm sure most people will like. I think I've followed all the rules; but if I haven't, I've certainly observed the most essential one, which is unity of place.

ORAZIO: Whoever told you that unity of place was an essential rule?

LELIO: Aristotle.

ORAZIO: Have you read Aristotle?

LELIO: To tell you the truth, I haven't, but I've heard this from others.

ORAZIO: Let me explain to you what Aristotle says. The philosopher began to write about comedy but never finished, and all we have from him on this subject are a few imperfect pages. In his *Poetics* he prescribed unity of place < 1:Cv/129> for tragedy,[5] but for comedy he said

---

[5] Unity of place, frequently and incorrectly attributed to Aristotle, actually stems from Castelvetro.

nothing. Some say that what he said for tragedy must be understood
for comedy as well < 1:In/10–11 >, and that had he finished his
treatise on comedy he would have prescribed unity of place. But it
can be objected that if Aristotle were still alive, he himself would do
away with an arduous rule which has begotten a thousand absurdities, a thousand improprieties and blunders. I distinguish between
two types of comedy: simple comedy and plotted comedy. Simple
comedy can be staged with a single set; plotted comedy cannot be
done this way without stiffness and incongruity. The ancients did
not have our facilities for changing scenes, and for this reason they
observed the unity. We will have observed it if the comedy takes
place in the same city, and all the more so if it takes place in the same
house, provided, however, the characters don't suddenly leap from
Naples to Castile[6] as they used to in some Spanish plays – though
nowadays they are beginning to correct such an abuse and have
scruples about distance and time < 1:Tm/208 >. I conclude, therefore,
that if a comedy can be presented without forced devices or incongruities in a single setting, then we should do so; but if for the sake of
unity of place we must introduce absurdities, then it is better to
change settings and respect the rule of verisimilitude.

Act 2, Scene 10

EUGENIO: Then do you think that we should do away with improvised
            comedies altogether?

ORAZIO: Altogether, no. In fact it's a good thing that Italians continue to do
            what other countries have never dared. The French say that Italian
            actors are rash for improvising before the public, but what may be
            considered rashness in an ignorant comedian is a virtue in a skilled
            one. We have some excellent actors in Italy who do our country and
            our profession great honor, and they achieve no less elegance
            through their admirable art of improvisation than a poet can achieve
            through writing.

EUGENIO: But our masked characters usually find it very difficult to act when
            their roles have been written out.

ORAZIO: Ah, but when a masked character is given a role that has been
            written with charm and wit and is well suited to his nature, then you
            can be sure that if he is worth his salt he will gladly memorize the
            part.

EUGENIO: Couldn't we do away with masks in our comedies?

ORAZIO: Heaven help us if we ever made such an innovation. The time is not
            ripe yet. In all things one should never try to go against the universal
            consensus. At one time people used to go to the theatre just to laugh;
            they wanted to see nothing but masks on stage, and whenever a
            serious character came out to recite a dialogue that was a little too
            long, they immediately grew bored. Now they are beginning to enjoy
            the serious roles, too; they like the dialogues and delight in unexpec-
            ted turns in the plot, they appreciate the moral and laugh at the
            quips and sallies contained in the serious scenes. But they also enjoy

---

6 As in *El burlador de Sevilla* by Tirso de Molina (1580–1648).

the masked characters, and we shouldn't eliminate them altogether. In fact, we should try instead to use them properly and to support them in their ridiculousness, even next to the most clever and graceful of serious characters.

EUGENIO: But to compose comedies in such a way is extremely difficult.

ORAZIO: It's a way of writing that was rediscovered only recently and charmed everyone at its first appearance; it won't be long before the most inventive minds will be aroused to improve it, as its originator desires with all his heart.

7

SAMUEL JOHNSON
(1709–84)

Dr. Johnson's criticism assumes a common discourse, heavily qualified by the contexts and material circumstances of authors and audiences,[1] and – at least "in questions that relate to the heart of man" – he was inclined to place less trust in abstractions than in "the common voice of the multitude, uninstructed by precept, and unprejudiced by authority."[2] Theatre was not special in this respect, as it was for Castelvetro <1:Cv/132>. Indeed, though he knew the theatre well,[3] Johnson scarcely differentiates between the activities of the spectator and the reader of plays, declaring them, in the Preface to his edition of Shakespeare to be much the same.

He speaks sardonically of the theatrical ambitions of Dryden and the rival who "placed their happiness in the claps of multitudes," and, in the same spirit, more than once remarks on "the capricious distribution of theatrical praise," the "ardour for theatrical entertainments" in his own time, and the money to be earned by writing for the stage (Waugh 1959, 246, 415, 166). But he also notices that the theatre may engage the feelings and imagination of the audience with a peculiar force, especially in the representation of domestic scenes, to which the audience has ready access. "What is nearest us, touches us most. The passions rise higher at domestic than at imperial tragedies," he writes.[4] And when, as in Rowe's *Jane Shore*, such scenes are found in context with conventional morality, the play remains popular and he, along with the public at large, approves.[5]

Though he by no means dismisses the art codified in neo-classical dramatic theory, Johnson is not disposed to govern, or be governed, by such prescriptive criteria as compliance with the unities of time and place (though he insists on unity of action), division into five acts, or, least of all, the purity of comic and tragic genres.[6] In *Rambler* 156 he further observes that "accidental prescriptions of authority, when time has procured them veneration, are often confounded with the laws of nature, and those rules are supposed coeval with reason, of which the first rise cannot be discovered." And in his "Preface" to Shakespeare (1765), he states what became a well-known axiom: that "there is always an appeal open from criticism to nature." But though this is undoubtedly the case with aesthetic

---

[1] See, for instance, *Rambler* 125.
[2] *Rambler* 52.
[3] Largely through his friend and former pupil David Garrick. Garrick produced Johnson's only play, *Irene*, at Drury Lane in 1749. It earned Johnson £300 but, understandably enough, no fame.
[4] To Mrs. Thrale, 11 July 1770 (Johnson/Redford 1992, 1:345).
[5] "This play, consisting of domestic scenes and private distress, lays hold upon the heart. The wife is forgiven because she repents, and the husband is honoured because he forgives. This therefore is one of those pieces which we still welcome on the stage" (Waugh 1959, 392).
[6] See, for instance, *Rambler* 125.

judgment, moral judgment, stemming from reason, which should be operative in the author no less than the critic is less open to appeal and more problematic for him.

One of Shakespeare's faults, noted in the "Preface," was that being "more careful to please than to instruct," he neglected the "writer's duty to make the world better." In Johnson, "poetical justice" <1:Rm/293> combines pleasure with instruction, but truth to nature and moral edification are not always consistent. Johnson's difficulties in dealing with this problem are indicated by comparison of the three passages placed together as the first selection below.

The author chooses what and what not to represent and the audience enables the representation by choosing to collaborate with it. The theatre audience, indeed, actually controls the drama of the age in that the "stage but echoes back the public voice."[7] The audience does not give itself up to an illusion that has, by some prescribed art, been perfected; nor does it lose sight of the real world in which the representation is taking place; nor relinquish its powers of moral judgment; but is somehow moved to, rather than argued into, a better moral understanding.

For further reading

Burwick 1991; Damrosch 1976; Hagstrum 1967; Keast 1952; Parker 1989; Wellek 1955: I.

[Truth to nature versus poetical justice]

(a) From *The Rambler*, No. 4[8]

The chief advantage these fictions have over real life is that their authors are at liberty, though not to invent, yet to select objects, and to cull from the mass of mankind those individuals upon which that attention ought most to be employed; as a diamond, though it cannot be made, may be polished by art, and placed in such a situation as to display that lustre which before was buried among common stones.

It is justly considered as the greatest excellency of art to imitate nature; but it is necessary to distinguish those parts of nature which are most proper for imitation: greater care is still required in representing life, which is so often discolored by passion or deformed by wickedness. If the world can be promiscuously described, I cannot see of what use it can be to read the account; or why it may not be as safe to turn the eye immediately upon mankind as upon a mirror which shows all that presents itself without discrimination.

It is therefore not a sufficient vindication of a character that it is drawn as it appears; for many characters ought never to be drawn: nor of a narrative that the train of events is agreeable to observation and experi-

---

[7] From the "Prologue, Spoken by Mr. Garrick, At the Opening of the Theatre in Drury Lane 1747" (Johnson/McAdam 1964, 89).

[8] *The Rambler* appeared twice weekly between March 1750 and March 1752. All but 7 of the 208 issues were written by Johnson himself. Number 4 is dated Saturday, 31 March 1750.

ence; for that observation which is called knowledge of the world will be found much more frequently to make men cunning than good. . . .

(b) From the notes on *King Lear*[9]

The injury done by Edmund to the simplicity of the action is abundantly recompensed by the addition of variety, by the art with which he is made to cooperate with the chief design, and the opportunity which he gives the poet of combining perfidy with perfidy, and connecting the wicked son with the wicked daughters, to impress this important moral, that villainy is never at a stop, that crimes lead to crimes, and at last terminate in ruin.

But though this moral be incidentally enforced, Shakespeare has suffered the virtue of Cordelia to perish in a just cause, contrary to the natural ideas of justice, to the hope of the reader, and, what is yet more strange, to the faith of the chronicles. Yet this conduct is justified by the Spectator,[10] who blames Tate[11] for giving Cordelia success and happiness in his alteration, and declares that, in his opinion, "the tragedy has lost half its beauty." Dennis < 1:Cg/299> has remarked, whether justly or not, that to secure the favorable reception of *Cato*, "the town was poisoned with much false and abominable criticism, and that endeavors had been used to discredit and decry poetical justice."[12] A play in which the wicked prosper, and the virtuous miscarry, may doubtless be good, because it is a just representation of the common events of human life: but since all reasonable beings naturally love justice, I cannot be easily persuaded that the observation of justice makes a play worse <Sl/199>; or, that if other excellencies are equal, the audience will not always rise better pleased from the final triumph of persecuted virtue. . . .

(c) From *Lives of the Poets: Addison*[13]

Whatever pleasure there may be in seeing crimes punished and virtue rewarded, yet, since wickedness often prospers in real life, the poet is certainly at liberty to give it prosperity on the stage. For if poetry has an imitation of reality, how are its laws broken by exhibiting the world in its true form? The stage may sometimes gratify our wishes; but, if it be truly the mirror of life, it ought to show us sometime what we are to expect.

---

[9] From the general note to the play in Johnson's edition of Shakespeare (1765).

[10] The *Spectator* was a daily, produced and mostly written by Steele and Joseph Addison (1672–1719). In number 40 Addison attacked the "ridiculous doctrine" of poetic justice, which his own *Cato* (1713) would eschew. Hence the accusation by Dennis <St/16> that Johnson reports.

[11] The version of Shakespeare's *King Lear* by Nahum Tate (1652–1715), in which Cordelia survives and marries Edgar, held the stage for many years.

[12] Dennis/Hooker 1939–43, II:43.

[13] The first part of Johnson's *Lives of the Poets* was published in 1779. The Addison life was finished early in the following year and published in Part II of the *Lives* in 1781. For a full text see Waugh 1959, 399ff.

From the "Preface" to Shakespeare[14]

... The poet of whose works I have undertaken the revision[15] may now begin to assume the dignity of an ancient, and claim the privilege of established fame and prescriptive veneration. He has long outlived his century, the term commonly fixed as the test of literary merit. Whatever advantages he might once derive from personal allusions, local customs, or temporary opinions, have for many years been lost; and every topic of merriment or motive of sorrow, which the modes of artificial[16] life afforded him, now only obscure the scenes which they once illuminated. The effects of favor and competition are at an end; the tradition of his friendships and his enmities has perished; his works support no opinion with arguments, nor supply any faction with invectives; they can neither indulge vanity nor gratify malignity, but are read without any other reason than the desire of pleasure, and are therefore praised only as pleasure is obtained; yet, thus unassisted by interest[17] or passion, they have passed through variations of taste and changes of manners and, as they devolved from one generation to another, have received new honors at every transmission.

But because human judgment, though it be gradually gaining upon certainty, never becomes infallible; and approbation, though long continued, may yet be only the approbation of prejudice or fashion; it is proper to inquire, by what peculiarities of excellence Shakespeare has gained and kept the favor of his countrymen.

Nothing can please many, and please long, but just representations of general nature. Particular manners can be known to few, and therefore few only can judge how nearly they are copied. The irregular combinations of fanciful invention may delight awhile by that novelty of which the common satiety of life sends us all in quest; but the pleasures of sudden wonder are soon exhausted, and the mind can only repose on the stability of truth.

Shakespeare is above all writers, at least above all modern writers, the poet of nature <Gt/136>; the poet that holds up to his readers a faithful mirror of manners and of life. His characters are not modified by the customs of particular places, unpracticed by the rest of the world; by the peculiarities of studies or professions, which can operate but upon small numbers; or by the accidents of transient fashions or temporary opinions: they are the genuine progeny of common humanity, such as the world will

---

[14] Johnson's eight-volume edition of Shakespeare's plays was announced in 1756 and published in 1765, the year in which the "Preface" was written. The first part of the "Preface" here omitted is largely concerned with earlier editions of Shakespeare's plays and with Johnson's own practice and principles as an editor. Johnson's punctuation has been slightly modified.

[15] Meaning the editing.

[16] The social life of the time.

[17] Self-interest.

always supply, and observation will always find. His persons act and speak by the influence of those general passions and principles by which all minds are agitated, and the whole system of life is continued in motion. In the writings of other poets a character is too often an individual; in those of Shakespeare it is commonly a species.

It is from this wide extension of design that so much instruction is derived. It is this which fills the plays of Shakespeare with practical axioms and domestic wisdom. It was said of Euripides, that every verse was a precept;[18] and it may be said of Shakespeare that from his works may be collected a system of civil and economical prudence. Yet his real power is not shown in the splendor of particular passages, but by the progress of his fable, and the tenor of his dialogue; and he that tries to recommend him by select quotations, will succeed like the pedant in Hierocles,[19] who, when he offered his house to sale, carried a brick in his pocket as a specimen.

It will not easily be imagined how much Shakespeare excels in accommodating his sentiments to real life, but by comparing him with other authors. It was observed of the ancient schools of declamation, that the more diligently they were frequented, the more was the student disqualified for the world because he found nothing there which he should ever meet in any other place.[20] The same remark may be applied to every stage but that of Shakespeare. The theatre, when it is under any other direction, is peopled by such characters as were never seen, conversing in a language which was never heard, upon topics which will never arise in the commerce of mankind. But the dialogue of this author is often so evidently determined by the incident which produces it, and is pursued with so much ease and simplicity that it seems scarcely to claim the merit of fiction, but to have been gleaned by diligent selection out of common conversation, and common occurrences.

Upon every other stage the universal agent is love <Vt/29>, by whose power all good and evil is distributed, and every action quickened or retarded. To bring a lover, a lady, and a rival into the fable; to entangle them in contradictory obligations, perplex them with oppositions of interest, and harass them with violence of desires inconsistent with each other; to make them meet in rapture and part in agony; to fill their mouths with hyperbolical joy and outrageous sorrow; to distress them as nothing human ever was distressed; to deliver them as nothing human ever was delivered, is the business of a modern dramatist. For this, probability is violated, life is misrepresented, and language is depraved. But love is only one of many passions, and as it has no great influence upon the sum of life, it has little operation in the dramas of a poet, who caught his ideas from

[18] Cicero, *Letters to his Friends* 16, 8.
[19] This Hierocles probably lived in the fourth century. A translation of his moral verse was attributed to Johnson.
[20] Petronius, *Satyricon* 1:1.

the living world, and exhibited only what he saw before him < 1:Cn/239–40>. He knew, that any other passion, as it was regular or exorbitant, was a cause of happiness or calamity.

Characters thus ample and general were not easily discriminated and preserved, yet perhaps no poet ever kept his personages more distinct from each other. I will not say with Pope[21] that every speech may be assigned to the proper speaker, because many speeches there are which have nothing characteristical; but perhaps, though some may be equally adapted to every person, it will be difficult to find any that can be properly transferred from the present possessor to another claimant. The choice is right, when there is reason for choice.

Other dramatists can only gain attention by hyperbolical or aggravated characters, by fabulous and unexampled excellence or depravity, as the writers of barbarous romances invigorated the reader by a giant and a dwarf; and he that should form his expectations of human affairs from the play, or from the tale, would be equally deceived. Shakespeare has no heroes; his scenes are occupied only by men, who act and speak as the reader thinks that he should himself have spoken or acted on the same occasion: even where the agency is supernatural the dialogue is level with life. Other writers disguise the most natural passions and most frequent incidents; so that he who contemplates them in the book will not know them in the world: Shakespeare approximates the remote, and familiarizes the wonderful; the event which he represents will not happen, but if it were possible, its effects would probably be such as he has assigned; and it may be said, that he has not only shown human nature as it acts in real exigences, but as it would be found in trials, to which it cannot be exposed.

This therefore is the praise of Shakespeare, that his drama is the mirror of life; that he who has mazed his imagination in following the phantoms which other writers raise up before him, may here be cured of his delirious ecstasies by reading human sentiments in human language; by scenes from which a hermit may estimate the transactions of the world, and a confessor predict the progress of the passions.

His adherence to general nature has exposed him to the censure of critics, who form their judgments upon narrower principles. Dennis and Rhymer < 1:Rm/291> think his Romans not sufficiently Roman; and Voltaire censures his kings as not completely royal.[22] Dennis is offended, that Menenius, a senator of Rome, should play the buffoon; and Voltaire perhaps thinks decency violated when the Danish usurper is represented as

---

[21] In the Preface to his edition of Shakespeare (1725), Alexander Pope (1688–1744) observes that "had all the speeches been printed without the very names of the persons, I believe one might have applied them with certainty to every speaker."

[22] The allusions are apparently to: John Dennis, *An Essay on the Genius and Writings of Shakespeare* (1712); Thomas Rhymer, *A Short View of Tragedy* (1692); and Voltaire, *Appel à toutes les nations de l'Europe* (1761).

a drunkard. But Shakespeare always makes nature predominate over accident; and if he preserves the essential character, is not very careful of distinctions superinduced and adventitious. His story requires Romans or kings, but he thinks only on men. He knew that Rome, like every other city, had men of all dispositions; and wanting a buffoon, he went into the senate house for that which the senate house would certainly have afforded him. He was inclined to show an usurper and a murderer not only odious but despicable; he therefore added drunkenness to his other qualities, knowing that kings love wine like other men, and that wine exerts its natural power upon kings. These are the petty cavils of petty minds; a poet overlooks the casual distinction of country and condition, as a painter, satisfied with the figure, neglects the drapery.

The censure which he has incurred by mixing comic and tragic scenes, as it extends to all his works, deserves more consideration.[23] Let the fact be first stated, and then examined.

Shakespeare's plays are not in the rigorous and critical sense either tragedies or comedies, but compositions of a distinct kind; exhibiting the real state of sublunary nature, which partakes of good and evil, joy and sorrow, mingled with endless variety of proportion and innumerable modes of combination; and expressing the course of the world, in which the loss of one is the gain of another; in which, at the same time, the reveller is hasting to his wine, and the mourner burying his friend; in which the malignity of one is sometimes defeated by the frolic of another; and many mischiefs and many benefits are done and hindered without design.

Out of this chaos of mingled purposes and casualties[24] the ancient poets, according to the laws which custom had prescribed, selected some the crimes of men, and some their absurdities; some the momentous vicissitudes of life, and some the lighter occurrences; some the terrors of distress, and some the gaieties of prosperity. Thus rose the two modes of imitation, known by the names of tragedy and comedy, compositions intended to promote different ends by contrary means, and considered as so little allied, that I do not recollect among the Greeks or Romans a single writer who attempted both <1:Ar/40>.

Shakespeare has united the powers of exciting laughter and sorrow not only in one mind but in one composition. Almost all his plays are divided between serious and ludicrous characters, and, in the successive evolutions of the design, sometimes produce seriousness and sorrow, and sometimes levity and laughter <Hu/260>.

That this is a practice contrary to the rules of criticism will be readily allowed; but there is always an appeal open from criticism to nature

---

[23] See also *Rambler* 156.
[24] Events.

<1:Lp/187>. The end of writing is to instruct; the end of poetry is to instruct by pleasing <1:Hr/73>. That the mingled drama may convey all the instruction of tragedy or comedy cannot be denied, because it includes both in its alternations of exhibition, and approaches nearer than either to the appearance of life by showing how great machinations and slender designs may promote or obviate one another, and the high and the low cooperate in the general system by unavoidable concatenation.

It is objected, that by this change of scenes the passions are interrupted in their progression, and that the principal event, being not advanced by a due graduation of preparatory incidents, wants at last the power to move, which constitutes the perfection of dramatic poetry. This reasoning is so specious, that it is received as true even by those who in daily experience feel it to be false. The interchanges of mingled scenes seldom fail to produce the intended vicissitudes of passion. Fiction cannot move so much but that the attention may be easily transferred; and though it must be allowed that pleasing melancholy be sometimes interrupted by unwelcome levity, yet let it be considered likewise that melancholy is often not pleasing, and that the disturbance of one man may be the relief of another; that different auditors have different habitudes; and that, upon the whole, all pleasure consists in variety <1:Dd/282>.

The players, who in their edition[25] divided our author's works into comedies, histories, and tragedies, seem not to have distinguished the three kinds by any very exact or definite ideas.

An action which ended happily to the principal persons, however serious or distressful through its intermediate incidents, in their opinion constituted a comedy. This idea of a comedy continued long amongst us, and plays were written, which, by changing the catastrophe, were tragedies today and comedies tomorrow.

Tragedy was not in those times a poem of more general dignity or elevation than comedy; it required only a calamitous conclusion, with which the common criticism of that age was satisfied, whatever lighter pleasure it afforded in its progress.

History was a series of actions, with no other than chronological succession, independent on each other, and without any tendency to introduce or regulate the conclusion. It is not always very nicely distinguished from tragedy. There is not much nearer approach to unity of action in the tragedy of *Antony and Cleopatra*, than in the history of *Richard the Second*. But a history might be continued through many plays; as it had no plan, it had no limits. . . .

The force of his comic scenes has suffered little diminution from the changes made by a century and a half, in manners or in words. As his

---

[25] The First Folio of Shakespeare's plays was compiled by the actors John Heming and Henry Condell in 1623.

personages act upon principles arising from genuine passion, very little modified by particular forms, their pleasures and vexations are communicable to all times and to all places; they are natural, and therefore durable; the adventitious peculiarities of personal habits are only superficial dyes, bright and pleasing for a little while, yet soon fading to a dim tinct, without any remains of former luster; but the discriminations of true passion are the colors of nature; they pervade the whole mass, and can only perish with the body that exhibits them. The accidental compositions of heterogeneous modes are dissolved by the chance which combined them; but the uniform simplicity of primitive qualities neither admits increase, nor suffers decay. The sand heaped by one flood is scattered by another, but the rock always continues in its place. The stream of time, which is continually washing the dissoluble fabrics of other poets, passes without injury by the adamant of Shakespeare.

If there be, what I believe there is, in every nation, a style which never becomes obsolete, a certain mode of phraseology so consonant and congenial to the analogy and principles of its respective language as to remain settled and unaltered; this style is probably to be sought in the common intercourse of life, among those who speak only to be understood, without ambition of elegance. The polite are always catching modish innovations, and the learned depart from established forms of speech, in hope of finding or making better; those who wish for distinction forsake the vulgar, when the vulgar is right; but there is a conversation above grossness and below refinement, where propriety resides, and where this poet seems to have gathered his comic dialogue. He is therefore more agreeable to the ears of the present age than any other author equally remote, and among his other excellencies deserves to be studied as one of the original masters of our language.

These observations are to be considered not as unexceptionably constant, but as containing general and predominant truth. Shakespeare's familiar dialogue is affirmed to be smooth and clear, yet not wholly without ruggedness or difficulty; as a country may be eminently fruitful, though it has spots unfit for cultivation: his characters are praised as natural, though their sentiments are sometimes forced, and their actions improbable; as the earth upon the whole is spherical, though its surface is varied with protuberances and cavities.

Shakespeare with his excellencies has likewise faults, and faults sufficient to obscure and overwhelm any other merit. I shall show them in the proportion in which they appear to me, without envious malignity or superstitious veneration. No question can be more innocently discussed than a dead poet's pretensions to renown; and little regard is due to that bigotry which sets candor higher than truth.

His first defect is that to which may be imputed most of the evil in books or in men. He sacrifices virtue to convenience, and is so much more careful to please than to instruct, that he seems to write without any moral purpose. From his writings indeed a system of social duty may be selected, for he that thinks reasonably must think morally; but his precepts and axioms drop casually from him; he makes no just distribution of good or evil, nor is always careful to show in the virtuous a disapprobation of the wicked; he carries his persons indifferently through right and wrong, and at the close dismisses them without further care, and leaves their examples to operate by chance. This fault the barbarity of his age cannot extenuate; for it is always a writer's duty to make the world better, and justice is a virtue independent on time or place. . . .

It will be thought strange that, in enumerating the defects of this writer,[26] I have not yet mentioned his neglect of the unities; his violation of those laws which have been instituted and established by the joint authority of poets and of critics.

For his other deviations from the art of writing, I resign him to critical justice, without making any other demand in his favor than that which must be indulged to all human excellence; that his virtues be rated with his failings: but, from the censure which this irregularity may bring upon him, I shall, with due reverence to that learning which I must oppose, adventure to try how I can defend him.

His histories, being neither tragedies nor comedies, are not subject to any of their laws; nothing more is necessary to all the praise which they expect than that the changes of action be so prepared as to be understood, that the incidents be various and affecting, and the characters consistent, natural and distinct. No other unity is intended, and therefore none is to be sought.

In his other works he has well enough preserved the unity of action. He has not, indeed, an intrigue regularly perplexed and regularly unravelled; he does not endeavor to hide his design only to discover it, for this is seldom the order of real events, and Shakespeare is the poet of nature: but his plan has commonly what Aristotle requires, a beginning, a middle, and an end < 1:Ar/44 >; one event is concatenated with another, and the conclusion follows by easy consequence. There are perhaps some incidents that might be spared, as in other poets there is much talk that only fills up time upon the stage; but the general system makes gradual advances, and the end of the play is the end of expectation.

To the unities of time and place he has shown no regard, and perhaps a nearer view of the principles on which they stand will diminish their value, and withdraw from them the veneration which, from the time of Corneille < 1:Cn/234ff >, they have very generally received, by discovering that they have given more trouble to the poet, than pleasure to the auditor.

The necessity of observing the unities of time and place arises from the

---

[26] In the omitted passage immediately above.

supposed necessity of making the drama credible <In/11>. The critics hold it impossible that an action of months or years can be possibly believed to pass in three hours; or that the spectator can suppose himself to sit in the theatre, while ambassadors go and return between distant kings, while armies are levied and towns besieged, while an exile wanders and returns, or till he whom they saw courting his mistress, shall lament the untimely fall of his son. The mind revolts from evident falsehood, and fiction loses its force when it departs from the resemblance of reality.

From the narrow limitation of time necessarily arises the contraction of place. The spectator, who knows that he saw the first act at Alexandria, cannot suppose that he sees the next at Rome, at a distance to which not the dragons of Medea could, in so short a time, have transported him; he knows with certainty that he has not changed his place; and he knows that place cannot change itself <Dt/37>; that what was a house cannot become a plain; that what was Thebes can never be Persepolis.

Such is the triumphant language with which a critic exults over the misery of an irregular poet, and exults commonly without resistance or reply. It is time therefore to tell him, by the authority of Shakespeare, that he assumes, as an unquestionable principle, a position, which, while his breath is forming it into words, his understanding pronounces to be false. It is false, that any representation is mistaken for reality; that any dramatic fable in its materiality was ever credible, or, for a single moment, was ever credited.

The objection arising from the impossibility of passing the first hour at Alexandria, and the next at Rome, supposes that when the play opens the spectator really imagines himself at Alexandria, and believes that his walk to the theatre has been a voyage to Egypt, and that he lives in the days of *Antony and Cleopatra*. Surely he that imagines this may imagine more. He that can take the stage at one time for the palace of the Ptolemies, may take it in half an hour for the promontory of Actium <Sl/203>. Delusion <Sd/251>, if delusion be admitted, has no certain limitation; if the spectator can be once persuaded, that his old acquaintance are Alexander and Caesar, that a room illuminated with candles is the plain of Pharsalia, or the bank of Granicus, he is in a state of elevation above the reach of reason, or of truth, and from the heights of empyrean poetry, may despise the circumscriptions of terrestrial nature. There is no reason why a mind thus wandering in ecstasy should count the clock, or why an hour should not be a century in that calenture of the brains that can make the stage a field.

The truth is, that the spectators are always in their senses, and know, from the first act to the last, that the stage is only a stage, and that the players are only players <Co/231>. They come to hear a certain number of lines recited with just gesture and elegant modulation. The lines relate to some action, and an action must be in some place; but the different actions that complete a story may be in places very remote from each other; and where is the absurdity of allowing that space to represent first Athens, and then Sicily, which was always known to be neither Sicily nor Athens, but a modern theatre <Vt/24>.[27]

By supposition, as place is introduced, time may be extended; the time required by the fable elapses for the most part between the acts; for, of so much of the action as is represented, the real and poetical duration is the same. If, in the first act, preparations for war against Mithridates are represented to be made in Rome, the event of the war may, without absurdity, be represented, in the catastrophe, as happening in Pontus; we know that there is neither war, nor preparation for war; we know that we are neither in Rome nor Pontus; that neither Mithridates nor Lucullus are before us.[28] The drama exhibits successive imitations of successive actions, and why may not the second imitation represent an action that happened years after the first; if it be so connected with it, that nothing but time can be supposed to intervene. Time is, of all modes of existence, most obsequious to the imagination; a lapse of years is as easily conceived as a passage of hours. In contemplation we easily contract the time of real actions, and therefore willingly permit it to be contracted when we only see their imitation.

It will be asked, how the drama moves, if it is not credited. It is credited with all the credit due to a drama. It is credited, whenever it moves, as a just picture of a real original; as representing to the auditor what he would himself feel, if he were to do or suffer what is there feigned to be suffered or to be done. The reflection that strikes the heart is not that the evils before us are real evils, but that they are evils to which we ourselves may be exposed. If there be any fallacy, it is not that we fancy the players, but that we fancy ourselves unhappy for a moment; but we rather lament the possibility than suppose the presence of misery, as a mother weeps over her babe, when she remembers that death may take it from her. The delight of tragedy proceeds from our consciousness of fiction; if we thought murders and treasons real, they would please no more <In/13; Hm/92>.

Imitations produce pain or pleasure, not because they are mistaken for realities, but because they bring realities to mind. When the imagination is recreated by a painted landscape, the trees are not supposed capable to give us shade, or the fountains coolness; but we consider, how we should

---

27 In his attack on Johnson's *Shakespeare*, William Kenrick made a critique of Johnson's idea of theatrical illusion <Co/230>, which goes, in part:

> Now, it is the senses and the passions, and not the imagination and understanding, that are … immediately affected. We do not pretend to say that the spectators are not always in their senses; or that they do not know (if the question were put to them) that the stage is only a stage, and the players only players. But we will venture to say they are often so intent on the scene as to be absent with regard to everything else. A spectator properly affected by a dramatic representation makes no reflections about the fiction or the reality of it, so long as the action proceeds without grossly offending or palpably imposing on the senses. (Vickers 1979, 189–90)

28 As in Nathaniel Lee's *Mithridates* (1678).

be pleased with such fountains playing beside us, and such woods waving over us. We are agitated in reading the history of Henry the Fifth, yet no man takes his book for the field of Agincourt. A dramatic exhibition is a book recited with concomitants that increase or diminish its effect. Familiar comedy is often more powerful in the theatre, than on the page; imperial tragedy is always less <Dt/48>. The humor of Petruchio may be heightened by grimace; but what voice or what gesture can hope to add dignity or force to the soliloquy of Cato?[29]

A play read, affects the mind like a play acted. It is therefore evident, that the action is not supposed to be real, and it follows that between the acts a longer or shorter time may be allowed to pass, and that no more account of space or duration is to be taken by the auditor of a drama than by the reader of a narrative, before whom may pass in an hour the life of a hero, or the revolutions of an empire.

Whether Shakespeare knew the unities and rejected them by design, or deviated from them by happy ignorance, it is, I think, impossible to decide, and useless to inquire. We may reasonably suppose that, when he rose to notice, he did not want the counsels and admonitions of scholars and critics, and that he at last deliberately persisted in a practice, which he might have begun by chance. As nothing is essential to the fable, but unity of action, and as the unities of time and place arise evidently from false assumptions, and, by circumscribing the extent of the drama, lessen its variety, I cannot think it much to be lamented, that they were not known by him, or not observed: nor, if such another poet could arise, should I very vehemently reproach him, that his first act passed at Venice, and his next in Cyprus. Such violations of rules merely positive, become the comprehensive genius of Shakespeare, and such censures are suitable to the minute and slender criticism of Voltaire:

> Non usque adeo permiscuit imis
> Longus summa dies, ut non, si voce Metelli
> Serventur leges, malint a Caesare tolli.[30]

Yet when I speak thus slightly of dramatic rules, I cannot but recollect how much wit and learning may be produced against me; before such authorities I am afraid to stand, not that I think the present question one of those that are to be decided by mere authority, but because it is to be suspected that these precepts have not been so easily received but for better reasons than I have yet been able to find. The result of my inquiries, in which it would be ludicrous to boast of impartiality, is that the unities of time and place are not essential to a just drama, that though they may

---

[29] In Act 5, scene 1 of Addison's *Cato*.

[30] From Lucan's epic, *Pharsalia* 3:138–40: "The changes wrought by the passing years are not so great that the laws would not rather be abolished by Caesar than upheld by Metellus."

sometimes conduce to pleasure, they are always to be sacrificed to the nobler beauties of variety and instruction; and that a play, written with nice observation of critical rules, is to be contemplated as an elaborate curiosity, as the product of superfluous and ostentatious art, by which is shown, rather what is possible, than what is necessary.

He that, without diminution of any other excellence, shall preserve all the unities unbroken, deserves the like applause with the architect, who shall display all the orders of architecture in a citadel, without any deduction from its strength; but the principal beauty of a citadel is to exclude the enemy; and the greatest graces of a play, are to copy nature and instruct life.

Perhaps what I have here not dogmatically but deliberatively written may recall the principles of the drama to a new examination. I am almost frighted at my own temerity; and when I estimate the fame and the strength of those that maintain the contrary opinion, am ready to sink down in reverential silence; as Aeneas withdrew from the defense of Troy, when he saw Neptune shaking the wall, and Juno heading the besiegers.[31]

---

[31] Virgil, *Aeneid*, 2. 610ff.

8

DAVID HUME
(1711–76)

The author of *A Treatise on Human Nature* (1739–40), *An Enquiry Concerning Human Understanding* (1758), and other philosophical and historical works of permanent interest, David Hume always thought of himself as pursuing, in these writings, as well as in his essays, a literary vocation. He had an intense concern with style not only as the means by which ideas might be clearly and persuasively presented or, on the other hand, made tedious and obscure; but also as an index to the character and quality of civilization at certain moments of its history. Indeed, a novelty of his *History of England* (1754–62) is the inclusion in it of descriptive and evaluative comments on the writers and artists of the periods surveyed; though the criteria he applies are the conventional ones of *his* time. Of Shakespeare, for instance, he remarks:

> His total ignorance of all theatrical art and conduct, however material a defect; yet, as it affects the spectator rather than the reader, we can more easily excuse than that want of taste which often prevails in his productions, and which gives way only by intervals to the irradiations of genius. A great and fertile genius he certainly possessed, and one enriched equally with a tragic and comic vein; but he ought to be cited as a proof, how dangerous it is to rely on these advantages alone for attaining an excellence in the finer arts.   (Hume 1823, VI:192)

His view of what a playwright should rely on, is indicated by his praise of *Douglas*, as a supreme example of "elegance, simplicity, and decorum."[1] Hume was well aware of the tendency of his age towards over-refinement but his own writings on literature are not free of it.

Despite – or perhaps because of – its immersion in the passions on which he supposes human nature and human understanding to be founded, Hume does not apply to tragedy the kind of skeptical scrutiny that he gives to philosophical questions, but his essay "Of Tragedy" (1757) is a significant development of such "sentimentalist" views as the one ascribed in it to Dubos. Though Hume does not relate his theory to the *Poetics*, his idea of the arousal of the passions by means of a painful subject and their transformation into pleasurable emotions by means of art is an alternative to those interpretations of Aristotelian catharsis that posit the evacuation of emotion – an idea that many eighteenth-century commentators found incomprehensible <Mt/31–2>. Instead of purgation of this kind, Hume proposes the artistic transmutation of emotions whereby they are purified or refined

---

[1] *Douglas* (1756) by John Home (1722–1808) is a once-popular romantic tragedy, notable for its pathetic incidents.

into aesthetic ones, which are felt to be pleasurably distinct from those arising from the unmediated experience of life.

The necessary conditions of this conversion are that the artistry be of a high order (beautiful and pleasurable in itself) and that the audience be conscious of the fictional, imitative character of the presentation, or distanced from its subject by time. Hume's idea of the pleasurability of aesthetic emotions anticipates Kant's in the *Critique of Judgement* (1790) and the similarity is heightened by the notable absence of any hint in Hume of a moral or didactic aspect of tragedy.

For further reading

Brunet 1965; Cohen 1962; Hipple 1956; Montgomery 1991; Wasserman 1947.

"Of Tragedy"[2]

It seems an unaccountable pleasure which the spectators of a well-written tragedy receive from sorrow, terror, anxiety, and other passions, that are in themselves disagreeable and uneasy <1:Ar/39>. The more they are touched and affected, the more delighted with the spectacle; and as soon as the uneasy passions cease to operate, the piece is at an end. One scene of full joy and contentment and security is the utmost that any composition of this kind can bear; and it is sure always to be the concluding one. If, in the texture of the piece, there be interwoven any scenes of satisfaction, they afford only faint gleams of pleasure, which are thrown in by way of variety, and in order to plunge the actors into deeper distress by means of that contrast and disappointment. The whole art of the poet is employed in rousing and supporting the compassion and indignation, the anxiety and resentment of his audience. They are pleased in proportion as they are afflicted and never are so happy as when they employ tears, sobs, and cries to give vent to their sorrow and relieve their heart, swollen with the tenderest sympathy and compassion.

The few critics who have had some tincture of philosophy have remarked this singular phenomenon and have endeavored to account for it <Sl/199; Sr/156>.

L'Abbé Du Bos, in his *Reflections on Poetry and Painting*,[3] asserts that nothing is in general so disagreeable to the mind as the languid, listless state of indolence into which it falls upon the removal of all passions and occupation <Sl/192>. To get rid of this painful situation, it seeks every amusement and pursuit; business, gaming, shows, executions; whatever will rouse the passions and take its attention from itself. No matter what the passion is: let it be disagreeable, afflicting, melancholy, disordered; it is

---

[2] First published in *Four Dissertations* (1757). The text is from Hume, 1904, 221–30.

[3] *Réflexions critiques sur la poésie et sur la peinture* (1719–33) by Jean-Baptiste Dubos (or Du Bos) (1670–1742) appeared in an English version by Thomas Nugent in 1748. See Adams & Hathaway 1950, 251–69.

still better than that insipid languor which arises from perfect tranquillity and repose <Sr/155-6; Sl/200>.

It is impossible not to admit this account as being, at least in part, satisfactory. You may observe, when there are several tables of gaming, that all the company run to those where the deepest play is, even though they find not there the best players. The view, or at least imagination, of high passions arising from great loss or gain affects the spectator by sympathy, gives him some touches of the same passions, and serves him for a momentary entertainment. It makes the time pass the easier with him and is some relief to that oppression under which men commonly labor when left entirely to their own thoughts and meditations.

We find that common liars always magnify, in their narrations, all kinds of danger, pain, distress, sickness, deaths, murders, and cruelties; as well as joy, beauty, mirth, and magnificence. It is an absurd secret which they have for pleasing their company, fixing their attention, and attaching them to such marvellous relations by the passions and emotions which they excite.

There is, however, a difficulty in applying to the present subject, in its full extent, this solution, however ingenious and satisfactory it may appear. It is certain that the same object of distress which pleases in a tragedy, were it really set before us, would give the most unfeigned uneasiness, though it be then the most effectual cure to languor and indolence. Monsieur Fontanelle seems to have been sensible of this difficulty and accordingly attempts another solution of the phenomenon, at least makes some addition to the theory above mentioned.[4]

"Pleasure and pain", says he, "which are two sentiments so different in themselves, differ not so much in their cause. From the instance of tickling, it appears that the movement of pleasure, pushed a little too far becomes pain, and that the movement of pain a little moderated becomes pleasure. Hence it proceeds as there is such a thing as sorrow soft and agreeable: it is a pain weakened and diminished. The heart likes naturally to be moved and affected. Melancholy objects suit it, and even disastrous and sorrowful, provided they are softened by some circumstance. It is certain that, on the theatre, the representation has almost the effect of reality; yet it has not altogether that effect. However we may be hurried away by the spectacle, whatever dominion the senses and imagination may usurp over the reason, there still lurks at the bottom a certain idea of falsehood in the whole of what we see <Jh/84–5>. This idea, though weak and disguised, suffices to diminish the pain which we suffer from the misfortunes of those whom we love, and to reduce that affliction to such a pitch as converts it

---

[4] In his *Réflexions sur la poétique*, published in 1742, but written long before that, Bernard le Bovier de Fontanelle (1657–1757) had insisted that, however persuasive the presentation, the audience always retains a sense of the fictiveness of the tragedy. See Adams & Hathaway 1950, 281–96.

into a pleasure. We weep for the misfortune of a hero to whom we are attached. In the same instant we comfort ourselves by reflecting that it is nothing but a fiction. And it is precisely that mixture of sentiments, which composes an agreeable sorrow, and tears that delight us <Sr/159>. But as that affliction which is caused by exterior and sensible objects is stronger than the consolation which arises from an internal reflection, they are the effects and symptoms of sorrow that ought to predominate in the composition."

This solution seems just as convincing, but perhaps it wants still some new addition in order to make it answer fully the phenomenon which we here examine. All the passions, excited by eloquence, are agreeable in the highest degree, as well as those which are moved by painting and the theatre. . . .

The genius required to paint objects in a lively manner, the art employed in collecting all the pathetic circumstances, the judgment displayed in disposing them: the exercise, I say, of these noble talents, together with the force of expression and beauty of oratorial numbers, diffuse the highest satisfaction on the audience, and excite the most delightful movements. By this means, the uneasiness of the melancholy passions is not only over-powered and effaced by something stronger of an opposite kind, but the whole impulse of those passions is converted into pleasure and swells the delight which the eloquence raises in us. The same force of oratory, employed on an uninteresting subject, would not please half so much, or rather would appear altogether ridiculous; and the mind, being left in absolute calmness and indifference, would relish none of these beauties of imagination or expression which, if joined to passion, give it such exquisite entertainment. The impulse, or vehemence, arising from sorrow, compassion, indignation, receives a new direction from the sentiments of beauty. The latter, being the predominant emotion, seize the whole mind and convert the former into themselves, at least tincture them so strongly as totally to alter their nature. And the soul, being at the same time roused by passion and charmed by eloquence, feels on the whole a strong movement which is altogether delightful.

The same principle takes place in tragedy; with this addition, that tragedy is an imitation, and imitation is always of itself agreeable <1:Ar/39>. This circumstance serves still further to smooth the motions of passion and convert the whole feeling into one uniform and strong enjoyment. Objects of the greatest terror and distress please in painting, and please more than the most beautiful objects that appear calm and indifferent.[5]

The affection, rousing the mind, excites a large stock of spirit and

---

[5] Hume notes that though painters represent "distress and sorrow" they dwell on such "melancholy affections" less than poets, who need them for variety and to motivate action.

vehemence, which is all transformed into pleasure by the force of the prevailing movement. It is thus the fiction of tragedy softens the passion, by an infusion of new feeling, not merely by weakening or diminishing the sorrow. You may by degrees weaken a real sorrow till it totally disappears; yet in none of its gradations will it ever give pleasure, except, perhaps, by accident to a man sunk under lethargic indolence, whom it rouses from that languid state.

To confirm this theory, it will be sufficient to produce other instances where the subordinate movement is converted into the predominant and gives force to it, though of a different, and even sometimes though of a contrary nature.

Novelty naturally arouses the mind and attracts our attention, and the movements which it causes are always converted into any passion belonging to the object and join their force to it. Whether an event excite joy or sorrow, pride or shame, anger or good-will, it is sure to produce a stronger affection when new or unusual. And though novelty of itself be agreeable, it fortifies the painful as well as agreeable passions.

Had you any intention to move a person extremely by the narration of any event, the best method of increasing its effect would be artfully to delay informing him of it and first excite his curiosity and impatience before you let him into the secret. This is the artifice practiced by Iago in the famous scene of Shakespeare, and every spectator is sensible that Othello's jealousy acquires additional force from his preceding impatience and that the subordinate passion is here readily transformed into the predominant one.

Difficulties increase passions of every kind; and by rousing our attention and exciting our active powers, they produce an emotion which nourishes the prevailing affection.

Parents commonly love that child most whose sickly, infirm frame of body has occasioned them the greatest pains, trouble, and anxiety in rearing him. The agreeable sentiment of affection here acquires force from sentiments of uneasiness.

Nothing endears so much a friend as sorrow for his death. The pleasure of his company has not so powerful an influence.

Jealousy is a painful passion; yet without some share of it, the agreeable affection of love has difficulty to subsist in its full force and violence. Absence is also a great source of complaint among lovers and gives them the greatest uneasiness; yet nothing is more favorable to their mutual passion than short intervals of that kind. And if long intervals often prove fatal, it is only because through time men are accustomed to them and they cease to give uneasiness. Jealousy and absence in love compose the *dolce peccante* of the Italians, which they suppose so essential to all pleasure.

There is a fine observation of the elder Pliny which illustrates the principle here insisted on. "It is very remarkable," says he, "that the last works of celebrated artists, which they left imperfect, are always the most prized, such as the Iris of Aristides, the Tyndarides of Nichomachus, the Medea of Timomachus, and the Venus of Apelles. These are valued even above their finished productions. The broken lineaments of the piece and the half-formed idea of the painter are carefully studied; and our very grief for that curious hand, which had been stopped by death, is an additional increase to our pleasure."[6]

These instances (and many more might be collected) are sufficient to afford us some insight into that analogy of Nature and to show us that the pleasure which poets, orators, and musicians give us, by exciting grief, sorrow, indignation, compassion, is not so extraordinary or paradoxical as it may at first sight appear. The force of imagination, the energy of expression, the power of numbers, the charms of imitation – all these are naturally, of themselves, delightful to the mind. And when the object presented lays hold also of some affection, the pleasure still rises upon us by the conversion of this subordinate movement into that which is predominant. The passion, though perhaps naturally, and when excited by the simple appearance of a real object, it may be painful, yet is so smoothed and softened and mollified when raised by the finer arts that it affords the highest entertainment.

To confirm this reasoning, we may observe that if the movements of the imagination be not predominant above those of the passion, a contrary effect follows, and the former, being now subordinate, is converted into the latter and still farther increases the pain and affliction of the sufferer. . . .

An action represented in tragedy may be too bloody and atrocious. It may excite such movements of horror as will not soften into pleasure, and the greatest energy of expression bestowed on descriptions of that nature serves only to augment our uneasiness. Such is that action represented in *The Ambitious Stepmother*[7] where a venerable old man, raised to the height of fury and despair, rushes against a pillar, and striking his head upon it, besmears it all over with mingled brains and gore. The English theatre abounds too much with such shocking images <Vt/28>.

Even the common sentiments of compassion require to be softened by some agreeable affection in order to give a thorough satisfaction to the audience. The mere suffering of plaintive virtue under the triumphant tyranny and oppression of vice forms a disagreeable spectacle and is carefully avoided by all masters of the drama. In order to dismiss the audience with entire satisfaction and contentment, the virtue must either convert itself into a noble courageous despair, or the vice receive its proper punishment. . . .

---

[6] Pliny, *Natural History* 30:6.
[7] By Nicholas Rowe, printed 1700.

9

MLLE DUMESNIL (MARIE-FRANÇOISE MARCHAND) (1713–1803)

In her *Memoirs* Mlle Dumesnil, one of the outstanding players of her time, carefully differentiates between the illusion created by playwrights and that created by actors. She challenges the views propounded by Mlle Clairon,[1] her rival of the Comédie-Française, which emphasized verisimilitude and contended that performance was the realization of the written drama. Dumesnil distinguishes the impact of the representation of an historical event from that of the performers' arousal of emotions, which have an immediacy not attainable through the playwright's historical imagination alone.

In opposition to Clairon's advocacy of careful study and accurate historical portrayal, Dumesnil proposes an analysis of the affective potentiality of the play, believing that the spectators will be reached through emotions rather than intellect. She recommends spontaneous outbursts of emotion as a means of impressing the spectators rather than an attempt to engage them by way of a carefully controlled and possibly stale depiction of a character. In this way, the actor will convey whatever is truly common in human experience, rather being a theatrical vehicle for a neo-classical dramatic decorum. Moreover, the performer should always be conscious of the effect she is making as a performer on the spectators, rather than confining her attention to the supposed reactions of the imaginary character. Diderot is critical of Dumesnil for this very reason, citing her predilection for inspiration which yields a "sublime moment"[2] without letting the spectator forget the presence of Dumesnil the performer; in contrast, he praises Mlle Clairon's careful study, which subordinates the performer to the role to the point where she is performing her "double."[3]

For further reading

Clairon [1800] 1971; Clairon [1822] 1968; Dumesnil [1823] 1968.

---

[1] Mlle Clairon was the stage name assumed by Claire Josèphe Hyppolite Léris de Latude (1723–1803).

[2] Diderot 1967, 130.

[3] Diderot/Vernière 1959, 309.

From *Memoirs*[4]

On "Reflections on Dramatic Art"[5]

One sees that Mlle Clairon begins, right from the title, to substitute pomposity for the truth. Your art, Mademoiselle, is not *dramatic* art; it is *theatrical* art <In/2>. The art of Corneille, Racine, and Voltaire is the art of drama. The distance between the art of composition and that of recitation is incommensurable. A writer who published reflections on the art of these great men could only entitle it *Reflections on Dramatic Art*; and nevertheless, his work would have nothing in common with yours under the same title.

On the article called "Strength"

I have found in my experience

– I have no need to warn that it is Mlle Clairon speaking –

many young authors and fashionable women, who thought nothing was easier than to play Mahomet, Mérope,[6] etc.; that the author had done everything; that to learn the lines and abandon oneself to nature was all that the actor had to do. Nature! that people should utter this word without knowing its meaning! Does not each sex, each age, each condition have its own distinct nature? Difference of period, of country, of customs, of manners does it not have the greatest influence? What study must not be undertaken in order to transform oneself?

– none –

To identify oneself with each role?

– none, when nature has endowed one with the fiery soul of a tragedian or a tragedienne –

to succeed in portraying

– so this is art: something learned –

love, hate, ambition, all the feelings of which humanity is capable, and every shade, every gradation by which these feelings arrive at their fullest expression.

All the arts, and all the professions have their known principles. None such exist for the tragic actor. It is from the history of all humanity that one's insights must be gathered: it is not enough to read about it; one must meditate upon it, make it familiar down to the smallest detail; in every role adapt to the genius of its nation. One must reflect intensely upon it, rehearse the same thing hundreds of times, in order to overcome the difficulties that one encounters at every step. It is not enough to

---

[4] Newly translated from Dumesnil [1823] 1968.
[5] This and the later sub-headings are titles of sections of Clairon's *Mémoires*. Dumesnil's method is to cite passages from Clairon under such titles and make a running commentary on them.
[6] *Mahomet* (1742) and *Mérope* (1736) are tragedies by Voltaire.

study one's role, one must study the whole work, in order to conceal its
weaknesses, to make its beauties felt, and to subordinate the role to the
totality of the work: one must study the taste of the public

– to please, yes: but to convey the meaning, no. His ear and his heart must
be his guides –

search the hearts of all those with whom one comes into contact,

– mercy! –

unravel the relationships in whatever one observes, whatever he hears.
That is the secret work of the actor.

– this belongs to the ethic of mystification of the great work. . . .

If *so many people utter this word, nature without knowing its meaning*, it
seems to me that you do not know its limits, and often confuse it with what
is of concern only to art. You ask, *Does not each condition have its own*
distinct nature? No, there is no doubt that it does not; but generally perhaps
each condition has a different way of expressing itself <Hu/265>. Last year
I saw a frenzied mother at the wheat market searching for her child whom
she had lost, asking everyone about it as she burst into tears, with all the
accents of despair. Never has an actress made more expressive, more
touching, truer, nobler gestures, than this mother transported by grief. I
pointed her out to one of my friends.

Difference of period, of country, of customs, and of manners does it not, adds
Mlle Hippolyte, *have the greatest influence?* All of those have no more
influence, than the diversity of languages in which tragedies are written,
on the great traits of nature which fuel the fire of tragedy, such as love,
jealousy, revenge, ambition, or maternal and filial love. These great
emotions of the soul are the same from one pole to the other, because they
enter into the fabric of humanity – the work of the Creator. To conceive
these great emotions, to experience them immediately and at will, to forget
oneself in the twinkling of an eye, in order to put oneself in the place of the
character whom one wishes to portray, is exclusively a gift of nature and
beyond all the efforts of art. As for vain conventions, more or less strange
customs, more or less different habits, more or less foolish prejudices, or,
more or less civil manners, human handiwork as variable and changeable
as they are, rarely does a role demand that an actor strongly express these
nuances; and when the role demands it, this technique, completely within
the resources of art, is easily acquired, provided that one have intelligence
and physical advantages: but the sacred fire of the great passions, the same
in all members of the human race, can only be lit by nature itself.

All arts, all professions have known principles. None such exist for the tragic
actor. What sophistry! The basis of theatrical art in tragedy, is first of all,
since we must always return to that point, "To have received from heaven
the secret influence," the source of pathos, of terror, and the spontaneous

forgetting of oneself, without any effort; a divine gift which can almost dispense with the beauties of art, as we have seen more than once. The existence of principles which have to do with everything that the actor did not receive from nature, which has no need of such principles, need not be put into doubt; and it seems to me that this is the whole treatise on the principles of the art of the theatre: Who am I *with respect to every other character?* Who am I in each scene? Where am I? What have I done? and what am I going to do? Applying these same questions to everyone on stage with me. . . .

On the article entitled "Referring Everything to Art"[7]

> *The same actress,* says Mlle Clairon, *is usually cast in the roles of Ariadne and Dido.*[8] *These two characters demonstrate the same love.*

– Basically the same love, yes; the same love in the nuances, no; but it is from nature itself, and not from art that one must take the expression of this essential difference.—

> *They must show the same fear and the same despair.*

– the same fear, yes; the same despair, no; because to Ariadne's despair of being abandoned by her lover, is added the despair of jealousy, a form of torture that Dido does not experience.—

> *If one relied on this nature which is so highly praised today, one might believe that what is sufficient for one role will suffice for the other.*

– On the contrary, it is by consulting this nature, which did not begin to be extolled recently, but has always been so, and without which there have never been and will never be true beauties; it is by consulting it, I say, that one will never believe that *what is sufficient for one role will suffice for the other.*—

Any two self-respecting princesses have doubtless only one manner of loving: it is an affection of the soul. Ariadne suffers the most from the torments of jealousy, as I have already observed of her: this is another affection of the soul. Theseus betrayed her for Phaedra; Aeneas was destined to leave Dido; she had no rival, but she adored her lover; this is another affection of the soul. Art intervenes only to supply certain means of realization. *Honestly,* exclaims Mlle Clairon to herself, after having indicated several of these means, and always kneeling before her idol, although she sometimes addresses these tributes involuntarily to nature, believing that she is addressing them to art: *honestly, will one succeed in all of this without art?* No, without a doubt; but nevertheless between two

---

[7] "De la nécessité de rapporter tout à l'art."

[8] In Greek mythology, Ariadne is the daughter of King Minos and Pasiphae. She gave Theseus, whom she loved, the thread that enabled him to find his way out of the labyrinth of the Minotaur; he later abandoned her. In Book 4 of Virgil's *Aeneid*, Dido, Queen of Carthage kills herself after Aeneas (at Jupiter's command) leaves her.

actresses, if one of them will feel more vividly, and if the other, less emotional and more skillful, will deploy all the beauties of art, the first will make a much greater impression: this is what proves that art, which Mlle Hippolyte always wishes to make supreme, is only an accessory. . . .

On the article entitled "The Danger of Traditions"[9]

> Ignorance and mere whim have led to so many contradictions in the theatre, that it is impossible to address all of them, but there is one that I cannot pass by in silence, and that is to see Cornelia arriving in black. The ship in which she fled, the passage of such a short time between the assassination of her husband and her arrival at Alexandria, could have left neither the time, nor the means to have made her widow's weeds; and certainly Roman women did not take the precaution of keeping them ready in their baggage. The famous Lecouvreur,[10] in having herself painted in this garment, proves that she wore it on stage. This ought to have been enough of an authority for even me:

– how modest this *even* is! –

> but according to the reputation that she has left behind, I dare to believe that she did not commit this error for a variety of reasons that I will pass over, and that she herself felt the ridiculousness of it.

You decide, Mlle Clairon, that it is *a mistake*, that this costume is *ridiculous*; but are you really sure that a Roman woman, to go into mourning, needed all the paraphernalia of a French woman? Are you sure that she had need of merchants of fashion, shoemakers, tailors, hair-dressers, jewellers, in order to change into mourning? It is probable that a shawl and a black veil which were all the expense necessary, would have been the trappings of her mourning. . . .

Even supposing that your sartorial criticism was well founded, would this still be not a *contradiction* as you put it, but a fault of *decorum*, mourning being the natural dress of a widow. After these facts and small observations, I will allow myself to suggest to you a middle way. The actress playing Cornelia will not henceforth be in total mourning, but she will wear a black veil, which will be raised and she will drape herself in black. It is believed that the famous Lecouvreur did not allow herself any innovation in the wearing of mourning in the role of Cornelia, it is believed that the actress who had preceded her used to play the role in the same costume *in front of* Corneille: there was no one more knowledgeable in Roman history than the great Corneille. This observation is also of some

---

[9] "Du danger des traditions."

[10] Adrienne Lecouvreur (1692–1730), of the Comédie-Française, was noted for a perform-ance style that exhibited naturalness and simplicity and so challenged the prevailing manners of declamation. Lecouvreur frequently played Cornelia in Corneille's *The Death of Pompey* (1642), and Charles Antoine Coypel (1694–1752) did a portrait in pastels of her holding the urn containing Pompey's ashes.

weight; it amounts to a kind of tradition, of which *the danger* did not appear so evident to us as it seems to Mlle Hippolyte.

The articles which deal briefly with the *use of white make-up*, and on the necessity for students to have at least a nodding acquaintance with *drawing*, *dance*, and *music* contain the most judicious reflections and advice, which could only have been given by such an accomplished artist as Mlle Clairon: but unfortunately these sketches seem all the more imperfect, since one expected so much more than these thumbnail sketches from this author. It is the same with articles which consider *language, geography*, and *literature*, of which it is doubtless essential that actors should acquire some knowledge, for the progress of their art; but one would not have guessed the primary motive for which Mlle Hippolyte advises her colleagues to give themselves to these studies; it is, she says, because actors have *the right* to judge writers who work for the theatre. Thus she reveals the absurd custom, which is absurd only in that it is exclusive, by which actors and especially actresses, propped up by the tyranny of their superiors, have made it [the right to judge authors] into a rule, which too often have brought shame to the French theatre. Mlle Hippolyte is convinced that the profession of an actor requires that he be knowledgeable, because he has *the right* to judge a tragic or comic writer, as a supreme court judge is bound to study law, because he has the right to pronounce on the fortune, the honor, and the life of Citizens. It is because actors have the sole right to judge plays without any consultation with the playwright that Mlle Hippolyte obliges all the members of this learned assembly to know mythology, history, geography, and language perfectly, to know all the genres of poetry, and all ancient and modern playwrights. *One can be aware then* she adds,

> if the author has made the most of his subject, if he has captured the times, the places, characters, if he is a creator, imitator, or plagiarist. Approbation is only flattery, criticism is only justified, to the extent that one is in a position to support one or the other. It is not enough to have the right to receive or reject a work, one must show oneself worthy of judging it.

This proposal by Mlle Hippolyte, justifying *the right* of judges on the basis of their incredible knowledge, in order to give them a majestic status worthy of these documents, is truly pompous. And where then were all the great men, all the women, prodigies of erudition, when the comic and tragic senate made such enormous blunders, so shamefully mistaken about those works which delight us, and those which will be admired by posterity? What! all these judges also had *the right* to judge, when had they not yet acquired all that Mlle Hippolyte demands that they must know to establish this right? This consideration alone makes a burlesque of all the majesty of this instruction. . . .

After having seen with surprise, that according to Mlle Hippolyte, *the wishes* of actors must be a rule for the public and for playwrights, astonishment increases, when one read in her *Memoirs, that fundamentally* playwrights are *nothing* without actors. For a long time Mlle Clairon has held that *when an author had finished his tragedy, only half the work was done, and that the actors did the rest*: at least there was something that this concession allowed in halves; but today, in the example of the lion, she claims the rest: she maintains that actors are all, and the playwrights *nothing*. This glorious queen does not want to share any more.

To say that a dramatic work is necessarily completed by performance is already no less than an extraordinary claim; because the author alone can commit the entirety to posterity. The success or failure, at the time of performance, cannot influence the opinion of posterity which is unapproachable by any illusion, impassive to any surprise, and infallible in its judgment. If it had not been thus, Pradon's *Phaedra* <Vt/24> would still be winning out over Racine's, and the masterpiece *Athalie*[11] would have been tainted by the stamp of mediocrity. A printer's claim to a proportion of ownership, would have been less foolish, since it would have been difficult, and often impossible, for the author to reach posterity without the participation of the printer. . . .

On the article entitled "General Reflections"[12]
. . . Voltaire also gave advice, and this advice was excellent.

> *One must not do as he does, said our Dumesnil, a long time ago; but one must always say and do as he advises: he is never wrong.*

This great man did not stop there: he gave you advice in writing, very systematic, very extensive, and admirable. His correspondence proves it.

Marmontel[13] <Lg/114> who gave you the lead role in all his plays, Marmontel who was so dear to you, Marmontel, whom you do not even mention in your *Memoirs*, fearing doubtless, to admit your weakness for this *bourgeois* playwright, gave you good advice for a long time.

Why do you say therefore that you have had neither a guide nor advice? You write in the same article *General Reflections*, that

> *the tragic actor must appropriate into daily life the tone, deportment, which he needs for theatre.*

Have you not said previously, that

---

[11] Racine's *Athalie* (1691) was first produced by students and did not receive professional production until 1716.

[12] "Réflexions générales."

[13] Jean-François Marmontel (1723–99) was the author of tragedies, *comédies larmoyantes*, and comic operas. He advised Clairon to adopt a more natural, less declamatory performance style. Marmontel was also a distinguished critic and theorist, and contributed articles on the theatre to Diderot's *Encyclopedia*. See Cardy 1982.

Le Kain[14] *is the closest to perfection that you have ever seen?*

Well! he never *appropriated into his daily life the tone, the deportment, that he had needed in the theatre.* Why then do you establish as a rule this eternal constraint that nature's rigor has imposed on you? ...

Why did Le Kain, once he had divested himself of his imperial robe, his uniform, or turban become once again a *bourgeois* of Paris? Why does Dumesnil, after having removed her diadem, return to simplicity? It is because the one and the other were always sure to rediscover nature without appealing to art; it was because they were by no means laboring to represent Genghis, Nero, Sémiramis, Agrippina in the theatre;[15] it is because they believed that they actually were these characters, and that we took them as such when we heard them; it is because they were suddenly raised up, exalted, embraced by the genius of nature; in a word, it is because these metamorphoses cost them nothing.

The work which you had imposed on yourself in public and in private exempted you, you add, *from that mental anguish which formerly tired you so much on stage.* But this two-hour struggle was less painful and shorter than what you had to withstand at home before your friends and your servants, by being a queen or empress ceaselessly. You still had twenty-two hours left, I allow ten for bed and boudoir, that leaves twelve hours of constraint, if, however, you deigned to abdicate to the boudoir. How will you manage to reconcile this continuous *rehearsal* with interaction with your friends and lovers, with so many domestic details which you surely approached with a dignity entirely different from the princess Nausicaa,[16] and not least with the indispensable intercourse between you and your domestic staff? Over and above so many obstacles, it was the last straw of art, never to escape from dramatic loftiness even in your own home: for, after all, in the theatre every single particular is noble, proud, majestic, terrible, or pitiful, worthy, in a word, of the buskin.

[14] Henri-Louis Lekain (1729–78), a leading actor of the Comédie-Française, was instrumental in such reforms as clearing spectators from the stage. Clairon praised him for his careful preparation of his roles.

[15] The allusion is to roles played by Lekain and Dumesnil: Nero and Agrippina in *Britannicus* (1669) by Racine in 1777; Dumesnil played Sémiramis, Queen of Babylon in *Sémiramis* (1748) by Voltaire, opposite Lekain as her son, D'Arzace, in 1756; Lekain played Genghis Khan, the Tartar emperor, in the first production of *The Orphan of China* (1755) by Voltaire.

[16] The shipwrecked Odysseus meets Nausicaa, who is doing laundry by the shore, in Book 6 of Homer's *Odyssey*. She takes him to her father's home, where he recounts his adventures.

10

CARLO GOZZI
(1720–1806)

Gozzi had considerable success in his own lifetime, as a dramatist and as an ideologue. In eighteenth-century Venice there was great resistance to the Enlightenment, with its challenge to the existing social order and its antagonism to patrician privileges. Goldoni is among those who favored the irradiation of the new culture and used his reformed comedy to promote social criticism and progress; Carlo Gozzi was a champion of the aristocratic opposition to these ideas, and he made every effort to put a stop to Goldoni's program of reform. If, by the gradual use of verisimilitude and socio-psychological typification, Goldoni nudges comedy toward social criticism, Gozzi seeks to counteract this design by reinvigorating a dramatic form long lacking any recognizable social content, its characters being mere abstractions in costume, without clear referents in reality.

Originally, to be sure, *commedia dell'arte* was itself an instrument of social criticism, satirizing such things as scholarship unrelated to the everyday reality of the audience in the figure of the Dottore and immigration from Bergamo[1] in the figures of Arlecchino and Brighella, but since the original social context no longer obtained in Venice neither did the original critical function of improvised comedy. Yet Gozzi could hardly fight the new liberalism of the times with a dramatic form divested of social content, and so, although he restores *commedia dell'arte* in his *Tales for the Theatre* (*Fiabe teatrali*) , he also turns it to ideological use in a manner parallel to Goldoni's use of his reformed comedies. And though the distinguishing feature of *commedia dell'arte* was stage improvisation, Gozzi, in his revival of the genre actually has to write out most of the speeches, since he would otherwise have no assurance of their ideological thrust. So, though he defends the *commedia dell'arte* in its most ephemeral and autonomous form, he also commits much of it to writing and thus sacrifices its autonomy. That Gozzi's return to the *commedia dell'arte* is part of a larger cultural and political strategy is clear not only from the *Tales* themselves but also from his autobiography, the *Useless Memoirs* (*Memorie inutili*). The chief instrument of this strategy is exotic theatricality, which Gozzi uses with consummate skill. From *Love of Three Oranges* (*L'amore delle tre melarance*) (in which the *commedia dell'arte*, personified by Truffaldino, successfully cures the audience of the melancholy brought upon it by the innovations of Goldoni and Chiari) to *The Green Bird* (*L'augellino belverde*) (in which the philosophy of the Enlightenment is repeatedly degraded and ridiculed) his *Tales for the Theatre* abound in such metamorphoses and other magical effects as only a brilliant baroque stagecraft and understanding of audience psychology could conceive.

---

[1] Bergamo was located in the poor, outermost region of the Republic of Venice. In the sixteenth and seventeenth centuries vast numbers of unskilled workers emigrated to the capital.

For further reading

Baretti 1768; Beniscelli 1986; Gozzi/Bermel & Emery 1989; Gozzi/Petronio 1962; Gozzi/Prezzolini 1934.

From *Ingenuous Dissertation and Sincere Account of the Origin of My Ten Tales for the Theatre*[2]

Improvised comedy, also known as *commedia dell'arte*, has always been found by Italian troupes to be the most useful type of comedy. It has been in existence for three hundred years. It has been opposed in every period of its existence, but it has not yet perished. It does not seem possible that some men who pass themselves off as authors in our times should remain unaware of the fact that they make themselves ridiculous when they lower their level of seriousness to that of a ludicrous expression of anger against the likes of Brighella, Pantalone, Dottore, Tartaglia, and Truffaldino.[3] Such anger, which seems rather the effect of too much wine, clearly demonstrates that *commedia dell'arte* is alive and well in Italy, to the shame of those attempts to persecute it, which are more ridiculous than the things that *commedia dell'arte* is itself about. The realization of this fact doubles their bile and causes them to rave in delirium, and that makes them appear even more ridiculous. We hear them say in desperation that, thanks to the so-called ingenious reformers of Italian theatre, the awkward plays of the *commedia dell'arte* have come to an end in Italy and their masked characters have been definitively suppressed, but the truth of the matter is that *commedia dell'arte* theatres are at present better attended than all others and that princes from all over call to their courts none other than those same masked characters for their entertainment.

Those clever, witty, and intelligent actors, capable of satisfying even the taste of our recently awakened talents, impersonate the ancient masked characters of our improvised comedy with the aid of their own ability to mimic and their characters' humorous costumes, which together constitute an instrument of laughter <St/17; Dt/67; Lg/116> so powerful, precise, concrete, and efficacious, that its effect will never diminish on the people, who will always have the right to enjoy what they like best, to laugh at what tickles them, and to pay no heed to those concealed Catos[4] who do not want them to take pleasure in what they like. . . .

In improvised comedy I see an honorable achievement for Italy, and I judge it to be a form of entertainment completely different from that of

---

[2] Newly translated from *Ragionamento ingenuo e storia sincera dell'origine delle mie dieci fiabe teatrali in Opere: Teatro e polemiche teatrali*, in Gozzi/Petronio 1962, 1035–37, 1040.

[3] Stock characters of the *commedia dell'arte*.

[4] A reference to Cato the Censor (234–149 B.C.), who prescribed great austerity and decried all extravagance.

written and meditated representations. I encourage men of culture and talent to write good plays, observing the rules of the art, and I am not so shameless as to call ignorant plebeians the noble spectators of improvised comedy, for I have seen with my own eyes that they are the same spectators that attend representations of premeditated plays. . . .

A thousand ingenious controversies and a thousand fine opinions which embellish books and which may be read on the subject of theatre, a thousand accusations and defenses of writers on ancient, modern, English, French, Spanish, and Italian theatre, are all superfluous, since theatrical performance is always ephemeral. What makes entertainment successful is the number of people that attend it, and written works meant to be staged have always fallen short of their intended lives, inducing boredom in a very short time unless they could count on something new to sustain them.

This demonstrates the great vigor of improvised Italian comedy, sustained by quick-witted actors and facetious masked characters. This miraculous prodigy derives from perhaps three hundred formless things, which include a choice of the best theatrical circumstances and comic routines, well rehearsed and refined, whose efficacy is assured by repetition and time. Improvised comedy remains always the same, its only variation being the difference that comes with the different wits that represent it. Although it has been continuously opposed in the past three centuries, it nevertheless continues to exist, and I leave to the Italians of the future the task of witnessing its survival in times to come.

11

GOTTHOLD EPHRAIM LESSING
(1729–81)

Lessing was Germany's first great critic and theorist of drama. He wrote a number of plays of lasting importance, including the first German domestic tragedy, *Miss Sara Sampson* (1755); *Minna von Barnhelm* (1767), which set new standards for German comedy; the tragedy *Emilia Galotti* (1772), a work made famous by Goethe's reference to it in *Werther* (1774); and the blank verse *Nathan the Wise* (*Nathan der Weise*) (1779), which promoted ideals of religious tolerance and humanity.

With Moses Mendelssohn and Friedrich Nicolai,[1] Lessing conducted a remarkable correspondence on the subject of tragedy, and he collaborated with them on the periodical *Letters on Contemporary Literature* (*Briefe, die neueste Literatur betreffend*) (1759–65). Evidence of Lessing's polemical style can be found in the seventeenth of these *Letters*, where the influential theatre critic Johann Christoph Gottsched (1700–66) is pilloried for creating a "frenchified" theatre rather than working to revitalize the German stage and bring into being an authentically national drama. Gottsched would have done better to seek inspiration from the English, from Shakespeare in particular, for "even if one judges according to the model of the ancients, Shakespeare is a far greater tragic poet than Corneille, in spite of the fact that the latter knew the ancients very well, and the former almost not at all. Corneille comes closer to them in mechanical arrangement, Shakespeare in the essentials" (Lessing/Göpfert 1970–79, v:71–72).

In 1767 Lessing became adviser and critic at the newly formed National Theatre in Hamburg, where he reviewed the work of the company in the essays subsequently published under the title *Hamburgische Dramaturgie* (1767–69).[2] Initially, the reviews appeared twice a week, but serial publication eventually became erratic and then ceased altogether. The nature of Lessing's assignment also changed. He began with discussions of actual productions, with particular attention to the art of the actor, about which he made incisive observations. Before long, this immediate concern with the theatre gave way to more general dramatic criticism. In No. 50, with characteristic irony, Lessing acknowledges that instead of the engaging theatrical newspaper his readers might have expected, they are getting only "long, serious, dry critiques of old, well-known plays, ponderous examinations of what tragedy should or should not be, at times even expositions of Aristotle." It is, however, "anything but a dramatic system," and the author feels no obligation "to resolve all the difficulties" he raises (No. 95).

---

1 The philosopher Moses Mendelssohn (1729–86) and Christoph Friedrich Nicolai (1733–1811), writer and publisher, were, with Lessing, leaders of the German Enlightenment.
2 By the time the entire *Dramaturgy* was published in 1769, the Hamburg National Theatre, a privately funded venture, had collapsed.

Hostility toward French neo-classicism continues throughout the *Dramaturgy*, with Corneille subject to the most vehement criticism. However, as the last essay in the *Dramaturgy* makes clear, neither Lessing's objections to the French insistence on regularity nor his obvious enthusiasm for Shakespeare prevented him from developing at the same time a skeptical attitude toward the *Sturm und Drang*[3] and its particular conception of genius. According to Lessing, a genius cannot be oppressed by rules and does not transcend them <Hu/265>, but rather "has the proof of all rules within himself" (No. 96). Moreover, great care is taken to distinguish Aristotle from his imitators, whose rules for the theatre consisted largely of misinterpretations and distortions of Aristotelian theory: "It is one thing to circumvent the rules, another to observe them. The French do the former; the latter was understood only by the ancients" (No. 46).

The aim of the theatre, in Lessing's view, is moral improvement: "the theatre is to be the school of the moral world" (No. 2). The purpose of drama is instruction, not in a narrowly didactic sense, but through "laughter itself" – as opposed to derision – in the case of comedy, and through the arousal of pity and fear in the case of tragedy; *catharsis* or "purification" consists in "the transformation of passions into virtuous habits" (No. 78). Pity and fear can only be aroused, however, if the spectator is drawn into the theatrical illusion and made to sympathize; nothing must disturb the illusion, and nothing must detract from its coherence or "inner probability." Theatre as the school of the moral world demands "purpose and harmony in all the characters a poet creates" (No. 34), and everywhere we are to see "nothing but the most natural and common course of events" (No. 32).

Like Diderot <Dt/35>, whose plays and accompanying discourses he had translated, Lessing was an advocate of the new domestic tragedy (*bürgerliches Trauerspiel*) and the greater realism it brought to the stage. In his discussion of the relation between tragedy and history, he argues that it is not the business of drama to keep alive the memory of great men; from the stage we are to learn not what a particular individual has done, but "what every person of a certain character would do under certain given circumstances" (No. 19). He never wrote the intended continuation – which would have focused on drama – of his semiotic study *Laocoön: An Essay on the Limits of Painting and Poetry* (*Laokoon: oder über die Grenzen der Malerei und Poesie*) (1766). However, the letter to Nicolai of 26 May 1769, written in response to a review of *Laocoön*, reveals his view of drama as the highest form of art because of its naturalization of the abstract: instead of relying on "arbitrary" signs, which have only a conventional relation to the signified, drama uses the "natural" signs of dialogue. To which one might add – as Lessing implies – that speech and gesture in the theatre take this process further.

For further reading

Burwick 1991; Kommerell 1960; Lamport 1981; Robertson 1939; Wellek 1955:1.

---

[3] Taking its name from the title of a play (1776) by Friedrich Klinger (1752–1831), "Storm and Stress" was an early expression of Romanticism, which arose in opposition to the perceived limitations of neo-classicism. Shakespeare enthusiasts such as Herder, Lenz, the young Goethe, and Schiller were associated with the *Sturm und Drang*.

From *Hamburg Dramaturgy*[4]

Preface

... This "Dramaturgie" is to form a critical index of all the plays performed, and is to accompany every step made here by the art of the poet as well as that of the actor.[5] ...

The great discrimination of a dramatic critic is shown if he knows how to distinguish infallibly, in every case of satisfaction or dissatisfaction, what and how much of this is to be placed to the account of the poet or the actor. To blame the actor for what is the fault of the poet is to injure both. The actor loses heart, and the poet is made self-confident. Above all, it is the actor who may in this particular demand the greatest severity and impartiality. The justification of the poet may be attempted at any time; his work remains, and can be always brought again before our eyes. But the art of the actor is transitory in its expression. His good and bad pass by rapidly, and not seldom the passing mood of the spectator is more accountable than the actor for the more or less vivid impression produced upon him.

A beautiful figure, a fascinating mien, a speaking eye, a charming gait, a sweet intonation, a melodious voice are things that cannot be expressed in words. Still they are neither the only nor the greatest perfections of the actor. Valuable gifts of nature are very necessary to his calling, but they by no means suffice for it. He must everywhere think with the poet; he must even think for him in places where the poet has shown himself human. ...

Number 1[6]

The theatre was successfully opened on the 22nd of last month with the tragedy *Olindo and Sophronia*.[7] ... The subject is derived from the well-known episode in Tasso.[8] It is not easy to convert a touching little story into a moving drama. True, it costs little trouble to invent new complications and to enlarge separate emotions into scenes. But to prevent these new complications from weakening the interest or interfering with probability; to transfer oneself from the point of view of a narrator into the real standpoint of each personage; to let passions arise before the eyes of the spectator in lieu of describing them, and to let them grow without effort in such illusory continuity that he must sympathize, whether he wants to or not: this it is which is needful, and which genius does without knowing it,

---

4 The translation, slightly modified, is from Lessing/Zimmern (first published c. 1890) 1962.

5 At the end of the *Dramaturgy*, lamenting the fact that "we have actors, but no mimetic art," Lessing explains how "the sensitivity of artists with regard to criticism" forced him to abandon the second part of his project.

6 Lessing's first essay is dated 1 May 1767.

7 An unfinished tragedy by Johann Friedrich von Cronegk (1731–58), published posthumously in 1760.

8 From Torquato Tasso's epic poem *Jerusalem Delivered* (1581) 2.1–54.

without tediously explaining it to itself, and which mere cleverness endeavors in vain to imitate.

... The good author, if he does not write merely to show his wit and learning, has ever the best and most enlightened of his time and country before his eyes, and he only condescends to write what can please and move them. If the dramatic author lowers himself to the rabble, he lowers himself only in order that he may enlighten and improve these people, and not to confirm them in their prejudices or in their ignoble mode of thought.

Number 2

Yet another remark, also bearing on Christian tragedies, might be made about the conversion of Clorinda. Convinced though we may be of the immediate operations of grace, they can please us little on the stage, where everything that has to do with the character of the personages must arise from the most natural causes. We can only tolerate miracles in the physical world <Dt/62>; in the moral everything must retain its natural course, because the theatre is to be the school of the moral world. The motives for every resolve, for every change of opinion or thought, must be carefully balanced against each other so as to be in accordance with the hypothetical character, and must never produce more than they could produce in accordance with strict probability. The poet, by beauty of details, may possess the art of deluding us to overlook misproportions of this kind, but he only deceives us once, and as soon as we are cool again we take back the applause he has lured from us. Applying these remarks to the fourth scene of the third act,[9] it will be seen that Sophronia's speeches and acts could have roused pity in Clorinda, but were much too impotent to convert a person who had no natural disposition to enthusiasm.[10] Tasso also makes Clorinda embrace Christianity, but only in her last hour, only after she has recently heard that her parents were also inclined to this faith:[11] subtle, weighty reasons by whose means the operations of a higher power are, as it were, entwined with the course of natural events. ...

Number 3

Why is it that we like to hear the commonest maxim spoken by this actor (Herr Eckhof)?[12] What is it that another must learn from him if we are to find him equally entertaining in the same case? All maxims must come from the abundance of the heart out of which the mouth speaks; we must appear to have thought of them as little as we intend to boast of them. It therefore follows as a matter of course that all the moral parts must be very

---

[9] Actually Act 4 scene 4 of *Olindo and Sophronia*.
[10] "enthusiasm" (*Enthusiasmus*) = extravagant religious emotion.
[11] Clorinda is loved by the crusader Tancred, who unknowingly wounds her in battle and baptizes her before she dies.
[12] Konrad Eckhof (1720–78), advocate of a more natural style of acting, was an important figure in German theatre who encouraged his colleagues to reflect on and discuss their art.

well learnt. They must be spoken without hesitation, without the faintest stammer, in an unbroken, easy flow of words, so that they may appear not a troublesome unburdening of memory, but spontaneous promptings of the actual condition. . . .

Every moral maxim is a general axiom, which as such demands a degree of calm reflection and mental composure. It must therefore be spoken with tranquillity and a certain coldness. But again, this general axiom is also the result of impressions made by individual circumstances on the acting personages. It is no mere symbolical conclusion; it is a generalized sensation, and as such it requires to be uttered with a certain fire and enthusiasm.

Consequently with enthusiasm and composure, with coldness and fire? Not otherwise; with a combination of both, in which, however, according to the conditions of the situation, now one and now the other predominates.

If the situation is a placid one, the soul must desire to gain a sort of elevation by the moral maxim; it must seem to make general observations on its happiness or its duties, in such a manner that by help of this very generalizing it may enjoy the former the more keenly and observe the latter the more willingly and bravely. If on the other hand the situation is turbulent, the soul must appear to recall itself by means of the moral axiom (under which definition I comprehend every general observation); it must seem to give to its passions the appearance of reason and to stormy outbursts the look of premeditated resolves. The former requires an elevated and inspired tone, the latter a tempered and solemn one. For in the one, reason must fire emotion, while in the other, emotion must be cooled by reason <In/6>.

Most actors exactly reverse this. In their agitated scenes they bluster out the general observations as excitedly as the other speeches, and in the quiet scenes repeat them just as calmly as the rest. It therefore follows that moral maxims are not distinguished either in the one or the other, and this is why we find them either unnatural or tedious and uninspiring. These actors have never reflected that embroidery must contrast with its ground, and that to embroider gold on gold is wretched taste. . . .

Number 4

. . . I seem to see a schoolboy say his task when the actor tenders to me moral reflections with the same movements with which a hand is given in the minuet, or as if he spun them down from a spindle. Every movement made by the hand in such passages should be significant. It is possible often to be picturesque if only the pantomimic be avoided. Perhaps another time I may find an occasion to explain by examples these various gradations from significant to picturesque and from picturesque to pantomimic gestures. Just now it would lead me too far, and I will only remark that among

significant gestures there is one kind that the actor must note above all and
with which alone he can impart life and light to the moral. These are in one
word the individualizing gestures. A moral maxim is a general axiom
extracted from the particular circumstances of the acting personages. By
means of its generality it becomes, so to speak, alienated from the action; it
becomes a digression whose connection with the actual present is not
noticed or comprehended by the less observant or less astute spectators. If,
consequently, a means exists to make this connection evident, to relate the
symbolical quality of the moral to the visible, and if this means lies in
certain gestures, the actor must on no account fail to make them. ...

Number 5

... It is easy to discover why, where the poet has not observed the least
moderation, the actor must moderate himself. There are few voices that do
not become displeasing at their utmost pitch, and movements that are too
rapid, too agitated, will rarely be dignified. Now our eyes and our ears are
not to be offended, and only when everything is avoided in the expression
of violent passion that can be unpleasant to these, can acting possess that
smoothness and polish which Hamlet demands [*Hamlet* 3.2] from it even
under these circumstances, if it is to make the deepest impression and to
rouse the conscience of stiff-necked sinners out of its sleep.

The art of the actor here stands midway between the plastic arts and
poetry <In/11>. As visible painting beauty must be its highest law, but as
transitory painting it need not always give to its postures the calm dignity
that makes ancient sculpture so imposing. It may, it must at times permit
to itself the wildness of a Tempesta,[13] the insolence of a Bernini <Kl/238>;
they have in this art all that which is expressive and peculiar without the
offensive element that arises in the plastic arts through their permanent
posture. Only it must not remain in them too long; it must prepare for them
gradually by previous movements, and must resolve them again into the
general tone of the conventional. Neither must it ever give to them all the
strength which the poet may use in his treatment. For though the art is
silent poetry, it desires to make itself comprehended immediately to our
eyes, and every sense must be gratified if it is to convey unfalsified the
proper impressions to the soul. ...

Number 7

... There are matters in the moral conduct of men which, in regard to their
immediate influence upon the well-being of society, are too insignificant
and in themselves too changeable to be worthwhile placing under the
protection of the law <Sr/157>. There are others again, against which the

---

[13] Pieter Mulier (1637–1701), the Dutch painter known as "Tempesta" on account of his
depictions of wild storms at sea.

whole force of legislation falls powerless. They are so incomprehensible in their mainsprings, so abnormal in themselves, and so unfathomable in their consequences, that they either escape totally from the penalty of the law or cannot possibly be punished according to their due. I do not attempt to restrict comedy to the former, as a species of the ludicrous, or tragedy to the latter, as extraordinary manifestations in the domain of morals that astonish our reason and rouse tumult in our breast. Genius laughs away all the boundary lines of criticism. Only so much is indisputable, that drama chooses its themes this side or beyond the frontiers of law, and only touches its objects insofar as they either lose themselves in the absurd or extend to the horrible. . . .

In England every new play has its prologue and epilogue composed either by the author himself or by a friend. They do not, however, employ it for the purpose for which the ancients used the prologue, namely, to inform the spectators of various matters that would help them to a more rapid comprehension of the main points of the play. But it nevertheless is not without its use. The English know how to say many things in it that serve to dispose the spectators in favor of the poet or of his subject, and that obviate unfavorable criticism both of him and of the actors. Still less do they employ the epilogue < 1:Rb/84 > as Plautus sometimes employed it, to tell the complete solution of the play for which the fifth act had not space. They use it as a kind of moral application, full of maxims and fine remarks on the morals portrayed and on the art wherewith they have been rendered, and all this is written in a droll, humorous tone. Nor do they alter this tone willingly even in the case of tragedies, so that it is nothing unusual that satire causes loud laughter to resound after the most piteous or murderous drama, and that wit becomes so wanton that it would seem to be express design that every good impression should be turned into an object of ridicule. . . . If, therefore, I wish that our new, original plays should not be brought before the public without introduction or recommendation, it goes without saying that in the case of tragedies I should wish the tone of the epilogue to be more suited to our German gravity. In England it is Dryden who has written masterpieces of this kind, and they are still read with the greatest pleasure, although many of the plays for which they were written have long been wholly forgotten. . . .

Number 9

. . . On the stage we want to see who the people are, and we can only see it from their actions. The goodness with which we are to credit them, merely upon the word of another, cannot possibly interest us in them. . . . It is true, a private person cannot achieve many great actions in the space of twenty-four hours. But who demands great actions? Even in the smallest, character can be revealed, and those that throw the most light upon character are the greatest according to poetical valuation. . . .

Number 11

... Very good then; all antiquity believed in ghosts. Therefore the poets of antiquity were quite right to avail themselves of this belief. If we encounter ghosts among them, it would be unreasonable to object to them according to our better knowledge. But does this accord the same permission to our modern poets who share our better knowledge? Certainly not <Vt/29>. But suppose he transfer his story into these more credulous times? Not even then. For the dramatic poet is no historian; he does not relate to us what was once believed to have happened, but he really produces it again before our eyes, and produces it again not on account of mere historical truth, but for a totally different and a nobler aim. Historical accuracy is not his aim, but only the means by which he hopes to attain his aim; he wishes to create an illusion and, through this illusion, to move us. If it be true, therefore, that we no longer believe in ghosts, and if this unbelief must of necessity hinder the illusion, if without this illusion we cannot possibly sympathize, then our modern dramatist injures himself when he nevertheless dresses up such incredible fables, and all the art he has lavished upon them is vain.

Consequently? It is never to be allowed to bring ghosts and apparitions on the stage? This source of terrible or pathetic emotions is exhausted for us? No, this would be too great a loss to poetry. Besides does poetry not own examples enough where genius confutes all our philosophy, rendering things that seem ludicrous to our cooler reason most terrible to our imagination? The consequence must therefore be different and the hypotheses whence we started false. We no longer believe in ghosts? Who says so? Or rather, what does this mean? Does it mean: we are at last so far advanced in comprehension that we can prove their impossibility; that certain incontestable truths that contradict a belief in ghosts are now so universally known, are so constantly present even to the minds of the most common people, that everything that is not in accordance with these truths seems ridiculous and absurd? It cannot mean this, but rather, in this matter concerning which so much may be argued for or against, that is not decided and never can be decided, the prevailing tendency of the age is to incline towards the preponderance of reasons brought to bear against this belief. Some few hold this opinion from conviction, and many others wish to appear to hold it, and it is these who raise the outcry and set the fashion. Meanwhile the great majority remain silent and indifferent, thinking now one way, now the other, delighting in hearing jokes about ghosts recounted in broad daylight, and listening with horror to ghost stories in the dead of night.

Now a disbelief in ghosts in this sense cannot and should not hinder the dramatic poet from making use of them. The seeds of possible belief in them are sown in all of us and most frequently in those persons for whom the poet chiefly writes. It depends solely on the degree of his art whether he can force these seeds to germinate, whether he possesses certain dexterous means to summon rapidly and forcibly arguments in favor of the existence of such ghosts. If he has them in his power, no matter what we may believe in ordinary life, in the theatre we must believe as the poet wills.

Such a poet is Shakespeare, and Shakespeare only and alone. His ghost in *Hamlet* makes our hair stand on end, whether it covers a credulous or an incredulous skull. M. de Voltaire did not do well when he referred to this ghost; he only made himself and his ghost of Ninus ridiculous by so doing.[14] Shakespeare's ghost appears really to come from another world. For it comes at the solemn hour, in the dread stillness of night, accompanied by all the gloomy, mysterious accessories wherewith we have been told by our nurses that ghosts appear. Now Voltaire's ghost is not even fit for a bugbear wherewith to frighten children. It is only a disguised actor, who has nothing, says nothing, does nothing that makes it probable that he is that which he pretends to be. All the circumstances, moreover, under which he appears, disturb the illusion and betray the creation of a cold poet who would like to deceive and terrify us without knowing how to set about it. Let us only consider this one thing. Voltaire's ghost steps out of his grave in broad daylight, in the midst of an assembly of the royal parliament, preceded by a thunder-clap. Now where did M. de Voltaire learn that ghosts are thus bold? What old woman could not have told him that ghosts avoid sunshine and do not willingly visit large assemblies? No doubt Voltaire knew this also, but he was too timid, too delicate to make use of these vulgar conditions. He wanted to show us a ghost, but it should be of a higher type, and just this original type marred everything. A ghost that takes liberties which are contrary to all tradition, to all spectral good manners, does not seem to me a right sort of ghost, and everything that does not in such cases strengthen the illusion seems to weaken it.

If Voltaire had paid some attention to mimetic action he would for other reasons have felt the impropriety of allowing a ghost to appear before a large assembly. All present are forced at once to exhibit signs of fear and horror, and they must all exhibit it in various ways if the spectacle is not to resemble the chilly symmetry of a ballet. Now suppose a large number of extras have been duly trained to this end, and, even assuming that they have been successfully trained, consider how all the various expressions of the same emotion must divide the attention of the spectator and withdraw it from the principal characters. For if these are to make their due impression on us, it is not only needful we should see them, but it is well we should see nothing but them. In Shakespeare, only Hamlet sees the ghost, and in the scene where his mother is present, she neither sees nor hears it.

---

[14] In his play *Sémiramis*, where Ninus, the murdered husband of the Assyrian queen, rises from his tomb upon hearing his wife's plan to marry the man who is, in fact, their son. In Voltaire's *Eriphyle* (1732), the appearance of the ghost of Amphiaraus, also modelled on the apparition of Hamlet's father, had likewise failed to impress the audience.

All our attention is therefore fixed on him, and the more evidence of terror and horror we discover in the fear-stricken soul, the more ready are we to hold the apparition that has awakened such agitation as that for which he holds it. The specter operates on us, but through him rather than by itself. The impression it makes on him passes on to us, and the effect is too vivid and apparent for us to doubt its supernatural cause. . . .

Number 14

Domestic tragedies found a very thorough defender in the person of the French critic who first made *Sara*[15] known to his nation. As a rule the French rarely approve anything of which they have not a model among themselves.

The names of princes and heroes can lend pomp and majesty to a play, but they contribute nothing to our emotion <Bm/130>. The misfortunes of those whose circumstances most resemble our own must naturally penetrate most deeply into our hearts, and if we pity kings, we pity them as human beings, not as kings. Though their position often renders their misfortunes more important, it does not make them more interesting. Whole nations may be involved in them, but our sympathy requires an individual object, and a state is far too much an abstract conception to touch our feelings. "We wrong the human heart," says Marmontel <Dl/96>, "we misread nature, if we believe that it requires titles to rouse and touch us. The sacred names of friend, father, lover, husband, son, mother – of mankind in general – are far more pathetic than aught else and retain their claims forever" <Dt/56>. . . .

But no matter how much their Diderots and Marmontels preach this to the French, it does not seem as though domestic tragedies are coming into vogue among them. The nation is too vain, too much enamored of titles and other external favors; even the humblest man desires to consort with aristocrats and considers the society of his equals bad society. It is true that a genius can exert great influence over his nation, and nature, which has nowhere resigned its rights, is perhaps only waiting there for the poet who is to exhibit all its truth and strength. . . .

Number 19

. . . Now Aristotle has long ago decided < 1:Ar/45–46> how far the tragic poet need regard historical accuracy: not farther than it resembles a well-constructed fable wherewith he can combine his intentions. He does not make use of an event because it really happened, but because it happened in such a manner as he will scarcely be able to invent more fitly for his present purpose. If he finds this fitness in a true case, then the true case is welcome, but to search through history books does not reward his

---

[15] Lessing's *Miss Sara Sampson* was partially translated and reviewed in the December 1761 issue of *Journal Étranger*.

labor. And how many know what has happened? If we only admit the possibility that something can happen from the fact that it has happened, what prevents us from deeming an entirely fictitious fable a really authentic occurrence, of which we have never heard before? What is the first thing that makes a history probable? Is it not its inner probability? And is it not a matter of indifference whether this probability be confirmed by no witnesses or traditions, or by such as have never come within our knowledge? It is assumed quite without reason that it is one of the objects of the stage to keep alive the memory of great men. For that we have history and not the stage. From the stage we are to learn not what this or that particular individual has done, but what every person of a certain character would do under certain given circumstances. The object of tragedy is more philosophical than the object of history, and it is degrading tragedy from its true dignity to employ it as a mere panegyric of famous men or to misuse it to feed national pride. . . .

Number 24

. . . In short, tragedy is not history in dialogue. History is for tragedy nothing but a storehouse of names wherewith we are used to associate certain characters < 1:Cv/1 30–32 >. If the poet finds in history circumstances that are convenient for the adornment or individualizing of his subject; well, let him use them. Only this should be counted as little a merit as the contrary is a crime. . . .

Number 25

. . . So much is the tragic poet dependent on his choice of subject. Through this alone the weakest and most confused play can achieve a kind of success, and I do not know how it is that in such plays good actors always show themselves to best advantage. A masterpiece is rarely as well represented as it is written. Mediocrity always fares better with the actors. Perhaps because they can put more of themselves into the mediocre < In/4 >; perhaps because the mediocre leaves us more time and repose to observe their acting; perhaps because in the mediocre everything turns upon one or two prominent characters, whereas in a more perfect play every character demands a first-rate actor, and if they are not this, in spoiling their part they also help to spoil the whole. . . .

Number 28

. . . Well, but now granted that absentmindedness[16] is incurable, where is it written that comedy should laugh only at moral faults and not at incurable defects? Every absurdity, every contrast of normality and deficiency, is laughable < St/1 7; Dt/5 9; Gl/70; Bm/1 30 >. But laughter and derision are far apart. We can laugh at a man, occasionally laugh about him, without in the least deriding him. Indisputable and well-known as this

---

[16] Lessing has been discussing *Le Distrait* (1697) by Jean-François Regnard (1655–1709).

difference is, all the quibbles which Rousseau <In/7> lately made against
the use of comedy only arose from the fact that he had not sufficiently
regarded it. He says, for instance, Molière makes us laugh at the misanthrope and yet the misanthrope is the honest man of the play;[17] Molière
therefore shows himself an enemy to virtue in that he makes the virtuous
man contemptible. Not so; the misanthrope does not become contemptible,
but remains what he was, and the laughter that springs from the situations
in which the poet places him does not rob him in the least of our esteem.
The same with the *distrait*: we laugh at him, but do we despise him on that
account? We esteem his other good qualities as we ought; why without
them we could not even laugh at his absentmindedness. Let a spiteful,
worthless man be endowed with this absentmindedness, and then see
whether we should still find it laughable. It will be disgusting, horrid, ugly
– not laughable. . . .

Number 29

Comedy is to do us good through laughter, but not through derision: not
just to counteract those faults at which it laughs, nor simply and solely in
those persons who possess these laughable faults. Its true general use
consists in laughter itself, in the practice of our powers to discern the
ridiculous, to discern it easily and quickly under all cloaks of passion and
fashion, in all admixture of good and bad qualities, even in the wrinkles of
solemn earnestness. Granted that Molière's Miser never cured a miser, nor
Regnard's Gambler, a gambler;[18] conceded that laughter never could
improve these fools: the worse for them, but not for comedy. It is enough
for comedy that, if it cannot cure an incurable disease, it can confirm the
healthy in their health. The Miser is instructive also to the extravagant
man, and to him who never plays, the Gambler may prove of use. The
follies they have not got themselves others may have with whom they
have to live. It is well to know those with whom we may come into
collision; it is well to be protected against certain impressions. A preserva-
tive is also a valuable medicine, and all morality has none more powerful
and effective than the ridiculous. . . .

Number 30

. . . This triple murder[19] should constitute only one action, that has its
beginning, its middle, and its end in the one passion of one person. What,
therefore, does it lack as the subject for a tragedy? Nothing for genius,
everything for a bungler. Here there is no love, no entanglement, no
recognition, no unexpected marvellous occurrence; everything proceeds

---

[17] In *Le Misanthrope* (1666).
[18] Molière's *L'Avare* (*The Miser*) (1668); Regnard's *Le Joueur* (*The Gamester*) (1696).
[19] Corneille's *Rodogune* (1645) is based on the historical account of the Syrian queen
Cleopatra, who murders her husband, one of her sons, and then is forced by her younger
child to drink the poison she had prepared for him.

naturally. This natural course tempts genius and repels the bungler. Genius is only busied with events that are rooted in one another, that form a chain of cause and effect <Dt/37>. To reduce the latter to the former, to weigh the latter against the former, everywhere to exclude chance, to cause everything that occurs to occur so that it could not have happened otherwise, this is the part of genius when it works in the domain of history and converts the useless treasures of memory into nourishment for the soul. Wit, on the contrary, that does not depend on matters rooted in each other, but on the similar or dissimilar, if it ventures on a work that should be reserved to genius alone, detains itself with such events as have not further concern with one another except that they have occurred at the same time. To connect these, to interweave and confuse their threads so that we lose the one at every moment in following out the other and are thrown from one surprise into another, this and only this is what wit can achieve. . . .

Number 32

. . . The poet finds in history a woman who murders her husband and sons. Such indeed can awaken terror and pity, and he takes hold of it to treat it as a tragedy. But history tells him no more than the bare fact, and this is as horrible as it is unusual. It furnishes at most three scenes, and, devoid of all detailed circumstances, three improbable scenes. What, therefore, does the poet do?

As he deserves this name more or less, the improbability or the meager brevity will seem to him the greatest want in this play. If he be in the first condition, he will consider above all else how to invent a series of causes and effects by which these improbable crimes could be accounted for most naturally. . . .

Number 34

. . . Harmony: nothing in the characters must be contradictory; they must ever remain uniform and inherently themselves; they must express themselves now with emphasis, now more slightly as events work upon them, but none of the events must be mighty enough to change black to white. . . .

Purpose: to act with purpose is what raises man above the brutes; to invent with purpose, to imitate with purpose, is that which distinguishes genius from the petty artists who only invent to invent, imitate to imitate. . . .

Number 35

. . . I have once before, elsewhere, drawn the distinction that exists between the action in an Aesopian fable and a drama.[20] What is valid for the former

[20] In the first of his "Abhandlungen über die Fabel" (1759), where he charges Charles Batteux (1713–80) with failing to draw such a distinction (Lessing/Göpfert 1970–79, v:352–85). Batteux <Gt/155>, a renowned classical scholar and theorist, attempted to

is valid for every moral tale that intends to bring a general moral axiom before our contemplation. We are satisfied if this intention is fulfilled, and it is the same to us whether this is so by means of a complete action that is in itself a rounded whole or not. The poet may conclude wherever he will as soon as he sees his goal. It does not concern him what interest we may take in the persons through whom he works out his intention; he does not want to interest but to instruct us. He has to do with our reason, not with our heart, and this latter may or may not be satisfied, so long as the other is illumined. Now the drama, on the contrary, makes no claim upon a single, definite axiom flowing out of its story. It aims at the passions which the course and events of its fable arouse and treat, or it aims at the pleasure accorded by a true and vivid delineation of characters and habits. Both require a certain integrity of action, a certain harmonious end, which we do not miss in the moral tale, because our attention is directed to the general axiom of whose especial application the story affords such an obvious instance. . . .

Number 42

. . . After the recognition <1:Ar/53–54> and Merope's discovery that she has twice been in danger of murdering her own son,[21] he makes Ismene exclaim with astonishment: "What a wonderful event, more wonderful than was ever conceived of on a stage!" . . . Maffei did not recollect that his play was set at a time when theatres were yet unknown, in the time before Homer, whose poems scattered the first seeds of the drama <1:Ar/40>. I would not have laid stress on this heedlessness to any person but to him who held it needful to excuse himself in the preface for employing the name Messene at a time when beyond doubt no town of this name existed, since Homer does not mention it. A poet can treat such trifles as he likes; we only demand that he should be consistent and that he should not in one instance have scruples which in another he boldly disregards, unless we are to believe that the omission has arisen from ignorance rather than from designed disregard. Altogether the lines quoted would not please me, even if they did not contain an anachronism. The tragedian should avoid everything that can remind the audience of their illusion <In/12; Sd/255>, for as soon as they are reminded thereof, the illusion is gone. It almost seems here as though Maffei sought to strengthen this illusion by assuming the idea of a theatre outside the theatre, but the mere words "stage" and "invention" are so prejudicial to the matter that they carry us straight thither whence he would divert us <Bm/132>. It is sooner permitted to the comic poet thus to place representation in apposition to represen-

---

reduce the five arts to the single principle of imitation of natural beauty. See also the seventieth *Literaturbrief*, v:228–34.

[21] The Italian dramatist Scipione Maffei (1675–1755), in his verse tragedy *Merope* (1713), upon which Voltaire's play of the same name is based.

tation, for to rouse our laughter does not require the same degree of illusion as to arouse our pity. . . .

Number 45

. . . Physical unity of time is not sufficient; the moral unity must also be considered, whose neglect is felt by everyone, while the neglect of the other, though it generally involves an impossibility, is yet not so generally offensive, because this impossibility can remain unknown to many. If, for instance, in a play a person must travel from one place to another, and this journey alone would require more than a day, the fault is only observed by those who know the distance of the locality. Not everybody knows geographical distances, but everybody knows for what actions he would allow himself one day, for what several. The poet, therefore, who does not know how to preserve physical unity of time except at the expense of moral unity, who does not hesitate to sacrifice the one to the other, consults his own interests badly and sacrifices the essential to the accidental < 1:Db/229>. . . .

Number 46

It is one thing to circumvent the rules, another to observe them. The French do the former; the latter was understood only by the ancients.

Unity of action was the first dramatic law of the ancients; unity of time and place < 1:Cv/129> were mere consequences of the former which they would scarcely have observed more strictly than exigency required had not the combination with the chorus arisen. For since their actions required the presence of a large body of people, always the same, who could go no further from their dwellings nor remain absent longer than it is customary to do from mere curiosity, they were almost obliged to make the scene of action one and the same spot and confine the time to one and the same day. They submitted *bona fide* to this restriction, but with a suppleness of understanding such that in nine cases out of ten they gained more than they lost thereby. For they used this restriction as a reason for simplifying the action and to cut away all that was superfluous; thus reduced to essentials, it became nothing but the ideal of an action, which was developed most felicitously in that form which required the least addition from circumstances of time and place.

The French, on the contrary, who found no charms in true unity of action, who had been spoilt by the wild intrigues of the Spanish school < 1:Cd/213–16>, before they had learnt to know Greek simplicity, regarded the unities of time and place not as consequences of unity of action, but as circumstances absolutely needful to the representation of an action, to which they must therefore adapt their richer and more complicated actions with all the severity required in the use of a chorus, which, however, they had totally abolished. When they found how difficult, indeed, at times how impossible this was, they made a truce with the tyrannical rules against which they had not the courage to rebel. Instead of a single place, they introduced an uncertain place, under which we could imagine now this, now that spot; enough if the places combined were not too far apart and none required special scenery, so that the same scenery could fit the one about as well as the other. Instead of the unity of a day they substituted unity of duration, and a certain period during which no one spoke of sunrise or sunset, or went to bed, or at least did not go to bed more than once, they allowed to pass as a day, however much might occur during this period.

Now no one would have objected to this, for unquestionably even thus excellent plays can be made, and the proverb says, cut the wood where it is thinnest. But I must also allow my neighbor the same privilege. I must not always show him the thickest part and cry, "There you must cut! That is where I cut!" Thus the French critics all exclaim, especially when they speak of the dramatic works of the English. What an ado they make of regularity, that regularity which they have made so easy for themselves! ... The strictest observation of the rules cannot outweigh the smallest fault in characterization. ...

Number 59

... Many hold pompous and tragic to be much the same thing <Sa/185>. Not only many readers, but also many poets themselves. Their heroes are to speak as ordinary mortals do? What sort of heroes would they be? ...

Diderot <Dt/46> might have added another reason why we cannot throughout take the old tragedies for our pattern. There all the personages speak and converse in a free public place, in the presence of an inquisitive multitude. They must, therefore, nearly always speak with reserve and due regard to their dignity; they cannot give vent to their thoughts and feelings in the first words that come, but must weigh and choose them. However, we moderns, who have abolished the chorus, who generally leave our personages between four walls, what reason have we to let them employ such stilted, rhetorical speech? Nobody hears it except those whom they permit to hear it; nobody speaks to them but people who are involved in the action, who are therefore themselves affected and have neither desire nor leisure to keep a check on verbal expression. This was only to be feared from the chorus, who never acted, however much they might be involved in the play, and always judged the acting personages more than they took a real part in their fate. It is as useless to invoke the high rank of the personages; aristocratic persons have learned how to express themselves better than the common man, but they do not affect incessantly to express themselves better than he. Least of all in moments of passion, since every passion has its own eloquence, is alone inspired by nature, is learnt in no school, and is understood by the most uneducated as well as by the most polished. There never can be feeling with a stilted, contrived, pompous language. It is not born of feeling, and cannot evoke it. But feeling agrees with the plainest, simplest, most common words and expressions. . . .

Number 70

. . . In nature everything is connected, everything is interwoven, everything changes with everything, everything merges from one into another. But according to this endless variety, it is only a play for an infinite spirit. In order that finite spirits may have their share of this enjoyment, they must have the power to set up arbitrary limits; they must have the power to eliminate and to guide their attention at will.

This power we exercise at all moments of our life; without this power there would be no life for us: from too many various feelings we should feel nothing, we should be the constant prey of present impressions, we should dream without knowing what we dream. The purpose of art is to save us this abstraction in the realms of the beautiful and to render the fixing of our attention easy to us. All in nature that we might wish to abstract in our thoughts from an object or a combination of various objects, be it in time or in place, art really abstracts for us, and accords us this object or this combination of various objects as purely and tersely as the sensations they are to provoke allow.

If we are witnesses of an important and moving event, and another event of trifling import traverses it, we seek to evade the distraction that threatens our attention. We abstract from it, and it revolts us to find that again in art which we wished away in nature. Only if this event in its progress assumes all shades of interest, and one does not merely follow upon the other, but of necessity evolves from it – if gravity provokes laughter, sadness pleasure, and *vice versa* – so directly that an abstraction of the one or the other is impossible to us, only then do we not demand it from art, and art knows how to draw a profit from this very impossibility. . . .

Number 75

. . . For it is certainly not Aristotle who has made the division so justly censured of tragic passions into terror and compassion. He has been falsely interpreted, falsely translated. He speaks of pity and *fear* < 1:Ar/46 >, not of pity and *terror*,[22] and his fear is by no means the fear excited in us by misfortune threatening another person. It is the fear which arises for ourselves from the similarity of our position with that of the sufferer; it is the fear that the calamities impending over the sufferer might also befall ourselves; it is the fear that we ourselves might thus become objects of pity. In a word, this fear is compassion referred back to ourselves.

. . . It is not that this fear is a passion independent of pity, which might be

---

[22] *Mitleid* = "pity" or "compassion"; *Furcht* = "fear"; *Schrecken* = "terror" <Gt/150>. Lessing begins only at this point in the *Dramaturgy* to translate the Aristotelian *phobos* as "fear" rather than "terror."

excited now with pity and now without it in the same way as pity can be excited now with and now without fear. This was Corneille's error < 1:Cn/ 245–46>, but this was not Aristotle's reason; according to his definition of compassion, it of necessity included fear, because nothing could excite our compassion which did not at the same time excite our fear. . . .

Number 76

. . . Compassionate emotions unaccompanied by fear for ourselves Aristotle designates philanthropy, and he only gives the name of compassion to the stronger emotions of this kind which are connected with fear for ourselves. . . .

Number 78

. . . Whoever has endeavored to arrive at a just and complete conception of Aristotle's doctrine of the purification of the passions will find that . . . since this purification consists in nothing else than the transformation of passions into virtuous habits, and since according to our philosopher each virtue has two extremes between which it rests, it follows that if tragedy is to change our pity into virtue, it must also be able to purify us from the two extremes of pity, and the same is to be understood of fear. Tragic pity must not only purify the soul of him who has too much pity, but also of him who has too little; tragic fear must not simply purify the soul of him who does not fear any manner of misfortune, but also of him who is terrified by every misfortune, even the most distant and most improbable. Likewise tragic pity in regard to fear must steer between this too much and too little, and conversely tragic fear in regard to pity. . . .

Number 80

To what end the hard work of dramatic form? Why build a theatre, disguise men and women, torture their memories, and invite the whole town to assemble at one place, if I intend to produce nothing more with my work and its representation than some of those emotions that would be produced as well by any good story that everyone could read comfortably at home? <ln/3–4>

The dramatic form is the only one by which pity and fear can be excited; at least in no other form can these passions be excited to such a degree. Nevertheless, it is preferred to excite all others rather than these, and it is preferred to employ the dramatic form for any purpose but the one for which it is so especially suited. . . .

It is well known how keen the Greek and Roman people were on their theatres – the former, in particular, on their tragic spectacles. Compared with this, how indifferent, how cold are our people toward the theatre! Whence this difference if it does not arise from the fact that the Greeks felt themselves animated by their stage with such intense, such extraordinary emotions, that they could hardly wait for the chance to experience them again and again, whereas we are conscious of such weak impressions from our stage that we rarely deem it worthwhile. Most of us go to the theatre out of idle curiosity or boredom, out of a desire to be fashionable or to see and be seen; few are those who go from any other motive.

I say we, our people, our stage, but I do not mean the Germans only. We Germans confess openly enough that we do not as yet possess a theatre. What many of our critics who join in this confession and are great admirers of the French theatre think about it, I cannot say, but I know well what I think. I think that not alone we Germans, but also those who boast of having had a theatre for a hundred years, indeed, who boast of having the best theatre in all Europe – that is, even the French – have as yet no theatre. They certainly have no tragic theatre, for the impressions produced by a French tragedy are so shallow, so cold! ...

Number 81

... Scarcely had Corneille wrested the theatre of the French a little from the state of barbarism than the French already believed themselves quite close to perfection. They deemed that Racine had given it the finishing touch, and after this no one questioned (which indeed they never had done) whether the tragic poet could not be yet more pathetic, more moving, than Corneille and Racine. It was taken for granted that this was impossible, and all the emulation of the successive poets was limited to the endeavor to be as like the one or the other as possible. For a hundred years they have thus deceived themselves and in part their neighbors. Now let someone come and tell them this, and see what they will reply.

Of the two it is Corneille who has done the greatest harm and exercised the most pernicious influence on these tragedians. Racine seduced only by his example, Corneille by his examples and doctrines together. The latter < 1:Cn/234–51 > especially, which were accepted as oracles by the whole nation (excepting a few pedants, an Hédelin < 1:Db/220 >, a Dacier < Vt/20 > who, however, often did not know themselves what they desired) and followed by all succeeding poets, could produce nothing but the most shallow, vapid, and untragical stuff.[23] ...

Aristotle says that tragedy is to excite pity and fear. Corneille says oh, yes, but as it happens, both together are not always necessary, and we can be contented with one of them: now pity without fear, another time fear without pity < 1:Cn/246 >. Else where should I be, I, the great Corneille, with my Rodrigue and my Chimène?[24] These good children awaken pity, very great pity, but scarcely fear. And again where should I be with my Cleopatra, my Prusias, and my Phocas?[25] Who can have pity on these

---

[23] In the passage that follows, Lessing focuses his critique on Corneille's second discourse < 1:Cn/244–48 >.

[24] Characters from *Le Cid* (1637) by Corneille.

[25] Characters from Corneille's *Rodogune*, *Nicomède* (1650), and *Héraclius* (1647).

wretches? But they create fear. So Corneille believed, and the French
believed it after him.

Aristotle says that tragedy should excite pity and fear, both, be it
understood, by means of one and the same person. Corneille says: if it so
happens, very good. It is not, however, absolutely necessary, and we may
employ two different persons to produce these two sensations as I have
done in my *Rodogune*. This is what Corneille did, and the French do after
him.

Aristotle says that by means of the pity and fear excited in us by tragedy,
our pity and our fear and all that is connected with them are to be purified.
Corneille knows nothing of all this and imagines that Aristotle wished to
say that tragedy excites our pity in order to awaken our fear, in order to
purify by this fear the passions which had drawn down misfortunes upon
the person we commiserate < 1:Cn/245 >. I will say nothing of the value of
this aim: enough that it is not Aristotle's. Since Corneille gave to his
tragedies quite a different aim, they necessarily became works totally
different from those whence Aristotle had deduced his theories; they
became tragedies which were not true tragedies. And such not only his,
but all French tragedies became, because their authors thought not of the
aim of Aristotle, but of the aim of Corneille. . . .

Number 89

. . . It is unquestionable that Aristotle makes no distinction between the
personages in tragedy and comedy with regard to their generality. Both,
not even excluding the persons in epic – all persons of poetical imitation
without distinction – are to speak and act not as would become them
individually and alone, but as anyone of their character in the same
circumstances would and must speak or act. In this generality lies the sole
reason why poetry is more philosophical and more instructive than
history, and if it is true that those comic poets who would give especial
physiognomies to their personages, so that only a single individual in the
world could be like them, would turn back comedy into its childhood and
pervert it into satire as Diderot says <Dt/53>, it is equally true that those
tragic poets who would only represent such and such a man, only Caesar
or Cato according to their individualities, without at the same time
showing how these individualities are connected with the character of
Caesar and Cato – a character that may be shared by others – weaken
tragedy and debase it to history. . . .

Numbers 101–04[26]

. . . What assures me that I do not mistake the essence of dramatic art is
this, that I acknowledge it exactly as Aristotle deduced it from the countless
masterpieces of the Greek stage. I have my own thoughts about the origin

---

[26] Nos. 101–04 constitute a single, final essay, dated 19 April 1768, but not published until
the entire *Hamburg Dramaturgy* appeared in two volumes in 1769.

and foundation of this philosopher's poetics which I could not bring forward here without prolixity. I do not, however, hesitate to acknowledge (even if I should therefore be laughed to scorn in these enlightened times) that I consider the work as infallible as the Elements of Euclid <Co/226; Sl/199>. Its foundations are as clear and definite, but certainly not as comprehensible, and are therefore more exposed to misconstruction. I would venture to prove incontrovertibly that tragedy cannot depart a step from the plumbline of Aristotle, without departing so far from its own perfection.

In this conviction I set myself the task of judging in detail some of the celebrated models of the French stage. For this stage is said to be formed quite in accordance with the rules of Aristotle, and it has been particularly attempted to persuade us Germans that only by these rules have the French attained to the degree of perfection from which they can look down on all the stages of modern peoples. We have long so firmly believed this, that among our poets, to imitate the French was regarded as tantamount to working according to the rules of the ancients.

Nevertheless, this prejudice could not eternally stand against our feelings. These were fortunately roused from their slumbers by some English plays, and we at last experienced that tragedy was capable of another quite different effect from that accorded by Corneille and Racine. But, dazzled by this sudden ray of truth, we rebounded to the edge of another prejudice. Certain rules with which the French had made us acquainted were too obviously lacking in the English plays. What did we conclude from this? That without these rules the aim of tragedy could be attained – indeed, that these rules were at fault if this aim were less attained.

Now even this deduction might have passed. But with *these* rules we began to confound *all* rules <In/15>, and to pronounce it generally as pedantry to prescribe to genius what it must do or leave alone <Hu/265>. In short we were on the point of wantonly throwing away the experience of all past times and rather demanding from the poet that each one should discover the art anew <Co/221>.

I should be vain enough to deem I had done something meritorious for our theatre if I might believe that I have discovered the only means of checking this fermentation of taste. I may at least flatter myself that I have worked hard against it, since I have had nothing more at heart than to combat the delusion concerning the regularity of the French stage. No nation has more misapprehended the rules of ancient drama than the French. They have adopted as the essential some incidental remarks made by Aristotle about the most fitting external division of drama, and have so enfeebled the essential by all manner of limitations and interpretations, that nothing else could necessarily arise therefrom but works that remained far below the highest effect on which the philosopher had reckoned in his rules. . . .

From a letter to Friedrich Nicolai, 26 May 1769[27]

... It is just as far from the truth to say that painting[28] uses only natural signs as it is to say that poetry uses only arbitrary signs. But it is certain that the further painting departs from natural signs, or mixes natural with arbitrary signs, the further away it gets from its own perfection, just as, on the other hand, poetry approaches perfection to the degree in which its arbitrary signs are brought closer to the natural. Consequently, the higher kind of painting is that which uses nothing but natural signs in space, and the higher kind of poetry is that which uses nothing but natural signs in time. Therefore neither historical nor allegorical painting can belong to the higher kind, for they only become comprehensible by means of arbitrary signs. ... Poetry must seek absolutely to raise its arbitrary signs to natural ones; only thus does it distinguish itself from prose and become poetry. The means by which it accomplishes this are tone, diction, the arrangement of words, metre, figures and tropes, similes, and so on. All these things bring arbitrary signs closer to the natural, but they do not make them natural signs; consequently, all genres that employ only these means must be regarded as lower kinds of poetry, and the highest kind of poetry is that which makes arbitrary signs wholly into natural signs. This is dramatic poetry, for here words cease to be arbitrary signs, and become *natural* signs of arbitrary things <In/6>. Aristotle has already said that dramatic poetry is the highest, indeed, the only poetry, and he grants the epic second place only insofar as it is, or can be, largely dramatic. ...

[27] Newly translated from Lessing/Kiesel 1987, XI/1:608–10.
[28] Lessing understands under the rubric of painting "the visual arts in general" (Lessing/Göpfert 1970–79, VI:11).

12

PIERRE-AUGUSTIN CARON DE BEAUMARCHAIS
(1732–99)

Although his fame rests on two brilliant comedies,[1] Beaumarchais began and ended his public[2] career as a dramatist with works in the "serious" genre which was increasingly practiced during the second half of the eighteenth century in France. His first published play, *Eugénie*, performed and printed in 1767, had as its preface the "Essay on the Serious Genre of Drama." In it, Beaumarchais states that an early draft of the "Essay" was written around 1759, and that he was soon led to attempt a play which would exemplify his critical principles. The project lagged until the performance, in 1761, of Diderot's *The Father* <Dt/36> rekindled Beaumarchais' enthusiasm and he was inspired to complete both the play and his critical preface.

Despite the numerous points of agreement between Diderot's *Conversations* and "Discourse" on the one hand and the "Essay" on the other – advocating a form of prose drama intermediate between tragedy and comedy which would deal with events from everyday life and exercise a morally improving effect on the audience – Beaumarchais' document is not a mere repetition of Diderot's position. In the first place, the conception of the new form of play is more precise: neither tragedy nor comedy (Diderot had used the hybrid terms "serious comedy" and "domestic tragedy"), what is proposed is a genre of its own, specifically identified as *drame* <Hu/256>.[3] (*Eugénie* was the first play performed in France to be so titled.) Second, Beaumarchais is somewhat less concerned with giving a theoretical foundation for the *drame* than with urging on audiences and playwrights alike its real and attractive merits, and thus contributing to a flowering of the genre. Finally, whereas Diderot's *Conversations* and "Discourse" tend to stress particularly the moral function of the new type of drama, Beaumarchais strikes more of a balance between emotional appeal (what he calls "interest") and moral consequence.

Beaumarchais later recanted these views about the *drame* and asserted that there was, after all, no intermediate genre between tragedy and comedy <In/14>. But the recantation was a heavily sarcastic performance and, in 1792, with *La Mère coupable* (*The Guilty Mother*) he returned to the domestic genre.

For further reading

Gaiffe [1910] 1980; Lioure 1968; Niklaus 1973; Proschwitz 1964.

---

[1] *Le Barbier de Séville* (1775) and *Le Mariage de Figaro* (1784).
[2] In the early 1760s, Beaumarchais composed several *parades*, amusing and scabrous playlets intended for private performance in the houses of the aristocracy.
[3] Diderot used the term *drame*, but in the general sense of "play" or "drama." Because of its specificity in the "Essay", the word *drame* has been retained in the translation.

From "Essay on the Serious Genre of Drama"[4]

I agree that a difficult truth will be more quickly recognized, more surely grasped, more soundly judged by a small number of enlightened people than by a tumultuous crowd, since otherwise such a truth would not be termed difficult. But since matters which pertain to taste, to feeling, to pure effect – in short, matters of spectacle – are sanctioned only on the basis of the immediate and powerful emotion which they arouse in all spectators, must they be judged by the same criteria? When it is not so much a question of discussion and analysis as of feeling, of being delighted or being moved, is it not as rash to say that the audience's spontaneous judgment is false and ill directed, as it would be to claim that a type of drama which has stirred a whole nation and which has been found generally pleasing, does not have the degree of excellence which is appropriate for that nation? ...

On all sides I hear lofty terms bandied about, as critics invoke, against the serious genre, Aristotle, the ancients, theories of poetry, theatrical practice, and the rules – above all, the rules, that eternal commonplace of critics, that fetish of small minds. Where have the rules ever produced masterpieces? Is it not rather great works which have always formed the basis of the rules? Inverting this natural order shackles the creative genius....

Let us reduce to simple terms a question which has never been properly formulated. Setting it before the court of reason, I would state it thus:

"Is it permissible in the theatre to attempt to engage the audience's sympathy, to cause tears to flow at the sight of an event which, if it were real and occurred in everyday life, would inevitably have the same effect?" For such is the intention of the upright, serious genre. If there is anyone so barbarous, so classical, as to claim the opposite, ask him whether per-chance by drama or play he means something other than a faithful portrayal of human actions.... [Various recent plays][5] have shown what beauties the serious genre is capable of producing, and have made us receptive to the pleasure that derives from the touching picture of domestic affliction, which is so much more moving since it seems to threaten us more immediately: an effect which all the great tableaux of heroic tragedy can never hope to achieve....

By its very nature, the serious genre presents a more compelling interest, a moral appeal which is more direct than in heroic tragedy and more profound than in amusing comedy, all else being equal....

---

[4] Newly translated from Beaumarchais/Allem & Courant 1973, 1–24.
[5] Beaumarchais refers to Voltaire's *L'Enfant prodigue* (*The Prodigal Son*) (1736), *Nanine* (1749), and *L'Écossaise* (*The Scottish Woman*) (1760); La Chaussée's *Mélanide* (1741); Mme de Graffigny's *Cénie* (1750); Diderot's *Le Père de famille* (*The Father*) (1758); and Michel-Jean Sedaine's *Le Philosophe sans le savoir* (*The Unwitting Philosopher*) (1765).

In the tragedy of the ancients,[6] an involuntary indignation against the cruel gods is the feeling which grips me as I view the misfortunes which they allow to befall an innocent victim. ... [The tragic protagonists are] devout and passive creatures, blind instruments of the wrath or the caprice of the gods. I am far more terrified than moved by their fate. Everything is larger than life in these plays: the unbridled passions, the appalling crimes, are as far removed from nature as they are unknown in our lives. ... Moreover, the ineluctable blows of fate offer the mind no moral sense; ... any belief in fatality degrades humanity by suppressing freedom, without which no action can be considered moral.

Further, if we examine what sort of interest the heroes and kings of tragedy arouse in us, we must acknowledge that these great events, these lofty personages, are merely snares for our pride, snares into which the sensitive heart rarely falls. Our vanity is pleased as we are made privy to the secrets of a haughty court, as we attend a council which will change the fate of a nation, as we enter the chamber of a queen of whom we would normally be allowed but a glimpse.

We like to see ourselves as the confidants of an unfortunate prince, because his woes, his tears, his weaknesses seem to bring his state down closer to our own, or console us for his superiority over us. ... But if our heart is in some way involved in the interest which we take in the characters of tragedy, it is less because they are heroes and kings than because they are unhappy human beings. ... Nature alone holds sway over the heart....

If the theatre is indeed a faithful reflection of what happens in the real world, then the interest which it arouses in us is necessarily related to the way we react to real objects. Thus I observe that frequently a great prince, at the height of his good fortune, covered with glory and success, arouses in us only the sterile reaction of admiration, which has nothing to do with our heart. ... The heart's true interest lies in the relationship between one human being and another, not between an ordinary mortal and a king <Lg/114>. Thus the splendor of rank does not increase the interest which I take in the tragic protagonist, but rather diminishes it. The nearer the suffering man's status is to my own, the more power his misfortunes have over my soul. ... What care I, a peaceful subject in an eighteenth-century monarchy, for the revolutions of Athens and Rome? What real interest can I take in the death of a tyrant from the Peloponnese? in the sacrifice of a young princess in Aulis?[7] None of that has anything to do with me; there is no moral consequence which applies to me <Hg/216; Co/227–9>. For

---

6 Beaumarchais means not only ancient Greek tragedy, but also seventeenth- and eighteenth-century imitations.

7 Aeschylus' Agamemnon is the tyrant; his daughter, Iphigenia, sacrificed in Euripides' *Iphigenia in Aulis*, is the princess. Beaumarchais may also have been thinking of Racine's *Iphigénie en Aulide*.

what is a moral consequence? It is the fruitful result and the personal application of the reflections which an event unleashes in us. What is interest? It is the involuntary feeling whereby we apply this event to our own lives, putting ourselves in the place of the person who is suffering. . . . This feeling exists in the heart of all human beings; it forms the basis of this irrefutable principle of art: that there is in the theatre neither moral consequence nor interest without a fundamental relationship between the dramatic subject and ourselves. It is certain therefore that heroic tragedy moves us only to the extent that it approaches the serious genre, by presenting human beings rather than kings; and that, since the subjects which it treats are so removed from our customs, and its characters so foreign to our daily life, its interest is less gripping than that of the serious *drame*, and its moral import less direct. . . .

It hardly seems necessary to demonstrate that there is more interest in a serious *drame* than in a comedy. It is generally recognized that we are more affected by touching subjects than by amusing ones, assuming all else is equal. . . .

[As for moral consequences,] while the comical portrayal of some ridiculous trait is a fleeting diversion in the theatre, experience shows that the laughter which a comic jibe arouses in us expends itself on the victim and has no effect on our own heart <St/17; Lg/115>. . . . This would be of no great consequence if the object of public ridicule were merely a pedant, a conceited ass, a coquette, an eccentric, a fool, . . .; [but,] though it shames our morality, the spectator all too often finds himself taking the side of a rogue against an honest man, for the latter is always the less amusing of the two. . . . Thus the moral consequence of amusing comedy is shallow, or nonexistent, or even contrary to what should obtain in the theatre.

This is not the case with a touching *drame*, rooted in our manners and customs. Whereas boisterous laughter prevents reflection, compassion is silent. It draws us into ourselves, isolates us from all else. The person who weeps in the theatre is alone; and the more he is moved, the more pleasurable is his weeping, especially at plays of the upright and serious genre, which stir the heart by means that are so authentic and so natural. . . . Moreover, compassion has a moral advantage over laughter in that it cannot be directed to any object without simultaneously producing a powerful reaction in ourselves. . . .

The serious and touching *drame* occupies a middle position between heroic tragedy and amusing comedy <Dt/50>. If I consider it in the light of its similarity to tragedy, I must ask: Do the vitality and force of a theatrical personage derive from social status or from fundamental character? A glance at the models that nature offers to art (which imitates nature) shows me that strength of character may be an attribute of a private citizen as much as of a prince. . . . Every man is what he truly is by his character; his status is determined by fate, but even here character has a role to play: hence, the serious *drame* which shows me human beings strongly affected by some event is as capable of vigor, power, and elevation as is heroic tragedy, which also shows me men who are strongly affected, but simply of loftier condition.

If I consider the noble and serious *drame* in relation to the comic, I grant that the *vis comica* is an indispensable element of a good comedy, but I ask why one should impute to the serious genre a lack of vitality – a lack which, if it exists, is attributable rather to the incompetence of the playwright. Since this genre derives its personages from daily social life, as does comedy, is it right to think that their characters will have less vigor or less delineation in the grief or anger provoked by an event which involves honor and one's very life, than when these characters are occupied with less pressing concerns, with simple predicaments, or with purely comic matters? Even if all of the particular *drames* to which I have referred lacked this *vis comica* – and I do not think this is the case – ... the discussion should turn on the greater or lesser skill of the playwrights, and not on the genre itself, which, by its very nature, is the least bombastic and the most vigorous of all. ...

The question is asked, whether the serious *drame* ... should be written in prose or in verse <Sa/185; Sd/254; Hu/264>. ... The example of de la Motte <In/11>, although slightly outside our problem, will nonetheless prove illuminating. His unhappy attempt to use prose in his *Oedipus* has prejudiced many and led them to take a stand in favor of verse <Vt/26>. On the other hand, Diderot, in his fine essay on dramatic art <Dt/48>, declares himself in favor of prose, but only on the basis of a feeling, and without developing any reasons for his preference. In the case of de la Motte, the partisans of verse also judged on the basis of a feeling. Both sides are perfectly correct, because they are in fact fundamentally in agreement. It is only because of a lack of explanation that they seem to be at odds, and this apparent opposition is precisely what provides the answer to our question.

Since de la Motte wanted to make the language which he used more natural, he should not have chosen the tragic subject of his play from the families of Cadmus, Tantalus, or the Atridae. These heroic, fabulous times, where we see gods and heroes all mingled together, exaggerate in our imagination the objects which are presented to us, and introduce a fantastic element for which the pompous and measured rhythm of verse seems to have been invented, and to which it is perfectly suited. ... It is therefore appropriate to blame de la Motte for treating the heroic subject of *Oedipus* in a familiar style. He would perhaps have committed an equally serious offense against truth, verisimilitude, and good taste, if he had used grandiloquent verse for a misfortune which had occurred in our time among people of ordinary station. ... If tragedy is to show men as greater, and comedy as lesser, than they are in reality <1:Ar/37, 41>, since the imitation used in both genres is at some remove from exact truth, the language used need not conform strictly to the norms of nature. Once the limits of what is natural have been passed, one can lead the human mind as far into the fantastical as one wishes; subjects have then only a poetic or conventional truth, and the mind easily adapts to anything. That is why tragedy is successfully written in verse, and comedy is at liberty to use either verse or prose. But the serious genre, which occupies a middle position between the other two, must show people exactly as they are, and therefore cannot take the slightest liberty with the language, manners, or characteristics of those it presents on stage. . . .

It must be noted that my argument [in favor of prose] applies only to the serious *drame*. If I were dealing with comedy, perhaps I would prefer that the charm of poetry be added to the gaiety of the subject.[8] Its coloring, less true but more brilliant than that of prose, would give the work the rich, flowery air of a garden. While the harmony of verse makes intense moments rather less natural, on the other hand it livens up weak parts and in particular is well suited for embellishing the frivolous details of a play which has no true source of interest. . . .

The serious genre, then, admits only a simple, unornamented style, devoid of flourishes. It must derive all its beauty from its subject, its composition, the interest and progression of its action. . . . Its characters must always be presented in such a way that they scarcely need to speak in order to involve the spectator. Its true eloquence is one of situations, and the only coloring that it may properly use is the lively, rapid, uneven, tumultuous language of the passions – so different from the regularity of meter and the affectation of rhyme, which no amount of effort can prevent from being obvious in a work in verse.

If the serious genre is to attain the full measure of truth which it ought to possess, the author's chief concern must be to transport me so far from the stage, to make me lose sight of the actors and the theatrical decor so completely, that I am not aware of them for a single moment throughout the whole course of the play. But the very first effect of rhymed conversation, which is considered "true" only by convention, is to bring me back to the theatre <Lg/118>, and thus to destroy utterly the illusion <In/12> which was supposed to be created. I felt I was in Vanderk's salon, and I quite lost sight of Préville and Brizard, so I saw only faithful Antoine and his exemplary master and truly shared their emotions.[9] Do you think I would have had the same experience if they had been speaking in verse? Not only would I have been aware of the actors behind the personages, but worse still, I would have been aware of the author behind the actors.

---

[8] Beaumarchais did not implement this idea when he came to write *The Barber of Seville* and *The Marriage of Figaro*.

[9] Pierre-Louis Dubus Préville (1721–99) played the retainer Antoine, and Jean-Baptiste Brizard (1721–91) played Vanderk, Sr., in Sedaine's *The Unwitting Philosopher*.

Whereupon, all of the truthfulness which is so essential to this play would have vanished; and Antoine, so real, so moving, would have appeared as awkward and morose, with his borrowed language, as a simple peasant decked out in fancy livery who was supposed to appear natural. With Diderot, then, I believe that the serious genre must be written in prose. I believe that this prose must not be laden with ornamentation, and that, if a choice must be made, elegance should always be sacrificed to energy.

13

JOHANN WOLFGANG VON GOETHE
(1749–1832)

As playwright, director, designer, and amateur actor, Goethe had intimate knowledge of the theatre. He had been interested in the stage ever since he was a boy, and after moving to Weimar in 1775, he became involved in private theatricals – acting, writing, and supervising the production of various court entertainments. He then assumed the directorship of the Weimar theatre (1791–1817), where, particularly during the years of his close association with Schiller (1794–1805), he worked to establish new standards for the German stage. Goethe's wide-ranging dramatic output includes the historical drama *Götz von Berlichingen* (1773), a play which reflects the extraordinary enthusiasm for Shakespeare shared by the writers of the *Sturm und Drang*; the "classical" plays *Iphigenie auf Tauris* (1787) and *Torquato Tasso* (1790), which would be recast in blank verse at the time of the author's Italian journey; and the immensely ambitious *Faust* (1832).

A deep appreciation of Shakespeare can be traced throughout Goethe's writings on the theatre, from the impassioned tribute of 1771 to the still laudatory but tempered discussion of Shakespeare as poet and playwright, "Shakespeare Once Again" ("Shakespeare und kein Ende," 1813, 1816). Along with contemporaries such as Johann Gottfried Herder (1744–1803) and J. M. R. Lenz (1751–92), Goethe saw Shakespeare as exemplary in his expressive power and scope. Shakespeare's plays, organized around a single unifying idea, provided a new model of drama which sanctioned the rejection of the traditional unities and generic distinctions. Above all Goethe admired Shakespeare's genius for characterization, and his own influential analysis of Hamlet in *Wilhelm Meisters Lehrjahre* (1796) contributes to the emphasis on character in the dramatic theory and criticism of the Romantic period.

Wilhelm Meister's Apprenticeship, a *Bildungsroman*, was an influential work; one of "the greatest tendencies of the age," according to the Romantic theorist Friedrich Schlegel (F. Schlegel/Eichner 1967, 198). In this account of a young man's quest for identity, which involves him in the world of the stage, different perspectives on the theatre are ironically juxtaposed within the context of the novel as a whole. As in the "Prelude" to *Faust*, Goethe presents both sympathetically and critically the individual perspectives of actor, theatre manager, and playwright, without necessarily endorsing any single view.

Goethe treats many issues in terms of polarities: poet versus playwright, drama versus stage play, reader versus spectator. These are part of a remarkably fluid structure of thought, in which the theoretical and the practical are closely linked, as can be seen in the passages about cutting a text for stage production. In the same spirit he explores the tensions between fidelity to the author's intentions and the demands of a contemporary audience or the actual resources available to any given theatrical company.

Much of Goethe's dramatic theory was developed in dialogue with Schiller. Questions of genre are raised in "On Epic and Dramatic Poetry" ("Über epische und dramatische Dichtung," 1797), a piece which reflects the conclusions of both writers. Goethe and Schiller were also united in their commitment to the aesthetic education of the public. In his observations on Aristotle's *Poetics* (1827), Goethe's reinterpretation of the notion of catharsis is based on his conviction that art has no immediate or direct effect on morality; the "neutralization and reconciliation" of emotions takes place in the structure of the play itself <Gt/151–2>.

For further reading

Carlson 1978; Hinck 1983; Lamport 1990; Wellek 1955:1.

From "Shakespeare: A Tribute"[1]

... The first page I read made me a slave to Shakespeare for life. And when I had finished reading the first drama, I stood there like a man blind from birth whom a magic hand has all at once given light. I realized and felt intensely that my life was infinitely expanded. Everything seemed new to me, unfamiliar, and the unaccustomed light hurt my eyes. Gradually I learned to see, and, thanks to my awakened spirit, I still feel intensely what I have gained.

I never doubted for a moment that I would renounce the traditional theatre. The unity of place seemed to me an oppressive prison, the unities of action and time burdensome fetters on our imagination. I struggled free – and knew for the first time that I had hands and feet. And now when I saw what harm the keepers of the rules had done me in their dungeon, and how many free spirits were still cowering there – my heart would have burst had I not declared war on them, had I not tried daily to destroy their prison towers.

The Greek theatre, which the French took as their model, was so constituted internally and externally that it would have been easier for a marquis to imitate Alcibiades[2] than for Corneille to follow Sophocles.

First in the service of religion, then solemnly political, the tragedy presented to the people with the simplicity of perfection great individual deeds of their forefathers. It aroused feelings of wholeness and greatness in the soul, for it was itself whole and great.

And in what souls!

Greek souls! I cannot find words to describe what that means, but I can feel it, and for brevity's sake I refer to Homer and Sophocles and Theocritus, who taught me to feel what it means.

---

[1] "Zum Shakespeares-Tag," written in 1771 for Shakespeare's name day, published in 1854. The translation is from Nardroff 1986, 163–65.

[2] Fifth-century B.C. Athenian patrician, politician, general, and friend of Socrates. He achieved brilliant military successes but was, with reason, distrusted by the Athenians.

Now I hasten to add: "Little Frenchman, why are you wearing Greek armor? It is much too big and heavy for you."

That is why all French tragedies are parodies of themselves.

How regulated everything is! They resemble each other like shoes and are not without their boring spots, typically in the fourth act – but sad to say, you gentlemen know that from your own experience, and I say no more.

I don't know who first had the idea of putting historical-political spectacles on the stage; that is a good question for anyone interested in writing a scholarly treatise. Whether or not the honor of being the originator falls to Shakespeare, it was he who raised this type of drama to a level that we must still take to be the highest, totally beyond the imagination of most. And so there is little chance that anyone will match, much less surpass him....

Shakespeare's theatre is a colorful gallery where the history of the world passes before our eyes on the invisible thread of time. The structure of his plays, in the accepted sense of the word, is no structure at all. Yet each revolves around an invisible point which no philosopher has discovered or defined and where the characteristic quality of our being, our presumed free will, collides with the inevitable course of the whole. Our corrupted taste, however, so beclouds our vision that we almost require a new Creation to escape the Darkness.

No Frenchmen, or Germans infected by their tastes, not even Wieland,[3] have come off very honorably in this regard, or in others either. Voltaire, who has always specialized in lese-majesty, has proved himself here as well to be a veritable Thersites. If I were Ulysses, he would cringe under the blows of my scepter.

Most of these gentlemen take particular offense at Shakespeare's characters.

But I cry: Nature! Nature! Nothing is so like Nature as Shakespeare's figures <Jh/77>.

Now they're coming at me from all sides!

If they would only give me room so that I can breathe and speak!

Shakespeare competes with Prometheus, imitating him by forming human beings feature by feature, but on a colossal scale – that is why we don't recognize them as our brothers. Then he brings them to life by breathing his spirit into them. He speaks through them all, and we recognize the kinship.

And how can our century dare judge Nature? How should we know Nature, we who from childhood have felt in ourselves and seen in others nothing but restraint and artificiality? I often feel shamed by Shakespeare,

---

[3] Christoph Martin Wieland (1733–1813), German writer and translator of Shakespeare, satirized by Goethe in *Götter, Helden und Wieland* (1774).

for it sometimes happens that at first glance I think, "I would have done that differently." Later I recognize that I am a poor wretch, that Nature proclaims her wisdom through Shakespeare, and that my characters are mere soap bubbles wafted about by fanciful whims.

Now let me finish – though I haven't even started yet.

What noble philosophers have said about the world applies to Shakespeare too: What we call evil is only the other side of good; evil is necessary for good to exist and is part of the whole, just as the tropics must be torrid and Lapland frigid for there to be a temperate zone. He guides us through the entire world, yet we pampered novices cry out at the sight of a grasshopper: "Master, it's going to eat us alive!"[4]

To work, gentlemen! Take your trumpets and drive forth those noble souls from the Elysium of so-called good taste, where, drowsy in monotonous twilight, they live, yet do not live; have passions in their hearts but no marrow in their bones, and, because they are not tired enough to rest and yet too lazy to act, they stroll aimlessly among the myrtles and laurels,[5] idling and yawning away their shadowy lives.

From *Wilhelm Meister's Apprenticeship*[6]

(4.3)   Seeing the company so favorably disposed, Wilhelm now hoped he might further have it in his power to converse with them on the poetic merit of the pieces which might come before them. "It is not enough," said he next day, when they were all again assembled, "for the actor merely to glance over a dramatic work, to judge of it by his first impression, and thus, without investigation, to declare his satisfaction or dissatisfaction with it. Such things may be allowed in a spectator, whose purpose it is rather to be entertained and moved than formally to criticize. But the actor, on the other hand, should be prepared to give a reason for his praise or censure: and how shall he do this, if he have not taught himself to penetrate the sense, the views, and feelings of his author? A common error is to form a judgment of a drama from a single part in it; and to look upon this part itself in an isolated point of view, not in its connection with the whole. I have noticed this within a few days, so clearly

---

[4] From one of the books of the Apocrypha, *Tobias* 6.3.

[5] An ironic allusion to the crowning of victorious poets, athletes, conquerors, and other "immortals" with wreaths made from these plants.

[6] From the translation (1824) by Thomas Carlyle. The numerical references are to book and chapter numbers. In the first excerpt, Wilhelm talks to his fellow actors, all members of an itinerant theatrical troupe. In 5.4 Wilhelm, who has signed a contract with the theatre manager Serlo, speaks from his position as actor (he will play the part of Hamlet) and *de facto* playwright (he will rewrite the play for their performance). In the last three excerpts, Wilhelm converses with Serlo and his sister Aurelia in the course of their preparations for the production of *Hamlet*.

in my own conduct, that I will give you the account as an example, if you please to hear me patiently.

"You all know Shakespeare's incomparable Hamlet: our public reading of it at the Castle yielded every one of us the greatest satisfaction. On that occasion, we proposed to act the piece; and I, not knowing what I undertook, engaged to play the Prince's part. This I conceived that I was studying, while I began to get by heart the strongest passages, the soliloquies, and those scenes in which force of soul, vehemence, and elevation of feeling, have the freest scope; where the agitated heart is allowed to display itself with touching expressiveness.

"I further conceived that I was penetrating quite into the spirit of the character, while I endeavored as it were to take upon myself the load of deep melancholy under which my prototype was laboring, and in this humor to pursue him through the strange labyrinths of his caprices and his singularities. Thus learning, thus practicing, I doubted not but I should by and by become one person with my hero.

"But the farther I advanced, the more difficult did it become for me to form any image of the whole, in its general bearings; till at last it seemed as if impossible. I next went through the entire piece, without interruption; but here too I found much that I could not away with. At one time the characters, at another time the manner of displaying them, seemed inconsistent; and I almost despaired of finding any general tint, in which I might present my whole part with all its shadings and variations. In such devious paths I toiled, and wandered long in vain; till at length a hope arose that I might reach my aim in quite a new way.

"I set about investigating every trace of Hamlet's character, as it had shown itself before his father's death: I endeavored to distinguish what in it was independent of this mournful event; independent of the terrible events that followed; and what most probably the young man would have been, had no such thing occurred.

"Soft, and from a noble stem, this royal flower had sprung up under the immediate influences of majesty: the idea of moral rectitude with that of princely elevation, the feeling of the good and dignified with the consciousness of high birth, had in him been unfolded simultaneously. He was a prince, by birth a prince; and he wished to reign, only that good men might be good without obstruction. Pleasing in form, polished by nature, courteous from the heart, he was meant to be the pattern of youth and the joy of the world." . . .

(5.4)   One of the conditions, under which our friend had gone upon the stage, was not acceded to by Serlo without some limitations. Wilhelm had required that *Hamlet* should be played entire and unmutilated; the other had agreed to this strange stipulation, in so far as it was *possible*. On this point they had many a contest; for as to what was possible or not possible, and what parts of the piece could be omitted without mutilating it, the two were of very different opinions.

Wilhelm was still in that happy season, when one cannot understand how, in the woman one loves, in the writer one honors, there should be anything defective. The feeling they excite in us is so entire, so accordant with itself, that we cannot help attributing the same perfect harmony to the objects themselves. Serlo again was willing to discriminate, perhaps too willing: his acute understanding could usually discern in any work of art nothing but a more or less *imperfect* whole. He thought, that as pieces usually stood, there was little reason to be chary about meddling with them; that of course Shakespeare, and particularly *Hamlet*, would need to suffer much curtailment.

But when Serlo talked of separating the wheat from the chaff, Wilhelm would not hear of it. "It is not chaff and wheat together," said he: "it is a trunk with boughs, twigs, leaves, buds, blossoms, and fruit. Is not the one there with the others, and by means of them?" To which Serlo would reply, that people did not bring a whole tree upon the table; that the artist was required to present his guests with silver apples in platters of silver. They exhausted their invention in similitudes; and their opinions seemed still farther to diverge.

Our friend was on the borders of despair, when, on one occasion, after much debating, Serlo counselled him to take the simple plan; to make a brief resolution, to grasp his pen, to peruse the tragedy; dashing out whatever would not answer, compressing several personages into one; and if he was not skilled in such proceedings, or had not heart enough for going through with them, he might leave the task to him, the Manager, who would engage to make short work with it.

"That is not our bargain," answered Wilhelm. "How can you, with all your taste, show so much levity?"

"My friend," cried Serlo, "you yourself will ere long feel it and show it. I know too well how shocking such a mode of treating works is; perhaps it never was allowed on any theatre till now. But where indeed was ever one so slighted as ours? Authors force us on this wretched clipping system, and the public tolerates it. How many pieces have we, pray, which do not overstep the measure or our numbers, of our decorations and theatrical machinery, of the proper time, of the fit alternation of dialogue, and the physical strength of the actor? And yet we are to play, and play, and constantly give novelties. Ought we not to profit by our privilege, then, since we accomplish just as much by mutilated works as by entire ones? It is the public itself that grants the privilege. Few Germans, perhaps few men of any modern nation, have a proper sense of an aesthetic whole; they praise and blame by passages; they are charmed by passages; and who has greater reason to rejoice at this than actors, since the stage is ever but a patched and piecework matter?"

"Is!" cried Wilhelm; "but must it ever be so? Must everything that is continue? Convince me not that you are right: for no power on earth should force me to abide by any contract which I had concluded with the grossest misconceptions."

Serlo gave a merry turn to the business; and persuaded Wilhelm to review once more the many conversations they had had together about *Hamlet*; and himself to invent some means of properly reforming the piece.

After a few days, which he had spent alone, our friend returned with a cheerful look. "I am much mistaken," cried he, "if I have not now discovered how the whole is to be managed, nay, I am convinced that Shakespeare himself would have arranged it so, had not his mind been too exclusively directed to the ruling interest, and perhaps misled by the novels, which furnished him with his materials."

"Let us hear," said Serlo, placing himself with an air of solemnity upon the sofa; "I will listen calmly, but judge with rigor."[7] . . .

(5.6)   . . . "You are entering on your new career with becoming conscientiousness," said Serlo. "The actor fits himself to his part as he can, and the part to him as it must <In/5>. But how has Shakespeare drawn his Hamlet? Is he then so utterly unlike you?"

"In the first place," answered Wilhelm, "he is fair-haired."

"That I call far-fetched," observed Aurelia. "How do you infer that?"

"As a Dane, as a Northman, he is fair-haired and blue-eyed by descent."

"And you think Shakespeare had this in view?"

"I do not find it specially expressed; but, by comparison of passages, I think it incontestable. The fencing tires him; the sweat is running from his brow; and the Queen remarks, *He's fat and scant of breath*. Can you conceive him to be otherwise than plump and fair-haired? Brown complexioned people, in their youth, are seldom plump. And does not his wavering melancholy, his soft lamenting, his irresolute activity, accord with such a figure? From a dark-haired young man, you would look for more decision and impetuosity <In/5>."

"You are spoiling my imagination," cried Aurelia: "away with your fat Hamlets! Do not set your well-fed Prince before us! Give us rather any *succedaneum* that will move us, will delight us. The intention of the author is of less importance to us than our own enjoyment, and we need a charm that is adapted for us."

(5.7)   One evening a dispute arose among our friends about the novel and the drama, and which of them deserved the preference. Serlo said it was a fruitless and misunderstood debate; both might be superior in their kinds, only each must keep within the limits proper to it.

---

[7] In the end, Serlo thinks Wilhelm's idea "extremely good: for, except these two distant objects, Norway and the fleet, the spectator will not be required to *fancy* anything; the rest he will *see*; the rest takes place before him; whereas, his imagination, on the other plan, was

"About their limits and their kinds," said Wilhelm, "I confess myself not altogether clear."

"Who *is* so?" said the other; "and yet perhaps it were worth while to come a little closer to the business."

They conversed together long upon the matter; and in fine, the following was nearly the result of their discussion.

"In the novel as well as in the drama, it is human nature and human action that we see. The difference between these sorts of fiction lies not merely in their outward form; not merely in the circumstance that the personages of the one are made to speak, while those of the other have commonly their history narrated. Unfortunately many dramas are but novels, which proceed by dialogue; and it would not be impossible to write a drama in the shape of letters.

"But in the novel, it is chiefly *sentiments* and *events* that are exhibited; in the drama, it is *characters* and *deeds*. The novel must go slowly forward; and the sentiments of the hero, by some means or another, must restrain the tendency of the whole to unfold itself and to conclude. The drama, on the other hand, must hasten, and the character of the hero must press forward to the end; it does not restrain, but is restrained. The novel-hero must be suffering, at least he must not in a high degree be active; in the dramatic one, we look for activity and deeds. Grandison, Clarissa, Pamela, The Vicar of Wakefield, Tom Jones[8] himself, are, if not suffering, at least retarding personages; and the incidents are all in some sort modelled by their sentiments. In the drama the hero models nothing by himself; all things withstand him, and he clears and casts away the hindrances from off his path, or else sinks under them."

Our friends were also of opinion, that in the novel, some degree of scope may be allowed to Chance; but that it must always be led and guided by the sentiments of the personages; on the other hand, that Fate, which, by means of outward unconnected circumstances, carries forward men, without their own concurrence, to an unforeseen catastrophe, can have place only in the drama; that Chance may produce pathetic situations, but never tragic ones; Fate, on the other hand, ought always to be terrible; and is, in the highest sense, tragic, when it brings into a ruinous concatenation the guilty man, and the guiltless that was unconcerned with him.

These considerations led them back to the play of *Hamlet*, and the peculiarities of its composition. The hero in this case, it was observed, is endowed more properly with sentiments than with a character; it is events alone that push him on; and accordingly the piece has in some measure

hunted over all the world" (Goethe/Carlyle 1962, 280). For a brief account of the relation between neo-classicism and Wilhelm's version of *Hamlet*, see Brown 1986, 110–11.

[8] In *Sir Charles Grandison* (1753–54), *Clarissa Harlow* (1747–48), and *Pamela* (1740–41) by Samuel Richardson (1689–1761); *The Vicar of Wakefield* (1762) by Oliver Goldsmith (c. 1730–74); and *Tom Jones* (1749) by Henry Fielding (1707–54).

the expansion of a novel. But as it is Fate that draws the plan, as the story issues from a deed of terror, and the hero is continually driven forward to a deed of terror, the work is tragic in the highest sense, and admits of no other than a tragic end.

They were now to study and peruse the piece in common; to commence what are called the book rehearsals. These Wilhelm had looked forward to as to a festival. Having formerly collated all the parts, no obstacle on this side could oppose him. The whole of the actors were acquainted with the piece; he endeavored to impress their minds with the importance of these book rehearsals. "As you require," said he, "of every musical performer, that he shall, in some degree, be able to play from the book, so every actor, every educated man, should train himself to recite from the book, to catch immediately the character of any drama, any poem, any tale he may be reading, and exhibit it with grace and readiness. No committing of the piece to memory will be of service, if the actor have not, in the first place, penetrated into the sense and spirit of his author; the mere letter will avail him nothing."

Serlo declared, that he would overlook all subsequent rehearsals, the last rehearsal itself, if justice were but done to these rehearsals from the book. "For commonly," said he, "there is nothing more amusing than to hear an actor speak of study: it is as if freemasons were to talk of building."

The rehearsal passed according to their wishes; and we may assert, that the fame and favor which our company acquired afterwards, had their foundation in these few but well-spent hours.

"You did right, my friend," said Serlo, when they were alone, "in speaking to our fellow-laborers so earnestly; and yet I am afraid they will scarcely fulfill your wishes."

"How so?" asked Wilhelm.

"I have noticed," answered Serlo, "that as easily as you may set in motion the imaginations of men, gladly as they listen to your tales and fictions, it is yet very seldom that you find among them any touch of an imagination you can call productive. In actors this remark is strikingly exemplified. Any one of them is well content to undertake a beautiful, praiseworthy, brilliant part: and seldom will any one of them do more than self-complacently transport himself into his hero's place, without in the smallest troubling his head whether other people view him so or not. But to seize with vivacity what the author's feeling was in writing; what portion of your individual qualities you must cast off, in order to do justice to a part; how by your own conviction that you are become another man, you may carry with you the convictions of the audience; how by the inward truth of your conceptive power, you can change these boards into a temple, this pasteboard into woods; to seize and execute all this is given to very few. That internal strength of soul, by which alone deception can be brought about; that lying truth, without which nothing will affect us rightly, have, by most men, never even been imagined." ...

(5.9) ... "Are you, then, inexorably bent on Hamlet's dying at the end?" inquired Serlo.

"How can I keep him alive," said Wilhelm, "when the whole piece is pressing him to death? We have already talked at large on that matter."

"But the public wishes him to live."

"I will show the public any other complaisance; but as to this, I cannot. We often wish that some gallant useful man, who is dying of a chronic disease, might yet live longer. The family weep, and conjure the physician, but he cannot stay him; and no more than this physician can withstand the necessity of nature, can we give law to an acknowledged necessity of art. It is a false compliance with the multitude, to raise in them emotions which they *wish*, when these are not emotions which they *ought*, to feel."

"Whoever pays the cash," said Serlo, "may require the ware according to his liking."

"Doubtless, in some degree," replied our friend; "but a great public should be reverenced, not used as children are, when peddlers wish to hook the money from them. By presenting excellence to the people, you should gradually excite in them a taste and feeling for the excellent; and they will pay their money with double satisfaction, when reason itself has nothing to object against this outlay. The public you may flatter, as you do a well-beloved child, to better, to enlighten it; not as you do a pampered child of quality, to perpetuate the error you profit from." ...

"On Epic and Dramatic Poetry"[9]

Both epic and dramatic writers are subject to general poetic laws, especially the laws of unity and development. In addition, both treat similar topics and can employ various structural devices. The fundamental difference between them is that the epic writer narrates an event as having happened in the past, while the dramatist represents an event as happening in the present. In order to define specifically the laws which they have to follow, it might help to say that the epic writer is by nature a rhapsodist and the dramatic writer an actor < 1:Ar/54 >. The rhapsodist is surrounded by a quiet group of attentive listeners, whereas the actor's audience is impatient both to watch and hear. If we keep this analogy in mind, it will not be difficult to determine what is most suitable to each genre, which subjects and literary devices each writer prefers. I say "prefers" because, as I suggested above, neither one has an absolute claim on anything.

[9] Written in 1797 in collaboration with Schiller, published in 1827. The translation is from Nardroff 1986, 192–94.

Epic poetry and tragedy should both be concerned with human issues, and the subject matter should be significant and elevated. Ideally, the characters should be living during a cultural period when spontaneous actions are still possible, when human beings do not act from moral, political or social motives, but from purely personal ones. In this respect, the Greek myths from the heroic era were especially suitable material.

The epic poem presents primarily individual action, the tragedy individual suffering. The epic poem depicts man's physical interaction with the world: battles, journeys, or any kind of enterprise which requires broad, descriptive treatment. Tragedy portrays man interacting with himself, with the result that the action of a genuine tragedy can be quite limited in scope.

Structural elements can be classified into five groups:
1 Progressive elements which promote the progress of the action and are used predominantly in drama.
2 Retrogressive elements which divert action away from its goal and are used almost exclusively in epic poetry.
3 Retarding elements which delay or prolong the action and are used effectively in both epic and dramatic writing.
4 Retrospective elements which incorporate previous events into the action.
5 Prospective elements which anticipate events that are to happen after the action; both retrospective and prospective elements are used by epic as well as dramatic writers to flesh out their work.

The worlds to be presented are the same for both.
1 The physical world:
   (a) The immediate world of the characters: the dramatist normally restricts himself to one locale, whereas the epic poet ranges more freely over a larger area.
   (b) The more distant world, in which I include all of nature: the epic poet, who appeals primarily to our imagination, makes this world more accessible through imagery, which the dramatist uses more sparingly.
2 The world of the mind:
   It is used by both and is best represented without embellishment in its normal and abnormal aspects.
3 The world of fantasies, premonitions, apparitions, chance, and fate:
   This world can be used by both; however, it must be represented concretely. This causes special problems for modern writers because, try as they may, they cannot easily find substitutes for the ancients' miraculous creatures, gods, soothsayers, and oracles.

Regarding the manner of treatment as a whole, we see the rhapsodist as a wise man who recites events which lie completely in the past and surveys them with serene detachment. His presentation aims at reassuring his audience so that they will listen to him willingly and patiently. He makes all parts of his recitation equally interesting, since he is not able immediately to counteract overly vivid impressions. He takes his audience back and forth in time, as he sees fit. His audience follows him wherever he leads them because he is only appealing to the imagination, which creates its own images, and to a certain degree it makes little difference to our imagination what kind of images are created. The rhapsodist himself should not appear as a higher being in his poem. It would be best for him to recite behind a curtain so that his audience will not associate any particular personality with what they hear and will imagine that they are listening only to the muses themselves.

With the actor it is just the opposite <In/5>. He represents a specific individual and wants us to concentrate exclusively on him and his immediate surroundings. His goal is to make us empathize with his mental anguish and his physical suffering, share his difficulties and forget ourselves. Like the rhapsodist, he must give his presentation a certain balance. However, he can afford to produce far more vivid impressions because, due to his physical presence, even a rather strong impression can be neutralized by a weaker one. It is an absolute necessity that the audience be constantly engaged and not be allowed to assume a position of detached contemplation. The actor wants them to be passionately involved and their imagination completely inactive; so he must not appeal to it, and even what is being narrated has to be made visual.

From "Shakespeare Once Again"[10]

So much has been said about Shakespeare that it would seem nothing more could be added. And yet it is characteristic of ideas that they stimulate new ideas. On this occasion, I intend to discuss Shakespeare from more than one point of view: first as a poet in general, then in comparison to ancient and contemporary writers, and finally as a playwright. . . .

I. Shakespeare as a Poet

The highest goal man can achieve is the awareness of his own attitudes and ideas – knowledge of himself which provides him with the means to gain intimate knowledge of the minds of others. There are people who have an innate talent for this and who, through experience, develop and refine it for practical purposes, deriving from it an ability to profit mainly from worldly matters. The poet too is born with this talent, except that he does not develop it for practical and mundane purposes, but rather for a higher, spiritual, universal one. By calling Shakespeare one of the greatest poets,

[10] Written in 1813 (Parts I and II) and 1816 (Part III), published in 1815 and 1826 respectively. The translation is from Nardroff 1986, 166–74.

we imply that there were few who perceived the world as he did, few who, by expressing their visions, allowed the reader to share so fully in their awareness of the world. Shakespeare makes the world completely transparent for us. All of a sudden, we find ourselves the confidants of virtue and vice, greatness, pettiness, nobility, and depravation – and all this, and even more, by the simplest of means. If we try to determine what those means are, it seems at first as if Shakespeare were appealing to our visual perception. But that is a delusion. Shakespeare does not write for the eye <Sr/168>. Let me attempt to explain what I mean.

The eye may be called the most perceptive of our senses, and hence the most effective means of communication. But the inner sense is even more perceptive, and it is to this sense that the word speaks most directly. After all, it is the word that comes to our aid when the object which our eyes perceive is strange and incomprehensible. Shakespeare addresses our inner sense, which immediately activates our creative imagination and brings about a total effect which is inexplicable to us. And that is the cause of the delusion I referred to, the impression that everything is happening right before our eyes. But if we examine Shakespeare's works carefully, we find that they contain much more action conveyed by the word than physical action. He makes things happen which are easily imagined, indeed are better imagined than seen. Hamlet's ghost, Macbeth's witches, many a gruesome scene become meaningful only through the power of the imagination, and this is true of many minor scenes as well. When reading we readily accept such things as a matter of course, whereas during a stage performance we may find them disturbing, even repugnant.

Shakespeare achieves his effects through the living word, and the living word is best conveyed by reading aloud because then the listener is not distracted by either a skillful or an awkward stage presentation <In/4>. There is no higher or purer pleasure than listening with closed eyes to a naturally expressive voice reciting, not declaiming, a Shakespeare play. We follow the simple thread of the plot and the unfolding events. To be sure, the description of certain characters causes us to form mental images of them, but actually, we are supposed to discover what is happening in the characters' minds through a sequence of words and speeches. All participants seem to have agreed among themselves not to leave us in the dark about anything. Heroes and foot soldiers, gentlemen and slaves, kings and messengers, all conspire to achieve this end. We may even say that minor figures are often more active in this regard than leading ones. Everything that fills the air, unspoken, during a historical event, everything that is lurking in the human heart in moments of great distress – it is all expressed in words. What the mind anxiously represses and conceals is revealed frankly and without inhibition. We experience the truth of life, and we do not know how.

Shakespeare resembles the world spirit in that he permeates the world as it does, and nothing remains hidden from either. But whereas it is the task of the world spirit to keep secrets before, and even after, the event, it is the poet's calling to reveal secrets and to take us into his confidence, if not before, then certainly during the event. The depraved man in power, the well-meaning dullard, the passionately involved man, the detached observer – they all wear their hearts on their sleeves, often improbably so. Everyone is eloquent and loquacious, and come what may, the secret must out, even if the stones have to speak! The inanimate world too is eager to hold forth, and all things participate: natural phenomena of heaven, earth and sea, and thunder and lightning. Wild beasts lift their voices, often seemingly as imagery, yet always as part of the revelation.

Even the civilized world must surrender its treasures. Art and science, craft and trade, they all bear gifts. Shakespeare's works are one great bustling fair, and he owes the richness of his wares to his native land.

England is ever present in Shakespeare's works, this land, surrounded by the sea, shrouded in mist and clouds, active in all corners of the earth. The poet lived during a great and important era, and he portrayed its culture, strengths and even weaknesses in a positive spirit. Indeed, he could not have such an effect on us had he not been a true child of his time. No one has more disdain for externals than he; his interest is directed toward man's inner self, and here all human beings are alike. Shakespeare's portrayal of Romans has been called superb. I disagree. His Romans are all Englishmen through and through – but they are human beings, thoroughly human, and may just as well wear the Roman toga as any other costume. Once we have accepted that, we look upon Shakespeare's anachronisms as admirable, for it is precisely his disregard for externals which makes his works so true to life.

I trust these few words will suffice, although they by no means do complete justice to Shakespeare's accomplishments. His friends and admirers will have much more to add. Let me conclude this part with the following observation: It would prove difficult to find another poet whose every work is based on a different idea which pervades the whole drama.

Coriolanus, for example, is permeated by anger at the refusal of the masses to recognize the superiority of able men. In *Julius Caesar*, everything hinges on the idea that able men refuse to accept a leader because they wrongly assume they can rule as a group. *Anthony and Cleopatra* says with a thousand tongues that pleasure and action are incompatible. We could continue in this vein and find ever more reasons for admiring Shakespeare.

II. Shakespeare in Comparison to Ancient and Contemporary Writers

... Ancient tragedy is based on an inescapable moral obligation [*Sollen*] which can only intensify and gain momentum if it clashes with an opposing desire [*Wollen*] <Hg/214>. Essentially, this is where the frightfulness of the oracles resides, a domain where Oedipus reigns supreme. In Antigone, however, obligation in the form of duty seems less harsh. Indeed, there are many variants of obligation, but it is always despotic, no matter whether it is embodied by reason, as in moral code or civil law, or by nature, as in the laws of birth, growth and decay, of life and death. We recoil from all these laws, without realizing that they serve the welfare of the whole. Desire, on the other hand, is free, is perceived as free and favors the individual. Therefore desire is insidious, and it took possession of man as soon as he encountered it. Desire is the god of modern times. Having become his worshippers, we are afraid of the opposing force, and that is the reason why our art and our way of thinking will always remain distinct from those of the ancients. Through moral obligation tragedy becomes great and powerful, through desire weak and insignificant. Desire gave rise not to tragedy but to so-called drama, in which desire takes the place of awesome moral obligation. But precisely because desire comes to the aid of our weakness, we feel grateful when in the end, after painful expectation, we receive some pitiful consolation.

If after these preliminary observations we return to Shakespeare, it is with the hope that the reader himself will be conducting his own comparisons and applying my theories. Shakespeare is indeed unique in that he fuses ancient and modern with such exuberance. In his plays, obligation and desire clearly try to counterbalance each other. Both are powerful contestants, yet Shakespeare always sees to it that desire remains at a disadvantage.

Perhaps no other poet has portrayed more magnificently the underlying connection between desire and moral obligation in individuals. As a character with a role in life, the individual is under an obligation, that is, he is constrained, destined for a specific function. Yet as a human being, he has desires; he is unconstrained, and his desires have no specific target. Already at this point, an inner conflict arises, and Shakespeare gives it special emphasis. But then an external conflict is added, a conflict which is often aggravated by the fact that, for various reasons, an unrealizable desire is raised to the level of a compelling obligation. I refer the reader to my earlier discussion of *Hamlet* where I demonstrated this theory.[11] The principle applies broadly in Shakespeare, however. Many of his characters get into predicaments which they are not equipped to handle. Hamlet does so because of the ghost, Macbeth because of the witches, Hecate and the superwitch, his wife, and Brutus because of his friends. Even in *Coriolanus* we find a similar pattern. In short, we may say that the motif of desire that overpowers the individual is characteristically modern. But since Shakespeare permits this desire to originate from without rather than from within, it becomes a type of obligation close to the ancients' concept. All

---

[11] In *Wilhelm Meister's Apprenticeship* 4.13.

protagonists in ancient literature desire only what is humanly possible, and that is the reason for the beautiful balance between desire, obligation, and fulfillment. However, their sense of obligation tends to strike us as too extreme and unconvincing, and as a result, despite our admiration, we are not deeply affected. A necessity that excludes freedom to some extent, or altogether, no longer appeals to our modern sensibilities. Shakespeare, on the other hand, closely approximates the modern view. To our amazement and joy, he fuses the ancient and the modern by changing necessity to moral necessity. If we want to learn anything from Shakespeare, this should be the subject of study....

III. Shakespeare as Playwright

... A universally recognized genius may use his talents in a problematical way; not everything the master does is masterful. While Shakespeare's name is an essential part of the history of literature, he is only a peripheral part of the history of the theatre. Yet, since he absolutely deserves our admiration as a writer for the theatre, we must examine the conditions under which he had to write, but without extolling those conditions as virtues or models.

There are closely related literary forms which in practice are often combined, such as epic, dialogue, drama, and stage play. The epic requires oral delivery by one individual to an audience; dialogue requires conversation in a closed circle to which an audience is allowed to listen; drama requires conversation supported by action, even if the action is only created by our imagination; a stage play requires all three together, and insofar as it also involves our visual sense, it can be effective as long as it presents a locale and characters to which we can relate.

In this sense, Shakespeare's works are predominantly drama. His method of revealing what happens in mind and soul captivates the reader. Stage requirements are unimportant to Shakespeare, so he does not pay much attention to them, nor do we as we read. We skip along from locale to locale, our imagination fills in all the episodes he omits, and we are even grateful to him for stimulating our minds in such a rewarding way. By presenting everything in the form of a stage play, Shakespeare facilitates the task of our imagination, for we are more familiar with the "stage that represents the world" than with the world itself. No matter how fantastic the things we read and hear, we still think that they would be effective in the theatre, which might explain why so many bad plays have been adapted from popular novels.

However, strictly speaking, nothing is truly suitable to the theatre which is not also perceived as symbolic: an important action which anticipates an even more important one. That Shakespeare knew how to achieve this supreme effect is evident in the scene where the heir to the throne takes the crown from the side of his sleeping, dying father, puts it on his own head and struts off [*Henry IV*, 2. 4. 5]. But such symbolic episodes are few, are isolated jewels in the midst of quantities of material which is not suitable for presentation on the stage. As a matter of fact, the stage almost always presents an obstacle to Shakespeare's creativity. His great talent is that of an epitomizer, one who extracts the essence, and since the poet is the very epitomizer of nature, we must acknowledge Shakespeare's great accomplishment in this regard as well. At the same time however – and this reflects well on him – we must reject the notion that the stage is a vehicle worthy of his genius. Yet it is precisely the limitations of the stage which force him to discipline his poetic talent. In adjusting to these constraints, he does not choose specific material for a specific work as some writers do, but rather, he decides on one idea as the central point, and then makes the world and the universe relate to it....

"On Interpreting Aristotle's *Poetics*"[12]

Anyone fairly well acquainted with the theory of poetics in general and the theory of tragedy in particular will recall a passage in Aristotle's *Poetics* which has caused interpreters much difficulty and whose exact meaning is still a matter of controversy. In his definition of tragedy, Aristotle seems to stipulate that the spectator's mind be purged of pity and fear through the presentation of actions and events that evoke these emotions <1:Ar/42>.

I think that I may best be able to convey my ideas and convictions regarding this passage by translating it.

"Tragedy is the imitation of a significant and complete action which has a certain length and is not narrated by a single character but presented in poetical language by separate characters, each of whom plays his own role. However, after a certain course of events which evoke pity and fear, the tragedy concludes by neutralizing those emotions."

By this translation I believe to have clarified the passage which has so far been considered obscure, and I would only add the following remarks: how could Aristotle possibly have thought of the effect – indeed the delayed effect – which a tragedy might have on the spectator, when in his characteristically objective way he was in fact discussing the structure of tragedy? Impossible! He states clearly and correctly: once tragedy has gone through a series of events arousing pity and fear, it must conclude on stage, before our eyes, with the neutralization and reconciliation of such emotions <1:In/7–8>.[13]

By catharsis he means this reconciliatory conclusion, which is actually expected of all drama, indeed of all poetic works.

---

[12] "Nachlese zu Aristoteles' *Poetik*" (1827). The translation is from Nardroff 1986, 197–99.
[13] "pity" = *Mitleid*; "fear" = *Furcht*; "with the neutralization and reconciliation of such emotions" = *mit Ausgleichung, mit Versöhnung solcher Leidenschaften* <Lg/121>.

In tragedy this is accomplished by some type of human sacrifice, either actually performed or, through divine intervention, replaced by a surrogate, as with Abraham or Agamemnon. In any case, a reconciliation, a solution is indispensable as a conclusion if the tragedy is to be a perfect work of art. However, the surrogate solution, which is prompted by the desire for a happy dénouement, brings the work closer to the intermediary form of the drama, as with the return of Alcestis. In comedy, on the other hand, we usually find marriage as a means of disentangling all sorts of predicaments, which are actually a lesser form of fear and hope. Although marriage may not be the end of life, it represents a significant and serious caesura in life. No one wants to die, everyone wants to get married: this is the half-facetious, half-serious difference between tragedy and comedy according to Aristotle's aesthetics.

Furthermore, we note that the Greeks used the trilogy for the purpose of catharsis. There is probably no more powerful example than *Oedipus at Colonus*. Because of daemonic personality traits, the somber intensity of his life, the propensity for precipitous actions, indeed, because of the very nobility of his character, this half-guilty criminal becomes the victim of ever inscrutable, inexplicably relentless forces and plunges himself and his family into deep and utterly hopeless misery. Yet in the end, after reconciliation and atonement, he is elevated to the company of the gods, becomes the benevolent guardian spirit of the land and is deemed worthy of the honor of a special sacrificial ceremony.

This is the principle on which the great master's maxim is based: the hero of a tragedy must be portrayed as neither completely guilty nor completely innocent < 1:Ar/49 >. In the first case, the catharsis would only follow from the plot itself. A murdered villain, for example, would seem only to have escaped punishment by law. In the second case, catharsis would be impossible: fate or human beings would have to bear the burden of too grave an injustice.

Although I do not wish to engage in polemics in discussing this or any other subject, I feel compelled to point out how others have dealt with the interpretation of this passage. Aristotle had said in his *Politics* [1342a] that music could be an aid to moral education because sacred melodies could soothe a mind that has been excited by orgies, and hence could have a similar effect in counterbalancing other emotions. I do not deny that an analogy exists between these two cases, but they are not identical. The type of music determines its effect, as Handel has shown in his *Alexander's Feast*, and as we can verify for ourselves at any dance when a waltz follows a dignified and proper polonaise and drives young people into a frenzy.

But music cannot affect morality, nor can the other arts, and it is always wrong to expect them to do so. Only philosophy and religion can achieve this; piety and a sense of duty require inspiration, and the arts can accomplish such an awakening only by chance. But what the arts can and do achieve is the softening of crude manners, which, however, may lead to effeminacy.

Whoever is in pursuit of truly moral education of the mind knows and will concede that tragedy and tragic novels do not soothe the spirit, but rather unsettle the emotions and what we call the heart. The result is a vague, uncertain mood, cherished by young people who, therefore, are passionately fond of literature of that kind.

Let us return to our original point and repeat: Aristotle speaks of the structure of the tragedy, with the dramatist in mind who contemplates producing a tragedy that is noble and appealing, pleasing to eyes and ears, and that is a unified whole.

Once the poet has fulfilled his duty, has tied significant knots and unravelled them appropriately, the same will happen in the spectator's mind. The complications will confuse him, the solution will enlighten him, but he will not go home a better person. Rather, he would be amazed at himself – if he were unusually observant – for coming back home just as frivolous or stubborn, as aggressive or meek, as kind or unkind as he was when he left. There would seem to be little more to say regarding this point, although further discussion could always shed more light on the theme.

14

FRIEDRICH VON SCHILLER
(1759–1805)

Schiller first received public attention in January 1782 with the première of *The Robbers* in Mannheim. Although Schiller's Preface warns that the play is not destined for the stage and that the theatre public is not yet ready for such a bold portrayal of vice, this powerful example of *Sturm und Drang* drama, admittedly toned down for the Mannheim audience, created a sensation (Sharpe 1991, 28–29). *The Robbers* explores the grand themes of tyranny and freedom, rebellion, power, and corruption in the context of fraternal hatred. The revolutionary spirit of the work prompted the French to proclaim its author an honorary citizen of the Republic in 1792. But in the Preface Schiller worries about the reception of his play, a sign that even at this early stage in his career he was concerned with the effect of theatre on society.[1] (In an earlier version of the Preface,[2] Schiller claims that there is a distinct advantage in writing a "dramatic narrative" rather than a "theatrical drama": the poet, subject only to general artistic principles, can ignore the particular rules prescribed by theatrical taste.)

In July 1783, Schiller was given a year's contract as playwright at the theatre in Mannheim, and it was here that he composed the first version of his essay "The Stage Considered as a Moral Institution." This programmatic statement of the public function of the theatre appears in its entirety here, for though the rhetoric is dated, the issues are still relevant. In one passage Schiller concedes that the stage may not have a direct effect on the behavior of the audience, but his own conviction – or at least his strong hope – is that the theatre will serve as a medium of enlightenment.

In 1789 Schiller was appointed Professor of History at the University of Jena, where, under the influence of Kant, he wrote a number of important essays on aesthetics, including "On Grace and Dignity," "On Pathos," "On the Aesthetic Education of Man," "On Naive and Sentimental Poetry," and "On the Sublime." He develops a theory of tragedy that moves away from the didacticism of the earlier essay to focus instead on the notion of the sublime: the effect of tragedy is to convey a sense of our own moral autonomy and freedom of spirit. "The ultimate aim of art is to represent the supersensuous," he claims in "On Pathos" ("Über das Pathetische"),[3] and the achievement of tragedy is to make us aware of our capacity for moral independence from suffering.[4]

---

[1] "The Effect of Theatre on the People" ("Vom Wirken der Schaubühne auf das Volk") was the original title of his address to a Mannheim cultural society, later revised and published as "The Stage Considered as a Moral Institution."

[2] "Unterdrückte Vorrede" (1781) in Schiller/Perfahl 1968, v:729–32.

[3] Schiller/Perfahl 1968, v:190.

[4] Wellek (1955, 1:246) points out that although "Schiller's main preoccupation ... was with tragedy," he does "speculate that perfect comedy would make all tragedy either superfluous or impossible."

Schiller provided the stimulus Goethe needed to make something of the Weimar stage, and together they worked for a decade to establish a high standard of theatre with its own distinctive aesthetic. As well as translating Shakespeare, Racine, and Gozzi, Schiller wrote new plays for the Weimar stage: the *Wallenstein* trilogy (1797–99), *Maria Stuart* (1799–1800), *The Maid of Orleans* (*Die Jungfrau von Orleans*) (1800–01), *The Bride of Messina* (*Die Braut von Messina*) (1802–03), and *Wilhelm Tell* (1803–04). The first performance of *Wallenstein's Camp* in October 1798 inaugurated not just the reconstructed Weimar court theatre but the age of Weimar classicism itself. The Prologue to *Wallenstein*, which was spoken on this occasion, marks a shift in Schiller's attitude toward the educative potential of the stage; the influence of Goethe is evident both in the absence here of a heavy didacticism and in the emphasis on the sublime effects of "art serene." In the Prologue Schiller also alludes to the power of historical drama to bring us closer to the essential truth of a matter.

The last lines of the Prologue suggest Schiller's antipathy toward "naturalism" in the theatre, a term that is actually used in the author's final theoretical pronouncement, "On the Use of the Chorus in Tragedy." As part of his battle against naturalism, Schiller had, in imitation of Greek tragedy, made use of the chorus <Vt/23> to create a distancing effect in his play *The Bride of Messina*. Although the 1803 première in Weimar was a success, Schiller felt that the public still clung to a desire for illusion in the theatre and he therefore wrote a theoretical justification for his use of the chorus, which he added as a preface to the drama when it was published several months later. This essay, also translated in its entirety here, argues that naturalism robs us of our freedom, whereas art that acknowledges its own artificiality – and is, paradoxically, more profoundly aligned with nature – has, in exercising our creative intellect, the power "to *make* us actually free."

For further reading

Bennett 1979; Bruford 1950; Lamport 1990; Sharpe 1991; Wellek 1955:1.

From "Preface to *The Robbers*"[5]

This play is to be regarded as nothing other than a dramatic narrative, which, in order to catch the most secret operations of the soul <In/8>, makes use of the dramatic method, without observing the limitations of a stage play or seeking the dubious advantage of theatrical performance.[6] One must acknowledge the absurdity of the expectation that three extra-ordinary characters, whose actions are subject to perhaps a thousand contingencies, be fully developed within three hours, for indeed three such remarkable people could not possibly, even in twenty-four hours, reveal their true natures to the most penetrating mind. It was impossible for me to

---

[5] "Zu den Räubern. Vorrede zur ersten Auflage" (1781). Newly translated from Schiller/ Perfahl 1968, v:732–36.

[6] In the suppressed preface, Schiller emphasizes that the dramatic method, the portrayal of events as present, need not be confined to writing for the stage but may be used to advantage in other literary forms.

restrict such a wealth of interconnected realities to the narrow confines prescribed by Aristotle and Batteux <Lg/117>.[7]

It is, however, not so much the bulk of my play as its content that banishes it from the stage. It is necessary that several characters appear, who offend the more delicate feelings of virtue and outrage our sense of decency. Every painter of human nature is faced with this necessity if he wants to produce a realistic portrait rather than a more easily digested outline or abstraction. It is the way of the world that the good should be shadowed by the bad and virtue receive its most vibrant coloring in contrast with vice. Whoever proposes to defeat vice and to vindicate religion, morality, and social order must expose vice in all its naked horror and place it before the eyes of humanity in its colossal magnitude. He must directly explore its dark labyrinths, and he must know how to penetrate feelings so perverted that his own soul rebels.

The innermost workings of vice are exhibited here. . . . I believe I have captured nature. . . . But if I am to portray human beings authentically, I must also include their good qualities, of which even the most wicked are never entirely destitute. If I want to warn against the tiger, I must, in order that he be recognized, not neglect his dazzling, beautifully marked coat. Moreover, a completely evil person is an entirely inappropriate subject for art, and would repulse the reader rather than rivet his attention. . . .

And this is why I would be ill advised to attempt my play on the stage. It takes a certain strength of mind on the part of the poet not to *adorn* vice, and on the part of the reader not to be seduced by attractive features into admiring what is fundamentally repugnant. Whether I have succeeded, I leave to others to judge, but the success of my readers is not at all assured. The vulgar – a term by no means synonymous with the poor – the vulgar are firmly rooted, and unfortunately set the fashion. Too myopic to grasp my full meaning, too narrow-minded to appreciate the scope of my vision, too petty to want to know the good I intend, they will, I fear, almost thwart my efforts, will perhaps misinterpret my play as an apology for the vice I am actually undermining, and make the poor poet, to whom everything except justice is given, pay for their simple-mindedness. . . .

"The Stage Considered as a Moral Institution"[8]

The stage came into being, according to Sulzer,[9] as the result of a general, irresistible longing for the new and extraordinary, a desire for passionate

---

[7] It was not until 1797 that Schiller, together with Goethe, actually began to study and appreciate Aristotle's *Poetics*.

[8] "Die Schaubühne als eine moralische Anstalt betrachtet," written in 1784, revised for publication in 1785 and 1802. Newly translated from Schiller/Perfahl 1968, v:92–101.

[9] Johann Georg Sulzer (1720–79) was well known for his writings on aesthetics. He was particularly concerned with the relation between the beauty necessary to art and art's educational value.

experience. Exhausted by the strenuous efforts of the mind, wearied by the monotonous, often depressing requirements of work, and satiated with sensuality, man felt a fundamental emptiness, which was at odds with his endless desire for activity <Hm/89>. Human nature, equally incapable of remaining in an animal state or of persisting in a state of refined intellectual work, demanded a middle condition, which would reconcile the two contradictory extremes, ease the severe tension into a gentle harmony, and facilitate the mutual transition from one state to the other. In general this is the province of the aesthetic sense, the sense of the beautiful. But since it must be the priority of a wise legislator, faced with two possible effects, to choose the higher, he will not be satisfied merely to have disarmed the impulses of his people; he will also, if at all possible, use these inclinations as instruments of a higher purpose and endeavor to transform them into sources of happiness. That is why he chose the stage, which opens up an endless sphere to the spirit thirsting for action, nourishes but does not strain our faculties, and combines the instruction of heart and mind with the noblest entertainment.

Whoever first observed that *religion* is the strongest pillar of the state – that without it the law itself loses its force – has, perhaps, unwittingly provided the stage with its noblest defense. This very inadequacy, the shaky foundation of political rule, which renders religion indispensable to the state, also determines the moral influence of the stage. To expand on the above observation, one might say that laws revolve around negative responsibilities, whereas religion extends its demands to actual behavior. Laws only inhibit actions that would effectively destroy society, whereas religion prescribes those which hold it together. Laws rule only manifest expressions of the will – only deeds are subject to them – whereas religion extends its jurisdiction to the hidden reaches of the soul and follows thought to its deepest source. Laws are flexible, as changeable as mood and passion, whereas religion binds forever. However, even if we were to assume something that is no longer the case, that religion has great power over every human heart, will it, or can it perfect human culture? Religion (I separate here its political side from its divine aspect) acts primarily on the senses, and it is perhaps by means of the sensuous alone that it exerts its influence. If we take this away, religion loses its power – and by what means does the stage produce its effect? To the majority of people there is nothing left of religion if we eradicate its images, its problems, if we destroy its pictures of heaven and hell – and yet they are only products of the imagination, insoluble riddles, frightening visions, and allurements from afar. How religion and law are strengthened when they enter into an alliance with the stage, where there is spectacle and living presence; where vice and virtue, happiness and misery, folly and wisdom pass before us in a thousand pictures, luminous and truthful; where Providence solves its riddles before our eyes; where the human heart confesses its faintest stirrings on the rack of passion, all masks are dropped, all adornment vanishes, and the truth sits in judgment, incorruptible as Rhadaman-thus.[10]

The jurisdiction of the stage begins where that of the law ends <Lg/110–11>. When justice is blinded by gold and revels in the wages of sin, when the crimes of the mighty mock its impotence and human fear ties the hands of authority, the stage takes up the sword and scales and drags vice before a terrible seat of judgment. The whole realm of the imagination and of history, of past and future, is at its command. Bold criminals, who have long since moldered in the grave, are summoned by the all-powerful call of poetry to reenact their shameful lives for the instruction of a horrified posterity. Impotent, like shadows in a concave mirror, they reproduce the terrors of their century before our eyes, and, in an ecstatic state of horror, we curse their memory. When morality is no longer taught, religion no longer finds adherents, and law no longer avails, we will still shudder at the sight of Medea as she staggers down the palace steps, the murder of her children accomplished. When Lady Macbeth, in a frightful somnambulistic trance, washes her hands and calls upon all the perfumes of Arabia to eradicate the repellent stench of murder, humanity will be seized with a wholesome sense of horror, and every spectator will silently rejoice in his own good conscience. Just as visual representation has a more powerful effect than the dead letter of narrative <Gt/145>, so the stage exercises a more profound and lasting influence than laws or morality.

Here, however, the stage is only *supporting* our laws – a still wider field is open to it. It punishes a thousand vices tolerated by our system of justice, and it encourages a thousand virtues about which the latter has nothing to say. Here the stage joins wisdom and religion. It creates its teachings and examples from these pure sources, and clothes stern duty in a charming and alluring garment. What magnificent feelings, resolutions, passions well up in our souls, what divine ideals present themselves for our emu-lation! When Augustus graciously extends his hand to the traitor Cinna,[11] who is prepared to hear the death sentence, and with godlike magnanimity says, "Let us be friends, Cinna!" – who among us at that moment would not gladly clasp the hand of his mortal enemy, in emulation of the divine Roman? When Franz von Sickingen, on his campaign against a prince and for alien rights, looks back and suddenly sees smoke rising from the castle where his wife and children have been left behind, and he continues on his way, a man of his word – how great human beings appear to me, how small and contemptible the dread power of fate![12]

---

[10] In Greek mythology a judge of the dead.
[11] In Corneille's *Cinna*.
[12] Schiller alludes to an anonymous play about the early sixteenth-century baron and fighter for justice, Franz von Sickingen. Von Sickingen is a character in Goethe's *Götz von*

In the mirror of the stage, the reflection of vice is as repellent as that of virtue is attractive. When the helpless, childlike Lear vainly appeals to his daughters for shelter; when, tearing his white hair in the tempestuous winds, he tells the raging elements of his unnatural offspring; when finally his fury and pain issue in the cry, "I gave you all!" – how abominable ingratitude appears to us! How highly we value respect and filial love!

But the sphere of influence of the stage extends still farther. The stage is active even in those areas of human culture which religion and law consider beneath their dignity. The happiness of society is disturbed as much by folly as by crime and vice. Experience teaches that in the web of human things, the heaviest weights are often suspended by the finest, most delicate threads; and, when we trace actions to their source, we are forced to smile ten times before being horrified even once. My register of criminals becomes shorter with each passing day, while my catalogue of fools increases in size. If the entire moral guilt of one class of people springs from one and the same source, if all the monstrous extremes of vice are merely altered forms, higher degrees of a quality that we ultimately regard with smiles and sympathy, why should nature not have followed the same course in the other class? I know of *one* way to preserve a human being from depravity, and that is to protect his heart from weakness.

We can expect the stage to be very effective at this. It holds the mirror up to the great class of fools and shames the manifold forms of their folly with wholesome ridicule. What we have described it as achieving by means of terror and emotion it achieves here (more quickly, perhaps, and infallibly) through satire and wit. If we were to compare comedy and tragedy with regard to their effectiveness, experience would probably decide in favor of the former. Ridicule wounds human pride to a greater degree than abhorrence tortures our conscience. Our cowardice retreats from what is terrifying, but this very cowardice exposes us to the sting of satire. Law and conscience often protect us from crime and vice – the ludicrous demands a peculiar sensitivity, which we exercise nowhere more than in the theatre. We may allow a friend to attack our morals and our beliefs, but it is difficult to forgive him a single laugh at our expense. Our offenses may tolerate an overseer and judge, our bad habits hardly a witness. The stage alone can laugh at our weaknesses, because it spares our sensitive feelings and preserves the guilty fool's anonymity. Without blushing, in its mirror we see our masks drop and are secretly grateful for the gentle warning.

But its vast sphere of influence extends even farther. The stage, more than any other public institution, is a school of practical wisdom, a guide through civil life, an infallible key to the most secret passages of the human soul. I admit that egotism and a lack of conscience often combine to negate

Berlichingen (1773) and would become the hero of a number of plays written long after Schiller's essay.

its effect, that a thousand vices still assert themselves, a thousand good feelings fail to take root in the cold heart of the spectator. I myself am of the opinion that Molière's Harpagon has possibly never reformed a single usurer, that the suicide of Beverley has not kept any of his brothers from a terrible addiction to gambling, that Karl Moor's unhappy fate as an outlaw will not make the highroads any safer[13] – but even if we allow the limits of this kind of direct effect, even if we want to be so unjust as to deny it altogether, does the stage not still exert an immense influence? If it fails to wipe out or even diminish the sum total of vice in the world, has it not acquainted us with the same? We have to live with these villains and fools, and we must either avoid them or confront them, defeat them or be ourselves defeated. But now they no longer surprise us. We are prepared for their assaults. The stage has given away the secret of finding them out and rendering them harmless. It has stripped the mask from the hypocrite's face and uncovered the net in which cunning and intrigue have entangled us. It has dragged deceit and falsehood from their subterranean labyrinths and exposed their horrible features to the light of day. The dying Sara[14] may not trouble a single debauchee, all the pictures of seduction avenged may not extinguish his ardor, and the artful actress may even try to prevent this effect – yet happily enough the unsuspecting innocent is now acquainted with the snares of the seducer; the stage has taught her to mistrust his promises and to beware his adoration.

The stage increases our awareness not only of human character, but also of fate, and it teaches us the great art of bearing our lot. In the web of life *chance* and *design* play an equally great role. The latter we can direct, but we must blindly submit to the former. It is enough if inevitable disasters do not find us completely resourceless, if our courage and intelligence have already been exercised in similar circumstances, and our hearts have been steeled for the blow. The stage presents us with many diverse scenes of human affliction. It involves us artificially in the distress of others, and rewards our momentary suffering with ecstatic tears and a marvellous increase of courage and experience <Hm/91>. Thus we join the abandoned Ariadne on Naxos, enter Ugolino's tower of starvation <Sd/252>,[15] ascend the appalling scaffold, and attend the solemn hour of death. Things of which we had only a faint idea we hear loudly and unequivocally confirmed by nature. In the Tower, the deceived favorite is abandoned by the queen. Now that he is to die, the frightened Moor finds that his

---

[13] The allusions are to: *The Miser* (1668) by Molière; *The Gamester* (1753) by Edward Moore (brought to the Hamburg theatre by Friedrich Ludwig Schröder); and Schiller's *The Robbers*.

[14] In Lessing's *Miss Sara Sampson*.

[15] Betrayed by a fellow conspirator in thirteenth-century Pisa, Ugolino was thrown into prison with his sons and grandsons and left to starve. He tells his story in Canto 33 of Dante's *Inferno*, but the allusion here is to Heinrich Wilhelm von Gerstenberg's drama *Ugolino* (1768).

treacherous sophistry deserts him.[16] Eternity releases the dead to reveal secrets that the living cannot know, and the confident villain loses his last ghastly refuge when even the tomb condemns him.

But beyond acquainting us with the destinies of humankind, the stage teaches us to be more just to the unfortunate, to judge them more leniently, for only when we can measure the depth of their suffering are we in a position to pass judgment on them. No crime is more shameful than that of a thief – but do we not all shed a tear of sympathy for Eduard Ruhberg, even as we condemn him, when we understand what drives him to commit the deed? Suicide is generally regarded with abhorrence; but when Mariane, oppressed by love, by the threats of an enraged father, and by the dreadful prospect of the convent walls, drinks the poison, who among us would rise to condemn her?[17] Humanity and tolerance are becoming the spirit of the age; their rays have penetrated to our courts of justice and even to the hearts of our princes. How great a share in this divine work belongs to our theatres? Have *they* not been responsible for acquainting man with man and uncovering the secret motives of his behavior?

One particular class of people has more cause than any other to be grateful to the stage. Only in the theatre do the great of the world hear what they seldom or never hear – truth; and what they seldom or never see, they see here – a human being.

The better drama has contributed greatly not just to our moral development, but to our whole intellectual enlightenment as well. In this higher sphere, the great mind, the ardent patriot, knows how to exploit the stage fully.

Scanning the human race, comparing different peoples and different centuries, he discovers how the great majority of people remain enslaved by prejudice and opinion, which forever work against their own happiness – and the purer rays of truth illuminate only the *individual* few, who perhaps bought this dividend at the price of lifelong effort. By what means can the wise legislator enable the whole nation to share in this enlightenment?

The stage is the common channel through which the light of wisdom streams down from the exceptional, thinking segment of the population; and from there it diffuses in milder rays through the entire state. More correct notions, clarified principles, purer feelings flow from here through the veins of the people; the darkness of barbarism and superstition vanishes; night gives way to the triumphant dawn. Among the many magni-

---

[16] Franz Moor, in *The Robbers*.

[17] The allusions are to *Ambition turns to Crime* (*Das Verbrechen aus Ehrsucht*) (1784) by August Wilhelm Iffland (1759–1814) and to *Mariane* (1776), an adaptation of Jean-François de la Harpe's play by Friedrich Wilhelm Gotter (1746–97). Iffland was the author of many plays, a director who conceived elaborate *mises en scènes*, and an actor noted for his realism. He created the role of Franz Moor in *The Robbers*.

ficent fruits of the better drama, I would like to single out two. How widespread has religious tolerance become in recent years! Even before Nathan the Jew and Saladin the Saracen made us feel ashamed with their preaching of the divine lesson that devotion to God remains independent of our misconceptions of Him, and before Joseph II fought the dreadful hydra of pious hatred, the stage had sown seeds of humanity and gentleness in our hearts; repugnant images of religious fanaticism taught us to avoid such hatred, and, seeing itself in this frightful mirror, Christianity washed its stains away.[18] Errors in *education* might be combated just as successfully, but we are still waiting for the play that will treat this particular theme. Because of its consequences, education is a matter of supreme importance to the state, and yet there is no matter left more unreservedly in the hands of a thoughtless citizenry, no affair more at the mercy of private whims and caprice. If the stage were to present us with unsettling pictures of unfortunate victims of a poor upbringing, our fathers might be moved to renounce inflexible maxims, and our mothers might learn to love more wisely. False notions lead the most sincere educators astray; it is even worse when they pride themselves on *method* and systematically destroy the tender shoots in hothouses.

The stage could also be used – if only the heads and guardians of the state understood how – to correct public opinion on various matters of government. Those with legislative power could speak indirectly to the citizenry, justify their actions even before complaints were uttered, and silence doubts without appearing to do so. The stage could and would even inspire industry and inventiveness, if poets thought it worthwhile to be patriotic and the state would condescend to hear them.

I cannot possibly fail to mention the great influence that a good, permanent theatre would exercise on the spirit of a nation. By national spirit I mean common opinions and tendencies, which differ from those found in other nations. Only the stage is able to bring about a high degree of concurrence, because it explores the whole field of human knowledge, exhausts all situations of life, and illuminates every corner of the human heart; because it unites people from all walks of life and clears the most accessible path to heart and mind. If *one* dominant feature characterized all of our plays, if our poets were to agree and establish a firm alliance to achieve this aim – if strict selection governed their work, and they dedicated their art to national subjects – in other words, if we had a national theatre, we would also be a nation. What bound the Greeks so firmly together? What drew the people so irresistibly to the stage? Nothing other than the patriotic content of the plays, the Greek spirit that breathed in them, the great, overwhelming interest in the republic and in the development of humanity.

---

[18] The allusions are to Lessing's *Nathan the Wise* and to the Edict of Toleration, by which Joseph II established religious equality before the law.

The stage has yet another merit – a merit that I mention all the more happily now, because I suspect the case against its detractors has been won. In doubt was the substantial influence of the stage on morals and enlightenment – but even enemies of the theatre have confessed that it is to be preferred to all other means of social indulgence and amusement. But what it achieves here is more important than people are accustomed to believe.

Human nature cannot bear the continuous, unrelenting pressure of business; and the appeal of sensual delight dies with gratification. Human beings, satiated with carnal pleasures, weary of long exertion, tormented by an endless desire for activity, thirst for superior, more refined amusement, or else dissipate their energies in ways which hasten their ruin and destroy the peace of society. Bacchanalian joys, ruinous gambling, a thousand mad diversions hatched by idleness are inevitable when the legislator does not know how to guide these tendencies in his people. The man concerned with public affairs, after a life of magnanimous sacrifice to the state, is in danger of becoming miserable and obsessive – the scholar of degenerating into a dull pedant – the common people of turning into a brutish mob. The stage is an institution where pleasure is combined with instruction, relaxation with exertion, entertainment with culture; where no single faculty is strained and no single pleasure is enjoyed at the expense of the whole. When grief gnaws at the heart, when melancholy poisons our solitary hours, when the business of the world disgusts us and a thousand cares oppress us, we dream away the real world in the artificial world of the theatre – we find ourselves again, our feeling revives, wholesome passions awaken our slumbering nature and blood flows in our veins once more. Unfortunate souls come to terms with their grief in weeping over another's misfortune, while the well-off become heedful, and the secure are made provident. The sensitive weakling toughens himself; the unfeeling brute begins for the first time to experience emotion. And then finally – what a triumph for you, oh nature! – so often trampled, just as often risen again! – when men and women from all walks of life, every shackle of affectation and fashion thrown off, torn away from every pressure of fate, united in a *single*, all-embracing sympathy, become *one* again, forget themselves and their world, and approach their divine origin. Each enjoys the raptures of all, cast back, intensified, and enlivened, from a hundred faces, and in each breast there is room for only a *single* emotion – that one is a *human being*.

From the Prologue to *Wallenstein*[19]

... swiftly flits the actor's wondrous art
Before our senses, leaving not a trace,
While mark of sculptor's chisel and the song
Of poets live a thousand years and more.
Here, when the artist dies, his spell dies with him,
And as the echoes fade within our ear,
The moment's swift creation is dissolved,
No lasting monument preserves its fame.
That art is hard, inconstant its reward,
The future winds no garlands for the actor;
So he must seize the present greedily,
Fulfil the moment that is his alone,
Win recognition from the world he lives in,
And in the best and noblest minds erect
Himself a living monument, that here
And now he may enjoy his fame immortal.
For he who satisfies the best of his
Own age, has lived for every age to come.

The fresh, new dawn Thalia's art begins
Upon this stage today, has also made
The poet bold to leave well-trodden paths,
And carry you beyond the confines of
Domestic life, on to a wider stage,
That will not be unworthy of the high,
Momentous times in which we live and strive.
Only an object of sublimity
Can stir the deepest depths within man's soul;
In narrow confines men grow narrow too,
But greater when their goals are higher set.
And as our century so gravely ends,
When truth, it seems, would take the shape of art,
When we behold a struggle of great natures
For a momentous goal before our eyes,
And for those objects men hold most sublime
They fight, for power and for liberty –
So art upon its shadow-stage as well
May strive for higher flights, indeed it must,
Or yield in shame before the stage of life.

... forgive the poet, if he does
Not sweep you all at once with rapid stride
To the catastrophe, but only brings
A row of captive scenes before your eyes,
In which those great events unfold themselves.
So let our play today win back again

---

[19] Spoken on the occasion of the reopening of the Weimar theatre in October 1798. The translation is from Schiller/Lamport 1979, 166–69.

Your ears and hearts to unaccustomed tones;
Let it transport you to that time of old,
On to that unfamiliar stage of war
Which soon our hero with his mighty deeds
Will fill.
         And if today the gentle muse,
The goddess of the dance and melody,
Should with due modesty insist upon
Her ancient native right, the play of rhyme,
Then do not scold her, but be thankful rather
That she should thus transform the somber hues
Of truth into the realm of art serene,
Create illusion, then in honesty
Reveal the trick she plays, and not pretend
That what she brings us is the stuff of truth.
Life is in earnest, art serene and free.

"On the Use of the Chorus in Tragedy"[20]

A poetic work must justify itself, and where facts do not speak, words will not be of much help. One might, therefore, leave it to the chorus to be its own advocate, if ever it were itself properly presented. But the work of tragic poetry becomes a whole only through theatrical performance: the poet simply supplies the words, which music and dance then bring to life. As long as the chorus lacks such sensuously powerful accompaniment, it will seem extraneous in the economy of the tragedy – a foreign body, an alien presence, which only interrupts the course of the action, destroys the illusion, and leaves the spectator cold. To do justice to the chorus, we must move from the actual stage to a *possible* one, a necessary move whenever one aims at something higher. What art does not yet have, it must acquire, and an incidental lack of resources ought not to limit the poet's creative imagination. He sets as his goal whatever is most worthy; he strives for an ideal; in practice art can accommodate itself to circumstances.

The common assertion that the public debases art is not true; the artist debases the public, and, historically, whenever art has declined, the artists have been responsible. The public needs nothing but receptivity, and this it has. People come to the theatre with an uncertain desire, with a multifarious capacity. They bring with them an ability to grasp the highest things, and they take pleasure in what is intelligent and true, but once they have begun to content themselves with something inferior, they will certainly cease to demand excellence.

One hears the objection that the poet may work according to an ideal,

[20] "Über den Gebrauch des Chors in der Tragödie" (1803). Newly translated from Schiller/ Perfahl 1968, II:245–53.

the critic may judge according to ideas, but in practice art is subject to contingencies and limitations; it rests upon needs. The manager wants to remain solvent, the actor wants to be seen, the spectator wants to be entertained. People seek pleasure, and are dissatisfied if some effort is required of them, when they are expecting amusement and relaxation.

However, in treating the theatre more seriously, we do not want to do away with the spectator's pleasure, but rather ennoble it. Theatre is to remain a diversion, but a poetic one. All art is dedicated to joy, and there is no higher, no more serious purpose than to make people happy. True art is that which provides the greatest pleasure – and the greatest pleasure is freedom of the spirit in the vital play of all its powers.

Everyone expects from the imaginative arts a certain liberation from the constraints of actuality; we want to give free rein to the imagination and delight in the possible. Even a person with the lowest expectations still wants to forget his everyday business, his ordinary life, his individual self; he wants to feel himself in extraordinary situations, to revel in the strangest workings of chance, and, if he is of a more serious nature, to discover on the stage the moral order that he finds lacking in real life. But he knows perfectly well that it is only an idle diversion, that he is feeding on dreams, and that when he returns from the theatre to the real world, it will press him once more with all its constricting force; he will be its victim as before, for it has remained what it was, and nothing in him has been changed. Nothing, therefore, has been gained beyond a pleasing momentary illusion, which vanishes upon his awakening.

And precisely because only a fleeting illusion is the object here, all that is necessary is a mere appearance of truth or the ever popular verisimilitude, so readily substituted for truth < 1:In/8–9>.

However, true art does not have as its object a mere passing diversion; its serious purpose is not to give us simply a momentary dream of freedom, but to *make* us actually free. It accomplishes this by awakening and developing a power within us to remove to an objective distance the sensuous world, which otherwise is only raw matter that burdens us or a blind force that oppresses us, to transform it into the free work of the spirit, to control materiality by means of ideas <In/13>.

And precisely because true art aims at something real and objective, it cannot be satisfied with the mere appearance of truth; it establishes its ideal structure upon truth itself, upon the deep and firm foundation of nature.

How art can be at once wholly ideal and yet in the deepest sense real – how it can entirely abandon actuality and yet accord exactly with nature – this is what few people grasp, this is what makes the common view of poetic and plastic works so distorted, because the two demands seem to be mutually exclusive.

Usually the attempt is made to achieve the one by sacrificing the other, and in this way both are missed. He whom nature has given discernment and depth of feeling, but denied creative imagination, will be a faithful painter of actuality; he will grasp casual appearances, but never the spirit of nature. He will reproduce the matter of the world, but it will not be our work, not the free product of our creative spirit, and therefore it cannot have the salutary effect of art, which consists in freedom. Serious, indeed, but joyless is the mood with which such an artist or poet leaves us, and we see ourselves painfully thrust back into the narrow sphere of common reality by the very art which should have freed us. On the other hand, he who is endowed with a lively imagination but lacks soul and character will not concern himself with truth; he will only play with the stuff of the world, seek to surprise us with fantastic and bizarre combinations, and as his whole enterprise is nothing but smoke and mirrors, he will certainly provide a moment's entertainment, but he will not establish or develop anything in our souls. His playfulness, like the seriousness of the other, is not poetic. To string together fantastic images in an arbitrary way is not to venture into the ideal, and to reproduce actuality in mimetic fashion is not to portray nature. Both demands stand so little in contradiction to each other that in fact they come to one and the same thing; art is only true if it wholly abandons actuality and becomes purely ideal. Nature itself is only an idea of the spirit, which never falls within reach of the senses <In/14>. It is veiled by appearances, but it itself never appears. Only to the art of the ideal is it given to grasp this spirit of the all and bind it in corporeal form. Art itself cannot present it to the senses, but it can, through its creative power, bring it before the imagination, and thereby be truer than all actuality and more real than all experience. It follows that the artist cannot use a single element of actuality as he finds it; his work must be ideal in *all* its parts if it is to have an integral reality and accord with nature.

What holds true for poetry and art as a whole is also valid for all their genres, and the above discussion may easily be applied to tragedy. Here too one must contend with the common conception of the *natural*, which is antithetic to all poetry and art. We allow a certain ideality in visual art – more because of convention than conviction – but from poetry, and from dramatic poetry in particular, we demand *illusion*, which, even if it really were possible to achieve, would always remain a pitiful deception. All the externals of a dramatic performance run counter to this conception – everything is only a symbol of the actual. Day itself in the theatre is only an artificial day, architecture is only symbolic architecture, metrical speech itself is ideal; yet the action is suddenly supposed to be real, and the part overwhelm the whole. Thus the French, who completely misunderstood the spirit of the ancients, introduced upon the stage the unities of time and place in the most vulgar empirical sense, as if it were a question here of any place other than a purely ideal space and a time other than simply the continuous unfolding of the action.

With the introduction of metrical speech, we have made an important step toward poetic tragedy <In/15>. Several lyrical attempts have been successfully realized on the stage, and poetry, by means of its own vital power, has won individual victories over prevailing prejudice. However, little is gained unless mistaken opinion as a whole is conquered, and it is not enough simply to tolerate as poetic license what is in fact the essence of all poetry. The introduction of the chorus would be the final, the decisive step – and if it served only to declare war openly and honestly on naturalism in art, it would be for us a living wall which tragedy draws about itself, in order to cut itself off entirely from the real world and preserve for itself its ideal ground, its poetic freedom.

Greek tragedy, as is well known, arose from the chorus. Even though historically it gradually became separate, one can still locate its poetic and its spiritual origins in the chorus, and without those persistent witnesses and bearers of the action, it would have developed into an altogether different sort of poetry. The abolition of the chorus and the shrinking of this sensuously powerful organ into the insipid and tiresomely recurrent figure of the confidant was, then, not as great an improvement of tragedy as the French and their imitators imagined.

Ancient tragedy, which originally concerned itself only with gods, heroes, and kings, used the chorus as an essential accompaniment, found in nature, and therefore employed. The actions and fates of heroes and kings, inherently public, were entirely so in antiquity. Consequently the chorus in ancient tragedy was more of a natural organ, consistent with the poetic shape of real life. In modern tragedy it becomes an artificial organ, which helps to *bring forth* poetry. Since the modern poet no longer finds the chorus in nature, he must create and introduce it poetically; that is, he must adapt the story he is treating in such a way that it is transposed back into that early age and that simple form of life.

Thus the chorus is of far more essential service to the modern tragedian than to the ancient poet, precisely because it transforms the ordinary modern world into the ancient poetic one; it renders useless to him everything that conflicts with poetry and impels him to take up the simplest, most original, and most naive themes. The palace of the kings is now closed; the courts of justice, formerly at the city gates, have moved indoors; writing has displaced the living word; the people itself, the sensuously vital collectivity, has, except when it operates as brute force, become the state, that is an abstract concept; and the gods have returned to the hearts of men. The poet must reopen the palaces; he must lead the courts of justice out under open skies; he must reestablish the gods; he must restore all immediacy, abolished by the artificial arrangement of real life, and cast off all artificial contrivances *in* and *around* human beings, which hinder the manifestation of our inner nature and our original character, just as the sculptor throws off modern garments and admits nothing of external circumstances except that which makes visible the highest of forms, the human.

But just as the visual artist drapes ample garments about his figures in order to fill out the spaces of his painting richly and gracefully, harmonize its separate parts, give scope to color which charms and refreshes the eye, and at once veil human form and make it visible, so the tragic poet interweaves and surrounds his strictly delimited action and the definite contours of his characters with a tissue of lyrical splendor in which, as in flowing robes of purple, the characters move freely and nobly, with a confident dignity and lofty serenity.

In a higher organization, substances or elementary forms of matter must no longer be visible; the pigment disappears in the delicate flesh color of the living subject. But even the elemental has its splendor, and can be taken up, as such, in an artistic body. But then it must earn its place by life and fullness and harmony, and confirm the forms that it surrounds, rather than crush them with its weight.

In works of visual art this is readily comprehensible, but the same thing holds true for poetry, and for tragic poetry as well, which is our subject here. Everything that the mind expresses in general is precisely like that which simply charms the senses – mere substance or raw material in a poetic work – and where it predominates, it will inevitably destroy the poetic, which is situated just at the point where the ideal and the sensuous cannot be differentiated. Now human beings are so constituted that we always want to move from the particular to the general, and so reflection must also have its place in tragedy. But if reflection is to deserve this place, it must regain through performance what it lacks in sensuous life, for if the two elements of poetry, the ideal and the sensuous, are not working in intimate *union*, then they must operate *side by side*, or poetry is defeated. If there is not a perfect balance, equilibrium can be restored only through an *adjustment* of both scales.

This is what the chorus does in tragedy. The chorus is itself a general concept rather than an individual, but this concept is represented by a sensuously powerful collective body, which makes an impression on the senses by means of its expansive presence <Sl/201>. The chorus abandons the narrow sphere of the action, in order to explore past and future, distant times and peoples, and humanity in general, to draw the great conclusions of life, and to pronounce the teachings of wisdom. But it does this with the full power of the imagination, with a bold lyrical freedom, which moves as with godlike steps about the high peaks of human experience – and it is accompanied by the entire sensuous power of rhythm and music in tones and gestures.

Thus the chorus *purifies* the tragic poem by separating reflection from the action, and thereby arming reflection itself with poetic power; just as the visual artist, by means of a rich drapery, transforms the ordinary need for clothing into a source of charm and beauty. But just as the painter finds himself compelled to intensify the color of the living subject, in order to counterbalance the power of elemental substances, so the lyrical speech of the chorus obliges the poet to elevate proportionally the entire language of the poem and thereby intensify the sensuous power of expression in general. Only the chorus gives the tragic poet grounds for this elevation of tone which fills the ear, enlarges the spirit, and expands the entire soul. This one giant form in his picture obliges him to put all his figures upon the cothurnus and thereby endow his painting with tragic grandeur. If one were to remove the chorus, the language of tragedy as a whole would deteriorate, or what is now great and powerful would appear forced and strained. The ancient chorus introduced into French tragedy would expose it in all its poverty and destroy it, while the same thing would doubtless reveal the true significance of Shakespearean tragedy.

Just as the chorus brings *life* to language, so it brings *repose* to the action – but the beautiful and lofty repose which is characteristic of a noble work of art. For the soul of the spectator must also retain its freedom in the midst of the most intense passion; it must not be the victim of impressions, but always detach itself clearly and serenely from the emotions that it suffers. Common criticism of the chorus, that it destroys the illusion and breaks the hold of the emotions, actually serves as its highest recommendation, for it is precisely such blind affective power that the true artist avoids; he scorns the creation of this kind of illusion. If the blows which tragedy inflicts upon our hearts were to follow one upon the other without interruption, passion would triumph over activity. We would involve ourselves confusedly with the subject matter and no longer remain above it. By keeping the different parts separate and interposing itself between displays of passion with its calming perspective, the chorus restores our freedom, which would other-wise be lost in the storm of emotion. Even the characters in tragedy have need of this respite, this repose, in order to collect themselves; for they are not actual beings, who merely represent individuals obeying the impulse of the moment, but ideal persons and representatives of a collectivity, who express the depth of humanity. The presence of the chorus, which, as a judging witness, hears them and subdues the first outbursts of their passion by its intervention, accounts for the equanimity with which they act and the dignity with which they speak. They stand as it were on a natural stage because they speak and act before onlookers, but precisely because of this they come to speak all the more appropriately to an audience in the theatre.

Such is my justification for bringing the ancient chorus back onto the tragic stage. Choruses are, to be sure, not unknown in modern tragedy, but the chorus of Greek tragedy, as I have understood it here – the chorus as a single ideal person, who bears and accompanies the entire action – is essentially different from those operatic choruses, and when I occasionally hear people speak, in relation to Greek tragedy, not of a chorus but of *choruses*, I suspect them of not really knowing what they are talking about. To the best of my knowledge, the chorus of ancient tragedy has never reappeared on the stage since its decline.

I have divided the chorus into two parts[21] and portrayed it in conflict with itself <Hg/210>; but this is the case only when it acts as an actual person or as a blind mob. As *chorus* and as ideal person it is always one with itself. The locale changes, and I have the chorus leave the stage several times, but Aeschylus, the creator of tragedy, and Sophocles, the greatest master of the art, also took such liberties.

Another liberty that I have allowed myself may prove more difficult to justify. I have intermingled Christianity and Greek mythology, and have even called to mind Moorish superstition. But the scene of the action is Messina, where these three religions continued both to have an effect on life and, partly through their various monuments, to speak to the senses. And I consider it a prerogative of poetry to treat different religions as a collective whole, in which everything that bears a particular character or expresses a particular way of feeling has its place. Beneath the exterior of all religions lies religion itself, the idea of a divine power, and the poet must be allowed to express this in whatever form he finds most appropriate.

---

[21] Schiller is now speaking of his practice in *The Bride of Messina*, where he uses two "semichoruses," each consisting of the retinue of one of the brothers in the play.

15

DECREES AND
DOCUMENTS OF THE
FRENCH REVOLUTION
(1789–94)

During the French Revolution, from 1789 to 1799, strenuous attempts were made to exercise official control over drama, music, graphic arts, sculpture, architecture, and urban planning. In keeping with a policy that redefined all public activity as acts of citizenship in the new republic, successive governments and their agencies[1] issued a series of decrees, which sought to regulate such activities. The Declaration of the Rights of Man and the Citizen (1798) distinguished the rights of an individual from civic welfare, and this attempt to balance personal freedom and the national good became the ideological basis for official policy on theatre. The first major references to theatre during the Revolution occur in a debate about the admissibility of actors and non-Catholics to citizenship,[2] and in the decree of the National Assembly outlining the powers of the municipal authorities for the maintenance of order at public gatherings.[3] The concept of citizenship and the exercise of municipal control underlie all subsequent legislation, including the series of decrees issued between 1789 and 1794,[4] which constitute the most aggressive attempts by government to commission theatre as an instrument of national culture.

The decrees which had the most far-reaching effect on theatrical repertoire were those of 13 January 1791 and 2 August 1793, since they specifically addressed the question of what kind of theatre would be appropriate for the Republic. They demonstrate the National Assembly's determination to break with the model of a theatre of privilege, as established by the old regime, notably in its creation of the Comédie-Française as a national theatre. The government sought to develop democratic forms of theatre, for which ancient Greece was often invoked for performance models and French neo-classical practice for dramaturgical ones.

The decrees of 1791 and 1793 abolished the restrictions linking genre and venue, so that every theatre was allowed to negotiate its own program, but the government made clear its preference for neo-classical tragedy, based on the lives of civic heroes of Greece and Rome – images of virtue for the citizens of the new republic – and provided production subsidies for tragedy, not comedy. (The highly

---

[1] Decrees were issued by the National Assembly, the National Convention, and the Directory as well as by the Commune of Paris and the Committees of Public Safety and of Public Instruction.
[2] 24 December 1789 (*Archives Parlementaires*, x:754–82).
[3] 16 August 1790 (*Archives Parlementaires*, xviii:109).
[4] Although decrees were issued until the end of the Revolution, in 1799, those after January 1796 concentrated primarily on ensuring the rights of the poor to access to the theatres.

topical sensational drama, exploiting the current events of the Revolution, and comedies of the boulevard stage were ignored in the decrees.)

Official intervention was thus a general endorsement of a programming policy not inconsistent with the productions of the former Comédie-Française, before its monopoly was broken, but with a special emphasis on the dramatization of civic responsibility and with a renewed emphasis on the theatre's potential influence on good spoken French, which verse drama was thought to encourage. The decrees of the Revolution, that is to say, were concerned with the production of ideal moral and linguistic models rather than with direct representations of the Republic.

For further reading

Carlson 1966; Lunel 1910; Moland 1877; Ozouf 1988; Pougin 1902; Rodmell 1990; Root-Bernstein [1981] 1984; Welschinger 1880.

Decree of 13 January 1791[5]

Upon the report of the Committee of the Constitution, the National Assembly passed the following decree:

Article 1:   Any citizen may establish a public theatre and put on plays of all genres, upon making a declaration of intent to the municipality where the theatre is to be located.

Article 2:   The works of authors who have been dead for five years or more are in the public domain and notwithstanding all the old privileges, which have been abolished, may be played in all the theatres without restrictions.

Article 3:   The works of live authors cannot be played in any public theatre anywhere in France, without the formal, written consent of the authors, on pain of the confiscation of the proceeds for the benefit of the authors.

Article 4:   The arrangements of article 3 apply to works already presented, regardless of any previous arrangements; an exception will be made for the arrangements which have already been made between actors and live authors, or those who died less that five years ago.

Article 5:   The heirs or trustees of the authors will be the proprietors of their works, in the five years time following the death of the author.

Article 6:   The managers or members of the various theatres, by reason of their status, will be subject to inspection by the municipal authorities. They will receive orders only from the municipal officers, who will not be able to stop or forbid the mounting of a play, except on the authority of the authors and the actors, and who can only charge the actors to conform with the laws of the land, and with the regulations

---

[5] Newly translated from *Archives Parlementaires*, XXII:214.

of the police and the laws to which the Committee of the Constitution constantly turns for such instruction and guidance. . . .

Article 7: There will be a guard only outside the theatre, which the military will not be responsible for unless formally requested by the municipal authorities. There will always be one or more civilian officials in the auditorium, and the military guard will not enter the auditorium except in the case when public safety is at risk, and on the express request of the civilian official, in accordance with the laws and police regulations. All the citizens are required to obey temporarily the civilian officials.

Decree of 2 August 1793[6]

[Proposal of the Committee of Public Safety made by Georges Couthon,[7] accepted by the National Convention]

. . . You would wound – you will greatly outrage – . . . republicans, should you allow the continued performance in their presence of an infinity of plays filled with injurious allusions to liberty, and which have no other goal but to deprave the spirit and the manners of the public; if also you did not order the performance of only such plays as are worthy to be heard and applauded by republicans. . . . Since [theatres] have too often served tyranny, they must also serve liberty. I have, as a consequence, the honor of proposing the following decree:

The National Convention decrees:

Article 1: As of the 4th of this month and until the 1st of September next, republican tragedies such as *Brutus* <Vt/29>, *William Tell*, *Caius Gracchus*,[8] and such plays as recount the glorious events of the Revolution, and the virtues of the defenders of liberty, will be performed three times a week in the theatres of Paris designated by the municipality. Once a week, these plays will be performed at the expense of the Republic.

Article 2: All theatres in which are performed plays that tend to deprave the public spirit and awaken the shameful superstitions reminiscent of monarchy will be closed, and the directors arrested and

---

6 *Archives Parlementaires*, LXX:134–35.

7 Georges Couthon (1755–94), who was closely associated with Robespierre (and went to the guillotine with him), was an impassioned advocate of the people's sovereignty.

8 Voltaire's *Brutus* is about Lucius Junius Brutus, who defended Rome from the tyranny of the Tarquins and, in the course of doing so, assented to his son's death. *William Tell* (1766) by Antoine-Marin Lemierre (1723–93) and *Caius Gracchus* (1792) by Marie-Joseph Chénier (1764–1811) also have heroes of the people for protagonists. In subsequent reports on theatrical activity, *Brutus* was apparently the most popular choice of theatre directors.

punished to the full extent of the law. The municipality of Paris is charged with the execution of this present Decree.

Decree of 10 March 1794[9]

[Decree of the Committee of Public Safety outlining the conditions under which the vacant Théâtre de la Nation ought to be reopened]

The Committee of Public Safety, after consideration of the petition presented by the associated sections of Marat, Mucius-Scaevola, the Bonnet, and L'Unité decrees:

Article 1:   That the former Théâtre Français,[10] which used to be a national building be reopened without delay, that it be dedicated exclusively to performances given by and for the People at fixed times each month.

Article 2:   The exterior of the building will be decorated with the following inscription: *Théâtre du Peuple*. The interior will be decorated with all the symbols of Liberty.

The companies of artists established in various theatres of Paris will be required to give performances in turn three times every ten days,[11] according to the schedule to be drawn up by the municipality.

Article 3:   No citizen will be allowed entry into the *Théâtre du Peuple* without a pass, which will only be issued to patriots. The municipality will arrange for the issuance of such documents. . . .

Article 5:   The repertoire of the plays to be played at the *Théâtre du Peuple* will be requisitioned from each theatre in Paris and shall be submitted for approval to the Committee.

Article 6:   In the communes in which performances are given, the municipality is charged with organizing civic performances, to be given free to the people every ten days. Only patriotic plays chosen from a repertoire approved by the municipality shall be given, under the surveillance of the district, answerable to the Committee of Public Safety.

Document of 3 May 1794[12]

[Concerning the use of titles: Report of the National Agent, to the Committee of Public Safety]

---

[9]   *Recueil des Actes du Comité de Salut Public*, XI:626.
[10]   Formerly the Comédie-Française (1690–1791) and then Théâtre de la Nation. The company was arrested in September 1793 for its unpatriotic repertoire.
[11]   The Revolutionary calendar replaced the week with the "décade," a unit of ten days.
[12]   As quoted in Welschinger 1880, 149–50. Newly translated.

Citizen representatives, I hasten to urge the administration of the police, to direct the administrators Lelièvre and Faro to reconsider or at least to modify their letter to the directors of theatres regarding the expressions "Monsieur" and "Citoyen." I hardly have to remind them that, in the revival of classical plays it is necessary to allow the retention of the costumes and modes of address appropriate to the time of writing or the country where the scene is supposed to occur <Hg/209>. Doubtless, one must find it just as ridiculous to say "Citizen Cataline" as to see Jupiter or Armide decorated with a tricolor rosette. Consequently, the police administration is writing to all the directors today informing them that they can leave as they are the tragedies written before the Revolution, or those in which the events portrayed are foreign, without changing the "Monsieur" or "Seigneur" or other titles. As for the old comedies, the administrators leave it to the shrewdness and the patriotism of the directors to decide when such changes are necessary. In a word, the adminstration proposes that new plays use the words "Citizen" and "Citizeness," unless "Monsieur" and "Madame" are employed as an insult or to designate an enemy of the Revolution.

Document of 4 June 1794[13]

In the name of the Committee of Public Instruction,[14] one of its members reports on the necessity of establishing standard usage for the French language.[15]

Let us hound immorality from the stage; furthermore, let us eradicate the linguistic usage by which a line of demarcation between equal citizens is still established. Under a despot,[16] Dufresny [and] Dancourt[17] could with

---

13 *Archives Parlementaires*, XCI:318–26.
14 On 15 November 1793 the Comité d'instruction publique was instructed by the Convention to oversee and report on theatrical performances, given that their influence on public education was too great for them to be left to private interests. The Committee was to consider how they could be made to serve the national interest and contribute to liberty and happiness in the Republic (*Archives Parlementaires*, LXXIX:278).
15 The member was Henri Grégoire (1750–1831), who dedicated himself to the work of the Committee of Public Instruction. He believed that education, technological and linguistic, was a way to combat tyranny and was especially concerned with literacy and language. His report discusses the importance of promoting a standard French throughout the Republic, whereby the people would be able to understand the country's laws and be empowered to pursue such "arts" as agriculture, navigation, and mining. In the process of (re-)education, the fine arts, including theatre, have a major role to play.
    The response of the National Convention to this report, was an authorization for the Committee of Public Instruction to proceed with a draft proposal for a new grammar and new vocabulary of the French language.
16 Louis XIV.
17 Charles Dufresny (1648–1724) was a playwright and journalist, the author of very successful domestic comedies. Florent Carton Dancourt (1661–1725) was an actor and

impunity bring to the theatre actors who, by speaking a semi-patois, excited laughter or pity. All present norms should proscribe this style. In vain you will raise the objection that Plautus introduced in his plays men who spoke the barbarous Latin of the Italian countryside; that the Italian comedians and recently also Goldoni <Gl/69>, produced on stage, their Venetian merchant and the bergamasque patois of Brighella, and so on. What is cited as an example for us to imitate is nothing but an abuse to reform. . . .

the author of many plays, notably realistic and topical comedies depicting a corrupt bourgeois society.

16

JOANNA BAILLIE
(1761–1851)

The first volume of plays on the passions by Joanna Baillie was remarkable for the fact that none of the plays in the book had ever been staged. It was published anonymously, in 1798,[1] with a long "Introductory Discourse" in which Baillie outlines her theory of the representation of the passions in relation to a scheme of dramatic genres. She supposes that such dramatic representations appease our deep curiosity about the motivation of all action in a common human psychology; and she appeared to be right, since the volume was very well received; by some as the finest collection of plays to appear for a hundred years or more. In due course Baillie revealed herself as the playwright, but not before, in April 1800, her *De Montfort*, was staged by John Philip Kemble at Drury Lane, with more critical than popular success. Years later (and after some intervening American productions) Byron – who called Baillie "our only dramatist since Otway and Southern" (Byron 1974, III:109) – urged the revival of *De Montfort* at Drury Lane, where he was a member of the Committee, and Edmund Kean was eventually persuaded to undertake it. The mixed reception (which included high praise) of the play was attributed by Kean to its being more poem than play (Carhart 1923, 127). Baillie had more success in the theatre with *The Family Legend*, which was staged in Edinburgh in January 1810, at the instigation of Walter Scott, who thought Baillie "the best dramatic writer ... since the days of Shakespeare and Massinger" (Carswell 1930, 280). Other productions of Baillie's plays were staged in Britain and America, some with considerable success. But in her later years her reputation declined as swiftly as it had grown, and she dropped out of sight as playwright and poet.

Various explanations of Baillie's much greater success as a playwright on the page than on the stage were proposed during her lifetime, one of which was "the bad taste of the public" (Carhart 1923, 121). Baillie herself admitted to serious faults in her dramaturgy but she also observed that there was a fundamental incompatibility between certain kinds of drama (including her own) and the size of the London theatres.[2] This is her theme in the extract below, which demonstrates an unusual interest in the relation between the writing and reception of plays and the buildings in which they are presented.

---

[1] *A Series of Plays: in which it is attempted to delineate the stronger passions of the mind, each passion being the subject of a tragedy and a comedy*. A second volume of plays on the passions appeared in 1802, *Miscellaneous Plays* in 1804, and a third volume of plays on the passions in 1812.

[2] Before her Richard Cumberland and after her Sir Walter Scott made similar critiques. See Kelly 1980, 99 and Scott 1834, 389ff.

For further reading
Carhart 1923; Carswell 1930.

[On the Effects of large theatres on plays and acting][3]

... The public have now to choose between what we shall suppose are well-written and well-acted plays, the words of which are not heard, or heard but imperfectly by two thirds of the audience, while the finer and more pleasing traits of the acting are by a still greater proportion lost altogether, and splendid pantomime, or pieces whose chief object is to produce striking scenic effect, which can be seen and comprehended by the whole. So situated, it would argue, methinks, a very pedantic love indeed, for what is called legitimate drama <In/2>, were we to prefer the former. A love for active, varied movement in the objects before us; for striking contrasts of light and shadow; for splendid decorations and magnificent scenery, is as inherent in us as the interest we take in the representation of the natural passions and characters of men: and the most cultivated minds may relish such exhibitions, if they do not, when both are fairly offered to their choice, prefer them. Did our ears and eyes permit us to hear and see distinctly in a theatre so large as to admit of chariots and horsemen, and all the "pomp and circumstance of war," I see no reason why we should reject them. They would give variety, and an appearance of truth to the scenes of heroic tragedy, that would very much heighten its effect. We ought not, then, to find fault with the taste of the public for preferring an inferior species of entertainment, good of its kind, to a superior one, faintly and imperfectly given. ...

The size of our theatres <Sl/197>, then, is what I chiefly allude to, when I say, present circumstances are unfavorable for the production of these plays. While they continue to be of this size, it is a vain thing to complain of either want of taste in the public, or want of inclination in managers to bring forward new pieces of merit, taking it for granted that there are such to produce. Nothing can be truly relished by the most cultivated audience that is not distinctly heard and seen, and managers must produce what will be relished. Shakespeare's plays, and some of our other old plays, indeed, attract full houses, though they are often repeated, because, being familiar to the audience, they can still understand and follow them pretty closely, though but imperfectly heard; and surely this is no bad sign of our public taste. And besides this advantage, when a piece is familiar to the audience, the expression of the actors' faces is much better understood, though seen imperfectly; for the stronger marked traits of feeling which

[3] From "To the Reader," Baillie 1812, xvi–xxvii. Spelling and punctuation have been modernized. The earlier part of this essay is a theoretical defense of her dramas of passion and thus a continuation of the "Introductory Discourse" in her first volume of plays.

even in a large theatre may reach the eyes of a great part of the audience, from the recollection of finer and more delicate indications, formerly seen so delightfully mingled with them in the same countenances during the same passages of the play, will, by association, still convey them to the mind's eye, though it is the mind's eye only which they have reached.

And this thought leads me to another defect in large theatres, that ought to be considered.

Our great tragic actress, Mrs. Siddons <Hz/245>, whose matchless powers of expression have so long been the pride of our stage, and the most admired actors of the present time, have been brought up in their youth in small theatres, where they were encouraged to enter thoroughly into the characters they represented; and to express in their faces that variety of fine fleeting emotion which nature, in moments of agitation, assumes, and the imitation of which we are taught by nature to delight in. But succeeding actors will only consider expression of countenance as addressed to an audience removed from them to a greater distance; and will only attempt such strong expression as can be perceived and have effect at a distance. It may easily be imagined what exaggerated expression will then get into use; and I should think, even this strong expression will not only be exaggerated but false. For, as we are enabled to assume the outward signs of passion, not by mimicking what we have beheld in others, but by internally assuming, in some degree, the passion itself; a mere outline of it cannot, I apprehend, be given as an outline of figure frequently is, where all that is delineated is true though the whole is not filled up. Nay, besides having it exaggerated and false, it will perpetually be thrust in where it ought not to be. For real occasions of strong expression not occurring often enough, and weaker being of no avail, to avoid an apparent barrenness of countenance, they will be tempted to introduce it where it is not wanted, and thereby destroy its effect where it is. – I say nothing of expression of voice, to which the above observations obviously apply. This will become equally, if not in a greater degree, false and exaggerated, in actors trained from their youth in a large theatre.

But the department of acting that will suffer most under these circumstances, is that which particularly regards the gradual unfolding of the passions, and has, perhaps, hitherto been less understood than any other part of the art – I mean soliloquy. What actor in his sense will then think of giving to the solitary musing of a perturbed mind that muttered, imperfect articulation which grows by degrees into words; that heavy, suppressed voice as of one speaking through sleep; that rapid burst of sounds which often succeeds the slow, languid tones of distress; those sudden, untuned exclamations which, as if frightened at their own discord, are struck again into silence as sudden and abrupt, with all the corresponding variety of countenance that belongs to it <Dt/43>; – what actor, so situated, will attempt to exhibit all this? No; he will be satisfied, after taking a turn or two across the front of the stage, to place himself directly in the middle of it; and there, spreading out his hands as if he were addressing some person whom it behoved him to treat with great ceremony, to tell himself, in an audible uniform voice, all the secret thoughts of his own heart. When he has done this, he will think, and he will think rightly, that he has done enough.

The only valuable part of acting that will then remain to us, will be expression of gesture, grace, and dignity, supposing that these also shall not become affected by being too much attended to and studied. . . .

All I have said on this subject, may still in a greater degree be applied to actresses; for the features and voice of a woman, being naturally more delicate than those of a man, she must suffer in proportion from the defects of a large theatre.

The great disadvantage of such oversized buildings to natural and genuine acting, is, I believe, very obvious; but they have other defects which are not so readily noticed, because they, in some degree, run counter to the common opinion of their great superiority in every thing that regards the general effect. The diminutive appearance of individual figures, and the straggling poverty of grouping, which unavoidably takes place when a very wide and lofty stage is not filled by a great number of people, is very injurious to general effect. This is particularly felt in comedy, and all plays on domestic subjects; and in those scenes also of the grand drama, where two or three persons only are produced at a time. To give figures who move upon it proper effect, there must be depth as well as width of stage; and the one must bear some proportion to the other, if we would not make every closer or more confined scene appear like a section of a long passage, in which the actors move before us, apparently in one line, like the figures of a magic lantern. . . .

Even in the scenes of professed show and spectacle, where nothing else is considered, it appears to me that a very large stage is in some degree injurious to the general effect. Even when a battle is represented in our theatres, the great width of the stage is a disadvantage; for as it never can nor ought to be represented but partially, and the part which is seen should be crowded and confused, opening a large front betrays your want of numbers; or should you be rich enough in this respect to fill it sufficiently, imposes on you a difficulty seldom surmounted, viz. putting the whole mass sufficiently in action to sustain the deception.[4] When a moderate number of combatants, so as to make one connected group, are fighting on the front of a moderately wide stage, which they sufficiently occupy, it is an easy thing, through the confusion of their brandished weapons and waving banners, to give the appearance of a deep active battle beyond them, seen, as it were, through a narrow pass; and beholding all the

---

[4] In a note, Baillie makes exceptions to the representations of sieges, using lots of walls, and the use of horses, which can readily fill the stage.

tumult of battle in the small view opened before us, our imagination supplies what is hid. If we open a wider view, we give the imagination less to do, and supply what it would have done less perfectly. In narrowing our battle, likewise, we could more easily throw smoke or an appearance of dust over the background, and procure for our fancy an unlimited space.

In processions, also, the most pleasing effect to our imaginations is, when the marshaled figures are seen in long perspective which requires only depth of stage; and the only advantage a wide stage has on such occasions is containing the assembled mass of figures, when the moving line stops and gathers itself together on the front. The rich confusion of such a crowd is indeed very brilliant and pleasing for a short time, but is dearly purchased at the price of many sacrifices.

On those occasions too, when many people are assembled on the front of the stage to give splendor and importance to some particular scene, or to the conclusion of a piece, the general effect is often injured by great width of stage. For the crowd is supposed to be attracted to the spot by something which engages their attention; and, as they must not surround this object of attention (which would be their natural arrangement) lest they should conceal it from the audience, they are obliged to spread themselves out in a long line on each side of it: now the shorter those lines or wings are, spreading out from the center figures, the less do they offend against natural arrangement, and the less artificial and formal does the whole scene appear.

In short, I scarcely know of any advantage which a large stage possesses over one of moderate size without great abatements, even in regard to general effect, unless it be when it is empty, and scenery alone engages our attention, or when figures appear at a distance on the background only. Something in confirmation of what I have been saying, has, perhaps, been felt by most people on entering a grand cathedral, where figures moving in the long aisles at a distance add grandeur to the building by their diminished appearance; but in approaching near enough to become themselves distinct objects of attention, look stunted and mean, without serving to enlarge by comparison its general dimensions.

There is also, I apprehend, greater difficulty, in a very wide and lofty stage, to produce variety of light and shadow; and this often occasions the more solemn scenes of tragedy to be represented in a full, staring, uniform light that ought to be dimly seen in twilight uncertainty; or to have the objects on them shown by partial gleams only, while the deepened shade around gives a somber indistinctness to the other parts of the stage, particularly favorable to solemn and terrific impressions. And it would be more difficult, I imagine, to throw down light upon the objects on such a stage, which I have never indeed seen attempted in any theatre, though it might surely be done in one of moderate dimensions with admirable effect. In short, a great variety of pleasing effects from light and shadow might be more easily produced on a smaller stage, that would give change and even interest to pieces otherwise monotonous and heavy; and it would often be very useful in relieving the exhausted strength of the chief actors, while want of skill in the inferior could be craftily concealed.[5] On this part of the subject, however, I speak with great diffidence, not knowing to what perfection machinery for the management of light may be brought in a large theatre. But at the same time, I am certain that, by a judicious use of light and scenery, an artificial magnitude may be given to a stage of a moderate size, that would, to the eye, as far as distance in perspective is concerned, have an effect almost equal to anything that can be produced on a larger stage; for that apparent magnitude arising from succession of objects, depends upon the depth of the stage, much more than its width and loftiness, which are often detrimental to it; and a small or moderate sized theatre may have, without injury to proportion, a very deep stage. . . .

[5] In a note, Baillie deplores the effects of the lamps used on the front of the stage (footlights), which distort both the impressions of groups and individual actors' features.

17

MME DE STAËL (ANNE-LOUISE-GERMAINE NECKER)
(1766–1817)

When Madame de Staël's *On Germany* was published in 1813,[1] it provided its French readers with a synthesis of her dramatic theory. In it, de Staël isolates drama as a distinct literary genre and, citing English and German examples, urges French playwrights to reconsider their (sometimes slavish) adoption of the neo-classical rules. Her argument is based largely on the importance of emotional response to literature in general, but she emphasizes that the specific kind of illusion created by drama enhances its powers of emotional arousal.

De Staël argues that drama achieves its effects on the spectators by the manipulation of such elements as the spatial, temporal, and visual relationships, which occur naturally in the experience of the audience and are compressed and intensified in drama. Strict adherence to the unities tends to destroy illusion and, she says, stylistic accomplishment may be at the expense of emotional inspiration.

As "literature in action" drama, according to de Staël, ought to affect the emotions more powerfully than other forms of literature. And, considering the prominent role of drama in ancient Greece, contemporary England, and Germany, she concludes that, in these countries, the development of drama has been in response to the spectators' demands, rather than to impersonal artistic criteria. Though she suggests that French playwrights look to other countries for the inspiration that would enable them to transcend the rules, de Staël, like Schlegel <Sl/189>, is alert to the danger of positing criteria that would serve the drama of all nations. She praises and follows the German example in opening up the discussion of drama as an art that transcends nationalism but de Staël also acknowledges the difficulty in simultaneously extending the appreciation of foreign drama and creating a dramatic literature that is specifically one's own.

For further reading

Eggli 1933; Henning 1929; Pange 1938; Staël/Folkenflik 1987; Wellek 1955: II; Whitford 1918.

---

[1] When the volume was first published in 1810 the French authorities ordered the destruction of all copies of what they took to be an excessively pro-German work, and immediately sent its author into exile. The book was republished in Paris in 1813.

From "On Dramatic Art"[2]

Theatre exercises a considerable influence over humanity. A tragedy which elevates the soul, or a comedy which depicts manners and characters, affects the mind like a real event <Lg/126; Hm/92>; thus, in order to be successful, a playwright must have studied the audience being addressed, and the grounds upon which it forms opinions. Knowledge of humanity is as important as imagination for a playwright; he must succeed in eliciting feelings of general interest, without losing sight of the particular circumstances which affect the spectators; theatre is literature in action, and the genius that it requires is so rare, because it is comprised of an exceptional combination of sensitivity to actuality with poetic inspiration. Nothing would be more absurd, therefore, than desiring to impose the same formula on all nations; for important modifications are inevitable when it is a matter of adapting universal art to each country, immortal art to contemporary manners; and it is from this that so many diverse opinions arise as to what constitutes dramatic talent; in all the other branches of literature, it is easier to find consensus.

One cannot deny, it seems to me, that of all the nations of the world, the French are most skilled in bringing together theatrical effects; they have surpassed others with the dignity of plotting and tragic style. But, even while recognizing this double superiority, one can experience more profound emotions in less well-ordered work; foreign plays in the way they are conceived are often more striking and more daring, and often they contain I don't know what kind of power that speaks more intimately to our hearts and affects us as much as emotions which have disturbed us personally....

The difference between French and German theatre can be explained by the characters of the two nations <In/2–3>; but, in addition to these natural differences, there are the systematized antinomies, the causes of which are important to know. What I have already said about classical and romantic poetry also applies to plays. The tragedies drawn from mythology are of a different nature than historical tragedies. ... The plot of tragedy, for the Greeks, is surprisingly simple; most of the events are foreseen and also predicted from the outset; it is a religious ceremony. ... When the same subjects were transported to the French theatre, our great poets gave them more variety; they multiplied the events, arranged surprises, and tightened the knot. They had, in effect, to replace the national and religious interests that the Greeks brought to these plays, but which we do not experience; often, not content with animating the Greek plays, we have lent the characters our manners and our responses, modern

[2] Newly translated from *De l'Allemagne* (*On Germany*) Part II, ch. 15, 'De l'art dramatique' in de Staël [1861] 1975, II:78–82.

politics and gallantry, and because of this a great number of foreigners do not understand the admiration that our great works inspire in us. In effect, when one hears them in another language, when they are stripped of their magical beauty of style, one is surprised that they arouse so little emotion, and at the improprieties that one finds in them; for, whatever neither fits in with the century, nor with the national manners of the persons being represented, is not that also indecorous? and is it not ridiculous in that these [manners] do not resemble ours?

Plays with Greek subjects do not lose anything by the severity of our dramatic rules; but if we would like to appreciate, as the English do, the pleasure of having an historical theatre, to take an interest in our past and be excited by our religion, how is it possible to conform so rigorously, on the one hand to the three unities, and on the other, to the kind of pomp which has been made a rule in our tragedies?

The question of the three unities is so overworked that one hardly dares to speak of it again <In/11>; but of these three unities, the only important one is that of action, the others do not need to be considered except as subordinate to it....

One must agree on [the meaning] of the word illusion in the arts; since we agree to believe that the actors separated by a few planks are Greek heroes who died three thousand years ago, then it is absolutely certain that what we call illusion, is not to imagine that what we see really exists <Jh/84>; a tragedy cannot seem real except by the emotion that it arouses in us <Hm/91>. If, in accordance with the kind of circumstances depicted, changes in the setting and prolongation of the fictional time add to the arousal of emotions, then the illusion becomes more vivid....

Historical subjects lend themselves less than fictional subjects to the conditions imposed on our writers; the etiquette of tragedy, which is rigorous in our theatre, is often opposed to new beauties, which would be appropriate for plays taken from modern history....

The pomp of alexandrine verse <Sd/254; Hu/264> is still a much greater obstacle, than even habitual good taste, to any changes in the form and content of French tragedy: one cannot say in alexandrine verse that one is entering or leaving, that one is sleeping or waking, without having to search for a poetic turn of phrase; and a mass of feelings and effects are banished from the theatre, not by the rules of tragedy, but by the requirements of versification <Vt/26; Sd/254>....

It will be agreed, perhaps, that catastrophes suit theatre more than subtle tableaux <Dt/39>; emotions excited by intense passions please most of the spectators more than the attention required to observe the human heart. Only national taste can determine these different dramatic systems; but we must acknowledge that if foreigners conceive of theatrical art differently from ourselves, this is neither out of ignorance, nor due to barbarity, but as a consequence of profound reflection which is worthy of examination. . . .

Shakespeare often combines opposite qualities and even faults; sometimes he is here and there in the realm of art; but he still possesses more knowledge of the human heart than of theatre. . . .

If one should risk any innovation in tragedy in France, one would be accused immediately of indulging in melodrama, but is it not important to know why melodramas please so many people? In England all classes of people are equally attracted to plays by Shakespeare. Our best tragedies do not interest the common people; under the pretext of a taste too refined and a sensibility too delicate to tolerate certain emotions, art is divided in two; bad plays contain touching situations ineptly expressed, and good plays admirably depict cold situations in order to be respected <Sd/253>; we possess few tragedies that can at once shake up the imagination of all classes.

The point is that if we continue to restrict ourselves as we now do, to imitating the masterpieces, never will there ever be anything new. Nothing in life should be static, and art is petrified when it no longer changes. Twenty years of revolution have given the imagination other needs than those it experienced, when Crébillon's novels depicted love and society of the time.[3] The Greek subjects are worn out . . . .

Tragedy is all in the events that interest nations; and this immense drama that humans have been playing out for six thousand years, would provide innumerable subjects for the theatre, if one allows more liberty to dramatic art. The rules are only travel guides for genius, they teach only that Corneille, Racine, and Voltaire passed by; but if one comes right down to it, why dispute about the route? Isn't the purpose to stir the soul while ennobling it? . . .

It would be desirable to throw off the constraints with which metre and rhyme have surrounded art <In/15>; more boldness must be permitted, a greater knowledge of history should be required; if one holds onto the pale copies of the same masterpieces exclusively, one will eventually see nothing more than heroic marionettes in the theatre, sacrificing love to duty, preferring death to slavery, inspired by contraries, in their actions as in their words, but without any relationship with this surprising creature one calls man, with the formidable fate which in turn drives and pursues him. . . .

In familiarizing others with a theatre founded on principles that are so different from ours, I neither claim that these principles are better, nor

---

[3] Claude Prosper Jolyot de Crébillon, *fils* (1707–77) served as an official censor of drama, as had his playwright father. His stories reflected and satirized contemporary society, especially its erotic activities.

specifically that we ought to adopt them in France; but these foreign combinations can excite new ideas; and when one sees the sterility which threatens our literature, it seems to me difficult not to desire that our writers review the milestones of their profession; and will it not do them good to become themselves conquerors in the empire of the imagination? It might be worth the effort for French playwrights to follow such advice.

18

AUGUST WILHELM
VON SCHLEGEL
(1767–1845)

August Wilhelm Schlegel was one of the most influential literary critics of his time. Together with his brother Friedrich, he edited the periodical *Athenäum* (1798–1800), the organ of German Romanticism, and his Berlin lectures on literature and aesthetics (1801–04) did much to popularize the ideas of the Romantic movement. Schlegel was an Orientalist, a poet, and author of a play (an adaptation of the *Ion* of Euripides) but his major works were his criticism, which brought together literary history and theory, and his translations of Shakespeare. Between 1797 and 1810 he translated seventeen of Shakespeare's plays, and between 1825 and 1833 Ludwig Tieck supervised the completion of the project: the so-called Schlegel–Tieck translation, which superseded existing attempts to render Shakespeare into German, and remains unsurpassed today.

Schlegel's *Lectures on Dramatic Art and Literature* (*Vorlesungen über dramatische Kunst und Literatur*), delivered in Vienna in 1808, provide us with "the major statement on the drama in the Romantic period" (Burwick 1991, 127). These lectures, which drew on many sources, including Kant, Lessing, Herder, Schiller, and, most notably, Friedrich Schlegel, were quickly translated into all the major European languages (Ewton 1972, 13–14) and in turn influenced such writers as Coleridge, De Quincey, de Staël, Stendhal, and Hugo. The first lecture develops the famous distinction between ancient and modern literature – and between the "classical" and the "romantic" <Hg/206> – and calls for a new historical awareness in criticism as opposed to the neo-classicist insistence on timeless values and standards. Schlegel's concern for the cultural and historical specificity of artistic production and reception forms the basis of his entire series of lectures, organized as a history of dramatic art from the theatre of ancient Greece to the modern German stage. In this historical survey, French neo-classical drama, as studied imitation of the Greek model, is regarded as an example of mechanical form, while the "romantic" drama of Shakespeare, neither tragedy nor comedy in the sense of the ancients,[1] is viewed as work of genius and the highest example of organic form <Co/222>.[2]

Schlegel explores in some detail the definitions of "dramatic," "theatrical," and "poetic." He regards drama as a synthesis of epic and lyric modes, and he defines it as the presentation of an action through dialogue. In the fourth lecture, the

---

[1] Schlegel's characterization of *Hamlet* as "ein Gedankentrauerspiel" (Schlegel/Lohner 1966–67, VI:168) ("a tragedy of thought" or "a philosophical tragedy") recalls the view of the play in Goethe's *Wilhelm Meister's Apprenticeship* <Gt/137> and anticipates Hegel's focus, in his *Lectures on Aesthetics*, on the centrality of character or individual passion in romantic tragedy <Hg/217–18>.

[2] The distinction between mechanical and organic form is elaborated in Lecture 25 (Schlegel/Lohner 1966–67, VI:109–10).

description of the ancient Greek stage both reveals the inappropriateness to it of neo-classical notions of verisimilitude < 1:In/8–9> and allows Schlegel to present his own views on the nature of dramatic illusion. Although he joins Schiller as a foe of naturalism, he argues that the chorus, "the ideal spectator," cannot be so easily transplanted onto the modern stage <Sr/169>. Schiller's views are also recalled in Schlegel's explanation of the pleasure we take in tragedy,[3] which he derives from Kant's discussion of the sublime, while Goethe's reading of Shakespeare is echoed in Schlegel's rejection of the three unities in favor of "a deeper, more mysterious unity."

For further reading

Burwick 1991; Carlson 1984; Ewton 1972; Wellek 1955:11.

From *Lectures on Dramatic Art and Literature*[4]

Lecture 1

The object of the present series of lectures will be to combine the theory of dramatic art with its history and to bring before my auditors at once its principles and its models. . . .

The history of the fine arts informs us what has been accomplished; the theory teaches what ought to be accomplished. But without some intermediate and connecting link, each would remain isolated and inadequate. This connecting link is furnished by criticism, which both elucidates the history of the arts and makes the theory fruitful. The comparison and assessment of the existing productions of the human mind necessarily throw light upon the conditions which are indispensable to the creation of original and masterly works of art.

Ordinarily we entertain a very erroneous notion of criticism, and understand by it nothing more than a certain shrewdness in detecting and exposing the faults of a work of art. As I have devoted the greater part of my life to this pursuit, I may be excused if, by way of preface, I seek to lay before my auditors my own ideas of the true genius of criticism.

We see numbers of people, and even whole nations, so fettered by the conventions of education and habits of life that, even in the appreciation of the fine arts, they cannot shake them off. Nothing which is alien to their own language, manners, and social relations appears to them natural, appropriate, or beautiful. With this exclusive mode of seeing and feeling, it is no doubt possible to attain, by means of cultivation, to great nicety of discrimination within the narrow circle to which it limits and circumscribes them. But no one can be a true critic without universality of mind, without that flexibility which enables us, by renouncing personal predilec-

---

[3] See Lectures 3 and 5.
[4] Published 1809–11. The translation, somewhat modified, is from Schlegel/Black 1973 (1815, revised by A. J. W. Morrison in 1846).

tions and blind habits, to adapt ourselves to the peculiarities of other ages and nations – to experience them, as it were, at their core – and to recognize and duly appreciate what ennobles human nature, everything beautiful and great, beneath the external accessories which were necessary to its embodiment, even though occasionally they may seem to disguise and distort it. There is no monopoly of poetry for particular ages and nations; consequently, that despotism in taste, which would seek to invest with universal authority the rules which at first, perhaps, were but arbitrarily advanced, is but a vain and empty pretension. . . .

. . . It is well known that almost four and a half centuries ago, the study of ancient literature received a new life, through the diffusion of the Greek language (for the Latin never became extinct): the classical authors were brought to light and rendered universally accessible by means of the press; the monuments of ancient art were diligently disinterred and preserved. All this powerfully excited the human mind and formed a decided epoch in the history of human civilization; its manifold effects have extended to our times, and will yet extend to an incalculable series of ages. But the study of the ancients was forthwith most fatally perverted. The learned, who were chiefly in the possession of this knowledge and who were incapable of distinguishing themselves by works of their own, claimed for the ancients an unlimited authority, and with great appearance of reason, since they are models in their kind. Maintaining that nothing could be hoped for the human mind but from an imitation of antiquity, in the works of the moderns they only valued what resembled, or seemed to bear a resemblance to, those of the ancients. Everything else they rejected as barbarous and unnatural. With the great poets and artists it was quite otherwise. However strong their enthusiasm for the ancients and however determined their purpose of entering into competition with them, they were compelled by their independence and originality of mind to strike out a path of their own and to impress upon their productions the stamp of their own genius. . . .

Matters continued in this state until a period not long ago, when several inquiring minds, chiefly Germans, endeavored to clear up the misconception and to give the ancients their due, without being insensible to the totally different merits of the moderns. The apparent contradiction did not intimidate them. The groundwork of human nature is no doubt everywhere the same, but in all our investigations we may observe that throughout the whole range of nature there is no elementary power so simple but that it is capable of dividing and diverging into opposite directions. The whole play of vital motion hinges on harmony and contrast. Why, then, should not this phenomenon recur on a grander scale in the history of man? In this idea we have perhaps discovered the true key to the ancient and modern history of poetry and the fine arts. Those who adopted it gave to the peculiar spirit of modern art, as contrasted with the antique or classical, the name of "romantic." ... the spirit of ancient art and poetry is plastic, but that of the moderns is picturesque.

By an example taken from another art, that of architecture, I shall endeavor to illustrate what I mean by this contrast. Throughout the Middle Ages there prevailed, and in the latter centuries of that era was carried to perfection, a style of architecture which has been called Gothic, but ought really to have been termed old German. When, with the general revival of classical antiquity, the imitation of Greek architecture became prevalent, and but too frequently without a due regard to the difference of climate and manners or to the purpose of the building, the zealots of this new taste, passing a sweeping sentence of condemnation on the Gothic, reprobated it as tasteless, gloomy, and barbarous. This was in some degree pardonable in the Italians, among whom a love for ancient architecture, cherished by hereditary remains of classical edifices and the similarity of their climate to that of the Greeks and Romans, might, in some sort, be said to be innate. But we Northerners are not so easily to be talked out of the powerful, solemn impressions which seize upon the mind at entering a Gothic cathedral. We feel, on the contrary, a strong desire to investigate and to justify the source of this impression. A very slight attention will convince us that the Gothic architecture displays not only an extraordinary degree of mechanical skill, but also a marvellous power of invention; on a closer examination, we recognize its profound significance and perceive that as well as the Greek it constitutes in itself a complete and finished system.

To the application! The Pantheon is not more different from Westminster Abbey or the church of St. Stephen at Vienna than the structure of a tragedy of Sophocles from a drama of Shakespeare. The comparison between these wonderful productions of poetry and architecture might be carried still farther. But does our admiration of the one compel us to depreciate the other? May we not admit that each is great and admirable in its kind, although the one is, and is meant to be, different from the other? The experiment is worth attempting. We will not quarrel with anybody for preferring one or the other. The world is wide, and affords room for a great diversity of objects. Narrow and blindly adopted prepossessions will never constitute a genuine critic, who ought, on the contrary, to possess the power of dwelling with liberal impartiality on the most discrepant views, renouncing the while all personal inclinations....

Lecture 2

What is dramatic? To many the answer will seem very easy: where various persons are introduced conversing together, and the poet does not speak in his own person. This is, however, merely the first, external foundation of the form; it is dialogical. But the characters may express thoughts and sentiments without operating any change on each other, and so leave the minds of both in exactly the same state in which they were at the commencement; in such a case, however interesting the conversation may be, it cannot be said to possess a dramatic interest. I shall make this clear by alluding to a more tranquil genre not intended for the stage, the philosophical dialogue. When, in Plato, Socrates asks the conceited sophist Hippias about the meaning of the beautiful, the latter is at once ready with a superficial answer, but is afterwards compelled by the ironical objections of Socrates to give up his former definition and to grope about him for other ideas, until, ashamed at last and irritated at the superiority of the sage who has convicted him of his ignorance, he is forced to quit the field: this dialogue is not only philosophically instructive, but also entertaining, as a drama in miniature. And justly, therefore, has this lively movement in the thoughts, this suspense regarding the outcome, in a word, the dramatic cast of the dialogues of Plato, always been celebrated.

From this we may conceive wherein consists the great charm of dramatic poetry. Action is the true enjoyment of life, nay, life itself <Hm/89>. Mere passive enjoyments may lull us into a state of listless complacency, but even then, if possessed of the least internal activity, we cannot avoid being soon wearied. The great bulk of mankind merely from their situation in life or from their incapacity for extraordinary exertions are confined within a narrow circle of insignificant operations. Their days flow on in succession under the sleepy rule of custom, their life advances by an insensible progress, and the bursting torrent of the first passions of youth soon settles into a stagnant marsh. From the discontent which this occasions they are compelled to have recourse to all sorts of diversions, which uniformly consist in an activity that involves a struggle with difficulties, yet presents no great challenge. Of all diversions, the theatre is undeniably the most entertaining. Here we see others act even when we cannot act to any significant purpose ourselves. The highest object of human activity is man, and in the drama we see men measuring their powers against one another, as intellectual and moral beings, either as friends or foes, influencing one another by their opinions, sentiments, and passions, and decisively determining their reciprocal relations and circumstances. The art of the poet accordingly consists in separating from the fable whatever does not essentially belong to it, whatever, in the daily necessities of real life and the petty occupations to which they give rise, interrupts the progress of important actions, and concentrating within a narrow space a number of events calculated to attract the minds of the hearers and to fill them with attention and expectation. In this manner he gives us a renovated picture of life, a compendium of whatever is moving and progressive in human existence.

But this is not all. Even in a lively oral narration, it is not unusual to introduce persons in conversation with each other and to give a corresponding variety to the tone and the expression. But the gaps which these conversations leave in the story, the narrator fills up in his own name with a description of the accompanying circumstances and other particulars. The dramatic poet must renounce all such expedients, but for this he is richly recompensed in the following invention. He demands that each of the characters in his story be represented by a living individual; that this individual not only match as far as possible the prevalent conceptions of his fictitious original in sex, age, and figure, but assume his entire personality <In/5>; that every speech be delivered in a suitable tone of voice and accompanied by appropriate action and gesture; and that those external circumstances be added which are necessary to give the hearers a clear idea of what is going forward. Moreover, these representatives of the creatures of his imagination must appear in the costume belonging to their assumed rank, age, and country, partly for the sake of greater resemblance, and partly because, even in dress, there is something characteristic. Lastly, he must see them placed in a locality which, in some degree, resembles that where, according to his fable, the action took place, because this also contributes to the vividness: he sets them in a scene. All this brings us to the idea of the theatre. It is evident that the very form of dramatic poetry, that is, the presentation of an action through dialogue without the aid of narrative, implies the theatre as its necessary complement <Hg/213>. We allow that there are dramatic works which were not originally designed for the stage and not calculated to produce any great effect there, which nevertheless afford great pleasure in the perusal. I am, however, very much inclined to doubt whether they would produce the same strong impression with which they affect us upon a person who had never seen or heard a description of a theatre. In reading dramatic works, we are accustomed ourselves to supply the representation. . . .

. . . Since, as we have already shown, visible representation is essential to the very form of the drama, a dramatic work may always be regarded from a double point of view – how far it is poetic, and how far it is theatrical. The two are by no means inseparable. Let not, however, the expression "poetic" be misunderstood. I am not now speaking of the versification and the ornaments of language, which, when not animated by some higher excellence, are the least effective on the stage; rather, I speak of the poetry in the spirit and design of a piece, and this may exist in as high a degree when the drama is written in prose as in verse. What is it, then, that makes a drama poetic? The very same, assuredly, that makes other works so. It must in the first place be a connected whole, complete and satisfactory within itself. But this is merely the negative definition of a work of art, by which it is distinguished from the phenomena of nature, which blur together and do not possess in themselves a complete and independent existence. To be poetic it is necessary that a composition should be a mirror of ideas, that is, thoughts and feelings which in their character are necessary and eternally true, and soar above this earthly life, and also that it should exhibit them embodied before us. What the ideas are, which in this view are essential to the different departments of the drama, will hereafter be the subject of our investigation. We shall also, on the other hand, show that without them a drama becomes altogether prosaic and empirical, that is to say, patched together by the understanding out of the observations it has gathered from literal reality.

But how does a dramatic work become theatrical, or fitted to appear with advantage on the stage? In single instances it is often difficult to determine whether a work possesses such a property or not. It is indeed frequently the subject of great controversy, especially when the self-love of authors and actors comes into collision <In/8>; each shifts the blame of failure on the other, and those who advocate the cause of the author appeal to an imaginary perfection of the histrionic art, and complain of the insufficiency of the existing means for its realization. But in general the answer to this question is by no means so difficult. The object proposed is to produce an impression on an assembled multitude: to rivet their attention and excite their interest and sympathy. In this respect the poet's occupation coincides with that of the orator. How then does the latter attain his end? By perspicuity, rapidity, and energy. Whatever exceeds the ordinary measure of patience or comprehension he must diligently avoid. Moreover, when a number of people are assembled together, they distract one another's attention whenever their eyes and ears are not drawn to a common object beyond themselves. Hence the dramatic poet as well as the orator must from the very commencement, by strong impressions, transport his hearers out of themselves, and, as it were, take bodily possession of their attention. ... Here the poet's great art lies in availing himself of the effect of contrasts, which enable him at one time to produce calm repose, profound contemplation, and even the self-abandoned indifference of exhaustion, or at another, the most tumultuous emotions, the most violent storm of the passions. With respect to theatrical fitness, however, it must not be forgotten that much must always depend on the capacities and humors of the audience, and, consequently, on the national character in general and the particular degree of mental culture. Of all kinds of poetry the dramatic is, in a certain sense, the most secular, for, issuing from the stillness of an inspired mind, it yet fears not to exhibit itself in the midst of the noise and tumult of social life. The dramatic poet is, more than any other, obliged to court external favor and loud applause. But of course it is only in appearance that he thus lowers himself to his hearers; in reality, he is elevating them to himself.

In thus producing an impression on an assembled crowd, the following circumstance deserves to be weighed, in order to ascertain its full importance. In ordinary intercourse people exhibit only the outward self to one another. They are withheld by mistrust or indifference from allowing others to look into what passes within them, and to speak with anything like emotion or agitation of that which is nearest our heart is considered unsuitable to the tone of polished society. The orator and the dramatist find means to break through these barriers of conventional reserve. While they transport their hearers into such lively emotions that the outward signs thereof break forth involuntarily, each perceives the other spectators to be affected in the same manner and degree, and those who before were strangers to one another become in a moment intimately acquainted. The tears which the dramatist or the orator compels them to shed for calumniated innocence or dying heroism make friends and brothers of them all. Almost inconceivable is the power of a visible communion of numbers to give intensity to those feelings of the heart which usually retire into privacy or only open themselves to the confidence of friendship. The faith in the validity of such emotions becomes unshakable through its diffusion; we feel ourselves strong among so many associates, and all hearts and minds flow together in one great and irresistible stream. . . .

The powerful nature of such an engine for either good or bad purposes has in all times justly drawn the attention of the legislature to the drama. Many regulations have been devised by different governments to render it subservient to their views and to guard against its abuse <Fr/173>. The great difficulty is to combine such a degree of freedom as is necessary for the production of works of excellence with the precautions demanded by the customs and institutions of the different states. In Athens the theatre enjoyed up to its maturity, under the patronage of religion, almost unlimited freedom, and the public morality preserved it for a time from degeneracy. The comedies of Aristophanes, which with our views and habits appear to us so intolerably licentious, and in which the senate and the people itself are unmercifully turned to ridicule, were the seal of Athenian freedom. Plato, however, who lived in the very same Athens, and either witnessed or foresaw the decline of art, proposed the entire banishment of dramatic poets from his ideal republic. Few states have considered it necessary to subscribe to this severe sentence of condemnation, but few also have thought it proper to leave the theatre to itself without any supervision. In many Christian countries dramatic art has been honored by being made subservient to religion, in the popular treatment and exhibition of religious subjects, and in Spain more especially competition in this department has given birth to many works which neither devotion nor poetry will disown. In other states and under other circumstances this has been thought both objectionable and inexpedient. Wherever, however, the subsequent responsibility of the poet and actor has been thought insufficient, and it has been deemed advisable to submit every piece before its appearance on the stage to a previous censorship, it has been generally found to fail in the very point which is of the greatest importance: namely, the spirit and general impression of a play. The nature of dramatic art requires that the poet put into the mouths of his characters much of which he himself does not approve; with respect to his own sentiments, he is to be judged by the spirit of the whole. On the other hand, it may happen that a play is perfectly inoffensive in its single speeches, and defies all censorship, while as a whole it is calculated to produce the most pernicious effect. . . .

Lecture 3

. . . The three principal kinds of poetry in general are the epic, the lyric, and the dramatic. . . .

The spirit of epic poetry, as we recognize it in its father, Homer, is clear self-possession. The epos is the calm, quiet representation of an action in progress. The poet relates joyful as well as mournful events, but he relates them with equanimity, and considers them as already past and at a certain remoteness from our minds.

The lyric poem is the musical expression of emotion through language. The essence of musical feeling consists in this, that we seek to dwell on and even to perpetuate in our souls a joyful or painful emotion. The feeling must consequently be already so far mitigated as not to impel us by the desire of its pleasure or the dread of its pain to tear ourselves from it, but rather to allow us, unconcerned about the changes produced by time, to dwell upon and be absorbed in a single moment of existence.

The dramatic poet, as well as the epic, represents external events, but he represents them as real and present.[5] In common with the lyric poet he also claims our mental participation, but not in the same calm composedness; the feeling of joy and sorrow which the dramatist excites is more immediate and vehement. He calls forth all the emotions which the sight of similar deeds and fortunes of living men would elicit, and it is only by the total sum of the impression which he produces that he ultimately resolves these conflicting emotions into a harmonious tone of feeling. As he stands in such close proximity to real life and endeavors to endue his own imaginary creations with vitality, the equanimity of the epic poet would in him be indifference; he must decidedly take part with one or other of the leading views of human life and constrain his audience also to participate in the same feeling.

. . . Earnestness, understood in the broadest sense, is the direction of our mental powers to some aim. But as soon as we begin to call ourselves to account for our actions, reason compels us to fix this aim higher and higher, until we come at last to the highest end of our existence, and here that longing for the infinite which is inherent in our being is baffled by the limits of our finite existence. . . . When we contemplate the relations of our existence to the extreme limit of possibilities . . . every heart which is not dead to feeling must be overpowered by an inexpressible melancholy, for which there is no other counterpoise than the consciousness of a calling

---

[5] In his fifth lecture, Schlegel states that epic is in poetry what bas-relief is in sculpture, while tragedy corresponds to the "isolated group" (Schlegel/Lohner 1966–67, v:69).

transcending the limits of this earthly life. This is the tragic tone of mind, and when the contemplation of the possible issues out of the mind as a living reality, when this tone pervades and animates a visible representation of the most striking instances of violent revolutions in human fortunes, in which the will is defeated or inner strength is proven, then the result is tragic poetry. We thus see how this kind of poetry has its foundation in our nature, while to a certain extent we have also answered the question of why we are fond of such sorrowful representations, and even find something consoling and elevating in them....

Lecture 4

When we hear the word "theatre," we naturally think of what with us bears the same name, and yet nothing can be more different from our theatre, in its entire structure, than that of the Greeks. If in reading the Greek plays we associate our own stage with them, the light in which we shall view them must be false in every respect....

The theatres of the Greeks were quite open above, and their dramas were always acted in day, and beneath the canopy of heaven. ... To have covered in the scene itself and imprisoned gods and heroes in a dark and gloomy apartment, artificially illuminated, would have appeared ridiculous to the ancients. An action which so gloriously attested their affinity with heaven could fitly be exhibited only in the open air, and, as it were, under the very eyes of the gods, for whom, according to Seneca, the sight of a brave man struggling with adversity is a suitable spectacle....

The theatres of the ancients were, in comparison with the small scale of ours, of colossal magnitude, partly for the sake of containing the whole of the people, with the concourse of strangers who flocked to the festivals, and partly to correspond with the majesty of the dramas represented in them, which required to be seen at a respectful distance <Bl/178>. The seats of the spectators were formed by ascending steps which rose round the semicircle of the orchestra (called by us the pit), so that all could see with equal convenience. The diminution of effect by distance was counteracted to the eye and ear by artificial contrivances consisting in the employment of masks, and of an apparatus for increasing the loudness of the voice, and of the cothurnus to give additional stature....

... The Greeks in general skillfully availed themselves even of extrascenic matters and made them subservient to the stage effect. Thus, I doubt not but that in the *Eumenides* the spectators were twice addressed as an assembled people: first, as the Greeks invited by the Pythoness to consult the oracle, and a second time as the Athenian multitude, when Pallas, through the herald, commands silence during the trial about to commence. So too the frequent appeals to heaven were undoubtedly addressed to the real heaven, and when Electra on her first appearance exclaims: "O holy light, and thou air co-expansive with earth!" she probably turned towards the actual sun ascending in the heavens. The whole of this procedure is highly deserving of praise, and though modern critics have censured the mixture of reality and imitation as destructive of theatrical illusion <Lg/118>, this only proves that they have misunderstood the essence of the illusion which a work of art aims at producing. If we are to be truly deceived by a picture, that is, if we are to believe in the reality of the object which we see, we must not perceive its limits, but look at it through an opening; the frame at once declares it for a picture. Now in stage-scenery we cannot avoid the use of architectural contrivances, productive of the same effect on dramatic representation as frames on pictures. It is consequently much better not to attempt to disguise this fact, but leaving this kind of illusion for those cases where it can be advantageously employed, to take it as a permitted license occasionally to step out of the limits of mere scenic decoration. It was, generally speaking, a principle of the Greeks, with respect to stage imitation, to require a perfect representation, and where this could not be accomplished, to be satisfied with merely symbolic allusions. . . .

Ancient tragedy was altogether ideal and rhythmical, and in forming a judgment of it, we must always keep this in view. It was ideal insofar as it aimed at the highest grace and dignity, and rhythmical insomuch as the gestures and inflections of voice were more solemnly measured than in real life. Just as the statuary of the Greeks <Hg/214>, with almost scientific strictness, began with the most general conception and sought to embody it in various general characters which were only gradually invested with the charms of life, so that the individual was the last thing to which sculpture descended, so in mimetic art the Greeks began with the idea (the delineation of persons with heroic grandeur, more than human dignity, and ideal beauty), then passed to character, and last of all to passion, which, in the collision with the requisitions of either of the others, was forced to give way. Fidelity of representation was less their object than beauty; with us it is exactly the reverse. On this principle, the use of masks, which appears astonishing to us, was not only justifiable, but absolutely essential; far from considering masks as a makeshift, the Greeks would certainly, and with justice too, have regarded as a makeshift the use of a player with vulgar, ignoble, or strongly marked features to represent an Apollo or a Hercules; indeed, they would have deemed it downright profanation. . . . In tragedy the great object in the art was the due subordination of every element; the whole was to appear animated by one and the same spirit, and hence, not merely the poetry, but the musical accompaniment, the scenic decoration, and the training of the actors all issued from the poet. The player was a mere instrument in his hands, and his merit consisted in the accuracy with which he filled his part, and by no means in arbitrary bravura or ostentatious display of his own skill. . . .

Ancient tragedy, because it involved music and dance, has frequently been compared with the opera. But this comparison betrays an utter ignorance of the spirit of classical antiquity. Its music and dance have nothing but the name in common with ours. In tragedy the primary object was the poetry, and everything else was strictly and truly subordinate to it. But in opera the poetry is merely an accessory, a means of connecting the different parts; it is almost lost amidst its many accompaniments. . . .

Lecture 5

. . . This is the essence of the tragic in the sense of the ancients.[6] We are accustomed to give to all terrible or sorrowful events the appellation of tragic, and it is certain that such events are selected in preference by tragedy, though a melancholy conclusion is by no means absolutely necessary, and several ancient tragedies – the *Eumenides*, *Philoctetes*, and in some degree also *Oedipus at Colonus*, not to mention many of the pieces of Euripides – have a happy and cheerful termination.

But why does tragedy select subjects so awfully repugnant to the wishes and the wants of our sensuous nature? This question has often been asked, and seldom satisfactorily answered <Hm/89>. Some have said that the pleasure of such representations arises from the comparison we make between the calmness and tranquillity of our own situation and the storms and perplexities to which the victims of passion are exposed. But when we take a warm interest in the persons of a tragedy, we cease to think of ourselves, and when this is not the case, it is the best of all proofs that we have taken but a feeble interest and that the tragedy has failed in its effect. Others again have had recourse to a supposed feeling for moral improvement, which is gratified by the view of poetic justice < 1:Rm/291; Jh/75–6> in the reward of the good and the punishment of the wicked. But he for whom the aspect of such dreadful examples could really be wholesome must be conscious of a base attitude very far removed from genuine morality, and would experience humiliation rather than elevation of mind. Besides, poetic justice is by no means indispensable to a good tragedy; it may end with the suffering of the just and the triumph of the wicked, if only the balance be preserved in the spectator's own consciousness by the prospect of futurity. Little does it mend the matter to say, with Aristotle, that the object of tragedy is to purify the passions through the arousal of pity and terror. In the first place commentators have never been able to agree about the meaning of this proposition and have had recourse to the most forced explanations of it < 1:In/7–8>. Look, for instance, into the *Hamburg Dramaturgy* of Lessing. Lessing gives a new explanation of his own, and fancies he has found in Aristotle a poetic Euclid <Lg/125; Co/226>. But mathematical demonstrations are liable to no misconce-

---

6 Schlegel has just finished discussing inner freedom and outer necessity as "the two poles of the tragic world. It is only by contrast with its opposite that each of these ideas is brought into full manifestation" (Schlegel/Lohner 1966–67, v:61).

ption, and geometrical evidence may well be supposed inapplicable to the theory of the fine arts. Supposing, however, that tragedy does operate this moral cure in us; it does so by arousing painful feelings – terror and compassion – and it remains to be proved how it is that we take pleasure in subjecting ourselves to such an operation.

Others have been pleased to say that we are attracted to theatrical representations from the want of some violent agitation to rouse us out of the torpor of our everyday life <Hm/89>. Such a craving does exist, and, when speaking of the attractions of the drama, I have already acknowledged the existence of this want, but to it we must equally attribute the fights of wild beasts among the Romans or even the combats of the gladiators. But must we, less indurated and more inclined to tender feelings, require demi-gods and heroes to descend, like so many desperate gladiators, into the bloody arena of the tragic stage, in order to agitate our nerves by the spectacle of their sufferings? No, it is not the sight of suffering which constitutes the charm of a tragedy, the games of the circus, or even the fights of wild beasts. In these we see a display of activity, strength, and courage: splendid qualities, related to the mental and moral powers of man. The satisfaction, therefore, which we derive from the representation, in a good tragedy, of powerful situations and overwhelming sorrows, must be ascribed either to the feeling of the dignity of human nature, excited in us by such grand instances of it as are therein displayed, or to the trace of a higher order of things <Hg/215>, impressed on the apparently irregular course of events and mysteriously revealed in them; or perhaps to both these causes conjointly.

The true reason, therefore, why tragedy need not shun even the harshest subject is that a spiritual and invisible power can only be measured by the opposition which it encounters from some external force capable of being appreciated by the senses. The moral freedom of man can only be displayed in a conflict with his sensuous impulses: so long as no higher call summons it to action, it is either actually dormant within him or appears to slumber, since otherwise it does but mechanically fulfill its part as a mere power of nature. It is only amidst difficulties and struggles that the moral part of man's nature avouches itself. If, therefore, we must explain the distinctive aim of tragedy by way of theory, we would give it thus: that to establish the claims of the mind to a divine origin, its earthly existence must be disregarded as vain and insignificant, all sorrows endured, and all difficulties overcome.

With respect to everything connected with this point, I refer my hearers to the section on the sublime in Kant's *Critique of Judgment*, to the complete perfection of which nothing is wanting but a more definite idea of the tragedy of the ancients, with which he does not seem to have been very well acquainted.

I come now to another feature which distinguishes the tragedy of the ancients from ours: the chorus. We must consider it as a personified reflection on the action which is going on, the incorporation into the representation itself of the sentiments of the poet as spokesman for all humankind. .... Whatever it might be and do in each particular play, it represents above all first the common mind of the nation and then a more general human sympathy. In a word, the chorus is the ideal spectator <Sr/169>. It mitigates the impression of a deeply moving or distressing representation by bringing to the actual spectator a lyrical and musical expression of his own emotions and elevating him to the region of contemplation. ...

Modern poets of the first rank have often, since the revival of the study of the ancients, attempted to introduce the chorus in their own plays, for the most part without a correct, and always without a vivid idea of its real import. They seem to have forgotten that we have neither suitable singing or dancing, nor, as our theatres are constructed, any convenient place for it.[7] On these accounts it is hardly likely to become naturalized with us.[8] ...

Lecture 17

The famous three unities < 1:In/10; In/11 >, which have given rise to a whole Iliad of critical wars, are the unities of action, time, and place.

The validity of the first is universally allowed, but the difficulty is to agree about its true meaning; it is no easy matter to come to an understanding on the subject.

The unities of time and of place are considered by some quite a subordinate matter, while others lay the greatest stress upon them and affirm that out of the pale of them there is no safety for the dramatic poet. In France this zeal is not confined merely to the learned world, but seems to be shared by the whole nation in common. Every Frenchman who has sucked in his Boileau[9] with his mother's milk considers himself a born champion of the dramatic unities, much in the same way that the kings of England since Henry VIII are hereditary defenders of the faith.

It is amusing enough to see Aristotle driven perforce to lend his name to these three unities, whereas the only one of which he speaks with any degree of fullness is the first, the unity of action. With respect to the unity of time he merely throws out a vague hint, while of the unity of place he says not a syllable < 1:In/10 >.

I do not, therefore, find myself in a polemical relation to Aristotle, for I by

---

[7] In his fourth lecture, Schlegel provides a physical description of the ancient Greek theatre and the place of the chorus in it.

[8] In his final lecture, Schlegel criticizes Schiller's use of the chorus in *The Bride of Messina*. Because the chorus is divided in two, with each half "contending against the other," it ceases to be "a true chorus, that is, the voice of human sympathy and contemplation elevated above personal considerations" (Schlegel/Lohner 1966–67, VI:283).

[9] *L'Art poétique (The Art of Poetry)* (1674) by Nicolas Boileau (1636–1711) was an epigrammatical formulation of neo-classical theory known throughout Europe.

no means contest the unity of action properly understood: I only claim a greater latitude with respect to place and time for many species of the drama, nay, hold it essential to them. . . .

De la Motte <In/11>, a French author who wrote against the unities in general, would substitute for unity of action the "unity of interest." If the term be not confined to the interest in the destinies of some single personage, but is taken to mean in general the direction which the mind takes at the sight of an event, this explanation, so understood, seems most satisfactory and very near the truth <Vt/25>. . . .

The separate parts of a work of art and, consequently, the separate parts of a tragedy must not be taken in by the eye and ear alone, but also comprehended by the understanding. Collectively, however, they are all subservient to one common aim, namely, to produce a joint impression on the mind. Therefore, the unity lies in a higher sphere, in the feeling or in the reference to ideas. This is all one, for the feeling, so far as it is not merely sensual and passive, is our sense, our organ for the infinite, which forms itself into ideas for us.

Far, therefore, from rejecting the law of a perfect unity in tragedy as unnecessary, I require a deeper, more intrinsic, and more mysterious unity than that with which most critics are satisfied. This unity I find in the tragical compositions of Shakespeare, in as great perfection as in those of Aeschylus and Sophocles, while, on the contrary, I do not find it in many of those tragedies which nevertheless are lauded as correct by "dissecting" criticism.

Logical coherence, the causal connection, I hold to be equally essential to tragedy and every serious drama, because all our mental powers act and react upon one another, and if the understanding be compelled to take a leap, imagination and feeling do not follow the representation with equal alacrity. But unfortunately the champions of so-called regularity have applied this rule with a degree of petty subtlety, which can have no other effect than that of cramping the poet and rendering true excellence impossible.

One should not think of the order of sequences in a tragedy as a slender thread, of which we are every moment in anxious dread lest it should snap (this simile is in any case inapplicable, for it is admitted that a plurality of subordinate actions and interests is inevitable); rather let us suppose it a mighty stream, which in its impetuous course overcomes many obstructions and loses itself at last in the repose of the ocean. It springs perhaps from different sources, and certainly receives into itself other rivers, which hasten towards it from opposite regions. Why should not the poet be allowed to carry on several, and, for a while, independent streams of human passions and endeavors, down to the moment of their raging junction, if only he can place the spectator on an eminence from whence he may overlook the whole of their course? And if this great and swollen body of waters again divide into several branches, and pour itself into the sea by several mouths, is it not still one and the same stream?

Lecture 18

... It will be objected that the ancient tragedians at least observed the unity of time. ... But what they observe is nothing but the seeming continuity of time. It is of importance to attend to this distinction – the seeming – for they unquestionably allow much more to take place during the choral songs than could really happen within their actual duration. ...

The moderns have, in the division of their plays into acts, which, properly speaking, were unknown to Greek tragedy < 1:Hr/69:189>, a convenient means of extending the period of representation without any ill effect. For the poet may fairly reckon so far on the spectator's imagination as to presume that during the entire suspension of the representation he will readily conceive a much longer interval to have elapsed than that which is measured by the rhythmical time of the music between the acts; otherwise to make it appear the more natural to him, it might be as well to invite him to come and see the next act tomorrow. ...

The objection to the change of scene is founded on the same erroneous idea of illusion which we have already discussed. To transfer the action to another place would, it is argued, dispel the illusion. But now if we are in reality to consider the imaginary for the actual place, then must stage decoration and scenery be altogether different from what it now is. Johnson, a critic who, in general, is an advocate for the strict rules, very justly observes that if our imagination once goes the length of transporting us 1800 years back to Alexandria, in order to figure to ourselves the story of Antony and Cleopatra as actually taking place before us, the next step, of transporting ourselves from Alexandria to Rome, is easier <Jh/84–5>. The capability of our mind to fly in thought, with the rapidity of lightning, through the immensity of time and space, is well known and acknowledged in common life; shall poetry, whose very purpose it is to add all manner of wings to our mind, and which has at its command all the magic of genuine illusion, that is, of a lively and enrapturing fiction, be alone compelled to renounce this universal prerogative? ...

But why are the Greek and romantic dramatists so different in their practice with respect to place and time? ... As to the ancients, besides the structure of their stage, which led naturally to the seeming continuity of time and to the absence of change of scene, the observance of this practice was favored by the nature of the materials on which the Greek dramatist had to work. These materials were mythology, and, consequently, a fiction, which, under the handling of preceding poets, had collected into continuous and perspicuous masses what in reality was detached and scattered about in various ways. Moreover, the heroic age which they painted was at once extremely simple in its manners and marvellous in its incidents, and hence everything of itself went straight to the mark of a tragic resolution.

But the principal cause of the difference lies in the plastic spirit of antique poetry and the picturesque spirit of romantic poetry. Sculpture directs our attention exclusively to the group which it sets before us; it divests it as far as possible from all external accompaniments, and where they cannot be dispensed with, it indicates them as slightly as possible. Painting, on the other hand, delights in exhibiting, along with the principal figures, all the details of the surrounding locality and all secondary circumstances. It can open a prospect into a boundless distance in the background, and light and shade with perspective are its peculiar charms. Hence the dramatic and especially the tragic art of the ancients annihilates in some measure the external circumstances of space and time, whereas, by their changes, romantic drama adorns its more varied pictures. In other words, the principle of antique poetry is ideal, while that of romantic poetry is mystical; the former subjects space and time to the inner free-agency of the mind, while the latter honors these incomprehensible essences as supernatural powers, in which there is somewhat of indwelling divinity.

Lecture 25

Works of genius cannot be permitted to be without form, but of this there is no danger. However, that we may answer this objection of want of form, we must understand the exact meaning of the term form, since most critics, and more especially those who insist on a stiff regularity, interpret it merely in a mechanical, and not in an organic sense. Form is mechanical when, through external force, it is imparted to any material merely as an accidental addition without reference to its quality, as, for example, when we give a particular shape to a soft mass that it may retain the same after its induration. Organic form, on the other hand, is innate; it unfolds itself from within, and acquires its determination contemporaneously with the perfect development of the germ. We everywhere discover such forms in nature throughout the whole range of living powers, from the crystallization of salts and minerals to plants and flowers, and from these again to the human body. In the fine arts, as well as in the domain of nature, the supreme artist, all genuine forms are organic, that is, determined by the quality of the work. In a word, the form is nothing but a significant exterior, the speaking physiognomy of each thing, which, as long as it is not disfigured by any destructive accident, gives true evidence of its hidden essence.

Hence it is evident that the spirit of poetry, which, though imperishable, migrates, as it were, through different bodies, must so often as it is newly born in the human race mould to itself, out of the nutrimental substance of an altered age, a body of a different conformation. The forms vary with the direction taken by the poetic sense, and when we give to new kinds of poetry the old names and judge of them according to the ideas conveyed by these names, the application which we make of the authority of classical antiquity is altogether unjustifiable. No one should be tried before a tribunal to which he is not amenable. We may safely admit that most English and Spanish dramatic works are neither tragedies nor comedies in the sense of the ancients: they are romantic dramas.

19

GEORG WILHELM FRIEDRICH HEGEL
(1770–1831)

Hegel's *Aesthetics: Lectures on Fine Art* (*Vorlesungen über die Asthetik*) is the post-humously edited version (based on students' notes, as well as his own) of the lectures on aesthetics that he delivered in Berlin in the 1820s.[1] *Aesthetics* culmi-nates in a discussion of drama, which, in Hegel's system is the supreme form of poetry, which, in its turn, is supreme among the five arts that Hegel designates as *the* "fine arts," or simply art. As to why drama should be accorded this priority (and be designated a branch of poetry), the major reasons would appear to be first that it combines the subjectivity and inwardness of lyric with the objectivity and social concerns of epic; and secondly that it combines complete sensuousness of apprehension with the conceptual power of language. Such views gather their force from a highly systematic and comprehensive account of the arts in human history and of their own histories related to their inherent structures and different modalities; and this account of the arts – or art – is itself integrated into a coherent system in which the roles of art, religion, and philosophy are related and differen-tiated as expressions of absolute truth.

Not only is the vast scope of Hegel's philosophical system-building daunting but the ambition itself of such a totalization is out of key with the philosophical temper of the late twentieth century. But what may now present most difficulty to Hegel's readers is the idealism whereby the progress of spirit manifests *itself* through human endeavors in the arts and philosophy, as well as in religion. On the other hand, the idea that there is a class of objects, produced in different media, that may sensibly be called "art" lives on, partly thanks to Hegel.

Art, religion, and philosophy in Hegel are ways of apprehending spirit, actually knowing – as opposed to what we are inclined to call scientific or objective "knowledge," which pretends to be unaffected by the knower. This interpenet-ration of the knower and the known, in Hegel, operates throughout the procession of human history, wherein spirit becomes manifest. And diachronic sequence is, at every instant, matched by synchronic oppositions – a source of difficulty in Hegel's thought.

Some of the more puzzling aspects of Hegel's discussion of the fine arts arise from the ways in which he relates historical sequence to modal difference. So "sym-bolic," "classical," and "romantic" – three key terms – follow each other as historical phases in which different arts are dominant; but they are also develop-mental phases within particular arts; and are also tendencies of different artistic media. So, the "symbolic" – a term that Hegel uses in an entirely different sense

---

[1] Editions by Heinrich G. Hotho appeared in 1835 and 1842 and a reissue, with emen-dations by F. Bassinger, in 1965. The English title used here is that of Hegel/Knox 1975, the translation used for the extracts that follow.

from any now current – is dominant in the pre-classical (i.e. pre-Attic) period, when architecture is the foremost artistic manifestation of spirit, and the "symbolic" relation with the absolute is a characteristic of architecture in general. More problematically, classical art is sculptural, sculpture is dominant in the classical phase, and sculpture, moreover – by reason of its commitment to the sensuous in apprehending the beautiful – is *the* preeminently artistic expression; but in classical antiquity, as always, poetry is supreme among the arts (though the era may not admit poetry this supremacy) and it is in Greek tragedy, with its combination of plastic representation with poetic abstraction, that Hegel finds artistic expression in its greatest perfection *as art*: "Here the art of speech is bound up with sculpture: the actor comes on the stage as a totally solid objective statue. But this statue is vitalized; it assimilates and expresses the subject-matter of the poetry; it is associated with every inner movement of passion and at the same time puts it into words and voices it. Consequently this presentation is more animated and is spiritually clearer than any statue or any picture" (Hegel/Knox 1975, II: 1186).

But art aspires beyond art, aspires in fact to a spiritual condition in which artistic expression itself is transcended, and the "romantic" or modern in art generally and in poetry especially has tended in this direction. With respect to drama, this tendency may even carry it away from the stage, though Hegel insists that the proper artistic realization of drama is necessarily in performance, and even argues against the printing of plays.

Hegel's rigorously systematic approach leads to a good deal of repetition – also due to the original lecture format, no doubt – in the filling out of the categories of his interlocking triadic paradigms. This is so both in the large categories of the system and in such subordinate ones as those applied in the discussion of drama. Bearing in mind the larger contexts in which the discussion of drama is set, the following bare outline may give both some sense of the systematic way in which Hegel approaches drama in the last part of *Aesthetics* and supply a framework for some of the extracts below:

DRAMATIC POETRY VERSUS EPIC AND LYRIC

PRINCIPLES OF DRAMATIC POETRY:
  National development is required.
  Conciliation of epic and lyric: epic objectification of national spirit, lyric individualism.
  Dissolution of one-sidedness: the dramatist understands both sides, unlike the lyrical poet, concerned with the subjective, and the epic poet who accepts what is.

WORK OF ART CHARACTERISTIC OF DRAMA:
  Unity, as distinct from epic and lyric, of: place; time; action.
  Structure: division and unfolding: scope; advancement; Act and Scene divisions.
  Attributes and media: dialogue; diction; meter.

RELATION TO PUBLIC: RIGHTS AND SUBMISSION:
  Limitations: universality or at least national interest.
  Illusion is required.
  Authorial viewpoint and objectivity.

SCENIC AND THEATRICAL ASPECTS

CLOSET DRAMA:
  Greek theatre.

Theatrical test of the dramatic.
Printing of plays questioned.
ACTING:
Declamation.
Gesture, movement, and posture.
"Liberation" from dance and song.
THEATRICALITY:
Theatrical improvisation.
Opera – its decadence.
Ballet – "a virtuosity of legs."

GENRES

PRINCIPLES OF TRAGEDY, COMEDY, AND DRAMA (THE NECESSITY FOR GENERIC DIVISION
  FROM POETIC COMPLETENESS AND PERFORMANCE; THE RELATION OF CHARACTER-
  IZATION TO THE MAIN AIM):
Tragedy: the range of supraindividual powers and the identification of the
  protagonist; opposition; resolution, transcending pity and fear.
Comedy (the triumph of the personal): powers of the individual; ratios of aims
  to efforts; resolution of contradiction.
Drama (and satire and tragicomedy): mixed genres, ancient and modern;
  blunted oppositions; mere theatrical effect.
ANCIENT AND MODERN:
The substantial *versus* the personal.
Will.
The modern concern with the exceptional: love and crime.
CONCRETE DEVELOPMENT OF TYPES:
Ancient tragedy and comedy.
Modern types.

Though Hegel ranges from ancient to modern drama and gives important
consideration to comedy, his discussion of Greek tragedy has an outstanding
importance, as A. C. Bradley so strongly and influentially argued. What is so
striking in Hegel's reading of his favorite Greek play, the *Antigone* of Sophocles, is
his notion of a resolution in the realm of spirit of opposing goods, which come into
conflict because of their partiality, a partiality which is the very condition of their
being in the world. This reading, which is a highly questionable one (Bungay
1984, 166–68), is an application of the idea that art is an attempt, which
necessarily falls short, at the sensuous realization of spirit. This attempt is manifes-
ted in terms of the content of the artistic representation and, even more perhaps, its
striving for an enabling form. In the thought of Hegel, that form, in its highest
development, is dramatic and its medium is the theatre.

For further reading

Bradley 1909; Bras 1989; Bungay 1984; Fulda 1990; Hegel/Knox 1975; Hegel/
Paolucci 1962; Kaminisky 1962; Knox 1936; Steinkraus 1980.

From *Aesthetics: Lectures on Fine Art*

[Art in Relation to the Public]

(I:263–64)[2] . . . But however far the work of art may form a world inherently harmonious and complete, still, as an actual single object, it exists not for *itself*, but for *us*, for a public which sees and enjoys the work of art. The actors, for example, in the performance of a drama do not speak merely to one another, but to us, and they should be intelligible in both these respects. And so every work of art is a dialogue with everyone who confronts it <In/8>. Now the truly ideal [work of art] is indeed intelligible to everyone in the universal interests and passions of its gods and men; yet since it brings its individuals before our eyes within a specific external world of customs, usages, and other particular details, there arises the new demand that this external world shall come into correspondence not only with the characters represented but equally with *us* too. Just as the characters in the work of art are at home in their surroundings, we require also for ourselves the same harmony with them and their environment. . . .

Now, given this clash between different ages, the question arises of how a work of art has to be framed in respect of the external aspects of locality, customs, usages, religious, political, social, moral conditions: namely whether an artist should forget his own time and keep his eye only on the past and its actual existence, so that his work is a true picture of what has gone; or whether he is not only entitled but in duty bound to take account solely of his own nation and contemporaries, and fashion his work according to ideas which coincide with the particular circumstances of his own time <Fr/173>. These opposite requirements may be put in this way: the material should be handled either objectively, appropriately to its content and its period, or subjectively, i.e. assimilated entirely to the custom and culture of the present. To cling to either of these in their opposition leads to an equally false extreme . . . .

[Supremacy of Drama]

(II:1158) Because drama has developed into the most perfect totality of content and form, it must be regarded as the highest stage of poetry and of art generally. For in contrast to the other perceptible materials, stone, wood, color, and notes, speech is alone the element worthy of the expression of spirit; and of the particular kinds of the art of speech dramatic poetry is the one which unites the objectivity of epic with the subjective character of lyric <Hu/259>. It displays a complete action as actually taking place before our eyes; the action originates in the minds of the characters who bring it about, but at the same time its outcome is decided by the really substantive nature of the aims, individuals, and

---

[2] References at the beginning of each extract refer to volume and page number in Hegel/ Knox 1975.

collision involved. But this conciliation of epic with the inner life of the person who is acting in front of us does not permit drama to describe, as epic does, the *external* aspect of the locality and the environment, as well as of what happens and is done, and it therefore demands a complete scenic production in order to give real life to the whole work of art. Lastly, the action itself in the entirety of its mental and physical actuality is susceptible of two opposed modes of treatment, tragic and comic, and the predominant principle of these provides us with a distinction in kind as a third chief aspect of dramatic poetry. . . .

The Principle of Dramatic Poetry
(II:1159)   What drama in general needs to be is the presentation, to our minds and imagination, of actual human actions and affairs and therefore of persons expressing their action in words. But a dramatic action is not confined to the simple and undisturbed accomplishment of a specific aim; on the contrary it rests entirely on *collision* of circumstances, passions, and characters, and leads therefore to actions and then to the reactions which in turn necessitate a resolution of the conflict and discord. . . .

[Three Act Structure]
(II:1169–70)   In every drama it suits the subject-matter best if the acts are three in number: in the first the emergence of the collision is explained; in the second, the collision comes to life as an encounter between interests, as struggle, difference, and complication; and then finally, in the third, when contradiction is at its peak it finds its necessary resolution. These sections of a drama are generally indistinct in Greek drama, but a corresponding analogy may be cited in the trilogies of Aeschylus in which, all the same, each part is rounded off into an independently complete whole. In modern dramatic poetry it is especially the Spanish who abide by a division into three acts < I:Lp/188 >; while the English, the French, and the Germans in the main generally divide the drama into five acts, where exposition falls into the first, the three inter-vening ones detail the quarrels and reactions, complications, and struggles of the opposing parties, and finally the fifth alone brings the collision to a complete conclusion. . . .

[Chorus, Monologue and Dialogue]
(II:1172–73)   . . . As everyone knows, the difference between chorus and dialogue was especially elaborated in Greek drama, whereas in modern drama this difference disappears because the material given to the chorus in Greek drama is now put into the mouths of the characters themselves. In contrast to the individual characters and their inner and outer strife, the *song of the chorus* expresses universal moods and feelings in language approaching now the solidity of the epic style, and now the impetuosity of lyric. In *monologues*, conversely, it is the inner life of an

individual which becomes objective to itself in a specific situation. They therefore have their genuine dramatic place at those moments especially when the heart simply sums itself up after earlier experiences, gives itself an account of its difference with others or of its own inner discord, or brings to final decision resolves either slowly ripened or suddenly made. But the completely dramatic form is the *dialogue*. For in it alone can the individual agents express face to face their character and aim, both their personal character and the substance of their animating "pathos"; in it alone can they come into conflict and so actually move the action forwards <In/6–7>. In dialogue too we can distinguish once more between a subjective and an objective "pathos". The former belongs rather to a casual particular passion, whether it be self-concentrated and expressed only aphoristically or whether it can storm out and explain itself completely. Poets who intend to move our personal feelings by touching scenes make special use of this kind of "pathos". But however far in that case they may depict personal suffering and fierce passion or an unreconciled inner discord of the soul, still the truly human heart is less moved by this than by a "pathos" in which something of objective worth is developed at the same time. . . . It does not matter how movingly the poet may describe passion; this is no help; our hearts are only rent, and we turn away. For in such a description there is nothing positive, none of the reconciliation which art should never lack. The Greeks, on the other hand, made their effect in tragedy principally by the objective sort of "pathos" in which human individuality was not lacking, so far as antiquity demanded it. Schiller's plays too have this "pathos" of a great mind, a "pathos" which is so poignant and is exhibited and expressed everywhere as the basis of the action. It is to this fact especially that we must ascribe the enduring effect which Schiller's tragedies have retained even at the present day, especially on the stage. For what creates a universal, lasting, and profound dramatic effect is what is really substantive in action – i.e. morality as a specific subject-matter, and greatness of spirit and character as form. And here too Shakespeare is supreme. . . .

[Authoriality in Drama]
(II:1179)   Now since drama produces an action in front of us so that we can see it going on, and individuals speak their own name and act their own person, it might seem that the author must withdraw to an altogether greater extent than he does in epic where he does at least appear as the narrator of the events. But this view of the matter is only partially correct. For, as I said at the start, drama owes its origin only to those epochs in which individual self-consciousness has reached a high stage of development both in its outlook on the world and in its artistic culture. Consequently a dramatic work need not give the impression of issuing, like an epic, from a national consciousness as such where the poet has been as it

were an impersonal tool for its affairs; on the contrary what we want to find in a perfect drama is the product of self-conscious and original creative activity and therefore also the art and virtuosity of an individual author. It is only in this way that dramatic creations acquire their proper peak of artistic life and determinacy in distinction from the actions and events of every day. . . .

[Drama for the Stage]

(II:1183–84)   But, unlike the Greeks, we are accustomed at times merely to *read* a drama as well as, at other times, to see it actually performed, and this fact has led dramatists themselves further astray by intending their work, to some extent, merely to be *read*, in the belief that this has no influence at all on the nature of the composition <In/3; Jh/86>. Of course there are certain isolated matters comprised in the mere externals of what is called "stagecraft", and infringement of these does not impair the value of a drama considered as poetry. For example, there is the calculation of how to set one scene in such a way that another, demanding considerable scenic preparations, may follow it conveniently, or how to give the actor time for rest or a necessary change of costume, etc. The knowledge and skill required in these matters provide no *poetic* advantage or disadvantage and depend more or less on theatrical arrangements which themselves are conventional and varying. But nevertheless there are other points in relation to which the poet, if he is to be really a dramatist, must keep essentially in view the live production of his piece, and he must make his characters speak and act with this in mind, i.e. with an actual and present performance in mind <1:Ar/54–55>. In these matters actual theatrical production is the touchstone. For in the eyes of the supreme tribunal – a healthy and artistically educated public – speeches and tirades <Dt/43; Gl/70; Hu/264> in what is called "flowery" language are in themselves futile if they lack dramatic truth. At certain epochs, indeed, the public may be corrupted by a highly praised "culture", i.e. by having put into its head the perverse opinions and follies of critics and connoisseurs; but if it still has some genuine taste of its own, it is satisfied only when the characters so express themselves and act as the living actuality of nature, and of art too, demands and involves. . . . But when a dialogue is actually going on in our *presence*, there is a valid presupposition that a man's will and heart, his decision and emotion, are direct, and that, in general, without any detour of prolonged reflections, man speaks to man directly, heart to heart, eye to eye, and face to face and is taken so to speak and reply. In that event, actions and speech spring alive in every situation out of the character as such, and this no longer leaves time for choosing between all sorts of different possibilities. In this respect it is by no means unimportant for the dramatist to keep in view, in his composition, the stage which demands such dramatic liveliness.

Indeed, in my opinion, no play should really be printed but should remain, more or less as the case was in antiquity, in manuscript for the theatre's repertory and get only an extremely insignificant circulation. If that happened, then at least we should not see so many dramas appearing which have indeed a cultivated style, fine feelings, excellent reflections, and profound thoughts, but which fail precisely in what makes drama dramatic, namely action and its vital movement. . . .

[Speech and Acting]

(ɪɪ:1187–89) In short, in Greece words and the spiritual expression of serious passions had full poetic rights, just as the external production was most completely elaborated by having an accompaniment of music and dancing. This concrete unity gives to the whole production a plastic character, because the spiritual element is not independently inwardized or expressed in the subjective experiences of these particular individuals; on the contrary it is perfectly married and reconciled with the equally justified external aspect, i.e. with what is seen on the stage.

Yet speech suffers under music and dancing <Bl/179> because it should be the *spiritual* expression of spirit, and so, after all, in modern times the actor's art has been able to liberate itself from these things. For this reason the poet has only now a relation to the actor as such because the actor is to bring a poetic work to life perceptibly by his declamation, gestures, and play of features. But this relation of the author to external material is of an entirely special kind, not shared by the other arts. In painting and sculpture it is the artist himself who carries out his conceptions in color, bronze, or marble; and, even if musical performance requires other hands and throats, what prevails there is, more or less, virtuosity and a finished mechanical skill, although it is true that the performance must not lack soul. On the other hand, the actor enters the work of art as an entire individual with his figure, countenance, voice, etc., and he has the task of absolutely identifying himself with the character he is representing.

In this matter the author has the right to demand from the actor that he shall think himself entirely into his given part, without adding anything of his own, and act it exactly as the author has conceived it and given it poetic form. The actor should be, as it were, the instrument on which the author plays, or the sponge that can absorb any color and give it back unchanged <In/5>. . . .

Shakespeare's figures above all are whole people, entire and unique, so that we require of the actor that he shall for his part bring them before our eyes in this entire completeness. Tone of voice, manner of recitation, gestures, facial expression, in short all outward appearance, and inner attitude of mind too, must be adapted by the individual actor to his specific part. Therefore, quite apart from the words, the manifold nuances and plays of gesture have a quite different importance: indeed the [modern] poet leaves to the actor's gestures a great deal which the Greeks would have put into words <Dt/42>. . . .

[Ethical Substance and Tragic Collision]

(II:1194–97)   The true content of the tragic action is provided, so far as concerns the *aims* adopted by the tragic characters, by the range of the substantive and independently justified powers that influence the human will: family love between husband and wife, parents and children, brothers and sisters; political life also, the patriotism of the citizens, the will of the ruler; and religion existent, not as a piety that renounces action and not as a divine judgment in man's heart about the good or evil of his actions, but on the contrary, as an active grasp and furtherance of actual interests and circumstances. A similar excellence belongs to the genuinely tragic *characters*. Throughout they are what they can and must be in accordance with their essential nature, not an ensemble of qualities separately developed epically in various ways; on the contrary, even if they are living and individual themselves, they are simply the *one* power dominating their own specific character; for, in accordance with their own individuality, they have inseparably identified themselves with some particular aspect of those solid interests we have enumerated above, and are prepared to answer for that identification. Standing on this height, where the mere accidents of the individual's purely personal life disappear, the tragic heroes of dramatic art have risen to become, as it were, works of sculpture <Sl/198> . . . .

Everything that forces its way into the objective and real world is subject to the principle of particularization; consequently the ethical powers, just like the agents, are differentiated in their domain and their individual appearance. Now if, as dramatic poetry requires, these thus differentiated powers ... are actualized ... then their harmony is cancelled and they come on the scene in *opposition* to one another . . . . The original essence of tragedy consists then in the fact that within such a conflict each of the opposed sides, if taken by itself, has *justification*; while each can establish the true and positive of its own aim and character only by denying and infringing the equally justified power of the other. The consequence is that in its moral life, and because of it, each is nevertheless involved in *guilt*.

The general reason for the necessity of these conflicts I have touched on already. The substance of ethical life, as a concrete unity, is an ensemble of *different* relations and powers which only in a situation of inactivity, like that of the blessed gods, accomplish the work of the spirit in the enjoyment of undisturbed life. But the very nature of this ensemble implies its transfer from its at first purely abstract *ideality* into its actualization in *reality* and its appearance in the mundane sphere. Owing to the nature of the real world, the mere *difference* of the constituents of this ensemble becomes perverted into *opposition* and collision . . . .

However justified the tragic character and his aim, however necessary the tragic collision, the third thing required is the tragic resolution of this conflict. By this means eternal justice is exercised on individuals and their aims in the sense that it restores the substance and unity of ethical life with the downfall of the individual who has disturbed its peace <Sl/200>. . . .

[Collision and Reconciliation in Greek Tragedy]

(ii:1212–15) The second chief feature, contrasted with the chorus, consists of the *individuals* who act and come continually into conflict. In Greek tragedy, as I have said more than once, the occasion for collisions is produced by the moral justification of a specific act, and not at all by an evil will, a crime, or infamy, or by mere misfortune, blindness, and the like. For evil in the abstract has no truth in itself and is of no interest. But, on the other hand, it must not look as if moral traits of character have been assigned to individuals merely by [the dramatist's] *intention*, for on the contrary their justification must be shown to lie in them *essentially*. Criminal types, like those of today, good-for-nothings, or even so-called "morally-noble" criminals with their empty chatter about fate, we therefore do not find in Greek tragedy any more than a decision or a deed resting on purely private interest and personal character, on thirst for power, lust, honor, or other passions, the right of which can be rooted only in an individual's private inclination and personality. But an individual's decision, justified by the object he aims at, is carried out in a one-sided and particular way, and therefore in specific circumstances, which already carry in themselves the real possibility of conflicts, he injures another and equally moral sphere of the human will. To this sphere another person clings as his own actual "pathos" and in carrying out his aim opposes and reacts against the former individual. In this way the collision of equally justified powers and individuals is completely set afoot <Gt/147>.

The range of the subject-matter here may be variously particularized but its essence is not very extensive. The chief conflict treated most beautifully by Sophocles, with Aeschylus as his predecessor, is that between the state, i.e. ethical life in its *spiritual* universality, and the family, i.e. *natural* ethical life. These are the clearest powers that are represented in tragedy, because the full reality of ethical existence consists in harmony between these two spheres and in absence of discord between what an agent has actually to do in one and what he has to do in the other. In this connection I need only refer to Aeschylus' *Seven Against Thebes* and, still more appositely, Sophocles' *Antigone*. Antigone honors the bond of kinship, the gods of the underworld, while Creon honors Zeus alone, the dominating power over public life and social welfare. In [Euripides'] *Iphigenia in Aulis*, in Aeschylus' *Agamemnon, Choephori*, and *Eumenides*, and in Sophocles' *Electra* we find a similar conflict. Agamemnon, as King and commander of the army, sacrifices his daughter in the interest of the Greeks and the Trojan expedition; thereby he snaps the bond of love for his daughter and his wife. This bond Clytemnestra, his wife and Iphigenia's mother, retains in the depths of her heart, and in revenge she prepares a shameful death for her home-coming husband. Orestes, her son, and the King's son, honors his mother but has to defend the right of his father, the King, and he slays the womb that bore him.

This is a subject valid for every epoch and therefore this presentation of it, despite all national differences, continues to excite our lively human and artistic sympathy <Bm/129>.

A second main type of collision is less concrete. The Greek tragedians are fond of portraying it especially in the fate of Oedipus. The most perfect example of this has been left to us by Sophocles in his *Oedipus Tyrannus* and *Oedipus Coloneus*. What is at issue here is the right of the wide awake consciousness, the justification of what the man has self-consciously willed and knowingly done, as contrasted with what he was fated by the gods to do and actually did unconsciously and without having willed it. Oedipus has killed his father; he has married his mother and begotten children in this incestuous alliance; and yet he has been involved in these most evil crimes without either knowing or willing them. The right of our deeper consciousness today would consist in recognizing that since he had neither intended nor known these crimes himself, they were not to be regarded as his own deeds. But the Greek, with his plasticity of consciousness, takes responsibility for what he has done as an individual and does not cut his purely subjective self-consciousness apart from what is objectively the case.

Lastly there are other collisions depending partly on special circumstances and partly on the general relation between an individual's action and the Greek μοῖρα [fate]. For our purpose these are of less importance.

But in considering all these tragic conflicts we must above all reject the false idea that they have anything to do with guilt or innocence. The tragic heroes are just as much innocent as guilty. On the presupposition that a man is only guilty if alternatives are open to him and he decides arbitrarily on what he does, the Greek plastic figures are innocent: they act out of this character of theirs, on *this* "pathos", because this character, this "pathos" is precisely what they are: their act is not preceded by either hesitation or choice. It is just the strength of the great characters that they do not choose but throughout, from start to finish, *are* what they will and accomplish. They are what they are, and never anything else, and this is their greatness. For weakness in action consists only in a cleavage between the individual and his object, in which case character, will, and aim do not appear as having grown into an absolute unity; and since no fixed aim is alive in the individual's soul as the substance of his own individuality, as the "pathos" and power animating his whole will, he may swither irresolutely from this to that and let caprice decide. From this swithering the

Greek plastic figures are exempt; for them the bond between the subject and what he wills as his object remains indissoluble. What drives them to act is precisely an ethically justified "pathos" which they assert against one another with the eloquence of their "pathos" not in sentimental and personal rhetoric or in the sophistries of passion, but in solid and cultivated objective language. (Sophocles above everyone else was a master in the depth, measure, and plastic and living beauty of language of this kind.) At the same time, however, their "pathos" is pregnant with collisions and it leads them to injurious and guilty acts. But they do not claim to be innocent of these at all. On the contrary, what they did, and actually had to do, is their glory. No worse insult could be given to such a hero than to say that he had acted innocently. It is the honor of these great characters to be culpable. They do not want to arouse sympathy or pity, for what arouses pity is not anything substantive, but subjective grief, the subjective depth of personality. But their firm and strong character is one with its essential "pathos", and what excites our admiration is this indestructible harmony and not the pity and emotion that Euripides alone has slipped into expressing.

The tragic complication finally leads to no other result or dénouement but this: the two sides that are in conflict with one another preserve the justification which both have, but what each upholds is one-sided, and this one-sidedness is stripped away and the inner, undisturbed harmony returns in the attitude of the chorus which clearly assigns equal honor to all the gods. The true development of the action consists solely in the cancellation of conflicts *as conflicts*, in the reconciliation of the powers animating action which struggled to destroy one another in their mutual conflict. Only in that case does finality lie not in misfortune and suffering but in the satisfaction of the spirit, because only with such a conclusion can the necessity of what happens to the individuals appear as absolute rationality, and only then can our hearts be morally at peace: shattered by the fate of the heroes but reconciled fundamentally. Only by adherence to this view can Greek tragedy be understood. . . .

[Modern Tragedy]
(II:1123)   Modern tragedy adopts into its own sphere from the start the principle of subjectivity. Therefore it takes for its proper subject-matter and contents the subjective inner life of the character who is not, as in classical tragedy, a purely individual embodiment of ethical powers . . . nevertheless in human action a basis of specific ends drawn from the concrete spheres of family, state, church, etc. is never missing. For, by acting, man, as man, enters the sphere of the real world and its particular concerns. But since now it is not the substantial element in these spheres which engrosses the interest of individuals, their aims are broadly and variously particularized and in such detail that what is truly substantial

can often glimmer through them in only a very dim way; and, apart from this, these aims acquire an altogether different form. . . . For since the principal of subjectivity itself has gained its right in the [religious, political, and social] spheres mentioned above, it follows that new features appear even in those which modern man is entitled to make the aim and guide of his action.

On the other hand, it is the right of personality as such which is firmly established as the sole subject-matter, and love, personal honor, etc., are taken as ends so exclusive that the other relationships either can only appear as the external ground on which these modern interests are played out or else stand on their own account in conflict against the demands of the individual's subjective heart. The situation is more profound when the individual character, in order to achieve his goal, does not shrink from wrong and crime, even if he has not envisaged himself as unjust and criminal in choosing his end. . . .

[Modern Comedy and the Dissolution of Art]

(ii:1236–37)   Now, with the development of the kinds of comedy we have reached the end of our philosophical inquiry. We began with symbolic art where personality struggles to find itself as form and content and to become objective to itself. We proceeded to the plastic art of Greece where the Divine, now conscious of itself, is presented to us in living individuals. We ended with the romantic art of emotion and deep feeling where absolute subjective personality moves free in itself and in the spiritual world. Satisfied in itself, it no longer unites itself with anything objective and particularized and it brings the negative side of this dissolution into consciousness in the humor of comedy. Yet on this peak comedy leads to the dissolution of art altogether. . . . [T]he Absolute no longer appears positively identified with the characters and aims of the real world but asserts itself only in the negative form of cancelling everything not correspondent with it, and subjective personality alone shows itself self-confident and self-assured at the same time in this dissolution.

Now at the end we have arranged every essential category of the beautiful and every essential form of art into a philosophical garland, and weaving it is one of the worthiest tasks that philosophy is capable of completing. For in art we have to do, not with any agreeable or useful child's play, but with the liberation of the spirit from the content and forms of finitude, with the presence and reconciliation of the Absolute in what is apparent and visible, with the unfolding of the truth which is not exhausted in natural history but revealed in world-history. Art is the most beautiful side of that history and it is the best compensation for hard work in the world and the bitter labor for knowledge. . . .

20

SAMUEL TAYLOR COLERIDGE
(1772–1834)

Though Coleridge is hardly known for his theatrical endeavors, he began his literary career as a playwright. Of his three plays, *Remorse* was successfully, though belatedly, staged at Drury Lane in 1813.[1] This play was so well received that its production looked like a revival of contemporary poetic drama in blank verse in the theatre. But Coleridge's own plays have an ambivalent relation to his dramatic criticism, which was ostensibly an effort to reform the theatre and, partly through it, the political life of the nation; both of which Coleridge came to see as too open to the influence of vulgar, leveling (or democratic) views (Moore 1982, 458–59). Though he was dismayed by what he saw as the degeneration of the theatre, Coleridge supposed that it might nevertheless be "a delightful, yet most effectual remedy for this dead palsy of the public mind" (Coleridge/Raysor 1930, I:209). He deplored the emphasis on spectacle <Bl/180>, the exaggerated acting styles, and the sentimentality of the theatre of his time and, above all, was concerned to discriminate between the potential of the theatre to convey poetic ideas sensuously and, on the other hand, to become mired in its material means. Despite his ambitions, personal and national, for the stage, Coleridge may be read as sharing with other Romantic critics a fundamental distrust of scenic aspects of performance and a strong conviction of the primacy of the auditory imagination. He frequently adverts to the potential value of a reformed theatre, undoubtedly, the kind of theatre that interested Coleridge was one that would be devoted to the service of dramatic poetry. It was on this basis that he contemplated an essay on the *necessary* "evils" of theatrical performance as distinct from those that should be extirpated from it.[2]

Coleridge's major debts to German predecessors are incontrovertible – in his dramatic criticism notably to A. W. Schlegel and Lessing[3] – but he may have been justified in declaring a certain independence, and even priority, for some of the views he shared with them. A key issue is the nature of stage illusion, which is central for all three theorists and, indeed, to their age <In/12>; and, whatever its

---

[1] *Remorse* had been written (under the title *Osorio*) in 1797. *The Fall of Robespierre* was written, in collaboration with Robert Southey, in 1794, very shortly after Robespierre's execution. *Zapolya* was written at Byron's urging but rejected by the Drury Lane management in 1816. (It was produced the following year at the Royal Circus and Surrey, an unlicensed theatre, but without any involvement by, or financial return to, Coleridge.) Coleridge also devised a Christmas entertainment, which was staged in 1818. His translations of two parts of Schiller's *Wallenstein* trilogy were not staged, though he had stage adaptation in mind.

[2] Letter of 8 May 1816 to John Murray (Coleridge/Griggs 1959, VI:637–38).

[3] Coleridge intended to write a biography of Lessing, whose works were the "chief object of [his] admiration" (Coleridge/Shawcross 1907, II:156) when he went to Germany in 1798.

origin as an idea, Coleridge's succinct formulation for the *reader's* response to *poetic illusion* as "that willing suspension of disbelief for a moment, which constitutes poetic faith" (Coleridge/Shawcross 1907, II:6) has proved memorable in English, especially in its adaptation (entirely justified by Coleridge's views) to dramatic and theatrical contexts.

Like that of many of his contemporaries in Britain and Germany, Coleridge's dramatic criticism was centered – one might say fixated – on Shakespeare's plays. For Coleridge, as for Hazlitt <Hz/241> and other Romantic theorists, Shakespeare possessed "that sublime faculty by which a great mind becomes that on which it meditates" (Coleridge/Foakes 1987, V, 1:80–81). (Keats' term for this aspect of poetic genius, especially in connection with Shakespeare, was "negative capability."[4]) For Coleridge, following Schlegel, Shakespeare's works were also the supreme examples of the artistic process of the fusion of the particular and the universal that could be described as organic form.

For further reading

Beer 1986; Burwick 1991; Carlson, J. 1988; Jackson 1964–65; Moore 1982.

[On Shakespeare as a deliberate artist][5]

The object which I was proceeding to attain in my last lecture was to prove that independently of his peculiar merits, which are hereafter to be developed, Shakespeare appears, from his poems alone, apart from his great works, to have possessed all the conditions of a true poet, and by this proof to do away, as far as may [be] in my power, the popular notion that he was a great dramatist by a sort of instinct, immortal in his own despite, and sinking below men of second- or third-rate character when he attempted aught beside the drama; even as bees construct their cells and manufacture their honey to admirable perfection, but would in vain attempt to build a nest. Now this mode of reconciling a compelled sense of inferiority with a feeling of pride, began in a few pedants, who having read that Sophocles was the great model of tragedy, and Aristotle the infallible dictator <1:Jn/194>, and finding that the *Lear*, *Hamlet*, *Othello*, and the rest, were neither in imitation of Sophocles, nor in obedience to Aristotle – and not having (with one or two exceptions) the courage to affirm that the delight which their country received from generation to generation, in defiance of the alterations of circumstances and habits, was wholly groundless – it was a happy medium and refuge, to talk of Shakespeare as a sort of beautiful *lusus naturae*, a delightful monster – wild, indeed, without taste or

---

[4] Letter to George and Tom Keats, 21, 27(?) December 1817; and letter to Richard Woodhouse, 27 October 1818 (Keats/Rollins 1958, I:193, 386–87).

[5] The text is based on Coleridge/Raysor 1930, I:219–20. (See also Coleridge/Foakes 1987, V, 1:78–80.) Punctuation and spelling have been modernized. Both Raysor and Foakes tentatively assign these fragmentary notes to Coleridge's lectures of 1808, and Foakes believes them to be for the lecture delivered on 1 April 1808.

judgment, but like the inspired idiots so much venerated in the East, uttering, amid the strangest follies, the sublimest truths <In/15>. In nine places out of ten in which I find his awful name mentioned, it is with some epithet of "wild," "irregular," "pure child of nature," etc., etc., etc. If all this be true, we must submit to it; though to a thinking mind it cannot but be painful to find any excellence, merely human, thrown out of all human analogy, and thereby leaving us neither rules for imitation, nor motives to imitate. But if false, it is a dangerous falsehood; for it affords a refuge to secret self-conceit – enables a vain man at once to escape his reader's indignation by general swollen panegyrics on Shakespeare, merely by his *ipse dixit* to treat what he has not intellect enough to comprehend, or soul to feel, as contemptible, without assigning any reason, or referring his opinion to any demonstrated principle <Lg/125>....

[On "what the drama should be"][6]

1 Illustration of principles my main object – therefore not so digressive as might appear.
2 With approved powers as a poet, Shakespeare commences a dramatist.
3 Finds the infant stage demanding an intermixture of ludicrous character, as imperiously as that of Greece and the chorus, and high language accordant.
4 Advantages of this – greater assimilation to nature, greater scope of power (more truths, more feelings) – effects of contrast, Lear and the Fool – and that the true language of passion becomes sufficiently elevated by having before heard the lighter conversation of men, in the same piece, under no strong emotion.
5 Nakedness of the stage. Drama then something betwixt recitation and a *re*-presentation. No scenes. Consequently, the laws of unity of place and unity of time,[7] the observance of which must either confine the drama to as few subjects as might be counted on the fingers, or involve gross improbabilities, far more striking than the violation would have been. Danger of a false ideal – *of aiming at more* than what is possible on the whole – *supermoralize and demoralize.* What play of the ancients – taking their ideal – does not hold out grosser absurdities than any in Shakespeare? On the Grecian [model] a man could be a poet, but rarely a

---

6 The text is based on Coleridge/Raysor 1930, I:203–07. (See also Coleridge/Foakes 1987, v, 1:82–87.) Punctuation and spelling have been modernized. Raysor (p. 199) supposes that these notes "may belong to the lectures of 1808" and Foakes (p. 72), though he acknowledges that they are not specifically linked with the lecture delivered on 1 April 1808, finds them consistent with that context.
7 Coleridge seems to mean that the (too limiting) doctrine of the unities was a hindrance not found in the Shakespearian theatre.

dramatist; on the present a dramatist, not a poet. Different states and degrees of illusion partly shown by others before me <Sl/198>.[8]

6 Not only are we never deluded, or anything like it; but the highest possible degree of delusion to beings in their senses sitting in a theatre <Jh/84> is a gross fault, incident only to low minds, who feeling unconsciously that they cannot affect the heart or head permanently, endeavor to call forth the momentary affections – pain no more than what is compatible with co-existing pleasure and to be amply repaid by thought – else onions, or shaving the upper lip.[9]

7 This leads us to what the drama should be. And first it is not a *copy*[10] of nature; but it is an imitation. This is the universal principle of the fine arts. In every well-laid out grounds, what we delight in we feel from that balance and antithesis of feelings and thoughts – how natural, we say! – but the very wonder that furnished the *how* implies that we perceived art at the same moment. We catch the hint from nature itself. Whenever in mountains or cataracts we discover a likeness to anything artificial which we yet know was not artificial, what pleasure! So in appearances known to be artificial that appear natural.[11] This applies in due degrees, regulated by steady good sense, from a clump of trees to the *Paradise Lost* or the *Othello*. It would be easy to apply it to painting, and even – though with much greater abstraction of thought, and by more subtle though just analogies – even to music. But this belongs to others. Suffice it that one great principle is common to all, a principle which probably is the condition of all consciousness, without which we should feel and imagine only by discontinuous moments, and be plants or animals instead of men. I mean that ever-varying balance – or balancing – of images, notions, or feelings (for I avoid the vague word, idea) conceived as in opposition to each other; in short, the perception of identity and contrariety, the least degree of which constitutes *likeness*, the greatest absolute difference; but the infinite gradations between these two form all the play and all the interest of our intellectual and moral being, till it lead us to a feeling and an object more awful than it seems to me compatible with even the present subject to utter aloud, though I am most desirous to suggest it. For there alone are all things at once different and the same; there alone as the principle of all things, does

---

8 Raysor (p. 204) suggests as precursors "Kames, Herder, Schiller, perhaps Schlegel."

9 Raysor (204) proposes that Coleridge intends that the pain for the spectators *should, indeed, be* no greater than is compatible with "co-existing pleasure" and *should be* compensated by thought; and that, otherwise, the pain of tragedy would be equivalent to that induced by onions or shaving. Raysor's interpretation is supported by a closely related remark in the extract from "Satyrane's Letters" below. The onions may derive from *Antony and Cleopatra* 1.2.177.

10 Coleridge deletes "not *an image*" in favor of "not a *copy*."

11 Raysor (p. 204) cites Kant/Meredith 1911, 167: "Nature proved beautiful when it wore the appearance of art; and art can only be termed beautiful, where we are conscious of its being art, while yet it has the appearance of nature."

distinction exist unaided by division – will and reason, succession of time and unmoving eternity, infinite change and ineffable rest.

> Return, Alpheus! the dread voice is past
> Which shrunk thy streams! ...
>   thou honor'd flood,
> Smooth-flowing Avon, crown'd with vocal reeds,
> That strain, I heard, was of a higher mood.
> But now my voice proceeds.[12]

We may divide a dramatic poet's characteristics, before we enter into the component merits of any one work, and speaking only of those things which are to be materials of all, into language, passion, and character, always bearing in mind that these must act and react on each other – the language inspired by the passion, the language and passion modified and differenced by the character. To the production of the highest excellencies in these three, there are requisite in the mind of the author: 1. good sense; 2. talents; 3. sensibility; 4. imagination; and to the perfection of a work, two faculties of lesser importance, but yet necessary to the ornaments and foliage of the column or roof, we should add fancy and a quick sense of beauty.

Language. It cannot be supposed that the poet should make his characters say *all* they would, or taking in his whole drama, that *each* scene or *paragraph* should be such as on cool examination we can conceive it likely that men in such situations would say, in that order and in that *perfection*. And yet, according to my feelings, it is a very inferior kind of poetry in which, as in the French tragedies, men are made to talk what few indeed even of the wittiest men can be supposed to converse in, and which both is, and on a moment's reflection appears to be, the natural produce of the hot-bed of vanity, namely an author's closet <In/3–4>, who is actuated originally by a desire to excite surprise and wonderment at *his* superiority to other men, instead of having felt so deeply on certain subjects, or in consequence of certain imaginations, as make it almost a necessity of his nature to seek for sympathy – no doubt, with that honorable desire of *permanent action* which distinguishes etc.

Where then the difference? Each part proportionate, to the whole, perhaps impossible – At all events, compatible with sound sense and logic, in the mind of the poet himself.

Judging of books by books, instead of referring what we read to our own experience, or making it a motive for observation – one great use of books.

Strong passions command[13] figurative language and act as stimulants.

German bad tragedies ridiculed – in which the dramatist becomes a novelist *in his directions to the actors*, and degrades tragedy to pantomime.

Yet still the consciousness of the poet's mind must be diffused over that of

---

[12] An adaptation of lines 132–33 and 85–88 of Milton's *Lycidas*.
[13] Foakes reads "commend."

the reader or spectator; but he himself, according to his genius, elevates us, and by being *always in keeping* prevents us from perceiving any strangeness, though we feel great exaltation. Very different kinds of style may be admirable, both in different men, and in different parts of the same poem. . . .

"Desultory Remarks on the Stage, and the present state of the Higher Drama"[14]

A theatre, in the widest sense of the word, is the general term for all places of amusement through the ear or eye in which men assemble in order to be amused by some entertainment presented to all at the same time. Thus, an old Puritan divine says: "those who attend public worship and sermons only to amuse themselves, make a theatre of the church and turn God's house into the devil's. *Theatra aedes diabololatricae.*" . . . The most important and dignified of this genus is, doubtless, the STAGE (*res theatralis histrionica*) which, in addition to the generic definition above given, may be characterized (in its *Idea*, or according to what it does, or ought to, *aim* at) as a combination of several, or of all the fine arts to an harmonious whole having a distinct end of its own, to which the peculiar end of each of the component arts, taken separately, is made subordinate and subservient; that, namely, of imitating reality (objects, actions, or passions) under a *semblance* of reality. Thus, Claude[15] imitates a landscape at sunset, but only as a *picture*; while a forest-scene is not presented to the audience as a *picture* but as a forest: and though in the *full* sense of the word we are no more *deceived* by the one than by the other, yet are our feelings very differently affected, and the pleasure derived from the one is not composed of the same elements as that afforded by the other, even on the supposition that the *quantum* of both were equal. In the former, it is a *condition* of all genuine delight, that we should *not* be deluded. See *Adam Smith's Posthumous Essays.*[16] In the latter (inasmuch as its principal end is not in or for itself, as is the case in a picture, but to be an assistance and means of an end out of itself) its very purpose is to produce as much illusion as its nature permits.[17] These and all other stage presentations are to produce a

---

14 The text is based on Coleridge/Raysor 1930, I:199–203. (See also Coleridge/Foakes 1987, v, I:129–35.) Punctuation and spelling have been modernized. Both Raysor and Foakes tentatively assign these fragmentary notes to Coleridge's lectures of 1808.

15 Claude Lorraine (1600–82): the French landscape painter, known for his picturesque canvases and his experiments with light. He influenced English landscape gardening.

16 An essay that Coleridge doubtless has in mind is "Of . . . the Imitative Arts" (Smith 1980, 176–213).

17 In an earlier draft of these notes, Coleridge adds that "the true stage illusion both in this and in all other things consists not in the mind's judging it to be a forest but in its remission of the judgment that it is not a forest" (Coleridge/Foakes 1987, v, I:130).

sort of temporary half-faith, which the spectator encourages in himself and supports by a voluntary contribution on his own part, because he knows that it is at all times in his power to see the thing as it really is <Sl/198>. I have often noticed that little children are actually deceived by stage-scenery, never by pictures, though even these produce an effect on their impressible minds which they do not on the minds of adults. The child, if strongly impressed, does not indeed positively think the picture to be the reality; but yet he does not think the contrary. . . . Now what pictures are to little children, stage illusion is to men, provided they retain any part of the child's sensibility, except that in the latter instance this suspension of the act of comparison, which permits this sort of negative belief, is somewhat more assisted by the will than in that of the child respecting the picture.

The subject of stage illusion is so important, and so many practical errors and false criticisms may arise, and indeed have risen, either from reasoning on it as actual delusion (the strange notion on which French critics built up their theory and the French poets justify the construction of their tragedies) or from denying it altogether (which seems the butt of Dr. Johnson's reasoning, and which, as extremes meet, would lead to the very same consequences by excluding whatever would not be judged probable by us in our coolest state of feeling with all our faculties in even balance <Jh/84–5>) that a short digression will, I hope, be pardoned, if it should serve either to explain or to illustrate the point.[18]

From "Satyrane's Letters: Letter Two"[19]

O dear lady! This is one of the cases,[20] in which laughter is followed by melancholy: for such is the *kind* of drama, which is now substituted everywhere for Shakespeare and Racine. You well know that I offer violence to my own feelings in joining these names. But however meanly I may think of the French serious drama, even in its most perfect specimens; and with whatever right I may complain of its perpetual falsification of the language and of the connections and transitions of thought, which Nature

---

[18] Coleridge goes on to compare dreams and nightmares but does not return to the subject of stage illusion.

[19] The pseudonym "Satyrane" signifies "the Idoloclast, or breaker of Idols" (Coleridge/Rooke 1969, IV, 2:185 and note 2). The original letters on which Satyrane's were based were written to Coleridge's wife, Sara (Fricker) and to Thomas Poole during Coleridge's stay in Germany in 1798–99. They were first published (in a revised form and with additions that include the following discussion of drama) in *The Friend* in 1809 and again revised to accompany *Biographia Literaria* in 1817. The text is from the 1817 version, as reprinted in Shawcross 1907, II:158–65. Spelling and punctuation have been modernized.

[20] The "case" in question was Coleridge's attendance at a performance of what he appears to have regarded as a generic "French comedy," though the play was actually a French translation of Heinrich Ferdinand Möller's *Der Graf von Walltron* (1776). See Coleridge/Rooke 1969, IV, 2:216 and note 3.

has appropriated to states of passion; still, however, the French tragedies are consistent works of art, and the offspring of great intellectual power. Preserving a fitness in the parts, and a harmony in the whole, they form a nature of their own, though a false nature. Still, they excite the minds of the spectators to active thought, to a striving after ideal excellence. The soul is not stupefied into mere sensations by a worthless sympathy with our own ordinary sufferings or an empty curiosity for the surprising, undignified by the language or the situations which awe and delight the imagination. What (I would ask of the crowd, that press forward to the pantomimic tragedies of Kotzebue[21] and his imitators) what are you seeking? Is it comedy? But in the comedy of Shakespeare and Molière the more accurate my knowledge, and the more profoundly I think, the greater is the satisfaction that mingles with my laughter. For though the qualities which these writers portray are ludicrous indeed, either from the kind or the excess, and exquisitely ludicrous, yet are they the natural growth of the human mind and such as, with more or less change in the drapery, I can apply to my own heart, or at least to whole classes of my fellow-creatures. How often are not the moralist and the metaphysician obliged for the happiest illustrations of general truths and the subordinate laws of human thought and action to quotations, not only from the tragic characters, but equally from the Jacques, Falstaff, and even from the fools and clowns of Shakespeare, or from the Miser, Hypochondriast, and Hypocrite of Molière! Say not, that I am recommending abstraction: for these class-characteristics, which constitute the instructiveness of a character, are so modified and particularized in each person of the Shakespearian drama, that life itself does not excite more distinctly that sense of individuality which belongs to real existence. Paradoxical as it may sound, one of the essential properties of geometry <Dt/63> is not less essential to dramatic excellence, and (if I may mention his name without pedantry to a lady) Aristotle[22] has accordingly required of the poet an involution of the universal in the individual < 1:Ar/45 >. The chief differences are that in geometry it is the universal truth itself which is uppermost in the consciousness, in poetry the individual form in which poetry is clothed. With the ancients, and not less with the elder dramatists of England and France, both comedy and tragedy were considered as kinds of *poetry*. They neither sought in comedy to make us laugh merely, much less to make us laugh by wry faces, accidents of jargon, slang phrases for the day, or the clothing of commonplace morals in metaphors drawn from the shops or mechanic occupations of their characters; nor did they condescend in

---

21 August Friedrich Ferdinand von Kotzebue (1761–1819) was a prolific playwright, whose
    works were frequently translated or adapted for the non-German stage.
22 The analogy with "geometry" in context with Aristotle is reminiscent of Lessing's claim
    that the *Poetics* is "as infallible as the Elements of Euclid" <Lg/125>.

tragedy to wheedle away the applause of the spectators by representing before them facsimiles of their own mean selves in all their existing meanness, or to work on their sluggish sympathies by a pathos not a whit more respectable than the maudlin tears of drunkenness. Their tragic scenes were meant to affect us, indeed, but within the bounds of pleasure and in union with the activity both of our understanding and our imagination. They wished to transport the mind to a sense of its possible greatness and to implant the germs of that greatness during the temporary oblivion of worthless "thing we are," and of the peculiar state in which each man *happens* to be; suspending our individual recollections and lulling them to sleep amid the music of nobler thoughts.

Hold! (methinks I hear the spokesman of the crowd reply, and we will listen to him. I am the plaintiff and be he the defendant.)

DEFENDANT: Hold! Are not our modern sentimental plays filled with the best Christian morality?

PLAINTIFF: Yes! Just as much of it, and just that part of it, which you can exercise without a single Christian virtue – without a single sacrifice that is really painful to you! – just as much as *flatters* you, sends you away pleased with your own hearts, and quite reconciled to your vices, which can never be thought very ill of when they keep such good company and walk hand in hand with so much compassion and generosity; adulation so loathsome, that you would spit in the man's face who dared to offer it to you in a private company, unless you interpreted it as insulting irony, you appropriate with infinite satisfaction, when you share the garbage with the whole sty, and gobble it out of a common trough. No Caesar must pace your boards – no Anthony, no royal Dane, no Orestes, no Andromache!

DEFENDANT: No: or as few of them as possible. What has a plain citizen of London, or Hamburg, to do with your kings and queens and your old schoolboy pagan heroes <Bm/129>? Besides, everybody knows the *stories*; and what curiosity can we feel –

PLAINTIFF: What, Sir, not for the *manner*? not for the delightful language of the poet? not for the situations, the action and reaction of the passions?

DEFENDANT: You are hasty, Sir! The only curiosity we feel is in the story: and how can we be anxious concerning the end of a play, or be surprised by it, when we know how it will turn out?

PLAINTIFF: Your pardon, for having interrupted you! We now understand each other. You seek, then, in a tragedy, which wise men of old held for the highest effort of human genius, the same gratification as that you receive from a new novel, the last German romance, and other dainties of the day, which *can* be enjoyed but once. . . . But why then do you pretend to admire *Shakespeare?* The greater part, if not all, of *his* dramas were, as far as the names of the main incidents are concerned, already stock plays. All the *stories*, at least, on which they are built, preexisted in the chronicles, ballads, or translations of contemporary or preceding English writers.

Why, I repeat, do you pretend to admire *Shakespeare?* Is it, perhaps, that you only *pretend* to admire him? However, as once for all you have dismissed the well-known events and personages of history, or the epic muse, what have you taken in their stead? Whom has *your* tragic muse armed with her bowl and dagger? The sentimental muse, I should have said, whom you have seated on the throne of tragedy? What heroes has *she* reared on her buskins?

DEFENDANT: O! Our good friends and next-door neighbors – honest tradesmen, valiant tars, high-spirited half-pay officers, philanthropic Jews, virtuous courtesans, tender-hearted braziers, and sentimental rat-catchers! (A little bluff or so, but all our very generous, tender-hearted characters *are* a little rude or misanthropic, and all our misanthropes very tender-hearted.)

PLAINTIFF: But I pray you, friend, in what actions great or interesting can such men be engaged?

DEFENDANT: They give away a great deal of money; find rich dowries for young men and maidens who have all other good qualities; they brow-beat lords, baronets, and justices of the peace (for they are as bold as Hector!); they rescue stage coaches at the instant they are falling down precipices; carry away infants in the sight of oppos-ing armies; and some of our performers act a muscular able-bodied man to such perfection that our dramatic poets, who always have the actors in their eye, seldom fail to make their favorite male character as strong as Samson. And then they take such prodigious leaps!! And what is *done* on the stage is more striking even than what is acted. I once remember such a deafen-ing explosion that I could not hear a word of the play for half an act after it; and a little real gunpowder being set fire to at the same time, and smelt by all the spectators, the naturalness of the scene was quite astonishing!

PLAINTIFF: But how can you connect with such men and such actions that dependence of thousands on the fate of one, which gives so lofty an interest to the personages of Shakespeare and the Greek tra-gedians. How can you connect with them that sublimest of all feelings, the power of destiny and the controlling might of heaven, which seems to elevate the characters which sink beneath its irresistible blow?

DEFENDANT: O mere fancies! We seek and find on the present stage our own wants and passions, our own vexations, losses, and embar-rassments.

PLAINTIFF: It is our own poor pettifogging nature, then, which you desire to have represented before you? Not human nature in its height and vigor? But surely you might find the former with all its joys and sorrows, more conveniently in your own houses and parishes.

DEFENDANT: True! But here comes a difference. Fortune is blind but the poet has his eyes open and is besides as complaisant as fortune is capricious. He makes everything turn out exactly as we would wish it. He gratifies us by representing those as hateful or contemptible whom we hate and wish to despise.

PLAINTIFF: (*aside*) That is, he gratifies your envy by libeling your superiors.

DEFENDANT: He makes all those precise moralists, who affect to be better than their neighbors, turn out at last abject hypocrites, traitors, and hard-hearted villains; and your young men of spirit, who take their girl and their glass with equal freedom, prove the true men of honor and (that no part of the audience may remain unsatisfied) reform in the last scene and leave no doubt on the minds of the ladies that they will make most faithful and excellent husbands; though it does seem a pity that they should be obliged to get rid of qualities which had made them so interesting! Besides, the poor become rich all at once; and in the final matrimonial choice the opulent and highborn themselves are made to confess that VIRTUE IS THE ONLY TRUE NOBILITY AND THAT A LOVELY WOMAN IS A DOWRY OF HERSELF!!

PLAINTIFF: Excellent! But you have forgotten those brilliant flashes of loyalty, those patriotic praises of the king and old England, which, especially if conveyed in a metaphor from the ship or the shop, so often solicit and so unfailingly receive the public plaudit. I give your prudence credit for the omission.

For the whole system of your drama is a moral and intellectual *Jacobinism* of the most dangerous kind[23] and those commonplace rants of loyalty are no better than hypocrisy in your playwrights, and your own sympathy with them a gross self-delusion. For the whole secret of dramatic popularity consists with you in the confusion and subversion of the natural order of things, their causes and their effects; in the excitement of surprise by representing the qualities of liberality, refined feeling, and a nice sense of honor (those things which rather pass among you for such) in persons and in classes of life where experience teaches us least to expect them; and in rewarding with all the sympathies that are the dues of virtue those criminals whom law, reason, and religion have excommunicated from our esteem!

And now good night! Truly! I might have written this last sheet without having gone to Germany;[24] but I fancied myself talking to you by your own fireside and can you think it a small pleasure to me to forget now and then that I am *not* there? Besides, you and my other good friends have made up your minds to me as I am, and from whatever place I write you will expect that part of my "Travels" will consist of the excursions of my own mind.

---

[23] See Moore 1982.
[24] He probably wrote it long afterwards!

From a letter to Daniel Stuart, 13 May 1816[25]

Dear Stuart

It is among the feeblenesses of our nature that we are often to a certain degree acted upon by stories gravely asserted, of which we do yet disbelieve every syllable – nay, which we perhaps happen to know to be false. The truth is, that images and thoughts possess a power in and of themselves, independent of that act of the judgment or understanding by which we affirm or deny the existence of a reality correspondent to them. Such is the ordinary state of the mind in dreams. It is not strictly accurate to say that we believe our dreams to be actual while we are dreaming. We neither believe it nor disbelieve it; with the will the comparing power is suspended, and without the comparing power any act of judgment, whether affirmation or denial, is impossible. The forms and thoughts act merely by their own inherent power; and the strong feelings at times apparently connected with them are in point of fact bodily sensations, which are the causes or occasions of the images, not (as when we are awake) the effects of them. Add to this a voluntary lending of the will to this suspension of one of its own operations (i.e. that of comparison and consequent decision concerning the reality of any sensuous impression) and you have the true theory of stage illusion; equally distant from the absurd notion of the French critics, who ground their principles on the presumption of an absolute *delusion* <Vt/24>, and of Dr. Johnson <Jh/84–5>, who would persuade us that our judgments are as broad awake during the most masterly representation of the deepest scenes of *Othello*, as a philosopher would be during the exhibition of a magic lantern with Punch and Joan, and Pull Devil Pull Baker, etc., on its painted slides. Now, as extremes always meet, this dogma of our dogmatic critic and soporific irenist would lead by inevitable consequence to that very doctrine of the Unities maintained by the French belletrists, which it was the object of his strangely overrated and contradictory and most illogical Preface (to Shakespeare) to overthrow.

Thus ... I have given you a theory which, as far as I know, is new, and which I am quite sure is most important, as the ground and fundamental principle of all philosophic and of all common-sense criticism concerning the drama and the theatre....

---

[25] The text is from Coleridge/Griggs 1959, IV:641–43. Spelling and punctuation have been modernized. Daniel Stuart (1766–1846) was an old friend, who owned newspapers to which Coleridge made contributions.

[*The Tempest* as a romantic drama][26]

We commence with *The Tempest* as a specimen of the romantic drama. But, whatever play of Shakespeare's we had selected, there is one preliminary point to be first settled, as the indispensable condition not only of just and genial criticism but of all consistency in our opinions. This point is contained in the words "probable," "natural." We are all in the habit of praising Shakespeare or of hearing him extolled for his fidelity to nature. Now what are we to understand by these words in their application to the drama? Assuredly not the ordinary meaning of them. Farquhar[27] the most ably and, if we except a few sentences in one of Dryden's prefaces[28] (written for a particular purpose and in contradiction to the opinions elsewhere supported by him) first exposed the ludicrous absurdities involved in the supposition, and demolished as with the single sweep of a careless hand, the whole edifice of French criticism respecting the so-called unities of time and place. But a moment's reflection suffices to make every man conscious of what every man must have before felt, that the drama is an *imitation* of reality, not a *copy*, and that imitation is contradistinguished from copy by this: that a certain quantum of difference is essential to the former and an indispensable condition and cause of the pleasure we derive from it; while in a copy it is a defect contravening its name and purpose. . . .

In evincing the impossibility of delusion, [Johnson] makes no sufficient allowance for an intermediate state, which we distinguish by the term illusion <Jh/84>.

In what this consists I cannot better explain than by referring you to the highest degree of it; namely dreaming. It is laxly said that during sleep we take our dreams for realities, but this is irreconcilable with the nature of sleep, which consists in the suspension of the voluntary, and therefore of the comparative, power. The fact is that we pass no judgment either way: we simply do not judge them to be unreal, in consequence of which the images act upon our minds, as far as they act at all, by their own force as images. Our state while we are dreaming differs from that in which we are in the perusal of a deeply interesting novel in the degree rather than in the kind, and from three causes. First, from the exclusion of all outward impressions on our senses, the images in sleep become proportionally more vivid than they can be when the organs of sense are in their active state. Secondly, in sleep the sensations, and with these the emotions and passions which they counterfeit, are the causes of our dream-images, while

---

[26] The text is from Coleridge/Raysor 1930, I:127–31. Punctuation and spelling have been modernized.

[27] In his "A Discourse upon Comedy" (1702), George Farquhar (1678–1707) attacked critical rule-mongering from the point of view of a practicing playwright.

[28] Dryden's *Essay of Dramatic Poesy* is his most sustained critique of the unities but his "Preface to *Don Sebastian*" fits Coleridge's description.

in our waking hours our emotions are the effects of the images presented to us. (Apparitions [are] *so detectible.*) Lastly, in sleep we pass at once by a sudden collapse into a suspension of this will and the comparative power; whereas in an interesting play, read or represented, we are brought up to this point, as far as it is requisite or desirable, gradually, by the art of the poet and the actors; and with the consent and positive aidance of our own will. We *choose* to be deceived. The rule, therefore, may be easily inferred. Whatever tends to prevent the mind from placing it[self] or from being gradually placed in this state in which the images have a negative reality must be a defect and consequently anything that must force itself on the auditors' mind as improbable, not because it *is* improbable (for that the whole play is foreknown to be) but because it cannot but *appear* as such.

But this again depends on the degree of excitement in which the mind is supposed to be. Many things would be intolerable in the first scene of the play that would not at all interrupt our enjoyment in the height of the interest. The narrow cockpit may hold,

> The vasty fields of France, or we may cram
> Within its wooden O the very casques
> That did affright the air at Agincourt.

[*Henry V*, Prologue 1–14]

And again, on the other hand, many obvious improbabilities will be endured as belonging to the groundwork of the story rather than to the drama, in the first scenes, which would disturb or disentrance us from all illusion in the acme of our excitement, as, for instance, Lear's division of his realm and banishment of Cordelia. But besides this dramatic probability, all the excellencies of the drama, as unity of interest <In/11; Sl/202>, with distinctness and subordination of the characters, appropriateness of style, nay, and the charm of language and sentiment for their own sakes, yet still as far as they tend to increase the inward excitement, are all means to this chief end – that of producing and supporting this willing illusion.

I have but one point more to add – namely, that though the excellencies above mentioned are means to this end, they do not therefore cease to be themselves *ends* and, as such, carry their own justification with them as long as they do not contravene or interrupt the illusion. It is not even always or of necessity an objection to them that they prevent it from rising to as great a height as it might otherwise have attained; it is enough if they are compatible with as high a degree as is requisite. If the panorama[29] had been invented in the time of Leo X, Raphael would still have smiled at the regret that the broom-twigs, etc., at the back of his grand pictures were not

[29] The first panorama (housing a cycloramic, pictorial representation) was exhibited in Edinburgh in 1788. Raphael (1483–1520), who painted a portrait of his patron Pope Leo X, was a forerunner of naturalism in art.

as probable trees as those in the panorama. Let me venture to observe that certain obvious, if not palpable, improbabilities may be hazarded in order to keep down a scene, [to keep it] merely instrumental <Sd/251>, and to preserve it in its due proportion of interest....

21

HEINRICH VON KLEIST
(1777–1811)

Kleist completed seven plays, all of them written in the last decade of his life. He never saw any of them performed, and most were not produced until well after his death. Goethe's strong dislike of his younger contemporary's work was decisive; the director of the Weimar theatre, responding to the selections from the tragedy *Penthesilea* that Kleist had sent him, rather condescendingly expresses his concern at seeing "young men of spirit and talent waiting for a theatre yet to come."[1] Today, however, Kleist is recognized as a writer "of uniquely dramatic genius," whose work has met with considerable success in the theatre, "no doubt in large measure because of that very modernity which so disturbed Goethe" (Lamport 1990, 160, 180).

Though Kleist offers us very little in the way of dramatic theory, the short work that follows has proved immensely influential. "Über das Marionettentheater" was published in four installments (12–15 December 1810) in the *Berliner Abendblätter*, Berlin's first daily newspaper, which Kleist edited until its demise in 1811. This was the year Kleist took his own life, which he regarded as "the most tormented" of all lives, made good only through "the most glorious and sensual of deaths,"[2] an elaborate double suicide.

"On the Marionette Theatre" has been used as a key to Kleist's work, and it has also been discussed as a significant contribution to Romantic aesthetic theory. Taking as its central topic the problem of self-consciousness and its relation to art, the work suggests the idea of "a return, via knowledge, to naïveté – to a second naïveté" (Hartman 1970, 300). Here the traditional biblical scheme of "Eden, Fall, and Redemption merges with the new triad of Nature, Self-Consciousness, and Imagination – the last term in both involving a kind of return to the first" (Hartman 1970, 307). The translation of the biblical pattern into a secular universal history (*Universalgeschichte*) has its roots in Rousseau, but it was elaborated primarily by the Germans: Lessing, Herder, Kant, Schiller, Fichte, Schelling, and Hegel (Abrams 1971, 199–225). Kleist contributes to this tradition, which focuses on the role of art and the creative imagination in the "circuitous" journey of humankind toward an ultimate, infinitely higher unity.

What is strikingly original in Kleist is the form itself of his discussion. He tells an unlikely story, which offers no clear answers, but raises a number of intriguing questions. The text poses a challenge for interpretation, as it sets out a theory of action, of beauty in movement, which proceeds in highly ironic fashion, often by way of paradoxical and outrageous statement. The narrator is drawn into the construction of the argument by the enigmatic Herr C–. Provoked by the latter's

---

[1] Letter from Goethe to Kleist, 1 February 1808 (Kleist/Sembdner 1982, IV:806).
[2] Letter to Marie von Kleist, 21 November 1811 (Kleist/Sembdner 1982, IV:887).

accusation that he has not read Genesis 3 closely enough, he offers his own example of the incompatibility of action and reflection, and thus unwittingly becomes a participant in the dialogical elaboration of an extraordinary thesis.

As Marvin Carlson has pointed out, Kleist's "Marionette Theatre" anticipates "the fascination the puppet exerted on drama theorists a century later" (Carlson 1984, 189). For the notion of the ideal actor as a kind of puppet, who simply reflects "the essential mood or soul of the drama" (Carlson 1984, 303), would be taken up by the symbolists – Maeterlinck, Appia, Lugné-Poe, Jarry, Arthur Symons, Yeats – and above all by Edward Gordon Craig in his famous essay "The Actor and the Über-Marionette" (1908). The idea of the actor as an instrument or medium for the compelling artistic vision of the director is clearly anticipated in Kleist's views on the role of the manipulator, as well as in his emphasis on competition, control, and mastery. The mysterious Herr C– himself, with his desire to exploit the skill of other artists[3] for his own purposes, already strongly suggests the controlling impulse of a "director's theatre."

For further reading

Abrams 1971; Carlson 1984; Hartman 1970; Lamport 1990; Sembdner 1967.

"On the Marionette Theatre"[4]

During the winter of 1801 which I spent in M–, I happened one evening, in the public gardens, to meet Herr C–, who had recently been engaged as the principal dancer at the opera in that town and was enjoying extra-ordinary popular success.

I told him that I had been astonished to see him several times at a marionette theatre, which had been hammered together in the market-place and was providing entertainment for the crowds by means of little dramatic burlesques interspersed with song and dance.

He assured me that the pantomime of these puppets afforded him much pleasure, and let it be known in no uncertain terms that a dancer who wanted to perfect his art could learn a few things from them.

Since this remark, from the way he expressed it, seemed to me to be more than a mere sudden whim, I sat down with him in order to question him more closely about the grounds he might have for such a strange claim.

He asked me if I had not, in fact, found some of the dance movements of the puppets, particularly of the smaller ones, very graceful.

---

[3] Herr C– speaks hypothetically of the craftsman (*Mechanikus*) who would construct a marionette according to his specifications, and then he refers to the craftsman (*Künstler*) who makes artificial limbs. The narrator suggests that Herr C– might find his hypothetical craftsman among the prosthetists. The words translated as "craftsman'" have very different connotations: *Mechanikus* = mechanic, *Künstler* = artist. However, the terms can be used interchangeably here, because the supreme artist is Herr C–.

[4] Newly translated from Kleist/Sembdner 1982, III:338–45.

I could not deny this fact. A group of four peasants, dancing a roundel in rapid tempo, could not have been painted more prettily by Teniers.[5]

I inquired about the mechanism of these figures and how it was possible, without having a myriad of strings on one's fingers, to control their individual limbs and extremities as the rhythm of their movements in the dance required.

He answered that I should not think of each individual limb as being placed and pulled by the manipulator during the various moments of the dance.

Each movement, he said, had its center of gravity. It suffices to control this in the innermost part of the figure; the limbs, which are nothing but pendulums, follow mechanically on their own, without any help whatsoever.

He added that this movement is very simple: whenever the center of gravity is moved in a *straight line*, the limbs describe *curves*; and often, when shaken in a merely random way, the whole figure comes to a kind of rhythmical movement which is similar to dance.

This observation seemed to me at first to shed some light on the pleasure he had claimed to find in the marionette theatre. I was still a long way from suspecting the conclusions that he would later draw.

I asked him if he believed that the manipulator who controlled these puppets must himself be a dancer or at least have some conception of the beautiful in relation to dance.

He replied that even if a task is easy from a mechanical point of view, it does not necessarily follow that it can be performed entirely without sensitivity.

The line that the center of gravity has to describe is indeed very simple and, so he believed, in most cases straight. In situations where it is curved, the law of its curvature seems to be of the first or at most of the second order, and even in the latter case only elliptical, a form of movement most natural for the extremities of the human body (because of the joints), which would demand no great artistic skill on the part of the manipulator.

From another perspective, however, this line is something very mysterious. For it is nothing less than the *path of the dancer's soul*, and he doubted that it could be found unless the manipulator were to transpose himself into the marionette's center of gravity – in other words, were to *dance*.

I replied that the business of a puppeteer had been presented to me as something fairly uninspired, rather like the turning of a crank on a barrel organ.

"Not at all," he answered. "In fact the relation of the movements of his fingers to the movement of the attached puppets is something quite artful,

---

[5] David Teniers the Younger (1610–90): the prolific Flemish painter famous for his genre scenes of peasant life.

rather like the relation of numbers to their logarithms or the asymptote to the hyperbola."

Meanwhile, he believed that even the last bit of vitality or spirit could be removed from the marionettes, that their dance could be transferred wholly into the realm of mechanical forces, and that it could be produced, just as I had imagined, by means of a crank.

I expressed my amazement at seeing him dignify with such attention this variety of fine art intended for the masses. Not only did he consider it capable of a higher development, he himself seemed to be preoccupied with such a thing.

He smiled and said he was confident in claiming that if a craftsman were to construct a marionette according to his specifications, he could use it to present a dance that neither he nor any other skillful dancer of his time, Vestris[6] himself included, would be capable of matching.

"Have you," he asked, when I silently cast my eyes at the ground, "have you heard of those mechanical legs that English craftsmen manufacture for unfortunate souls who have lost their limbs?"

I said no, I had never come across such things.

"I am sorry to hear that," he replied, "for when I tell you that these unfortunate individuals dance with them, I am almost afraid that you will not believe me. What do I mean, 'dance'? The range of their movements is indeed limited, but those they do have at their command are executed with a serenity, ease, and grace that must astonish every thinking soul."

Jokingly, I responded that he had now found his man. For the craftsman who was capable of constructing such a remarkable limb would doubtless be able to put together an entire marionette according to his specifications.

"What," I asked, as he in his turn, slightly embarrassed, looked down at the ground, "what, then, are the specifications that you would expect his skill to meet?"

"Nothing," he answered, "that is not already to be found here – balance, agility, ease – but a higher degree of everything, and in particular a natural arrangement of the centers of gravity."

"And the advantage that this puppet would have over living dancers?"

"The advantage? First of all a negative one, my excellent friend, namely this, that it would never act *affectedly*. For affectation, as you know, appears when the soul (*vis motrix*)[7] is situated somewhere other than in a movement's center of gravity. Since the manipulator, using a wire or string, has absolutely no other point in his power, all the remaining limbs are what they should be – dead, pure pendulums – and they follow the basic law of gravity – an excellent quality, which one looks for in vain in most of our dancers.

[6] Gaetan Vestris (1729–1808), soloist in the Paris Opéra ballet and the finest dancer of his time, was known as "the god of the dance."

[7] "*vis motrix*" = the animating force.

"Just observe P–," he continued, "when she plays Daphne, and, pursued by Apollo, looks back at him: her soul is located in the small of her back; she bends as though she were about to break, like a naiad out of the school of Bernini <Lg/110>.[8] Or look at young F–, when, as Paris, he stands among the three goddesses and extends the apple to Venus: his soul is lodged (it is a fright to behold) in his elbow.

"Such mistakes," he added, breaking off, "are unavoidable, since we have eaten of the tree of knowledge. Paradise is locked and the cherubim behind us; we must journey around the world and see if it is perhaps open again somewhere at the back."

I laughed. Certainly, I thought, the human spirit cannot err where none exists. But I could see that he had more on his mind and asked him to continue.

"In addition," he said, "these puppets have the advantage of *antigravity*. They know nothing of the inertia of matter, that property most inimical to the dance, for the force that lifts them into the air is greater than that which holds them to the ground. What would our dear G– give to be sixty pounds lighter or to be aided in her entrechats and pirouettes by such a force? Puppets, like elves, need the ground only so that they can *touch* on it and renew the vigor of their limbs through this momentary check; we need it in order to *rest* and recover from the exertions of the dance – a moment which is clearly not part of the dance, and with which we can do nothing except make it as inconspicuous as possible."

I said that no matter how skillfully he might present his paradoxes, he would never make me believe that a mechanical puppet could be more graceful than the human body.

He retorted that it was absolutely impossible for a human being to match the grace of a puppet. Only a god could compete with matter in this respect, and here was the point where both ends of the ring-like world came together.

I became more and more astonished, and did not know what I should say to such strange claims.

It would seem, he retorted, as he took a pinch of snuff, that I had not read the third chapter of the Book of Genesis very carefully; and if a person is unfamiliar with this first stage of all human development, one can hardly speak with him about the later stages, let alone the final one.

I said that I knew very well what disorders consciousness produces in the natural grace of human beings. A young man of my acquaintance had lost his innocence right before my eyes, as it were, through a mere observation, and afterward he was unable ever to find paradise again, in

---

[8]   Gian Lorenzo Bernini (1598–1680), the outstanding sculptor of the Baroque period in Italy, was also the creator of spectacular architectural and theatrical works. In Kleist's time, Bernini's art was regarded by many as hopelessly elaborate, ornate, and exaggerated.

spite of every conceivable effort. But what conclusions, I added, can you draw from this?

He asked me what incident I had in mind.

"About three years ago," I related, "I was bathing with a young man whose development at the time was suffused with a wonderful grace. He would have been just approaching the age of sixteen, and only the first traces of vanity were beginning to appear – a result of the favor he enjoyed with women. It happened that shortly before this, in Paris, we had seen the statue of the youth removing a thorn from his foot; copies of the statue are well known and can be found in most German collections. Just as my friend was putting his foot on a stool in order to dry it, a momentary glance in a large mirror reminded him of the statue; he smiled and told me the discovery he had made. In actual fact I had seen the same thing in exactly the same instant, but, whether it was to test the sureness of the grace he possessed or to counter his vanity in a salutary way, I laughed and replied that he must be seeing things! He reddened and raised his foot a second time in order to show me; however, as one might easily have guessed, the attempt failed. Flustered, he raised his foot a third and fourth time; he must have raised it about ten times: in vain! He was incapable of producing the same movement again – what am I saying? The movements he did make had such a comical aspect that I had trouble holding back my laughter.

"From that day – from that moment, as it were – an inconceivable change came over the young man. He began to spend entire days in front of the mirror; and bit by bit his charm deserted him. An invisible and incomprehensible power, like an iron net, seemed to spread over the free play of his gestures, and, after a year had gone by, there was no longer any trace of the loveliness which had once delighted those who surrounded him. There is someone still living today who was witness to this strange and unfortunate occurrence and can confirm it, word for word, just as I have related it."

"At this point," said Herr C– amicably, "I must tell you another story; you will easily see how it fits in here.

"On a journey to Russia, I was visiting the estate of Herr von G–, a Livonian nobleman, whose sons were at that time very involved in fencing. The eldest in particular, just home from the university, was playing the virtuoso, and he offered me a rapier one morning when I was in his room. We fenced, but it happened that I was better than he was. He became flustered, partly because of his own passion, and almost every thrust I made found its mark, until finally his rapier went flying into the corner. Picking it up, he said, half jokingly, half irritably, that he had met his match, but sooner or later we all encounter our master, and now he wished to lead me to mine. The brothers burst out laughing and shouted, 'Let's go! Down to the stall!' Taking me by the hand, they led me to a bear that their father, Herr von G–, was having raised on the estate.

"Astonished, I went up to the bear who was standing on his hind legs, with his back against a post to which he was chained and his right paw poised to strike. He looked me straight in the eye: this was his fencing posture. I thought I must be dreaming to find myself facing such an opponent, but Herr von G– said, 'Go ahead, attack! See if you can hit him!' When I had recovered somewhat from my astonishment, I lunged at him with my rapier; the bear made a very quick movement with his paw and parried my thrust. I tried misleading him with feints; the bear did not move. I lunged at him again with concentrated skill, and I definitely would not have failed to hit a human breast, but the bear made a very quick movement with his paw and parried the thrust. I was now almost in the situation of the young Herr von G–. The bear's soberness robbed me of my composure, thrusts alternated with feints, I was dripping with sweat: in vain! It was not only that the bear, like the premier fencer in the world, parried all my thrusts, but he did not react at all to feints (no fencer in the world copies him in this). His paw poised to strike, he stood with his eyes fixed on mine as though he could read my soul therein; and when my thrusts were not in earnest, he did not move.

"Do you believe this story?"

"Absolutely!" I cried, applauding enthusiastically. "I'd believe it of any stranger, it is so plausible;[9] how much more, then, of you!"

"Now, my excellent friend," said Herr C–, "you have everything you need to understand me. We see that in the organic world, as reflection grows darker and weaker, grace emerges more radiant and powerful. But just as two lines intersecting on one side of a point, after their passage through infinity, suddenly reappear on the other side, or just as the image in a concave mirror, after moving out into the infinite, suddenly becomes visible again, so too grace returns, when knowledge has, as it were, gone through an infinity; thus, grace appears most purely in that human form which has either no consciousness at all or an infinite one – that is, in a puppet or in a god."

"Therefore," I said, somewhat abstracted, "we would have to eat once more of the tree of knowledge in order to fall back into the state of innocence?"

"Yes, indeed," he answered. "That is the final chapter in the history of the world."

---

[9] The word *wahrscheinlich* ("plausible" or "probable") appears here as part of an extended ironic play on notions of probability, credibility, and verisimilitude < 1:In/8–9>.

22

WILLIAM HAZLITT
(1778–1830)

In his series of essays on Shakespeare's characters,[1] Hazlitt not only discusses them sympathetically and inventively, but almost communes with them; and this approach is founded on his most fundamental ideas about drama, poetry, and art. Like Keats and Coleridge <Co/220>, Hazlitt avers that Shakespeare was able to realize his characters so fully and concretely because he could assume their identities: "He was the least of an egotist that it was possible to be. He was nothing in himself; but he was all that others were, or that they could become" (Hazlitt/ Howe 1930–34, V:47). Characterization in Shakespeare is not a matter of "words, a set speech or two, a preconcerted theory of a character" but of the dramatic personages being "present in the poet's imagination, as at a kind of rehearsal ..." (Hazlitt/Howe 1930–34, V:48). Aristotle advocated a kind of pre-performance by the writer of tragedies <1:Ar/54> but Hazlitt goes much further in this direction: Shakespeare's empathy with his characters is the enabling constituent of his genius for dramatic poetry; and, moreover, this creative genius has its counterpart in a criticism that involves itself through an equivalent imaginative appropriation of the dramatist's *personae*.

In his essays on the theatre and his theatre reviews Hazlitt concerned himself primarily with actors, and in a similar but more complex way. He is most attentive to the ways in which the given role is – as it must be – informed by both the natural attributes and the talents of the actor. He is sympathetically alert to the presence, needs, and efforts of the performer and, though he often judges the performances with some rigor, he is acutely aware of the ways in which his writing is involved with them, not something objective and detached. This is partly the attitude of a reviewer – one with scruples – but also one who, like Hegel <Hg/206> insists on the arts as intersubjective media rather than egotistical expressions.

One of the apparent paradoxes of Hazlitt's writing on the theatre is his great enthusiasm for a social activity which he views, at the same time, as an impossible art in certain vital respects, and notably in the staging of Shakespeare's plays. In most cases Hazlitt would rather read the plays than see them played, since he finds that theatrical representation, or "pantomime" as he often calls it <Dt/68>, falls far short of the poetry, not only for accidental reasons but for the intrinsic one that "the imagination cannot sufficiently qualify the actual impressions of the senses" (Hazlitt/Howe 1930–34, IV:248). In the playing of Restoration drama Hazlitt finds no such difficulty and is exceptionally appreciative of it.

---

[1] These essays were collected as *The Characters of Shakespear's Plays* (1817). Other collections of essays by Hazlitt having to do with drama and theatre are: *A View of the English Stage* (1818); *Lectures on the English Comic Writers* (1819); and *Lectures Chiefly on the Dramatic Literature of the Age of Elizabeth* (1820).

His writing about theatre is alive both to its own involvement in the pleasures of theatre-going and to its relative durability. It will outlast its particular occasions and itself become part of theatrical tradition and a layer of the social memory of past performances, which each new performance renews.

For further reading

Hazlitt/Howe 1930–34; Heller 1990; Kinnaird 1978; Park 1971; Schneider 1933; Whitely 1955.

"On Actors and Acting"[2]

Players are "the abstracts and brief chronicles of the time [*Hamlet* 2.2.548]"; the motley representatives of human nature. They are the only honest hypocrites. Their life is a voluntary dream; a studied madness. The height of their ambition is to be *beside themselves*. Today kings, tomorrow beggars, it is only when they are themselves that they are nothing. Made up of mimic laughter and tears, passing from the extremes of joy or woe at a prompter's call, they wear the livery of other men's fortunes; their very thoughts are not their own. They are, as it were, train-bearers in the pageant of life, and hold up a glass to humanity, frailer than itself. We see ourselves at second-hand in them: they show us all that we are, all that we wish to be, and all that we dread to be. The stage is an epitome, a bettered likeness of the world, with the dull part left out: and indeed with this omission, it is nearly big enough to hold all the rest. What brings the resemblance nearer is that, as *they* imitate us, we, in our turn, imitate them. How many fine gentlemen do we owe to the stage? How many romantic lovers are mere Romeos in masquerade? How many soft bosoms have heaved with Juliet's sighs? They teach us when to laugh and when to weep, when to love and when to hate, upon principle, and with a good grace! Wherever there is a playhouse, the world will go on not amiss. The stage not only refines the manners, but it is the best teacher of morals, for it is the truest and most intelligible picture of life. It stamps the image of virtue on the mind by first softening the crude materials of which it is composed, by a sense of pleasure. It regulates the passions by giving a loose to the imagination. It points out the selfish and depraved to our detestation, the amiable and generous to our admiration; and if it clothes the more seductive vices with the borrowed graces of wit and fancy, even those graces operate as a diversion to the coarser poison of experience and bad example, and often prevent or carry off the infection by inoculating the

---

[2] The original "Round Table" essay appeared in the *Examiner* for 5 January 1817. It was collected in *The Round Table: A Collection of Essays on Literature, Men and Manners* (1817). The present text is from Hazlitt/Howe 1930–34, IV:153–60, with minor modifications in punctuation.

works remain. When a great actor dies, there is a void produced in ciety, a gap which requires to be filled up. Who does not go to see Kean? no, if Garrick were alive, would go to see him? At least one or the other ist have quitted the stage. We have seen what a ferment has been cited among our living artists by the exhibition of the works of the old isters at the British Gallery.[14] What would the actors say to it, if, by any ell or power of necromancy, all the celebrated actors, for the last ndred years, could be made to appear again on the boards of Covent rden and Drury Lane, for the last time, in all their most brilliant parts? hat a rich treat to the town, what a feast for the critics, to go and see tterton, and Booth, and Wilks,[15] and Sanford, and Nokes, and Leigh,[16] d Penkethman, and Bullock, and Estcourt,[17] and Dogget,[18] and Mrs. rry,[19] and Mrs. Montfort,[20] and Mrs. Oldfield, and Mrs. Bracegirdle,[21] d Mrs. Cibber, and Cibber himself, the prince of coxcombs,[22] and

In his "On the Catalogue Raisonné of the British Institution" (*Examiner*, 3, 10, and 17 November 1816) Hazlitt attacked the idea that the work of modern British artists might be promoted by the depreciation of old masters.

Thomas Betterton (c. 1635–1710) excelled in such roles as Sir Toby Belch and Falstaff. Barton Booth (1681–1733) acted for him during Betterton's management of Lincoln's Inn Fields. Robert Wilks (1665–1732) was Booth's rival as an actor and later his fellow manager of Drury Lane.

Samuel Sanford was an actor and singer of the late seventeenth century, notable for his portrayals of villains. James Nokes (d. 1696) excelled in comic roles. Anthony Leigh (d. 1692) was also known for his comic roles, especially (with Nokes) for his fops. He played for the Duke's, King's, and United Companies.

William Penkethman (d. 1725) was a comedian whose roles included some written for him by Colley Cibber. William Bullock, the elder (c. 1667–1742) was an actor closely associated with the Drury Lane management. He was noted for farce and comedy and also for his female roles, which included Kate Matlock in *The Funeral*. He often played alongside Penkethman. In connection with his part in *The Fox* by Thomas Baker, he was tried for participating in an obscene performance, and acquitted. The mimicry of Dick Estcourt (1668–1712), a member of the Drury Lane company, is described by Steele in *The Spectator* 468.

Congreve wrote the parts of Fondlewife and Ben Legend for Thomas Dogget (1670–1721), who retired from the joint-management (with Wilks and Cibber) of Drury Lane when, and because, Barton Booth joined it.

Elizabeth Barry (1658–1713) created many roles, including Monimia in Otway's *The Orphan* (1680) and Belvedera in his *Venice Preserv'd*. She and Betterton were highly successful in staging the pathos of Otway's characters and scenes.

Among the roles played by Susanna Percival (Mrs. Mo[u]ntfort) (1667–1703) was Melantha in Dryden's *Marriage à-la-Mode*. Hazlitt goes on to quote at length Cibber's description of her in the part (Hazlitt/Howe 1930–34, IV:157–58).

Anne Oldfield, a member of the Drury Lane company, excelled in both comic and tragic roles and was notable for the clarity of her diction. Cibber, Farquhar, and Voltaire were among those who admired her acting. Oldfield was considered a worthy successor to Anne Bracegirdle (c. 1673–1748), whose retirement was precipitated by Oldfield's success. Among Bracegirdle's famous roles were Congreve's Angelica and his Millamant. The Mrs. Cibber here referred to is Susannah Maria Arne (1714–66), a principal in Garrick's company at Drury Lane and the daughter-in-law of Colley Cibber – not his daughter, the remarkable transvestite Charlotte Charke. As well as being a comedian, a playwright, and the Poet Laureate, Colley Cibber (1671–1757) was also one of the managerial triumvirate for whom Penkethman acted at Drury Lane. As noted above, Cibber's *Apology* is Hazlitt's main source of information about Restoration actors.

mind with a certain taste and elegance. To show how little we agree with the common declamations against the immoral tendency of the stage on this score, we will hazard a conjecture, that the acting of *The Beggar's Opera* a certain number of nights every year since it was first brought out has done more towards putting down the practice of highway robbery than all the gibbets that ever were erected. A person, after seeing this piece, is too deeply imbued with a sense of humanity, is in too good humor with himself and the rest of the world, to set about cutting throats or rifling pockets. Whatever makes a jest of vice, leaves it too much a matter of indifference for anyone in his senses to rush desperately on his ruin for its sake. We suspect that just the contrary effect must be produced by the representation of *George Barnwell* <Dt/48>, which is too much in the style of the Ordinary's[3] sermon to meet with any better success. The mind, in such cases, instead of being deterred by the alarming consequences held out to it, revolts against the denunciation of them as an insult offered to its free-will, and, in a spirit of defiance, returns a practical answer to them, by daring the worst that can happen. The most striking lesson ever read to levity and licentiousness is in the last act of *The Inconstant*,[4] where young Mirabel is preserved by the fidelity of his mistress, Orinda [= Oriana], in the disguise of a page, from the hands of assassins, into whose power he has been allured by the temptations of vice and beauty. There never was a rake who did not become in imagination a reformed man, during the representation of the last trying scenes of this admirable comedy.

If the stage is useful as a school of instruction, it is no less so as a source of amusement. It is a source of the greatest enjoyment at the time, and a never-failing fund of agreeable reflection afterwards. The merits of a new play, or of a new actor, are always among the first topics of polite conversation. One way in which public exhibitions contribute to refine and humanize mankind, is by supplying them with ideas and subjects of conversation and interest in common. The progress of civilization is in proportion to the number of commonplaces current in society. For instance, if we meet with a stranger at an inn or in a stage-coach, who knows nothing but his own affairs – his shop, his customers, his farm, his pigs, his poultry – we can carry on no conversation with him on these local and personal matters: the only way is to let him have all the talk to himself. But if he has fortunately ever seen Mr. Liston act,[5] this is an immediate topic of mutual conversation, and we agree together the rest of the evening in discussing the merits of that inimitable actor, with the same satisfaction as in talking over the affairs of the most intimate friend.

If the stage thus introduces us familiarly to our contemporaries, it also

[3] The Ordinary was a clergyman who visited prisoners sentenced to death.

[4] A comedy (1702) by Farquhar.

[5] John Liston (1776–1846), one of Hazlitt's favorite actors, was an immensely successful comedian, who also played some tragic roles.

brings us acquainted with former times. It is an interesting revival of past ages, manners, opinions, dresses, persons, and actions – whether it carries us back to the wars of York and Lancaster, or half-way back to the heroic times of Greece and Rome, in some translation from the French, or quite back to the age of Charles II in the scenes of Congreve and of Etherege (the gay Sir George!) – happy age, when kings and nobles led purely ornamental lives; when the utmost stretch of a morning's study went no further than the choice of a sword-knot, or the adjustment of a side-curl; when the soul spoke out in all the pleasing elegance of dress; and beaux and belles, enamored of themselves in one another's follies, fluttered like gilded butterflies in giddy mazes through the walks of St. James's Park!

A good company of comedians, a Theatre-Royal judiciously managed, is your true Herald's College; the only Antiquarian Society that is worth a rush. It is for this reason that there is such an air of romance about players, and that it is pleasanter to see them <1:Lp/190>, even in their own persons, than any of the three learned professions. We feel more respect for John Kemble[6] in a plain coat than for the Lord Chancellor on the woolsack. He is surrounded, to our eyes, with a greater number of imposing recollections: he is a more reverend piece of formality; a more complicated tissue of costume. We do not know whether to look upon this accomplished actor as Pierre, or King John, or Coriolanus, or Cato, or Leontes, or the Stranger. But we see in him a stately hieroglyphic of humanity; a living monument of departed greatness; a somber comment on the rise and fall of kings. We look after him till he is out of sight, as we listen to a story of one of Ossian's[7] heroes, to "a tale of other times!" ...[8]

The most pleasant feature of the profession of a player, and which, indeed, is peculiar to it, is that we not only admire the talents of those who adorn it, but we contract a personal intimacy with them. There is no class of society whom so many persons regard with affection as actors. We greet them on the stage; we like to meet them in the streets; they almost always recall to us pleasant associations; and we feel our gratitude excited, without the uneasiness of a sense of obligation. The very gaiety and popularity, however, which surrounds the life of a favorite performer, make the retiring from it a very serious business. It glances a mortifying reflection on the shortness of human life, and the vanity of human

pleasures. Something reminds us that "all the world's a stage men and women merely players" [*As You Like It* 2.7.139–40]

It has been considered as the misfortune of first-rate talents that they leave no record behind them except that of vague that the genius of a great actor perishes with him, "leaving t copy" [*Twelfth Night* 1.5.261]. This is a misfortune, or unpleasant circumstance, to actors; but it is, perhaps, an adva stage. It leaves an opening to originality. The stage is alway anew; the candidates for theatrical reputation are always afresh, unencumbered by the affectation of the faults or excelle predecessors. In this respect, we should imagine that the aver of dramatic talent remains more nearly the same than that walk of art. In no other instance do the complaints of the dege moderns seem so unfounded as in this; and Colley Cibber's ac regular decline of the stage, from the time of Shakespeare to th II, and from the time of Charles II to the beginning of Georg quite ridiculous. The stage is a place where genius is sure to c legs, in a generation or two at farthest. In the other arts (as in poetry) it has been contended that what has been well done giving rise to endless vapid imitations, is an obstacle to what n well hereafter: that the models or *chef-d'oeuvres* of art, wh accumulated, choke up the path to excellence; and that genius, where they can be rendered permanent and handed age to age, not only prevent, but render superfluous, future p the same kind. We have not, neither do we want, two Shak Miltons, two Raphaels, any more than we require two suns sphere. Even Miss O'Neill[10] stands a little in the way of our re Mrs. Siddons.[11] But Mr. Kean[12] is an excellent substitute for th Garrick,[13] whom we never saw. When an author dies, it is n

---

6   John Philip Kemble (1757–1853). Hazlitt goes on to mention some of his most famous roles from: Thomas Otway's *Venice Preserv'd* (1682); *King John* and *Coriolanus* by Shakespeare; Addison's *Cato*; Shakespeare's *A Winter's Tale*; and *The Stranger*, Benjamin Thompson's translation of von Kotzebue's *Menschenhass und Rue* (1789). Hazlitt's "Mr. Kemble's Retirement" (*The Times*, 25 June 1817) is an assessment of the actor's talents and career.

7   The epic poems concocted by James Macpherson (1736–96) and attributed by him to Ossian, supposedly an ancient Gaelic poet, were much admired for their Romantic qualities. Hazlitt (mis)quotes the first line of the poems.

8   Hazlitt interpolated here a passage from his "Theatrical Examiner" article for 4 June 1815. This passage ends with the quotation from *As You Like It*. The omitted part concerns the retirement from the stage of John Bannister (1760–1836).

9   In Chapter 4 of his *Apology for the Life of Mr. Colley Cibber, Comedian* (17 names most of the Restoration actors mentioned by Hazlitt in this arti lively sketches of the acting of many of them.

10   Eliza O'Neill (1791–1872), who came to London from Ireland in I considered to be Mrs. Siddons' successor, as in "Miss O'Neill's Retir *Magazine*, 2, February 1820), in which Hazlitt admiringly reviews her car how much better it is for an actor to retire at the height of her powers tha their decline.

11   Sarah Siddons (1755–1831) was the outstanding female tragedian of London stage, from which she first retired in 1812. In "Mrs. Siddons" (E 1816) Hazlitt reviews her Lady Macbeth and finds her return to the stag

12   Edmund Kean (1789–1833) earned renown with his playing of Shylock 1814 and achieved his greatest successes in his playing of roles such as N III, and Iago.

13   David Garrick (1717–79) not only transformed acting style in England v naturalness in a great variety of stage roles but also exercised an enorm European ideas of the theatre – those of Diderot and Lessing for examp many plays and was a distinguished and innovative manager of Drury

Macklin, and Quin, and Rich,[23] and Mrs. Clive, and Mrs. Pritchard, and Mrs. Abington,[24] and Weston, and Shuter,[25] and Garrick, and all the rest of those who "gladdened life," and whose death "eclipsed the gaiety of nations"![26] We should certainly be there. We should buy a ticket for the season. We should enjoy *our hundred days* again. We should not miss a single night. We would not, for a great deal, be absent from Betterton's Hamlet or his Brutus, or from Booth's Cato, as it was first acted to the contending applause of Whigs and Tories. We should be in the first row when Mrs. Barry (who was kept by Lord Rochester, and with whom Otway was in love) played Monimia or Belvidera; and we suppose we should go to see Mrs. Bracegirdle (with whom all the world was in love) in all her parts. We should then know exactly whether Penkethman's manner of picking a chicken, and Bullock's mode of devouring asparagus, answered to the ingenious account of them in the *Tatler*,[27] and whether Dogget was equal to Dowton[28] – whether Mrs. Montfort or Mrs. Abington was the finest lady – whether Wilks or Cibber was the best Sir Harry Wildair,[29] – whether Macklin was really "the Jew that Shakespeare drew," and whether Garrick was, upon the whole, so great an actor as the world would have made him out! Many people have a strong desire to pry into the secrets of futurity: for our own parts, we should be satisfied if we had the power to recall the

---

[23] Charles Macklin (1700–97) achieved prominence with his Shylock in 1741, which earned him the couplet, attributed to Alexander Pope and quoted below. James Quin[n] (1693–1766) was known for his varied Shakespearean roles and the declamatory style in which he played them, which Garrick made outmoded. John Rich (1692–1761) produced Gay's *The Beggar's Opera* in 1728 at the Lincoln's Inn Fields, which he owned. For many years he produced and acted in an annual pantomime, creating a vogue for the genre. (Hazlitt substituted Rich's name for that of Peg Woffington in his revision of the *Examiner* article.)

[24] Kitty Clive (1711–85), who played at Drury Lane under Garrick, was outstanding in low comedy though she aspired to tragic roles. Hannah Pritchard (1711–68) became known for her playing of light comedy but her most famous role was Lady Macbeth, which she played opposite Garrick. Frances Abington (1737–1815) was a longtime member of Garrick's company at Drury Lane, where she played leading roles.

[25] Thomas Weston (1737–76), an outstanding comedian, was a notable Scrub in Farquhar's *The Beaux Stratagem*. Edward (Ned) Shuter (c. 1728–76) was an actor and singer, who was hired by Garrick for Drury Lane in 1774 but went on to act mostly at Covent Garden. He had a large repertoire of comic roles (including Farquhar's Scrub). Shuter was known for his badinage with audiences, and was reputed to be an excellent reciter of prologues and epilogues.

[26] A misquotation of Dr. Johnson's epitaph on Garrick.

[27] No. 188.

[28] William Dowton (1764–1851) was an actor and manager in London and the provinces. He was notable for his comic roles in Restoration drama and Shakespeare, displaying mercurial qualities on and off stage. His revival of Samuel Foote's *The Tailors* at the Haymarket in 1805 was the occasion for a riot by the London tailors.

[29] In *The Constant Couple; or, a Trip to the Jubilee* (1699) and its sequel *Sir Harry Wildair* (1701) by Farquhar.

dead, and live the past over again, as often as we pleased![30] Players, after all, have little reason to complain of their hard-earned, short-lived popularity. One thunder of applause from pit, boxes, and gallery, is equal to a whole immortality of posthumous fame; and when we hear an actor, whose modesty is equal to his merit, declare that he would like to see a dog wag his tail in approbation, what must he feel when he sees the whole house in a roar! Besides, Fame, as if their reputation had been entrusted to her alone, has been particularly careful of the renown of her theatrical favorites: she forgets, one by one, and year by year, those who have been great lawyers, great statesmen, and great warriors in their day; but the name of Garrick still survives with the works of Reynolds[31] and of Johnson. . . .[32]

[30] From the original periodical publication Hazlitt cut the following: "We have no curiosity about things or persons that we never heard of. Mr. Coleridge professes in his Lay Sermon to have discovered a new faculty, by which he can divine the future. This is lucky for himself and his friends, who seem to have lost all recollection of the past."

[31] Sir Joshua Reynolds (1723–92): foremost among the portrait painters of his time; friend of Garrick and Johnson; first President of the Royal Academy; and the chief exponent of neo-classical aesthetic theory in England. His annual lectures to the Academy were published as *Discourses on Art* (1790).

[32] In the 1817 volume the article continues with another short interpolation and the remainder of the original *Examiner* article, which together constitute a brief defense of actors from "common cant" criticisms of their lives and characters.

23

STENDHAL (HENRI BEYLE)
(1783–1842)

Stendhal composed the first part of *Racine and Shakespeare* in response to an event which had aroused his indignation. At the end of July 1822, a troupe of English actors presented (or tried to present) *Othello* in Paris at the theatre of la Porte Saint-Martin, but met with such a hostile reception, fired by chauvinism and memories of 1815, that the play was virtually inaudible. The company was able to continue its performances of Shakespeare in Paris only by moving to a small, ill-equipped theatre and restricting admission to subscribers. In October 1822, Stendhal published in the *Paris Monthly Review* an article which contained the essential material of the first chapter of the pamphlet which he would publish in the following March as *Racine and Shakespeare*.[1]

In his initial reaction and in the more elaborated *Racine and Shakespeare*, Stendhal pursued several complementary programs. Most immediately, he denounced the narrow-minded attitude of the French towards things English, but he understood that it was related to a larger problem. At the risk of simplifying a complex situation, we may say that in 1823 it was the political conservatives who were most sympathetic to the Romantic movement in literature, whereas the liberals (bourgeois and Bonapartist) were the defenders of the neo-classical tradition. Stendhal, a convinced liberal, was strongly opposed to what he saw as the outmoded, irrelevant, and oppressive literary heritage of the *ancien régime*. He therefore felt a pressing need to correct a misconception among those who should have been his allies, and demonstrate not only the superiority of Shakespeare, but more generally the need to overcome the influence of habit and create a form of drama truly suited to contemporary society. Stendhal offers examples of possible subjects (such as the death of Henri III or of Henri IV) which would be appropriate for treatment in the kind of play which he was advocating.

Drama is the particular focus, but it is set in the larger context of an aesthetic of Romanticism which Stendhal defines in the third chapter. There the matter might have rested, but in a session of the French Academy held on 24 April 1824, the permanent secretary, Auger, delivered a public denunciation of Romanticism and a defense of the national literary heritage. Stendhal replied with *Racine and Shakespeare II*, published in March 1825.

This second pamphlet takes the form of an exchange of letters between a Romantic and a Classicist.[2] The debate is markedly one-sided: of the ten letters, the

---

[1] Similarly, the *Paris Monthly Review* presented in January 1823 a second article which would become the second chapter of the pamphlet. (The third chapter did not make a prior appearance.)

[2] Stendhal had used a dialogue between a Romantic and an Academician in Chapter 1 of the 1823 pamphlet, in a passage which was essentially a translation of Ermes Visconti's

Classicist has only three (two are very brief) and does little more than provide the
Romantic with a pretext for expounding his ideas. There is a certain amount of
repetition of positions already expressed in 1823,[3] but there is now a stronger
political undercurrent, particularly in the condemnation of censorship.

Stendhal's ideas in the two parts of *Racine and Shakespeare* are summarized in his
long note near the end of the second pamphlet. With this in mind, two comments
may be useful. First, unlike Diderot and Beaumarchais, Stendhal does not envisage
the creation of a new, intermediate genre. He retains the traditional categories of
tragedy and comedy, but seeks to remake them in forms suited to his age. Second,
his antipathy to verse in drama should be understood in light of both the stereo-
typed "poetic" language used in the plays of his time and the relatively rigid form of
the alexandrine line, with its fixed caesura and rejection of run-on lines. Stendhal is
opposed, not to all verse (he recognizes the supple and expressive qualities of
English and Italian verse), but to the codified and restrictive practice which habit
had established and maintained in France.

For further reading

Crouzet 1983–84; Gould 1989; Scelfo 1984; Stendhal/Martino 1970; Talbot
1983.

From *Racine and Shakespeare* (1823)[4]

Chapter 1

> To write tragedies which will appeal to an audience in 1823,
> should we follow Racine's procedures or Shakespeare's? . . .

The whole quarrel between Racine and Shakespeare comes down to
deciding whether, by observing the unities of place and time, we can write
plays which will have a strong appeal for nineteenth-century audiences –
in other words, which will offer them *dramatic* pleasures rather than *epic*
pleasures . . . .

I claim that respect for the unities of place and time is a French habit, a
deeply rooted habit from which it will be difficult to free ourselves, because
Paris is the salon of Europe and sets the tone; but I maintain that these
unities are in no way necessary for producing deep emotion and a true
dramatic effect. . . .

[THE ROMANTIC:] You must agree that the illusion which we [nor-
mally] seek in the theatre is not a perfect illusion <Jh/84; Co/230> . . . . You
must agree that audiences are aware that they are seeing a representation
of a work of art, not a real event. . . . [But] do you [also] think that now and

---

Dialogo sulle unità drammatiche di luogo e di tempo (*Dialogue on the Dramatic Unities of Place
and Time*) (1819).

[3] There is also some repetition within the two pamphlets. *Racine and Shakespeare* is a form of
crusading journalism, albeit of high quality.

[4] Newly translated from Stendhal/Martino 1970.

then, say two or three times in an act, for a second or two, the illusion is total?

THE ACADEMICIAN: I'm not sure. To answer you, I would have to go back to the theatre several times and observe my own reactions.

THE ROMANTIC: Ah, that's a delightfully honest answer. ... It seems to me that these moments of total illusion are more frequent than is generally believed ... . But these moments last only a fleeting second. ... These delightful instants do not occur when a scene changes, nor when the author makes the spectator leap over twelve or fifteen days, nor when he is obliged to put a long narration in the mouth of one of his characters in order to inform the audience of some event which must be made known, nor when we encounter three or four lines which are admirable *as verse*. These wonderful rare moments of perfect illusion can be found only in the heat of an animated scene, as the exchanges come hard on the heels of each other. ... We will never find these moments of perfect illusion when a murder is committed on stage, or when guards come to arrest someone and take him off to prison. We cannot believe such things to be real, and they will never produce illusion. Such events are employed simply to lead up to the scenes <Co/231> during which the audience will encounter those wonderful split seconds; and I maintain that those brief moments of perfect illusion *are found more frequently in Shakespeare's tragedies than in Racine's*. All of the pleasure which we find in tragic drama depends on the frequency of these short moments of illusion, *and on the emotional state in which they leave the spectator's soul during the intervals between them*. One of the greatest obstacles to these moments of illusion is admiration, however justified, for the fine verse <Sa/185> of a tragedy. ...

Chapter 3 [What Romanticism Is]

Romanticism is the art of presenting to nations the literary works which, in the present state of their habits and beliefs, are likely to give them the greatest possible amount of pleasure.

Classicism, on the contrary, offers them the type of literature which gave the greatest possible pleasure to their great-grandfathers.

Sophocles and Euripides were eminently romantic: they gave the Greeks assembled in the theatre of Athens the tragedies which, in accordance with that people's moral habits, religion, and ideas on what constitutes human dignity, were likely to offer the greatest possible pleasure.

Imitating Sophocles and Euripides today, and claiming that these imitations won't make nineteenth-century Frenchmen yawn, is the hallmark of classicism <Vt/20>. ...

Never, within historical memory, has a people undergone, in its customs and its pleasures, a more rapid and more radical change than occurred between 1780 and 1823: and we are given the same old literature! Let our grave opponents simply look around them: the fool of 1780 spouted stupid, flat jokes, he was always laughing; the fool of 1823 spouts vague, trite, boring philosophical utterances, he is always long-faced. There [for example] is a noteworthy revolution. A society in which an element so essential and so recurring as *the fool* has changed to this extent, can no longer tolerate the same form of the *ridiculous* or of *the pathetic*. . . .

The romantic poet *par excellence* was Dante: he adored Virgil, but he created the *Divine Comedy*, and the episode of Ugolino <Sr/159>,[5] totally unlike the *Aeneid*, because he understood that in his own time people were afraid of hell.

Romantics don't advise anyone to imitate directly Shakespeare's dramas. What we must imitate in this great man is his way of studying the world in which we live, and the art of giving our contemporaries exactly the kind of tragedy they need, but which they don't have the boldness to demand, intimidated as they are by the reputation of the great Racine.

By chance, this new French tragedy might bear a considerable resemblance to Shakespeare's. But that would be solely because our circumstances are the same as those of England in 1590. We too have factions, punishments, conspiracies. . . . Since we are intellectually far superior to the English of that period, our *new tragedy* will have greater simplicity. . . . The French mentality will especially reject the German gibberish which many people call *romantic* today. Schiller *copied* Shakespeare and his rhetoric; he didn't have the wit to give his countrymen the tragedy which their mores required. . . .

From *Racine and Shakespeare* II (1825)

. . . A romantic tragedy is written in prose; the succession of events which it presents before the spectator lasts several months and they occur in different places. . . .

[A Hypothetical Romantic Comedy][6]

That's what I call a romantic comedy: the events last three and a half months; it takes place in various parts of Paris; . . . and it is written in prose, in very common prose. . . . *Lefranc, or the Poet* is a romantic comedy because the events *resemble* what happens before our eyes every day. The writers, noblemen, judges, lawyers, men of letters, spies, etc., who speak and act in this comedy are like those we meet every day in drawing-rooms: no more affected, no more stiff than they are in reality, and indeed that is more than enough. The characters in classical comedy, on the other hand,

---

[5] In the *Inferno* (canto 33), Count Ugolino is represented as gnawing on the skull of his enemy Archbishop Ruggieri.

[6] Stendhal first outlines the plot of a hypothetical work, which he titles *Lefranc, ou le poète*. It is a bitter little sketch of a comedy in five acts about the stifling of a dramatist with genius but no talent for self-promotion.

seem to be wearing a double mask: first, the dreadful affectation which we are obliged to put on in society if we want to be esteemed; and in addition the affectation of nobility, still more ridiculous, with which the author endows them on his own by making them speak in alexandrines. ... The comedy *Lefranc, or the Poet* has no [distinctive] style, and that, in my opinion, is its strong point, that is what I prize in it. ...

Need I add that what I have said about the comedy *Lefranc* is no guarantee at all of talent. If this play has no vivacity, no genius, it will be even more boring than a classical comedy, which, lacking dramatic pleasure, at least offers the pleasure of *fine verse*. A romantic comedy devoid of talent, lacking fine verse to impress the audience, will be a bore from the very first performance. So, you see, we come back to this truth which the Academicians, and those who aspire to the Academy, decry as being a proof of bad taste: *the alexandrine is frequently just a veil to hide incompetence*. (English or Italian verse can express anything and presents no obstacle to dramatic beauties.) ...

Molière was a romantic in 1670, because at that time the court was full of Orontes, and provincial châteaux were full of very discontented Alcestes.[7] Rightly viewed, all great authors were romantic in their time. A century after their death, it is the writers who copy them, rather than opening their eyes and imitating nature, who are the classics. ...

[Stendhal's Summary][8]

1. Never any battles or executions on stage: such things are epic, not dramatic. In the nineteenth century, audiences dislike horror, and when, in Shakespeare, we see a torturer come forward to burn out the eyes of small children [*King John* 4.1], instead of shuddering we laugh at the broomsticks with red paint on the end which are supposed to represent red-hot irons.

2. The more the ideas and events of a play are romantic (that is, based on present-day needs), the more one must respect language – which is a matter of convention – in the turns of phrase no less than in the words. ...

3. The passionate interest with which we follow the emotions of a personage constitutes tragedy; the simple curiosity which leaves our attention free for a hundred different details constitutes comedy. The interest which Julie d'Étanges[9] inspires in us is tragic; Shakespeare's *Coriolanus* is comic. The mixing of these two types of interest seems to me very difficult.

4. Unless the intention is to portray the successive changes which time produces in a man's character, it may be found that, if a tragedy is to please in 1825, its action should not extend over several years. Once

---

[7] Oronte and Alceste are characters in Molière's *Le Misanthrope*.

[8] The following note, in which Stendhal summarizes many of his ideas on the form of drama which he would like to see practiced in his time, appears near the end of the 1825 pamphlet.

[9] The heroine of Jean-Jacques Rousseau's novel *La Nouvelle Héloise* (*The New Eloise*) (1761).

dramatists have tried their own experiments, it may turn out that one year is a suitable average. If a tragedy were extended much beyond that, the hero would no longer be the same man at the end as he was at the beginning. ...

5. It is Shakespeare's *art* that we must borrow. ... The English of 1600 were quite different from the French of 1825. But it is the latter we must please. ... In order to write romantic dramas (that is, suited to the needs of our time), we must diverge considerably from Shakespeare's manner, and, for example, avoid the *tirade* <Dt/43; Gl/70; Hg/212; Hu/264> with an audience which grasps perfectly the sense of innuendos, whereas things had to be explained at length, with powerful images, for an English audience in 1600.

6. After deriving our *art* from Shakespeare, we must turn to Gregory of Tours, Froissart, Livy, the Bible, and the modern Greeks for the subjects of tragedy.[10] What subject is more beautiful or more moving than the death of Jesus? ...

7. We are told: "Verse is the ideal beauty of expression: once a thought has been conceived, verse is the most beautiful way to express it, the way which gives it its greatest effect." Yes, for satire, epigrams, satirical comedy, epic poetry, or mythical poetry such as *Phaedra* and *Iphigenia*. No, if we are dealing with the kind of tragedy which derives its effects from the accurate portrayal of the movements of the soul and events from the life of the moderns <Hu/264>. The idea or the emotion must *above all* be expressed with clarity in drama, which in this respect is very different from the epic. "The table is full," cries Macbeth, trembling with fear as he sees the ghost of Banquo, whom he has just had murdered, sit at the royal table in the place reserved for Macbeth himself [*Macbeth* 3.4]. What verse, what rhythm could add to the beauty of this phrase? It is a cry from the heart, and a cry from the heart has no place for inversions. Is it for their function as part of an alexandrine that we admire, "Let us be friends, Cinna," or Hermione's question to Orestes, "Who bade you do it?"[11]

It is precisely these words that the situation requires, and no others. When the demands of metre do not allow the exact term that an agitated person would use, what do our academic poets do? They sacrifice the emotion to the alexandrine. ...

Verse is intended to condense, by dint of ellipses, inversions, juxtapositions of words, etc. (those dazzling privileges of poetry), the reasons for

---

10 The choice of Gregory of Tours (c. 538–94), author of the *Historia Francorum*, and Jean Froissart (c. 1337-c. 1410), chronicler of the Hundred Years War, is consistent with the preference which Stendhal expresses in several places for French historical subjects, especially those drawn from the Middle Ages, but the inclusion of the Roman historian Livy (Titus Livius, 59 B.C.–A.D.17) is surprising. As for the modern Greeks, Stendhal is thinking of the struggle for Greek independence, which was a topic of vital interest at the time he was writing.

11 Corneille, *Cinna*, 5.3.1701; Racine, *Andromaque* (1667), 5.4.1543.

feeling a beauty of nature. In drama, it is the *preceding scenes* which give its full effect to what we hear being said in the present scene. ...

A character becomes nothing more than a rhetorician *whom I distrust* if I have even a minimal experience of real life, once he attempts to add to the power of what he is saying by the beauty of the expression.

The fundamental condition of drama is that the action takes place in a room from which Melpomene's magic wand has removed one of the walls and replaced it with the auditorium. The characters do not know that there is an audience. ... The moment there is an apparent concession to the audience <Lg/118>, the dramatic characters cease to exist. I see only rhapsodes reciting an epic poem which may or may not be beautiful. ...

24

VICTOR-MARIE HUGO
(1802–85)

Hugo's Preface to his play *Cromwell* (1827) is a major dramatic manifesto with strongly polemical elements, such as the criticism of the unities of place and time <In/11>, and the defense of historical plays. But these elements need to be interpreted in light of the overall perspective of the argument, in which Hugo views drama in the context of a cultural and psychological evolution, and elaborates a theory of art which would allow it to encompass the richness of human experience. So he militates for "the freedom of art against the despotism of systems, codes, and rules," as he says at the end of the programmatic part of the Preface.

As Hugo explains in his theory of the three successive ages, drama is above all a way of viewing and communicating the human condition. It is here that Hugo's conception of the inseparable coexistence of the sublime and the grotesque, in life and therefore in art, assumes its capital importance. He considers that "beauty has but one type, ugliness has a thousand" (Hugo/Souriau 1897, 207), and hence only the recognition and inclusion of the "grotesque" will allow the dramatist to achieve an adequate perception of the sublime and to recreate a sense of the *totality* of experience.

The result will not be a simple juxtaposition of comic and tragic elements, but frequently a simultaneous presence of antithetical impulses, sometimes within a single character.[1] Hugo calls the type of play which will achieve this vision a *drame*. But with him the term is radically different from its use in Beaumarchais' "Essay" <Bm/127>. In Hugo, *drame* does not designate a genre halfway between tragedy and comedy; rather it transcends and subsumes both tragedy and comedy (each of which is incomplete on its own), and becomes the archetype of drama as it should be. (Accordingly, it is translated as "drama" below.)

Such drama will draw its subjects from history, but history conceived as the incarnation of the characteristic spirit of an age, interpreted by the "focusing mirror" of art <Hu/263>, and speaking across time to the present. "It is the present as we create it, viewed in the light of history as our forefathers created it," says Hugo in the Preface to his play *Mary Tudor* (1833). For its full effect, drama must avoid "the ordinary," and thus Hugo defends the use of poetic language and of the alexandrine <Sa/185; Sd/254>, which he intends however to make more flexible and thus more expressive. Hugo shares with many other theorists a desire for greater "realism," but his is a transformed realism.

---

[1] The protagonist of Hugo's own *Ruy Blas* (1838) describes himself as "an earthworm enamored of a star."

For further reading

Duchet 1967; Hugo/Reynaud 1985; Hugo/Souriau 1897; Lioure 1968; Scelfo 1984; Ubersfeld 1974.

From the Preface to *Cromwell*[2]

...[3] A spiritual religion, supplanting a material, external paganism, insinuated itself into the heart of ancient society, killed it, and in the body of a decrepit civilization sowed the seed of modern civilization. .... Among its fundamental verities, it taught mankind that there are two lives to be lived, the one transitory, the other immortal; the one pertains to the earth, the other to heaven. It shows that both the nature and the fate of humanity are dual; that in each human being coexist an animal and an intelligence, a body and a soul....

Paganism, which forged all its creations from the same clay, abases the divine and exalts the human. Homer's heroes have almost the same stature as his gods. ... Christianity, on the contrary, ... establishes an abyss between soul and body, between God and humanity.... With Christianity, there was introduced into the human psyche a new feeling which was unknown to the ancients and which has become remarkably developed among the moderns, a feeling which is more than seriousness and less than sadness: melancholy....

Christianity brought poetry around to truth. Like Christianity, the modern muse will see[4] things in a higher and broader perspective. It will sense that not everything in creation is *beautiful* in human terms, that the ugly exists alongside the beautiful, the misshapen near the graceful, the grotesque on the other side of the sublime, evil with goodness, shadow with light. It will ask whether the narrow, relative reason of the artist is to prevail over the infinite, absolute reason of the Creator; if it is the human being's right to improve on God's work; ... if, in short, being incomplete is really the right way to be harmonious. It is then that, with its gaze firmly fixed on events which are simultaneously laughable and awe-inspiring, and directed by the spirit of Christian melancholy and philosophical criticism, poetry will take a great, decisive stride, a stride which, like the

---

[2] Newly translated from Hugo/Souriau 1897, 169–292.

[3] At the beginning of the Preface, Hugo sketches his theory of the "three ages," each with a corresponding form of literature: first, the primitive period, which is lyric; second, the ancient or heroic age, which is epic. Like lyric, "epic" is a matter of subject and of attitude, rather than external form and thus "it is especially in ancient tragedy that the epic is most apparent." Third, Hugo arrives at the beginning of the modern era at the advent of Christianity.

[4] Hugo is viewing the "modern" (which is opposed to classical antiquity and thus dating from before the Renaissance) from a point of view in the historical past. From this perspective the "modern" will unfold in the future.

shock of an earthquake, will change the whole face of the intellectual world. Poetry will begin to act as nature does, mingling its creations together, but without confusing them, shadow with light, the grotesque with the sublime; in other words, body with soul, the animal and the spiritual. The point of departure for religion is always the point of departure for poetry. Everything is bound up together.....

It is from the fruitful union of the grotesque and the sublime that the modern spirit is born – so complex, so varied in its forms, so inexhaustible in its creations, and so distinct therein from the uniform simplicity of the spirit of antiquity; ... this is the basis of the radical and indisputable difference between the two literatures. Not that the comic and the grotesque were absolutely unknown to the ancients; ... but this part of art was still in its infancy.....

In the thought of the moderns, on the contrary, the grotesque plays an enormous role: on the one hand, it produces the deformed and the horrible; and on the other, the comic and the clownish.....

The grotesque, this germ of comedy which will be taken up by the modern muse, will grow and flourish once it is transplanted to a more favorable soil than paganism and the epic. In the new poetry, whereas the sublime will represent the soul as it is, purified by Christian ethics, the grotesque will play the part of the human animal. The first type, freed from every impurity, will have all charms, graces, and forms of beauty as its attributes; it will be called on one day to create Juliet, Desdemona, Ophelia. The second type will assume all follies, weaknesses, and forms of ugliness. In this division of humanity – indeed, of all creation – it will be the repository of passions, vices, crimes; it will be lascivious, servile, gluttonous, treacherous, quarrelsome, hypocritical; by turns it will be Iago, Tartuffe, Basile; Polonius, Harpagon, Bartholo; Falstaff, Scapin, Figaro.[5] ...

[In the sixteenth century,] the moment came when a balance would be established between the two principles [the sublime and the grotesque]. One man, a supreme poet, ... was about to set all in order. The two rival spirits united their double flame, and from that flame sprang Shakespeare.

We have now reached the leading light of modern times. Shakespeare is drama; and drama – which commingles the grotesque and the sublime, the dreadful and the farcical, tragedy and comedy – is the distinguishing feature of the third period of poetry, of modern literature.....

Primitive times are lyric, ancient times are epic, modern times are dramatic. The ode sings of eternity, the epic solemnizes history, drama paints life. (But, it may be objected, drama also portrays the story of peoples. Yes, but as *life*, not as *history*. It leaves to history the exact

---

[5] Basile and Bartholo are characters from Beaumarchais' *The Barber of Séville* and *The Marriage of Figaro*; Harpagon from Molière's *The Miser*; and Scapin from *Scapin's Tricks* (1671) and other plays by Molière.

sequence of events, the order of dates, ... all of the externals of history. It takes the internal. What history forgets or neglects – details of costumes, of manners, of physiognomies, the hidden side of events – belongs to drama. ... Don't look for pure history in drama, even if it is *historical* drama. It writes legends, not descriptions. It is a chronicle, not a chronology.)[6] ...

It is not my intention to assign to each of the three periods of poetry an exclusive area, but to identify the dominant characteristic of each. The Bible, that divine monument of lyricism, contains ... embryonic forms of epic and of drama: *Kings* and *Job*. In the Homeric poems one is aware of a residue of lyric poetry and of an incipient dramatic poetry. ... But in each form there is a generating element to which all others are subordinate and which gives the totality its specific character.

Drama is complete poetry. The ode and the epic contain drama only in its rudimentary form; fully developed, drama is capable of subsuming and encompassing both lyric and epic <Hg/209>. ... It is clear that Shakespeare's series of chronicle-dramas presents a considerable epic element. But it is especially lyric poetry which is compatible with drama; lyricism is supple and unconstraining, adaptable to all of drama's forms, sublime in Ariel, grotesque in Caliban. Our era, which is above all dramatic, is, by that very fact, eminently lyrical. ... Thus drama is the culminating point of modern poetry, *Paradise Lost* is a drama even more than it is an epic. ...

Once Christianity had said to mankind: You are dual, you are composed of two creatures, the one perishable, the other immortal; the one fleshly, the other spiritual; the one chained by appetites, needs, and passions, the other borne up on the wings of inspiration and imagination; the one always stooped towards its mother, the earth, and the other constantly soaring towards heaven, its true home – from that moment, drama was created. Is drama in fact anything other than the contrast which we see every day, the perpetual struggle between two opposing forces which characterize our lives, warring over humanity from the cradle to the grave?

The poetry which was born of Christianity, the poetry of our era, is thus drama. The distinguishing trait of drama is the real; the real results from the natural combination of two types, the sublime and the grotesque, which commingle in drama as they do in life and in all creation. For true poetry, complete poetry, lies in a harmony of opposites <Hg/215>. ...

If we systematically separate these two trunks of art [the grotesque and the sublime], preventing their branches from intermingling, the only fruit they will produce will be, on the one hand, abstract representations of vices and follies; and, on the other, abstract representations of crimes, heroism, and virtues. The two types, separated and on their own, will go their individual ways, on each side abandoning the real. Hence, after these

---

[6] This passage in parentheses appears as a note in Hugo's text.

abstractions, there will be something left which needs to be represented: humanity; after these tragedies and comedies, something which needs to be created: drama.

In drama (at least as it can be conceived, even if not executed), everything is bound up together, as in reality. The body has a role to play as does the soul; and the people and events activated by this dual agency appear as alternatively comical and terrible, sometimes simultaneously comical and terrible. ... Great men, for all their greatness, always have within them a lower self which makes a mockery of their intelligence. That is what makes them human, and that is what makes them dramatic....

One of the supreme beauties of drama is the grotesque. It is not simply an appropriate element, it is often a necessity. Sometimes it takes the form of homogeneous, complete characters: Dandin, Prusias, Trissotin, Brid-'oison,[7] Juliet's nurse; sometimes it bears the stamp of terror, as in Richard III, Bégearss, Tartuffe, Mephistopheles;[8] sometimes it is even cloaked in grace and elegance, as in the case of Figaro, Osric, Mercutio, Don Juan. It turns up everywhere, for just as the basest people often show flashes of sublimity, so too the greatest frequently pay tribute to what is coarse and ridiculous.... Thanks to [the grotesque], there is no monotony. By turns it introduces laughter and horror into tragedy. It brings Romeo face to face with the apothecary, Macbeth with the witches, Hamlet with the gravediggers. And sometimes, as in the scene of King Lear with his fool, it can, without dissonance, add its harsh voice to the most sublime, the most dismal, or the most dreamlike music of the soul....

We can see how quickly the arbitrary distinction among genres collapses when it is examined by reason and taste. It would be just as simple to destroy the so-called rule of the two unities. I say two unities, not three, since it has long been recognized that unity of action or of the totality, the only true, sound unity, is not at issue....

What is odd is that the slaves of habit claim to base their rule of the two unities on verisimilitude < 1:In/8–10>, whereas it is precisely the real which destroys it. What could be more improbable than the antechamber, that trite location in which our tragedies take place, where conspirators come – God knows how – to rant against the tyrant, and where the tyrant himself comes to rail against the conspirators.[9] ... Where did one ever see an antechamber like that? What could be more contrary, I won't say "to truth," for the classicists pay little heed to truth, but even to plausibility?

---

7 A Dandin appears in both Molière's *Georges Dandin* (1669) and Racine's *Les Plaideurs* (*The Litigants*) (1668). Prusias is from Corneille's *Nicomède*; Trissotin from Molière's *Les Femmes savantes* (*The Learned Ladies*) (1672); and Brid'oison from Beaumarchais' *Le Mariage de Figaro*.

8 Bégearss is from Beaumarchais' *L'Autre Tartufe, ou la Mère coupable* (*The Other Tartuffe, or The Guilty Mother*) (1792). The Mephistopheles Hugo has in mind is probably the one from Goethe's *Faust*.

9 Hugo is probably thinking of Corneille's *Cinna*, but the situation is stereotypical.

Hence everything that is too specific, too intimate, too local to take place in the antechamber or the public square – in other words, the real heart of the drama – takes place in the wings. We see on stage only the elbows of the action; its hands are elsewhere. Instead of scenes, we have narrations; instead of tableaux, descriptions....

We are beginning to understand nowadays that the specific place is one of the prime elements of reality. The characters who speak and act are not the only ones who leave a true imprint of events in the mind of the audience. The place in which some catastrophe took place becomes a dreadful, essential witness.... How can Henri IV be stabbed anywhere but in the rue de la Ferronnerie, cluttered with carts and coaches? How can Joan of Arc be burned anywhere but in the Vieux-Marché? ...

The rule of unity of time is no sounder than that of unity of place. Squeezing the action into twenty-four hours is as ridiculous as squeezing it into an antechamber. Every action has its own duration as well as its own place. Crossing unity of time and unity of place like the bars of a cage, and pedantically imprisoning, in the name of Aristotle, all of those events, peoples, and figures which Providence distributes so profusely in reality, mutilates men and things, and distorts history. To be more precise, everything will die in the process, and thus the dogmatic mutilators reach their usual result: what was alive in the chronicle is dead in the tragedy. That is why the cage of the unities so often contains only a skeleton....

One final argument, derived from the very core of art, will suffice to show the absurdity of the rule of the two unities. This is the existence of a third unity, unity of action, the only one universally accepted, because it results from a fact: neither the human eye nor the human mind can grasp more than one ensemble at a time. This unity is as necessary as the other two are useless. It is what establishes the point of view of the play; and by that very fact it excludes the other two. There can no more be three unities in a play than three horizons in a landscape. Further, let us be careful not to confuse unity of action with simplicity of action. Unity of the whole in no way excludes secondary actions on which the main action is to be based. It is necessary only that these parts, carefully subordinated to the whole, be constantly directed towards the central action and take their place around it on the different levels or rather on the different planes of the drama. Unity of the whole constitutes the law of perspective in the theatre.[10]

"But," cry the jailors of the mind, "great geniuses followed these rules which you reject!" <Lg/125> Yes, alas! And what might those admirable men have accomplished if they had been allowed to act freely? ... So Corneille found himself condemned, the lion was muzzled <1:Cd/212>. The painful aspect of this grotesque affair is that, after having been struck

---

[10] Throughout this passage, Hugo is establishing an analogy between drama and painting ("the human eye ... horizons in a landscape ... planes ... law of perspective").

down in his very first flight, this genius, so modern, so imbued with Spain and the Middle Ages, forced to be untrue to himself and to turn to antiquity, offered us a Castilian Rome ... in which we can recognize neither the real Rome nor the real Corneille. Racine experienced the same difficulties, but without putting up the same resistance. He had none of Corneille's haughty fierceness. He bowed in silence. ... What beauties *men of taste* have cost us, from Scudéry < 1:Cd/212> to La Harpe![11] ... Yet our great poets managed to manifest their genius despite all these constraints. ...

Nonetheless, we hear the repeated refrain, and will doubtless hear it for some time yet: "Follow the rules! Imitate the models! It was the rules that formed the models!" Just a moment! There are two kinds of models: those who were formed by the rules, and, before them, those on whom the rules were formed. ... And as for imitating! Is a reflection as worthy as the light? Is the satellite which endlessly follows the same circular path as important as the central life-giving sun? For all his poetic talent, Virgil is merely Homer's moon. And besides, whom should we imitate? The ancients? I have shown that their theatre has no relationship to ours. ... The moderns? Hah! imitate imitations! Please!

"But," someone will object, "given the way you conceive of art, you seem to expect only great poets, you always count on genius?" Art doesn't count on mediocrity. It prescribes nothing for mediocrity, it does not recognize it, it is utterly indifferent to its existence. Art provides wings, not crutches. ...

The time has come to state our position boldly; and indeed it would be strange if in this era freedom, like light, should manage to penetrate into every domain except the one which is the most naturally free of all, the life of the mind. Down with theories, arts of poetry, and systems. Away with the old layer of plaster which hides the beauty of art. There are neither rules nor models; or rather there are no rules but the general laws of nature, which reign over all art <Dl/95>, and the particular laws which, for each work, derive from the conditions which are appropriate to each subject < 1:In/2>. The former are eternal, internal, and durable; the latter are variable, external, and function only once. The former are the framework which holds up the building; the latter are the scaffolding which is used during construction and which is dismantled when the task is done. ... For each work, the man of genius, who intuits rather than learning [by precept], extracts the first kind of laws from the general order of things and the second kind from the particular totality of the subject he is treating. ...

I stress the fact that the poet should consult only nature, truth, and inspiration (which is also a form of truth and nature). Lope de Vega said:

---

[11] Jean-François de la Harpe (1739–1803) wrote tragedies but is better known for his dogmatically neo-classical lectures collected as *Lycée, ou Cours de la littérature ancienne et moderne* (1799–1805).

"When I have to write a comedy, I lock up the precepts with six keys" < 1:Lp/184>. To lock up the rules, six keys are not too many. Above all, the poet must not copy anyone, not Shakespeare, not Molière, not Schiller, not Corneille. If genuine talent were to abdicate its true nature to this extent, abandoning its own individuality in order to become someone else, it would lose everything by assuming the function of a *doppelgänger*....

Nature, then! Nature and truth. And here, in order to show that, far from destroying art, these new ideas seek rather to rebuild it on a firmer foundation, let us attempt to indicate what is the impassable boundary which separates reality according to art from reality according to nature. It would be folly to confuse the two.... The truth of art cannot be *absolute* reality. Art cannot reproduce the thing itself. ... Unless we wish to be ridiculous, we must recognize that the domains of art and of nature are quite distinct....

It has been said that drama is a mirror which reflects nature < 1:Dn/79>. But if this mirror is an ordinary one, with a flat, even surface, it will reflect only a dull two-dimensional image, accurate but drab. We know that color and light are lost in the process of simple reflection. So drama must be a focusing mirror which collects and concentrates the rays of light, rather than weakening them: from a glimmer it must make light; from light, a flame. Only then can drama be acknowledged as art.

Theatre is a point of view. Everything which exists in the world, in history, in life, in mankind, can and must be reflected in it, but under the magic wand of art. Art scans the centuries, scans nature, scans chronicles, strives to reproduce reality – especially that of customs and characters, which is much less subject to doubt and contradiction than are facts. It restores what annalists have cut out, ... intuits their omissions and remedies them, fills in their lacunae with imaginings which bear the stamp of the period, brings together what they have left scattered, reestablishes the workings of Providence's strings behind human marionettes, clothes the whole thing with a form which is both poetic and natural, and gives it that life of truth and specificity which produces illusion. ... Thus the goal of art is almost divine: to bring back to life, if writing history; to create, if writing poetry.... [In drama, art aims] at illuminating both the inner and the outer elements of human beings: the outer, by their speeches and actions; the inner, by asides and monologues. In short, it seeks to mingle, in a single presentation, drama of life and drama of conscience.

It follows, then, that for such a work, the poet must choose, not what is *beautiful*, but what is *characteristic*. That does not mean, as is said nowadays, *creating local color*, which consists of simply adding a few gaudy strokes here and there to a work which is in all other respects false and conventional. It is not on the surface of a play that we should find local color, but in the very heart of the work, so that it spreads outward on its own, naturally and evenly.... The play should be totally suffused with this color of the period; it must be in the very air, so that it is only on entering and on leaving the theatre that we notice that there has been a change of century and of atmosphere. It requires a certain amount of study and toil to achieve this; so much the better. ... It is also such study, sustained by powerful inspiration, that will save the play from a mortal defect: *the ordinary*. ... In this theatrical perspective, every figure must be focused on its most salient, individual, precise trait. ... My next statement will prove once more to people of good will that I have no intention of disfiguring art: I consider verse to be one of the best ways of safeguarding drama from the scourge which I have just identified, ... the infestation of the ordinary <Sd/254>....

Only by sheer luck can a few remnants survive this cataclysm of false art, false style, false poetry. And there we find the reason for the misunderstanding on the part of several distinguished reformers. Shocked by the stiffness and pomp of this so-called dramatic poetry, they came to believe that our poetic language is incompatible with naturalness and truth. They had been bored so often by the alexandrine <Sa/185>, that they condemned it, in a sense without a hearing, and concluded rather hastily that drama must be written in prose.

They are mistaken. If the style, as well as the action, of certain French tragedies rings false, we should blame the versifiers rather than the verse itself. ...

Verse constitutes the optics of thought. That is why it is especially suited to the theatrical perspective. Properly handled, it gives particularity to things which would otherwise seem trite and insignificant. ... It is the belt which holds up the garment and creates its folds. What then could nature and truth lose by being incorporated into verse? ... Does wine cease to be wine just because it is bottled?

If I may state my opinion on what should be the style of drama, I would want verse which is free, honest, straightforward, devoid of all prudishness or affectation; moving easily from comedy to tragedy, from the sublime to the grotesque; now concrete, now poetic; both artistic and inspired; profound and abrupt; broad and true; capable of shifting the caesura in order to hide the monotony of the alexandrine; preferring run-on lines which extend the idea rather than inversion which muddles it; preserving the use of rhyme, which is both slave and queen,[12] and which is the supreme grace of our poetry; ... avoiding the *tirade* <Dt/43; Gl/70; Hg/212>; sprightly in dialogue; always subordinate to the character; ... lyric, epic, or dramatic as required <In/2>; capable of spanning the full poetic gamut, ... without ever exceeding the limits of a spoken scene. ... An idea which is cast in verse suddenly becomes more incisive and more striking. Iron becomes steel. ...

---

[12] In his *Art of Poetry*, Boileau had said: "Rhyme is a slave and must only obey."

A language is not something fixed. The human mind is always on the move, and languages move with it. .... Nineteenth-century French can no more be eighteenth-century French than the latter can be seventeenth-century French. ... Every period has its own ideas, and must have the words which are appropriate for these ideas....

My intention has been to eliminate arts of poetry, rather than to write one. ... My plea has been for the freedom of art against the despotism of systems, codes, and rules <Lg/125>....[13]

[13] In the final section of the Preface Hugo turns to a discussion of *Cromwell*.

BIBLIOGRAPHY

The names of authors whose works appear in this volume are in bold type.

Abrams, M. H. 1971. *Natural Supernaturalism: Tradition and Revolution in Romantic Literature.* New York.

Adams, Henry Hitch, and Baxter Hathaway. 1950. *Dramatic Essays of the Neoclassic Age.* New York.

Albrecht, W. P. 1965. *Hazlitt and the Creative Imagination.* Lawrence, KA.

Arcari, Pietro. 1902. *L'arte poetica di Pietro Metastasio.* Milan.

Archives Parlementaires. See Madival, M. M., and E. Laurent, eds.

Aulard, F. A., ed. 1899–1911. *Recueil des Actes du Comité de Salut Public.* 20 vols. Paris.

Baillie, Joanna

   1812. *A Series of Plays in which it is attempted to delineate the stronger passions of the mind . . . .* Vol. III. London.

Barba, Eugenio and Nicola Savarese. 1991. *A Dictionary of Theatre Anthropology: The Secret Art of the Performer.* Ed. Richard Gough; trans. Richard Fowler. London.

Baretti, Giuseppe Marco Antonio. 1768. *An Account of the Manners and Customs of Italy: With Observations on the Mistakes of Some Travellers, with Regard to that Country, by Joseph Baretti.* London.

Barish, Jonas. 1981. *The Antitheatrical Prejudice.* Berkeley and Los Angeles.

Beaumarchais, Pierre-Augustin Caron de

   Allem, Maurice, and Paul Courant, eds. 1973. *Théâtre complet et lettres relatives à son théâtre.* Paris.

   Larthomas, Pierre, ed. 1988. *Oeuvres.* Paris.

Beer, John. 1986. Coleridge's originality as a critic of Shakespeare. *Studies in the Literary Imagination* 19 (2):51–69.

Beniscelli, Alberto. 1986. *La finzione del fiabesco.* Casale Monferrato.

Bennett, Benjamin. 1979. *Modern Drama and German Classicism: Renaissance from Lessing to Brecht.* Ithaca, NY.

Besterman, Theodore. 1968. *Voltaire.* London.

Binni, Walter. 1963. *L'Arcadia e il Metastasio.* Florence.

Bradley, A. C. 1909. Hegel's Theory of Tragedy. In Hegel/Paolucci 1962.

Bras, Gérard. 1989. *Hegel et l'art.* Paris.

Brown, Jane K. 1986. *Goethe's Faust: The German Tragedy.* Ithaca, NY.

Brown, Joseph E., comp. 1926. *The Critical Opinions of Samuel Johnson: a Compilation and Interpretation.* Princeton.

Bruford, W. H. 1950. *Theatre, Drama and Audience in Goethe's Germany.* London.

Brunet, Olivier. 1965. *Philosophie et ésthétique chez David Hume.* Paris.

Bungay, Stephen. 1984. *Beauty and Truth: A Study of Hegel's Aesthetics.* Oxford.

Burney, Charles. 1796. *Memoirs of the Life and Writings of the Abbate Pietro Metastasio.* London.

Burwick, Frederick. 1991. *Illusion and the Drama: Critical Theory of the Enlightenment and Romantic Era.* University Park, PN.

Butwin, Joseph. 1975. The French Revolution as *Theatrum Mundi. Research Studies* 43:141–52.

Byron, Lord George Gordon. 1844. *The Poetical Works of Lord Byron.* London.

   1974. 'Alas! the love of Women!': Byron's Letters and Journals, ed. Leslie A. Marchand. Vol. III: 1813–1814. Cambridge, MA.

Cardy, Michael. 1982. *The Literary Doctrines of Jean-François Marmontel.* Oxford.

Carhart, Margaret. 1923. *The Life and Works of Joanna Baillie.* New Haven.

Carlson, Julie. 1988. An active imagination: Coleridge and the politics of dramatic reform. *Modern Philology* 86:22–33.

Carlson, Marvin. 1966. *The Theatre of the French Revolution*. Ithaca, NY.

1978. *Goethe and the Weimar Theatre*. Ithaca, NY.

1984. *Theories of the Theatre: A Historical and Critical Survey, from the Greeks to the Present*. Ithaca, NY.

Carswell, Donald. 1930. *Sir Walter: A Four-part Study in Biography (Scott, Hogg, Lockhart, Joanna Baillie)*. London.

Chatfield-Taylor, H. C. 1913. *Goldoni: A Biography*. New York.

Chouillet, Jacques. 1973. *La Formation des Idées esthétiques de Diderot 1745–1763*. Paris.

Clairon, Hyppolite [Claire Josèphe Hippolyte Légris de Latude]. [1800] 1971. *Memoirs of Hyppolite Clairon, the Celebrated French Actress: with Reflections upon Dramatic Art*, by Hyppolite Clairon. New York.

[1822] 1968. *Mémoires écrits par elle-même: nouvelle edition*. Geneva.

Cohen, Ralph. 1962. The transformation of passion: a study of Hume's theories of tragedy. *Philological Quarterly* 41:450–64.

Cole, Toby, and Helen Krich Chinoy, eds. 1970. *Actors on Acting*. New York.

Coleridge, Samuel Taylor

Foakes, R. A., ed. 1987. *The Collected Works of Samuel Taylor Coleridge: Lectures 1808–1819 on Literature*. Vol. v parts 1 and 2. London and Princeton.

Griggs, E. L., ed. 1956. *Collected Letters of Samuel Taylor Coleridge*. Vol. III. Oxford.

1959. *Collected Letters of Samuel Taylor Coleridge*. Vol. IV. Oxford.

Raysor, Thomas Middleton. 1930. *Coleridge's Shakespearean Criticism*. 2 vols. Cambridge, MA.

Rooke, Barbara E., ed. 1969. *The Collected Works of Samuel Taylor Coleridge: The Friend*. Vol. IV, parts 1 and 2. London and Princeton.

Shawcross, J., ed. 1907. *Biographia Literaria, with his Aesthetical Essays*. 2 vols. Oxford.

Crane, R. S., ed. 1952. *Critics and Criticism: Ancient and Modern*. Chicago.

Crouzet, Michel. 1983–84. A propos de *Racine et Shakespeare*: tradition, réforme et révolution dans le romantisme. *Nineteenth-Century French Studies* 12:1–35.

Damrosch, Leopold. 1976. *The Uses of Johnson's Criticism*. Charlottesville, VA.

Daniels, Barry V. 1983. *Revolution in the Theatre: French Romantic Theories of Drama*. Westport, CN.

Davis, James Herbert Jr. 1967. *Tragic Theory and the Eighteenth-Century French Critics*. Chapel Hill, NC.

Dennis, John. 1939–43. *The Critical Works of John Dennis*, ed. Edward Niles Hooker. 2 vols. Baltimore, MD.

Diderot, Denis

1967. *Paradoxe sur le comédien, précédé des entretiens sur Le Fils naturel*. Chronologie et préface par Raymond Laubreaux. Paris.

Caput, Jean-Pol, ed. 1973. *Le Fils naturel et les Entretiens sur Le Fils naturel*. Paris.

Chouillet, Jacques and Anne-Marie, eds. 1980. *Oeuvres complètes*. 10 vols. Paris.

Green, F. C., ed. 1936. *Diderot's Writings on the Theatre*. Cambridge.

Vernière, Paul, ed. 1959. *Diderot: Oeuvres esthétiques*. Paris.

Duchet, Claude. 1967. Victor Hugo et l'âge d'homme (*Cromwell* et sa Préface). In Hugo/Mass 1967, 5–38.

Dumesnil, Mlle (Marie Françoise Marchand)

[1823] 1968. *Mémoires en réponse aux mémoires d'Hippolyte Clairon*. Geneva.

Eggli, Edmond and Pierre Martino. 1933. *Le Débat romantique en France, 1813–1830*. Paris.

El Nouty, Hassan. 1978. *Théâtre et pré-cinéma*. Paris.

Ewton, Ralph W. 1972. *The Literary Theories of August Wilhelm Schlegel*. The Hague.

Fido, Franco. 1977. *Guida a Goldoni*. Turin.

1984. *Da Venezia all'Europa: Prospettive sull'ultimo Goldoni*. Rome.

Fielding, Henry. 1950. *The History of Tom Jones: A Foundling*. Introduction by George Sherburn. New York.

Fischer-Lichte, Erika, Josephine Riley, and Michael Gissenwehrer, eds. 1990. *The Dramatic Touch of Difference*. Tübingen.

Fulda, Friedrich, ed. 1990. *Hegel und die Kritik der Urteilskraft*. Stuttgart.

Gaiffe, Félix. [1910] 1980. *Le Drame en France au XVIIIe siècle*. Paris.

Goethe, Johann Wolfgang von

Carlyle, Thomas, trans. [1824] 1962. *Wilhelm Meister's Apprenticeship*. New York.

Eastlake, Charles Lock, trans. [1840] 1967. *Theory of Colours*. London.

Nardroff, Ellen and Ernest H. von, trans. 1986. *Essays on Art and Literature*, ed. John Geary. *Goethe's Collected Works: Suhrkamp Edition*. Vol. III. New York.

Trunz, Erich, ed. 1981. *Goethes Werke*. Hamburger Ausgabe in 14 Bänden. Munich.

Goldoni, Carlo

Miller, John W., trans. 1969. *The Comic Theatre, a Comedy in Three Acts*. With an introduction by Donald Cheney. Lincoln, NB.

Gould, Evelyn. 1989. *Virtual Theater: From Diderot to Mallarmé*. Baltimore and London.

Gozzi, Carlo

Bermel, Albert, and Ted Emery, eds. and trans. 1989. *Five Tales for the Theatre*. Chicago.

Petronio, Giuseppe, ed. 1962. *Opere: Teatro e polemiche teatrali*. Milan.

Prezzolini, Giuseppe, ed. 1934. *Memorie inutili*. Bari.

Hagstrum, Jean H. 1967. *Samuel Johnson's Literary Criticism*. Chicago.

Hartman, Geoffrey H. 1970. Romanticism and Anti-Self-Consciousness. In his *Beyond Formalism: Literary Essays 1958–1970*. New Haven.

Hartnoll, Phyllis, ed. 1985. *The Oxford Companion to the Theatre*. 4th ed., repr. with corrections. Oxford.

Hazlitt, William

Howe, P. P., ed. 1930–34. *The Complete Works of William Hazlitt*. Vols. IV and V. London.

Hegel, Georg Wilhelm Friedrich

Knox, T. M., trans. 1975. *Aesthetics: Lectures on Fine Art*. 2 vols. Oxford.

Paolucci, Anne and Henry, eds. 1962. *Hegel on Tragedy*. New York.

Heller, Janet Ruth. 1990. *Coleridge, Lamb, Hazlitt and the Reader of Drama*. Columbia, MO.

Henning, Ian Allan. 1929. *L'Allemagne de Madame de Staël et la polémique romantique*. Paris.

Herry, Ginette. 1976. Il teatro comico o il prezzo della riforma. *Studi Goldoniani* 4:7–47.

Highfill, Philip H., Kalman A. Burnim, and Edward A. Langhans. 1973–1991 (in progress). *A Biographical Dictionary of Actors, Actresses, Musician, Dancers, Managers and other Stage Personnel in London, 1660–1800*. Vols. I–XIV. Carbondale, IL.

Hinck, Walter. 1983. Man of the Theatre. In *Goethe Revisited*, ed. Elizabeth M. Wilkinson. New York.

Hipple, W. J., Jr. 1956. The Logic of Hume's essay 'Of Tragedy'. *Philosophical Quarterly* 6:43–52.

Hobson, Marian. 1982. *The Object of Art: The Theory of Illusion in Eighteenth-Century France*. Cambridge.

Hugo, Victor-Marie

Mass, Jean, ed. 1967. *Oeuvres complètes*. Vol. III. Paris.

Reynaud, Jean-Pierre. 1985. *Oeuvres complètes: Critique*. Paris.

Souriau, Maurice, ed. 1897. *La Préface de Cromwell*. Paris.

Ubersfeld, Annie, ed. 1968. *Cromwell*. Paris:

Hume, David

1823. *The History of England from the Invasion of Julius Caesar to the Revolution in 1688, in Eight Volumes*. Vol. VI. London.

1904. *Essays: Moral, Political and Literary*. London.

Hume, Robert D. 1988. *Henry Fielding and the London Theatre 1728–1737*. Oxford.

Jackson, J. R. de J. 1964–65. Coleridge on dramatic illusion and spectacle in the performance of Shakespeare's plays. *Modern Philology* 62:13–21.

Johnson, Samuel

Bate, W. J., and Albrecht B. Strauss, eds. 1969. *The Yale Edition of the Works of Samuel Johnson*. Vols. III–IV: *The Rambler*. New Haven.

McAdam, E. L., Jr., with George Milne, eds. 1964. *The Yale Edition of the Works of Samuel Johnson*. Vol. VI: *Poems*. New Haven.

Redford, Bruce, ed. 1992. *The Letters of Samuel Johnson*. Vol. I: 1731–1772. Princeton.

Sherbo, Arthur, ed. 1968. *The Yale Edition of the Works of Samuel Johnson*. Vols. VII–VIII: *Johnson on Shakespeare*. New Haven.

Waugh, Arthur, ed. [1906] 1959. *Lives of the English Poets*. 2 vols. London.

Jones, Thora Burnley, and Bernard de Boer Nicol. 1976. *Neo-classical Dramatic Criticism, 1560–1770*. New York.

Jordain, Eleanor. 1968. *Dramatic Theory and Practice in France 1690–1808*. New York.

Kallich, Martin. 1946. The associationist criticism of Francis Hutcheson and David Hume. *Studies in Philology*, 13:644–68.

Kaminisky, Jack. 1962. *Hegel on Art*. Albany, NY.

Kant, Immanuel. 1911. *Kant's Critique of Aesthetic Judgement: translated with seven introductory essays, notes and an analytical index*. Trans. James Creed Meredith. Oxford.

Keast, William R. 1952. The Theoretical Foundation of Johnson's Criticism. In Crane 1952.

Keats, John. 1958. *The Letters of John Keats 1814–1821*. Ed. Hyder E. Rollins. Vol. I. Cambridge, MA.

Kelly, Linda. 1980. *The Kemble Era: John Philip Kemble, Sarah Siddons and the London Stage*. London.

Kinnaird, John. 1978. *William Hazlitt: Critic of Power*. New York.

Kleist, Heinrich von

Sembdner, Helmut, ed. 1982. *Sämtliche Werke und Briefe in Vier Bänden*. 4 vols. Munich.

Knox, Israel. 1936. *The Aesthetic Theories of Kant, Hegel and Schopenhauer*. New York.

Kommerell, Max. 1960. *Lessing und Aristoteles: Untersuchung über die Theorie der Tragödie*. Frankfurt am Main.

Lamb, Charles and Mary. 1912. *Miscellaneous Prose: The Works of Charles and Mary Lamb*, ed. E. V. Lucas. Vol. I. London.

Lamport, F. J. 1981. *Lessing and the Drama*. Oxford.

1990. *German Classical Drama: Theatre, Humanity and Nation 1750–1870*. Cambridge.

Langer, Susanne K. K. 1953. *Feeling and Form: A Theory of Art*. New York.

Lessing, Gotthold Ephraim

Göpfert, Herbert G., ed. 1970–79. *Werke*. 8 vols. Munich.

Kiesel, Helmuth, ed. 1987. *Briefe von und an Lessing 1743–1770*. Werke und Briefe. Vol. XI/1. Frankfurt am Main.

McCormick, Edward Allen, trans. 1962. *Laocoön. An Essay on the Limits of Painting and Poetry*. Baltimore, MD.

Zimmern, Helen, trans. 1962. *Hamburg Dramaturgy*. New York.

Lioure, Michel. 1968. *Le Drame*. Paris.

Loftis, John. 1952. *Steele at Drury Lane*. Berkley and Los Angeles.

Lunel, Ernest. [1910] 1970. *Le Théâtre et la Révolution: histoire anecdotique des spectacles, de leurs comédiens et leur public par rapport à la Révolution française*. Geneva.

Madival, M. M., and E. Laurent, eds. 1862–1991. *Archives Parlementaires de 1787–1860, Recueil complet des débats législatifs et politiques des Chambres françaises*. First series. 93 vols. Paris.

Metastasio, Pietro

Brunelli, Bruno, ed. 1951. *Tutte le opere di Pietro Metastasio*. Milan.

Moland, Louis Emile Dieudonné. 1877. *Théâtre de la Révolution, ou Choix de pièces de théâtre qui ont fait sensation pendant la période révolutionnaire*. Paris.

Montgomery, Robert L. 1991. *Terms of Response: Language and Audience in Seventeenth- and Eighteenth-Century Theory*. Pennsylvania.

Moore, John David. 1982. Coleridge and the 'Modern Jacobinical Drama': Osario, remorse, and the development of Coleridge's critique of the stage 1797–1816. *Bulletin of Research in the Humanities* 85:443–64.

Naves, Raymond. 1938. *Le Goût de Voltaire*. Paris.

Nicastro, Guido. 1974. *Goldoni e il teatro comico del secondo Settecento*. Bari.

Niklaus, Robert. 1963. La Portée des théories dramatiques de Diderot et ses réalisations théatrales. *Romanic Review* 54:6–19.
    1973. Beaumarchais et le drame. In *Missions et démarches de la critique. Mélanges offerts au Professeur J. A. Vier.* Paris. 491–99.
Ozouf, Mona. 1988. *Festivals of the French Revolution.* Trans. Alan Sheridan. Cambridge.
Pange, Comtesse Jean de. 1938. *Auguste-Guillaume et Madame de Staël.* Paris.
Park, Roy. 1971. *Hazlitt and the Spirit of the Age.* Oxford.
Parker, G. F. 1989. *Johnson's Shakespeare.* Oxford.
Paulson, Ronald. 1989. *Breaking and Remaking: Aesthetic Practice in England, 1700–1820.* New Brunswick, NJ.
Pougin, Arthur. 1902. *La Comédie-Française et la Révolution.* Paris.
Proschwitz, Gunnar von. 1964. "Drame": Esquisse de l'histoire du mot. *Studia Neophilologica* 36:9–50.
Recueil des Actes du Comité de Salut Public. See Aulard, F. A., ed.
Riccoboni, François. 1750/1971. *L'Art du théâtre à Madame ..., suivi d'une Lettre de M. Riccoboni fils à Monsieur ... au sujet de l'Art du théâtre.* Geneva.
Robertson, J. G. 1939. *Lessing's Dramatic Theory.* Cambridge.
Rodmell, Graham. E. 1990. *French Drama of the Revolutionary Years.* London.
Root-Bernstein, Michèle. [1981] 1984. *Boulevard Theatres and Revolution in Eighteenth-Century Paris. Theater and Dramatic Studies*:22. Ann Arbor.
Russo, Luigi. 1921. *Metastasio.* Bari.
Scelfo, Maria Luisa. 1984. *Le teorie drammatiche nel Romanticismo tra Manzoni e Hugo.* Catania.
Schiller, Friedrich von
    Lamport, F. J., trans. 1979. *The Robbers* and *Wallenstein.* Harmondsworth.
    Perfahl, Jost, ed. 1968. *Sämtliche Werke in 5 Bänden.* 5 vols. Munich.
Schlegel, August Wilhelm von
    Black, John, trans. (rev. A. J. W. Morrison). 1973. *Course of Lectures on Dramatic Art and Literature.* New York.
    Lohner, Edgar, ed. 1966–67. *Vorlesungen über dramatische Kunst und Literatur. Kritische Schriften und Briefe.* Vols. v–vi. Stuttgart.
Schlegel, Friedrich von. 1967. *Charakteristiken und Kritiken 1.* Ed. Hans Eichner. *Kritische Friedrich Schlegel Ausgabe.* Vol. II. Munich.
Schneider, Elisabeth. 1933. *The Aesthetics of William Hazlitt: A Study of the Philosophical basis of his Criticism.* Philadelphia.
Scott, Sir Walter. 1834. *The Miscellaneous Prose Works of Sir Walter Scott, Bart.* Vol. VI: *Essays on Chivalry, Romance, and the Drama.* Edinburgh.
Sembdner, Helmut, ed. 1967. *Kleists Aufsatz über das Marionettentheater: Studien und Interpretationen.* Berlin.
Sharpe, Lesley. 1991. *Friedrich Schiller: Drama, Thought and Politics.* Cambridge.
Smith, Adam. 1980. *Essays on Philosophical Subjects.* Ed. W. P. D. Wightman and J. C. Bryce. London.
Smith, Patrick J. 1970. *The Tenth Muse: A Historical Study of the Opera Libretto.* New York.
Staël, Mme de (Anne-Louise-Germaine Necker)
    [1861] 1975. *Oeuvres complètes.* Vol. II. Geneva.
    Folkenflik, Vivian. 1987. *An Extraordinary Woman: Selected Writings of Germaine de Staël.* New York.
States, Bert O. 1987. *Great Reckonings in a Little Room: On the Phenomenology of Theater.* Berkeley and Los Angeles.
Steele, Sir Richard
    Kenny, Shirley Strum, ed. 1971. *The Plays of Richard Steele.* Oxford.
Steinkraus, W. E., and K. I. Schmitz, eds. 1980. *Art and Logic in Hegel's Philosophy.* Atlantic Highlands, NJ.
Stendhal (Henri Beyle)
    Daniels, Guy, trans. 1962. *Racine and Shakespeare.* New York.
    Martino, Pierre, ed. 1970. *Racine et Shakespeare.* Paris.

Stone, P. W. K. 1967. *The Art of Poetry, 1750–1820: Theories of Poetic Composition and Style in the late Neo-classic and Early Romantic Periods*. New York.

Talbot, Emile J. 1983. Stendhal et le/la politique: Autour de *Racine et Shakespeare*. *Stendhal Club* 15:227–234.

Ubersfeld, Anne. 1974. *Le Roi et le bouffon*. Paris.

Vickers, Brian, ed. 1979. *Shakespeare: the Critical Heritage*. Vol. v: 1765–1774. London.

Voltaire (François-Marie Arouet)

Moland, Louis, ed. 1877. *Oeuvres complètes*. Vol. II. Paris.

Wasserman, Earl R. 1947. The pleasures of tragedy. *ELH* 14:283–307.

Wellbery, David. 1984. *Lessing's Laocöon: Semiotics and Aesthetics in the Age of Enlightenment*. London.

Wellek, René. 1955. *A History of Modern Criticism: 1750–1950*. Vol. I: *The Later Eighteenth Century*; Vol II: *The Romantic Age*. New Haven.

Welschinger, Henri. 1880. *Le Théâtre de la Révolution; avec documents inédits*. Paris.

Whitely, Alvin. 1955. Hazlitt and the theatre. *University of Texas Studies in English* 34:67–100.

Whitford, Robert Calvin. 1918. *Madame de Staël's Literary Reputation in England*. Urbana, IL.

Williams, David. 1966. *Voltaire: Literary Critic*. Geneva.

Williams, Raymond. 1983. *Keywords: A Vocabulary of Culture and Society*. London.

INDEX